Shanghai Sojourners

INSTITUTE OF EAST ASIAN STUDIES
UNIVERSITY OF CALIFORNIA • BERKELEY
CENTER FOR CHINESE STUDIES

Shanghai Sojourners

EDITED BY
Frederic Wakeman, Jr., and Wen-hsin Yeh

A publication of the Institute of East Asian Studies, University of California at Berkeley. Although the Institute of East Asian Studies is responsible for the selection and acceptance of manuscripts in this series, responsibility for the opinions expressed and for the accuracy of statements rests with their authors.

Correspondence may be sent to:
Ms. Joanne Sandstrom, Managing Editor
Institute of East Asian Studies
University of California
Berkeley, California 94720

The China Research Monograph series, whose first title appeared in 1967, is one of several publications series sponsored by the Institute of East Asian Studies in conjunction with its constituent units. The others include the Japan Research Monograph series, the Korea Research Monograph series, the Indochina Research Monograph series, and the Research Papers and Policy Studies series. A list of recent publications appears at the back of the book.

Library of Congress Cataloging-in-Publication Data

Shanghai sojourners / Frederic E. Wakeman, Jr., Wen-hsin Yeh, editors.
     p. cm. — (China research monograph ; no. 40)
  Includes bibliographical references and index.
  ISBN 1-55729-035-0 (paper) : $20.00
  1. Shanghai (China)—History. I. Wakeman, Frederic E. II. Yeh, Wen-Hsin. III. Series.
DS796.S257S57 1992
951.1'32—dc20   92-70468
                                                CIP

Contents

Acknowledgments

We would like to thank the Committee on Scholarly Communication with the People's Republic of China, the National Endowment for the Humanities, and the Shanghai Academy of Social Sciences for sponsoring the September 1988 conference in Shanghai that featured most of the papers in this volume. That symposium was convened by Professor Zhang Zhongli and Professor Sherman Cochran. We would also like to express our gratitude to Professor Thomas Gold, chair of Berkeley's Center for Chinese Studies, for his encouragement and support. Susan Stone and Elinor Levine put the final version of the manuscript together for Joanne Sandstrom, who edited and produced the book at the Institute of East Asian Studies.

Contributors

Marie-Claire Bergère is Professor of Chinese Civilization at the Institut National des Langues et Civilisations Orientales of the Institut de la Sorbonne Nouvelle.

Sherman Cochran is Professor and Chair of History at Cornell University.

Bryna Goodman is Associate Professor of History at the University of Oregon.

Gail Hershatter is Professor of History at the University of California, Santa Cruz.

Emily Honig is Associate Professor of Women's Studies at Yale University.

Brian G. Martin is a foreign policy specialist in the Australian Parliamentary Research Service.

Elizabeth J. Perry is Professor of Political Science at the University of California, Berkeley.

Frederic Wakeman, Jr., is Walter and Elise Haas Professor of Asian Studies and Director of the Institute of East Asian Studies at the University of California, Berkeley.

Jeffrey Wasserstrom is Associate Professor of History at the University of Indiana.

Wen-hsin Yeh is Assistant Professor of History and Vice-chair of the Center for Chinese Studies at the University of California, Berkeley.

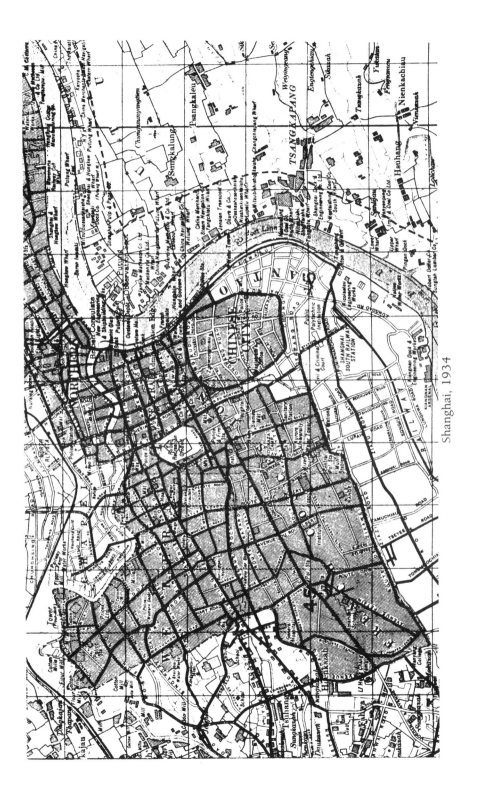

Shanghai, 1934

Introduction

FREDERIC WAKEMAN, JR., and WEN-HSIN YEH

Shanghai was formally opened to foreign trade on November 17, 1843. When the first party of English traders arrived, they saw the future International Settlement—a strip of land to the north of the Chinese city bordering the riverine area where Suzhou Creek ran into the Huangpu before entering the sea—"in the shape of sundry reed-beds, swamps, ponds and other malarious constituents."[1] These Englishmen were soon joined by an ever increasing number of Western traders and missionaries, of whom many were French and American. After the turn of the century other foreign sojourners arrived: Japanese, White Russians, Indians, Vietnamese, Prussians, Portuguese, Italians, Spanish, Poles, Greeks, and so forth. Shanghai's foreign community in its heyday was said to represent no fewer than fifty-eight nationalities. But the size of this foreign community never seemed to have exceeded a total of 150,000 people.[2]

The tenfold increase of Shanghai's population between 1842 and 1945 was largely a result of Chinese immigration from the countryside into the city, especially into the International Settlement (which doubled in numbers between 1895 and 1910 and doubled again between 1910 and 1930) and the French Concession (which almost tripled between 1895 and 1915 and more than tripled again between 1915 and 1930). From the 1850s on, each new social disturbance in the interior sent tens of thousands of Chinese refugees to Shanghai, seeking protection under the English and French flags. In the late 1850s the rebel troops of the Kingdom of Heavenly Peace (the Taipings), which ravaged eighteen provinces in fourteen years (1850–1864), swept through the lower Yangzi Valley, capturing such major cities as Nanjing, Suzhou, and Hangzhou.

---

[1] Shanghai Mercury, *Shanghai by Night and Day* (Shanghai, 1902), p. 4.

[2] Zou Yiren, *Jiu Shanghai renkou bianqian de yanjiu* [A study of the changes in population of old Shanghai] (Shanghai, 1980), pp. 68, 81.

The Taipings did not take Shanghai, but the Chinese part of the city was occupied by the Cantonese and Fukienese dock workers and by sailors of the Small Swords Society. Between 1855 and 1865, the population of the International Settlement swelled from approximately 20,000 to 90,000. The French Concession at the same time gained about 40,000. The foreign consuls and residents viewed this influx of Chinese with alarm and set up the first Municipal Council of the International Settlement on July 22, 1854, in part to deal with the emergency.[3]

The newcomers to Shanghai in the 1860s included a large number of gentrymen from such leading Jiangnan cities as Suzhou, Nanjing, Songjiang, and Hangzhou—all elite refugees from areas that had fallen to the Taipings. When these men fled to Shanghai, they brought their wealth and cultural tastes with them. New styles of cultured life began to appear in Shanghai's concessions, and by the time the Taipings were put down, many of the newcomers had come to regard Shanghai as a new home. Movements of this sort, along with the changing patterns of trade and transportation after the opening of the treaty ports, were largely responsible for the long-term shifts in Jiangnan's regional geography. By the third quarter of the nineteenth century, Shanghai had emerged to become the leading metropolis of the lower Yangzi Valley. Traditional Jiangnan cities lost their preeminence as traders went elsewhere, artisans emigrated, and the gentry were attracted to the new cosmopolitanism of Shanghai.

Commerce expanded and light industry developed in Shanghai at the turn of the twentieth century. Along the Bund stood the imposing high-rise offices of major Western banking corporations and trading houses. In the early stage of modern urban development many firms on Nanjing Road and the cotton mills along Yangshupu were financed mainly with foreign capital. Although the first Chinese-owned machine-powered rice-grinding concern was founded in 1863, indigenous industrial capitalism was repeatedly hampered by structural weaknesses in the investment environment that led to major recessions such as the one engendered by the credit crisis of 1883.[4] Between 1915 and 1919, when the European powers were engaged in war, however, Shanghai's light industry enjoyed a major boom. The benefits were shared primarily by Japanese and Chinese investors. Flour mills, shipping concerns, textile mills, silk

---

[3] Shanghai Mercury, *Shanghai by Night and Day*, p. 15. Crowding and poor accommodations apparently led to an outbreak of cholera and other epidemic diseases.

[4] Yen-p'ing Hao, *The Commercial Revolution of Nineteenth-Century China: The Rise of Sino-Western Mercantile Competition* (Berkeley and Los Angeles: University of California Press, 1984), pp. 329, 331–334.

filatures, paper mills, coal mining concerns, and facilities for the manufacture of tobacco products, matches, cement, light bulbs, and so forth, multiplied in the ensuing decades.[5] The fortunes amassed by wealthy entrepreneurs and shareholders during the Nanjing decade 1927–1937 were impressive. The leading members of this bourgeoisie, the Rong brothers, for example, opened a total of nine textile mills and twelve flour mills between 1902 and 1932 and accumulated no less than 2,913,000 silver dollars' worth of capital.[6] Although the size of this urban bourgeoisie, especially its upper crust, was relatively insignificant, the financial power that it wielded in the Republican period was disproportionate to its size.[7]

The development of light industry and commerce induced a second type of immigration from the countryside. Tens of thousands of able-bodied villagers from Jiangnan, Subei, Anhui, and Zhejiang were drawn to the city in search of opportunities. Women and youngsters were brought in as contract laborers, domestic helpers, apprentices, and prostitutes. Many arrived with the help of kinsmen and fellow villagers. The reliance upon such native-place ties profoundly shaped the recruitment patterns of labor.[8] In the early industries labor was cheap, and personal financial security hardly existed. Wages were low and living conditions poor; many lived with relatives and friends in crowded quarters. Large numbers of workers were promptly laid off when recession hit. Although the census taken by the new government in 1949 showed that Shanghai employed a total of 840,000 artisans and industrial, construction, and transportation workers in addition to 370,000 shop clerks and apprentices, the authorities also discovered 400,000 cases of adult male unemployment.[9]

---

[5] Jiu Zhongguo de ziben zhuyi shengchan guanxi bianxie zu, ed., *Jiu Zhongguo de ziben zhuyi shengchan guanxi* [Capitalist relations of production in old Shanghai] (Shanghai, 1977), p. 24.

[6] Ibid., p. 35.

[7] After the socialist government took over, 102,607 individuals registered themselves as owners and shareholders of industries and trading concerns in the following January. Another 51,760 were registered and assigned jobs as former entrepreneurs and managers of private industrial and commercial concerns by the Shanghai municipal government in 1956. Zou Yiren, *Jiu Shanghai renkou bianqian de yanjiu*, pp. 30–31.

[8] Emily Honig's research on the conditions of women workers in Shanghai's cotton mills shows that the textile labor force was not only divided by native-place ties but was also controlled by the Green Gang through its influence over matters of recruitment and its ability to threaten physical harm. See Emily Honig, *Sisters and Strangers: Women in the Shanghai Cotton Mills, 1919–1949* (Stanford, Calif.: Stanford University Press, 1986), pp. 57–69, 123–124.

[9] Zou Yiren, *Jiu Shanghai renkou bianqian de yanjiu*, pp. 36, 104, 110–111.

Single male workers often went home to their villages to marry. The majority of these men, unable to afford the higher expenses of urban housing and food, left their wives behind upon returning to Shanghai, both to observe the traditional norm and to take advantage of the lower living costs in the rural areas. The demographic composition of Shanghai reflected these patterns of immigrants' lives. During the Nanjing decade less than 30 percent of Shanghai's population was native to the area. In the early 1930s the male to female ratio was 142 to 100. Because few unskilled laborers were accompanied by their families, less than a quarter of Shanghai's presocialist population was younger than fourteen years old.[10] Many neighborhoods that were spawned in the back alleys in the commercial and industrial districts of the city, meanwhile, retained the essentially village characteristics of the home towns of their residents.

The third and most dramatic increase in Shanghai's population took place between 1937 and 1941, when war broke out and Japanese troops occupied coastal China. The foreign concessions became "lone islets" (*gudao*) in a sea of Japanese invading forces, used by Chinese resisters to launch sniper attacks on enemies and collaborators alike. While the population of the Chinese portion of Shanghai declined during the war, that of the foreign concessions reached a total of 2,430,000, a gain of 780,000 from 1937.[11] The push of social disturbances and the pull of economic opportunities thus combined to alter the social geography and demographic profile of Shanghai in the century after the Opium War. While in the 1840s less than 1 percent of Shanghai's population was to be found outside the Chinese city and its suburbs, in the 1940s no less than 65 percent sought security and employment in the two foreign concessions, which together comprised less than 6 percent of the total area of metropolitan Shanghai.

The spectacular growth of population and wealth that Shanghai experienced between 1842 and 1949 resulted in a city of extreme complexity, which was often divided along cultural, national, and class lines. The concessions, ever growing and expanding, nearly displaced the former Chinese magistrate's seat (referred to as the "native city" in Settlement English) as a metropolitan center. Chinese political authority and police power were, until 1942, kept out of the concessions by the treaty rights of extraterritoriality.[12] After the Nationalists took power in

---

[10] Ibid., pp. 47, 53–55.

[11] Ibid., pp. 3–4.

[12] The treaty rights of extraterritoriality exempted the foreign nationals on Chinese soil from the rule of Chinese law. The Land Regulations, signed by the Shanghai *taotai* and the English and French consuls, permitted the foreign community the use of land in designated areas. Neither constituted explicit legal concession of Chinese sovereign rights in the

1927, it had become a point of national pride to revive the Chinese city and build it into a viable rival civic center to the foreign concessions. But paradoxically, the very notion of a civic center itself was taken from the West; and the city hall, the court house, the auditorium, the library, the square, the museum, the hospital, the athletic stadium, and other public buildings were all admittedly inspired by Western examples. The very model of a modern municipal government, as opposed to the old district magistrate's *yamen,* was taken from the English example.[13]

Socially and economically, a small number of financiers and entrepreneurs, foreign as well as Chinese, controlled a disproportionately large share of resources and led a life that contrasted sharply with that led by those who lived in the urban slums. Such disparity aroused the indignation of social critics and intellectuals alike. In film, drama, and fiction, the 1930s was a decade of prolific literary and artistic representations of social tension, exploitation, and injustice. The most gripping image of Shanghai capitalism and private ownership in its prime was captured perhaps by Xia Yan, the writer and journalist, in his classic reportage of the system of teen-age women contract labor in the city's cotton mills. Shanghai, wrote Xia Yan, was "a city of forty-eight-storey skyscrapers built upon twenty-four layers of hell."[14]

Sojourners

Shanghai was more than just two cities, vertically divided, or four cities, horizontally bounded. A patchwork of sojourners living in and between these various cities made up the total urban complex. Traditional Chinese sojourners (*youyu,* "travelers in residence") were simply people come from elsewhere who had either attained enough distinction to be mentioned in the district gazetteer or else were exiles who had sought temporary shelter and succor. The very term suggested a transient local identity, as though the "real" existence of traditional sojourners had to be in some other part of the empire where the family graves were kept and where one eventually had to return.

---

foreign concessions. The Land Regulations, however, were invoked as the legal foundation of a self-governing foreign concession. Through the establishment of an elected Municipal Council and the vigorous assertion of extraterritoriality in a Mixed Court with token Chinese representation, the International Settlement succeeded in turning itself into a political entity that claimed substantial rights. See Nicholas R. Clifford, *Shanghai 1925: Urban Nationalism and the Defense of Foreign Privilege* (Ann Arbor, Mich.: Center for Chinese Studies, 1979), pp. 1–4. See also Frederic Wakeman, Jr., "Policing Modern Shanghai," *China Quarterly,* no. 115 (September 1988): 408–440.

[13] Shen Yi, "Shanghai shi gongwuju shi nian" [Ten years in the Shanghai Municipal Bureau of Works], *Zhuanji wenxue,* part 1: vol. 70, no. 2, pp. 11–18 (August 1970).

[14] Xia Yan, *Baoshen gong* (Reprint Beijing, 1978), p. 26.

Shanghai sojourners (*lühu*,[15] "travelers in Shanghai") were also transients from somewhere, but the term in this case did meaningfully emphasize the place where they sojourned: Hu, or Shanghai. It thereby summed up the central ambiguity of sojourning in this particular metropolis. Shanghai sojourners were more than persons passing through; they were denizens. Their stay was on the way to becoming permanent residence, while their loyalties fluctuated strategically between attachment to native place and the announcement of a new identity as *Shanghai ren* (Shanghai people).

The residents of Shanghai were sojourners in another sense as well: they lived between the various cities that comprised the whole. Indeed, they were often able to benefit from Shanghai's being such a congeries of cities, each with its own jurisdiction under the treaty-guaranteed protection of extraterritoriality. Criminal elements were particularly favored in this respect. As Brian Martin argues in his essay in this volume, Shanghai gangsters successfully transferred to this Sino-foreign urban environment the rural bandits' classic strategy of establishing their "lairs" in the no-man's-land between two or more county or prefectural administrations: "By 1920 Shanghai had become a veritable urban Liangshanpo."

The disunity of administrative control in the city—the fact that there were multiple civic authorities—gave sojourners and their native-place networks an important role to play as intermediating organizations.[16] "Shanghai was a city of immigrants," Martin points out, "and one where the social cohesion of the Chinese population was tenuous at best. In this situation the role of native-place networks gained in significance, and these provided the basis for whatever social organization existed among the Chinese population." The native-place system consequently constituted "the basic building block" of gangster organizations:

> The gangsters used native-place networks to organize protection rackets, to interpose themselves as middlemen between their native-place group and other such groups, to mediate relations between their fellow-provincials and petty officialdom in the various municipalities of Shanghai, and to gain control of the labor market and transform it into a lucrative racket. (Chapter 8)

---

[15] As in Jianghuai lühu tongxianghui (Association of Jianghuai Sojourners in Shanghai), which was the city's single most powerful Subei association, established in 1919.

[16] See, for example, the role played by the Pudong Association (which was financially supported by the gangster Du Yuesheng) as described in Bryna Goodman, "Urban Identity and the Question of a Public Sphere in Chinese Cities: Regional Associations in 1930s Shanghai," paper delivered at the Regional Seminar of the Center for Chinese Studies, Berkeley, November 1990.

One of the most obvious examples of this was prostitution, the sojourner's vice above all others. According to Gail Hershatter, the prostitution industry was the largest single employer of female labor in Shanghai. In 1930, approximately one in every thirty residents "sold sex for a living." Brothels were at the very heart of the city's commerce. When the Shanghai Municipal Council initiated a plan in May 1920 to phase out legal houses of prostitution, "panic" reportedly spread among the International Settlement's Chinese shopkeepers who argued, with the endorsement of the Chinese General Chamber of Commerce, that first-class brothels were meeting places for merchants and therefore good for business. The termination of the licensed brothel system in 1924 did not put an end to prostitution. In addition to ordinary streetwalkers, there was a growth of ancillary occupations that served the same function: masseuses, tour guides, tea hostesses, taxi dancers, and so on. And new illegal brothels opened up and persisted simply because they offered sojourning prostitutes a niche in the city.

Prostitution was protected, furthermore, because the sojourners who ran the industry enjoyed nonnative sources of power. In this sense, Shanghai truly was a comprador society, down to and including instruments of government. Martin makes the important point that even the Chinese police were "compradors of violence." The major gang leader of the early 1920s, Huang Jinrong, owed his prominence not so much to his own membership in the Green Gang as to his being on the French police force. The gangsters' ability to "police" Shanghai's streets effectively reduced police costs for the French and the International Settlement forces, so that within both concessions a kind of informal headman/security-merchant system was adopted by co-opting the more powerful of the sojourners and transforming them into "civic leaders."

The system was particularly attractive to the French, who, as they became outnumbered seven to one in their own concession by other foreign nationalities, turned to Chinese for help on their Municipal Council. The "Gentry-Councillor Clique" appointed to serve was composed of Chinese who had studied in France or were Roman Catholics. This clique functioned, in some respects at least, like other native-place groups (except that its leaders received papal decorations and ran Catholic hospices) such as the Ningbo financial clique of Zhu Baosan and Yu Xiaqing, with which it was closely connected. In this regard one might well ask whether or not compradorism led more readily to municipal self-government in Shanghai than in other cities administered by Chinese national authorities.

Sojourning Capitalists

The most prominent sojourners besides the top gangsters were big capitalists, both foreign and Chinese. Sherman Cochran's "sojourning capitalists" competed to dominate mass consumption businesses like the match industry, whether as members of Japan's largest marketing firm, Mitsui Trading Company; of the West's biggest match manufacturer, Swedish Match Company; or of China's leading match producer and distributor, China Match Company. The last of these eventually dominated the industry precisely because it so skillfully used native-place ties to advance its marketing strategies.

The founder of the China Match Company, Liu Hongsheng, was born and raised in Shanghai, but he maintained strong particularistic ties with cohorts from his native place of Dinghai county in Ningbo prefecture. In 1920, the year Liu began manufacturing matches, he was appointed head of the Association of Ningbo Sojourners in Shanghai. At the same time he helped establish a middle school in his home county in Ningbo prefecture. The Dinghai Middle School charged no tuition and admitted only county residents. Liu proceeded thereafter to staff his match company with the school's graduates, thereby recruiting—in Cochran's words—"a steady flow of young Ningbo native-place cohorts all beholden to Liu for their educations and their jobs."

After buying out several other Chinese match manufacturing companies, Liu incorporated his particularistic network of Ningbo distributors into a marketing system staffed by salaried employees responsible both for recruiting local Chinese commission agents and for monitoring the agents' activities in cities and towns way down the urban hierarchy outside Shanghai. Paid high wages while controlling these commission agents by a system of guarantors that did not require the agents themselves to pay cash in advance for the match consignments, the China Match Company's Ningbo cadres customized their products for local consumers. Eventually China Match Company came to dominate the middle and lower Yangzi markets, forming a cartel that brought the company immense profits in the late 1930s.

Native-place ties were also of paramount influence in banking and commerce. In the first place, such ties helped one gain employment. As Wen-hsin Yeh points out with respect to apprentices and clerks,

> contemporary sources agreed almost unanimously that kinship ties and personal connections outweighed all other factors when it came to placement in Shanghai's job market. Tradesmen were often interconnected through native-place associations and master-disciple relationships, and these ties grew even stronger when lines of professional transmission were conjoined with matrimonial affiliations. Normative claims that

governed familial relationships were extended to work relationships as well. (Chapter 6)

Marie-Claire Bergère's study of the Shanghai Banker's Association not only shows how important Zhejiang provenance was, but also demonstrates how flexible such a network could be, especially when it came to admitting outsiders like the Jiangsu bankers Chen Guangfu and Zhang Jia'ao. Indeed, Bergère maintains that the professional association (*fatuan*) both institutionalized local solidarities and produced a more open *société civile*.[17]

At first glance, civil society hardly appeared to be the prevailing order of Republican Shanghai. Although the most recent historical literature by Western scholars claims to find evidence of a new public municipal order (deparochialization of native-place ties, blurring of boundaries between gentry and merchant elites, growing traditions of institutionalized municipal self-governance) in several late imperial and early Republican Chinese cities, some of the essays in this volume hardly support that assertion in the case of Shanghai.[18] Above all, Martin's study of the Green Gang's role in the French Concession suggests that, from a political perspective at least, municipal institutions were ad hoc, elites were in continuing conflict among themselves, colonial concerns overrode pleas for political autonomy, and local government depended upon organized crime as an instrument for social control.

Nevertheless, Bergère is not the only contributor to this volume on Shanghai sojourners to detect strains of civic order within parochial organizations. Bryna Goodman stresses the importance of particularistic organizations to the political order: she views the proliferation of native-place associations (*tongxianghui*) during the early Republic as key

---

[17] This last role was especially striking in 1920–1921 when the National Bankers' Association (Quanguo yinhang lianhehui), which was dominated by the "Zhejiang clique," paid off the national government's debts in exchange for financial reform.

[18] This form of circumscribed self-government is the "gentry democracy" that Mark Elvin wrote about in describing the local elite management systems around Shanghai in the early years of this century. Mark Elvin, "The Administration of Shanghai, 1905–1914," in Mark Elvin and G. William Skinner, eds., *The Chinese City between Two Worlds* (Stanford, Calif.: Stanford University Press, 1974), p. 250; and idem, "The Gentry Democracy in Chinese Shanghai, 1905–1914," in Jack Gray, ed., *Modern China's Search for a Political Form* (London: Oxford University Press, 1969), pp. 41–65. See also William T. Rowe, *Hankow: Commerce and Society in a Chinese City, 1796–1889* (Stanford, Calif.: Stanford University Press, 1984), p. 344; Susan Mann Jones, "Merchant Investment, Commercialization, and Social Change in the Ningpo Area," in Paul A. Cohen and John Schrecker, eds., *Reform in Nineteenth-Century China* (Cambridge: Harvard University Press, 1976), pp. 41–48; Mary Backus Rankin, *Elite Activism and Political Transformation in China: Zhejiang Province, 1865–1911* (Stanford, Calif.: Stanford University Press, 1986), pp. 136–169.

evidence of a civil society emerging in Shanghai. Arguing that particularistic associations flourish in "open" cities under circumstances of
extraordinary social change, Goodman seeks to show that *tongxianghui*
provided native-place community members with a multitude of welfare
services ranging from coffin repositories to hospices. They even constituted a form of traditional political representation in an "egalitarian
language of native-place sentiment" that allowed wealthy and poor to
share equally in these bonds.

Native-place associations are also said to have abetted modern political movements—movements that Jeffrey Wasserstrom, building on the
work of Charles Tilly, reminds us were sometimes conducted by protesters favoring tactics based on traditional "scripts."[19] The native-place
groups (*bang*) of Shandong, Ningbo, and Guangdong played especially
active roles during the height of the May Fourth Movement of 1919 in
Shanghai. Though their inherent parochialism may have inhibited trade
unionism, native-place ties and preexisting brother/sisterhoods also
helped labor movements spread, as in the March 1934 Meiya strike.
Viewed in this way, however, native-place identity ultimately worked
against class identity—or so at least claimed Communist organizers who
felt that native-place *bang*, which were actual subdivisions in the work
place, prevented unionwide allegiances.

As parochial and primordial solidarities, did native-place groups flourish most among more "traditional" workers who retained strong roots in
the countryside? So it would seem. Elizabeth Perry's Hangzhou-
Huzhou-Suzhou peasant-artisans wore country clothes, were often deeply
religious Buddhists or Christians, entered into traditional marriages that
reinforced native connections, and maintained strong kinship ties that
sometimes brought entire families into the same factory. Emily Honig
describes how Shanghai sojourners emulated gangsters rather than students, swearing brother/sisterhoods and specializing in locale-specified
occupations: Yangzhou people's "three knives" (barbers, cooks, and
pedicurists), Yancheng and Funing rickshaw pullers, Nantong drayers,
Taizhou peanut peddlers, Gaoyou wok repairers, and so on.

---

[19] Charles Tilly, *From Mobilization to Revolution* (Reading, Mass.: Addison and Wesley,
1978). In *The Contentious French,* Tilly argues that the tactics of protesters in seventeenth-
century France were variations on everyday routines, rituals, and ceremonies. To him, protest can best be seen as a form of "learned" behavior from preexisting models (or
"scripts") used to help people gain collective redress for their grievances. Charles Tilly,
The Contentious French (Cambridge, Mass.: Harvard University Press, 1986), pp. 116–117.

Shanghai Identities

The people who comprised the lowliest of these native-place groups did not actually share an identity before coming to Shanghai. The groups were, so to speak, the product of epithets directed against the least advantaged of the sojourners: *Subei ren* (people from northern Jiangsu) or *Jiangbei ren* (people from north of the Yangzi River). Often poverty-stricken refugees, they were cast as stereotypes of coarseness and dirtiness: shack dwellers who ate yams instead of rice, rickshaw pullers and collectors of night soil, criminal elements who ultimately collaborated with the Japanese. Moreover, their ascription as "Subei ren" served mainly as a way for other immigrants from "south of the Yangzi River" to distinguish themselves as "real" Shanghai people speaking a variant of the Wu dialect, eating Jiangnan cuisine, and listening to southern opera. "Shanghai identity," Honig contends, "can be understood only in contradistinction to 'the other' against which it defined itself, and Subei people represented that 'other'."

Was it difficult, then, to become a *Shanghai ren?* Much depended upon one's background. As we see in Perry's chapter on weavers and the labor movement, workers in the silk industry could be divided into two very different kinds of proletarians. One kind came from the traditional rural handicraft areas of Hangzhou, Huzhou, and Suzhou, where their families had woven for generations. Older and poorly educated (only 20–30 percent of the males could read), they were driven to the city by the decline of rural handicrafts. For them the move to Shanghai was an unwelcome "proletarianization," characterized by work in smaller factories for lower wages and much less job security than the second, much more "modern" work force that hailed from counties like Shengxian and Dongyang in eastern Zhejiang enjoyed.

This second group of "labor aristocrats" (*guizu gongren*) consisted of young men and women from peasant families who had at least an elementary education (95 percent of the men and 35 percent of the women could read). For them, the move to Shanghai to work at companies like Meiya with its generous wages, free clinic and library, night school, and recreation club was upwardly mobile. They soon "converted" to a new, modern, urban life style, adopting Western clothing, leather shoes, movie going, and foreign food. Eschewing traditional sworn brotherhoods, full of admiration for middle school and university students, they fell in love with one another and lived together, enjoyed forming opera troupes, and belied their "labor aristocracy" standing by responding to the great strike waves that student agitators often led after 1927. They were by then seasoned *Shanghai ren*.

Traditional apprentices and clerks also turned relatively quickly into urbanites. Categorized as "vocational youth" (*zhiye qingnian*) by the urban reformist gentry of Jiangsu, the 300,000 or so literate clerks and apprentices in trade, manufacturing, the professions, the public and private service sectors, as well as among elementary and normal school teachers in Shanghai, constituted a huge new urban audience for periodicals like *Shenghuo* (Life). These "petty urbanites" (*xiao shimin*) were told, in Wen-hsin Yeh's words,

> to make the best of their circumstances, to exercise self-control, and to cultivate spiritual composure. Poverty was no hindrance to a young man's eventual advancement, because personal success was not the gift of birth, but the result of discipline and resolve. The essential message was simply that steady effort to perfect one's performance might make it possible for any young man to rise to the top of Shanghai's commercial and industrial world. (Chapter 6)

In truth, however, opportunities for advancement may have declined during this period. Most of the vocational press's success stories—the neo-Confucian equivalent of Horatio Alger's rise—concluded with the hero becoming the master of his own enterprise. As a store or factory owner, these successful men were usually depicted as heads of large households with an entourage of apprentices, clerks, accountants, secretaries, and other employees. But as Shanghai modernized, the increasing numbers of competitors and the larger scale of investment deprived "vocational youth" of the opportunity to own their own businesses. And the "households" they headed frequently consisted of a mother, wife, and small child in the countryside back home, their bonds with whom had often attenuated. At the same time, Shanghai itself remained a source of deep and abiding ambivalence, a lure that could easily beckon one to ruin.

Ambivalence

Part of the sojourners' ambivalence toward Shanghai stemmed from the Sino-Western quality of the city—what John Fairbank once called "rickshaw culture." Shanghai was regarded as unique because it was built with the help of *yang guizi* (foreign devils). The colorfulness of Annamese constables, of baton-wielding blue-eyed Scottish police, of White Russian prostitutes was both an attraction and a matter of national shame. Everyday life was suffused with ambivalence. Students loathed the foreign imperialists yet emulated—in an antinomian way—their rituals. Wasserstrom shows us how even student protest movements against the Westerners were influenced by the flag-raising ceremonies of British Empire Day rituals.[20] This ambivalence is one reason why it was difficult to come up with a sense of community in Shanghai, even though its urban culture was so fascinating in and of itself. The very guidebooks that introduced the city to rustic "hayseeds" (*tubaozi*) visiting the exotic city also inhibited a ready identification with Shanghai. To sojourners, Shanghai's "identity" was both the foreign city with its movie theaters, street lights, and "civilized" (*wenming*) creature comforts such as running water and heat, and the native city inhabited by "shed people" (*penghu*), with the homeless sleeping in coffins or begging on the streets.

This confusion of Shanghai's multiple identities, which reinforced the sojourners' native-place ties, in turn made it possible for émigrés from various parts of Jiangnan to proudly retain their local identities as Shaoxing or Wuxi people while simultaneously claiming a more general status as the real *Shanghai ren* vis-à-vis the convenient Subei outsiders. But this may have been a somewhat stunted municipal identity; there may not have been, even by the 1920s, a transformation into Shanghainese that decisively cut native roots. It would be extremely misleading to point to a single, discrete moment when individuals supposedly stopped being from Ningbo and started thinking of themselves as *Shanghai ren*.

It is important, therefore, to distinguish the rise of Shanghai urban culture from an individual's own geographical identity, which was closely connected with pride of place. If it seemed better to be from Suzhou than from Shanghai, then sojourners from the former would claim native-place ties and assert a Suzhou identity as long as they wished—and certainly several generations beyond actual residence or natality there.

Because of Shanghai's sheer foreignness, native-place identity could more easily accommodate a national identity, although there was inevitable tension between the two. Goodman notes that members of native-place associations consciously sought to connect the formation of a *tongxianghui* with the political strengthening of the larger entity of China: "Love the native place, love the country." As a metonymy, native place could stand for nation, concretizing abstract ties through local community, using *xiao tuanti* (small groups) to form *da tuanti* (a large group, the nation).

---

[20] To be sure, this was an instance, like Natalie Davis' examples, of inverted versions of authorized rituals, rearrangements of official scripts, in which ordinary people usurp roles normally played by powerholders. See, for examples, Natalie Davis, *Society and Culture in Early Modern France* (Stanford, Calif.: Stanford University Press, 1975).

Of course, the presence of the foreigners in the settlements continuously reminded Chinese sojourners in Shanghai of the importance of standing together as fellow countrymen. Foreigners, who were paradigmatic sojourners in their own right, had little direct contact with Chinese beyond their servants until the late 1920s. But foreign cultural influence penetrated deeply, inciting nationalistic self-awareness among Chinese. Because of the foreign presence, any political organization that arose to represent Chinese interests quickly took on the hue of national representation. Criminal elements thus could wrap themselves in the cloak of patriotism. A good example of this ploy was the French Concession Chinese Ratepayers' Association, which after 1927 was dominated by Du Yuesheng and the other Green Gang bosses, who became legitimate spokesmen for the French Concession's 300,000 Chinese residents.

Japanese aggression aroused nationalistic passions among Shanghai's citizens even more. As conflict with Japan intensified, Shanghai's keenly status-conscious "petty urbanites" were quick to identify their own self-esteem with national self-esteem. After September 18, 1931, this segment of the population was aroused to a high patriotic pitch. The full-scale war that eventually broke out in 1937 between China and Japan had the additional effect of throwing some of these Shanghai sojourners—white-collar workers, middle-class professionals, artists, and intellectuals—back into the countryside. This forced rustication of the urban-based intelligentsia brought an end for the time being to Shanghai as a progressive base for sojourners.

Many returned in 1945 after the war with Japan was over. By then *Shanghai ren* had firmly established their own identity, although sojourners kept on coming and going. The prostitution industry, for example, continued to attract thousands of women to Shanghai every year. All of that changed after the Communist victory in 1949. It took some time, but the creation of an urban residential registration system by the new authorities restricted legal sojourning in the city. The foreign "Shanghailanders" departed of their own accord or were forced to leave later. The criminal gangs were curtailed. Even the prostitutes were finally taken off the streets and put in reform schools. By 1953, after suitable reeducation, one group of former prostitutes was sent back to the women's native places in the countryside. A second group was released to assume factory jobs in Shanghai proper. And a third group went far west, to farms in Gansu, Ningxia, and Xinjiang, where they hoped to find husbands. The era of ambivalent sojourning was over, and the exotic, disturbing, polymorphous quality of the semicolonial city was lost. Cosmopolitan Shanghai had become securely Chinese.

CHAPTER ONE

The Shanghai Bankers' Association, 1915–1927

Modernization and the Institutionalization of Local Solidarities

MARIE-CLAIRE BERGÈRE

From 1917 to 1927 the Shanghai Bankers' Association (SBA) was one of the most assertive organizations of the Shanghai business class. It represented the interests and promoted the views of a remarkable group of young bankers who struggled for the development of banking and the adoption of various financial and monetary reforms. In a more general way, they also advocated the modernization of the economic system and political institutions.

The SBA was one of the professional associations (*fatuan*) established in the early twentieth century under a series of laws promulgated by the government between 1903 and 1915 requiring the regulation of certain infant professions, including industry, law, and banking. Moreover, the associations were charged with various official functions, and consequently, they came to be considered to have a legitimate voice in public affairs.[1]

The chambers of commerce were established in 1903 and the lawyers' associations in 1912. Although traditional banks (*qianzhuang*) had already organized themselves into the Native Bankers' Guild (Qianye gonghui) in 1911, it was not until August 1915 that the Beijing government required banking associations (*yinhang gonghui*) to be established in each important financial center for the self-regulation of modern banks.[2]

The creation of the Shanghai banking association took some time. The association began as an informal group of young managers—Zhang

---

[1] See Andrew Nathan, *Peking Politics, 1918–1923* (Berkeley and Los Angeles: University of California Press, 1976), pp. 13–14.

[2] See *Shanghai qianzhuang shiliao* [Materials on the history of Shanghai native banks] (Shanghai: Shanghai renmin chubanshe, 1960), p. 645.

Jia'ao (Bank of China), Li Ming (Zhejiang Provincial Bank), and Chen Guangfu (Shanghai Commercial and Savings Bank)—who regularly lunched together to discuss business. According to Zhang Jia'ao, they were "friends with common interests in promoting modern banking." This solidarity stimulated Zhang to undertake a plan to establish a regular organization.[3] In summer 1917, the group was made into an official association the regulations of which comprised no fewer than six chapters and forty-five articles! At the same time, this banking group established the *Yinhang zhoubao* (Bankers' weekly) as the mouthpiece of the SBA. It was soon to become one of the most influential Chinese financial and economic magazines.

Chinese modern (private) banking developed quite late and started to expand only at the time of World War I. In 1913–15 Chinese modern bankers were newcomers on the Shanghai scene. How is it, then, that they were able to become so rapidly and powerfully organized? Part of the answer lies in the relations that modern bankers maintained with the regional associations (*bang*) and professional guilds established by the traditional bankers during the previous years. As these relations generally developed by means of individual contacts, they may be approached through biographical studies of the main modern bankers.

The Founding of the SBA

Distrust of Official Interference

Eight banks took part in founding the SBA in 1917–18: the Bank of China (Zhongguo yinhang), the Bank of Communications (Jiaotong yinhang), the National Commercial Bank (Zhejiang xingye yinhang), the Chekiang Industrial Bank (Zhejiang difang shiye yinhang), the Shanghai Commercial and Savings Bank (Shanghai chuxu yinhang), the Salt Gabelle Bank (Yanye yinhang), the Chungfoo Union Bank (Zhongfu yinhang), and the Ningbo Commercial Bank (Siming yinhang). Several of these establishments were official banks (the Bank of China, the Bank of Communications, the Salt Gabelle Bank) whose head offices were in the north, in Beijing or Tianjin, and whose presidents and general managers were linked to the Beiyang political and military clique. In 1916, Yuan Shikai, who needed funds to carry out his monarchical plans, ordered the Bank of China and the Bank of Communications to freeze assets and suspend the redemption of notes. The local managers of the Bank of

---

[3] "Autobiography of Chang Chiao-ao [Zhang Jia'ao]," unpublished manuscript, Oral History Project, Columbia University, ca. 1960, pp. 5–6.

China succeeded in keeping their bank independent of the government and militarists, refusing Yuan Shikai's order. The Bank of Communications complied with the order and, as a consequence, was discredited. It had to be reorganized in 1917. Thereafter, the Shanghai branches of the two official banks became almost autonomous, and their managers ran them more and more as private banks.

Distrust of official interference was common among young Shanghai bankers. Chen Guangfu, who started his banking career as general manager of the Jiangsu (Provincial) Bank in 1911, tried to get full power for the board of directors, which included no officials but only compradors. After being dismissed from the bank in 1914 for refusing to loan money to the government, Chen got the financial support of Zhang Jia'ao and Li Ming to start his own private bank, the Shanghai Commercial and Savings Bank. Zhang Jia'ao had little money of his own, but he transferred 50,000 Chinese dollars from the Bank of China to open an account with the new bank.[4]

Native-Place Ties

By birth, most managers of both "official" and private banks belonged to the Zhejiang-Jiangsu clique, which for more than a century had controlled Shanghai (traditional) banking activities. A brief glance at the biographies of the founding fathers of the SBA reveals the importance of these native-place ties. Most of these bankers—or their families— came from Zhejiang province. Such was the case for Song Hanzhang (Bank of China), a native of Yuyao district; Qian Yongming (Bank of Communications), a native of Wuxing district; Xu Jijin (National Commercial Bank), a native of Yongjia district; Li Ming (Chekiang Industrial Bank), who was born in Shaoxing; and Sun Hengfu (Ningbo Commercial Bank), who came from Ningbo.[5] The Zhejiang entrepreneurs had played a predominant role in the development of the Shanghai traditional banks during previous decades.[6]

---

[4] "Reminiscences of Ch'en Kuang-fu as told to Julie Lien-Ying How, December 6, 1970 to June 5, 1961," unpublished manuscript, Oral History Project, Columbia University, pp. 33–35.

[5] The most important sources for biographical data are Howard L. Boorman and Richard C. Howard, eds., *Biographical Dictionary of Republican China* (New York: Columbia University Press, 1967–1971); *Who's Who in China* (Shanghai: China Weekly Review, 1925 [3d ed.] and 1931 [4th ed.]); Li Xun and Sun Sibai, eds., *Minguo renwuzhuan* [Biographies of the Republican Period] (Beijing, Zhonghua shuju, 1978–1987), 6 vols.; *Zhongguo jindai mingren tujian* [Repertory of famous Chinese of modern times] (Shanghai, 1925; Taipei, 1977); and the two unpublished manuscripts from Columbia University's Oral History Project, "Autobiography of Chang Chiao-ao" and "Reminiscences of Ch'en Kuang-fu."

[6] On the history of *qianzhuang* bankers, see Andrea MacElderry, *Shanghai Old-Style Bank-*

It was no wonder that Shanghai modern bankers came from the same regional group. Some of them, in fact, were *qianzhuang* owners turned into modern bank managers. For example, this was the case with Sun Hengfu, who owned five *qianzhuang* and to whom Yu Xiaqing (another Zhejiang man, from Zhenhai) entrusted the management of his newly founded Ningbo Commercial Bank. Zhejiang modern bankers not only enjoyed the professional experience accumulated by their fellow country-men, but they also received financial support from them when they established their own banking firms: Both Yu Xiaqing and Chen Guangfu relied on this support for funding the Ningbo Commercial Bank and the Shanghai Commercial and Savings Bank, respectively.

Although Chen Guangfu was not a Zhejiang man (he was born in Jin-jiang [Jiangsu], a town that had produced many traditional bankers), by virtue of personal and business relations, the Jiangsu modern bankers were considered to belong to the Zhejiang financial clique. Among them was one of the most active leaders of the SBA, Zhang Jia'ao (Chang Kiang-au; vice-manager of the Shanghai branch of the Bank of China), a native of Baoshan, near Shanghai. Also integrated into the Zhejiang clique were some bankers from Anhui province, such as Sun Yuanfang (manager of the Shanghai branch of the Chungfoo Union Bank), who, like the founders of this bank, Sun Duosen and Sun Duoyu, was born in Shouxian district. Through family- and native-tie connections, Jiangsu and Anhui entrepreneurs had developed relations with the Beiyang refor-mists and bureaucratic capitalists of the last imperial decade and the early Republican period. Through men like Zhang Jia'ao and Sun Yuan-fang, the SBA could strike various alliances with the communications clique in Beijing and Tianjin.[7]

Cosmopolitanism

Although these men were linked with (and sometimes supported by) the traditional financial circles, their world outlook was different. When

ers (ch'ien-chuang), 1880–1935, Michigan Papers in Chinese Studies, no. 25 (Ann Arbor: University of Michigan, 1976); Susan Mann, "The Ningpo Pang and Financial Power in Shanghai," in The Chinese City Between Two Worlds, ed. Mark Elvin and William Skinner (Stanford, Calif.: Stanford University Press, 1973), pp. 73–96; and Shanghai qianzhuang shi-liao.

[7] The connections between some of the most important entrepreneurs of Jiangsu and Anhui provinces and the political and business circles in the north (Beijing-Tianjin) had been built up by Zhou Xuexi. The son of an official-gentry family of Anhui, Zhou Xuexi had been one of the most active assistants of Yuan Shikai, overseeing and coordinating the poli-cy for industrialization in Zhili province during the early decades of the twentieth century.

Zhang Jia'ao joined the Bank of China as assistant manager of its Shanghai branch in December 1913, he supplemented his formal (Japanese) education by learning from native bankers. According to his testimony, he benefited greatly from their experience. But in the course of these contacts with native bankers, he "was keenly aware of a large gulf" between his and their ideas.[8]

The persistence and relevance of particularistic solidarities in the 1920s should not obscure the modernizing role of the new Shanghai bankers. Many of them had the opportunity to learn foreign languages in the missionary or Chinese modern-style schools of the treaty ports. Except for their *doyen,* Song Hanzhang, they had studied business and finance abroad: Zhang Jia'ao, Li Ming, Qian Yongming, and Xu Jijin in Japan; Chen Guangfu and Sun Yuanfang in the United States.[9] They had been initiated into Western public and social institutions and belonged to the modern and cosmopolitan world. According to Chen Guangfu, Zhang Jia'ao advocated not only new banking methods but also a parliamentary government supported by a rising middle class. "Other scholars wanted parliamentary government but did not know how to achieve it. Zhang Jia'ao's idea was to begin with new banks, business, commerce, education. . . . He held such views [since] as long ago as 1913–1914."[10]

Even though they relied on native-place ties, the Shanghai bankers felt the need for an association that would be more professional (only managers or owner-managers of the main banks could become members) and at the same time could provide an organizational basis for promoting broader goals, such as nationalism, economic modernization, and state building. The traditional guilds did not give way to the modern syndicate. They coexisted as complementary (rather than antagonistic) forces. The SBA helped the Ningbo and other guild leaders to adjust to new

---

[8] "Autobiography of Chang Chiao-ao," p. 34.

[9] Zhang Jia'ao first studied at the Institute of Modern Languages in Shanghai and then in 1905 went to Japan and enrolled at Keio University (Tokyo) to study finance and economics. Li Ming first enrolled at a Baptist college in Hangzhou run by American missionaries. In 1905 he went to Japan and studied at Yamaguchi Commercial College, where he majored in banking. Xu Jijin was also a graduate from Yamaguchi Commercial College. Qian Yongming was educated in the Polytechnic Institute (later known as Nanyang College) of Shanghai and then graduated from Kobe Commercial College. Chen Guangfu enrolled in Wesleyan University at Delaware (Ohio) from 1904 to 1906, then studied at the University of Pennsylvania, where he took a degree in business. Sun Yuanfang went to the United States in 1903. He first studied at Wesleyan University, then at MIT (from 1906 to 1909), and finally at Brown University (1909 to 1912). Although Song Hanzhang did not study abroad, he had, according to Zhang Jia'ao, "a good English," having previously served in the customs service.

[10] "Reminiscences of Ch'en Kuang-fu," pp. 36–37.

socioeconomic and political circumstances. The Zhejiang clique lent its well-entrenched influence to the new SBA.

The Ways and Means of the SBA: Organizational Capacities and *Guanxi*

The SBA was one of the modern institutions that appeared in China during the first half of this century and through which Chinese urban society developed from an archaic and particularistic stage toward a more open *société civile*. This transition was apparently very rapid in the case of the SBA. It took only three years for the "lunching club" of 1915 to become a formal organization with a very complex legal status and detailed regulations for recruitment, meetings, and voting procedures.

The SBA was organized in 1917, but the formal establishment did not take place until August 1918. By that time, five new banks had joined the original eight. The first formal meeting of the new association was held on August 8 in a recently purchased office on Xianggang lu. The chairman, vice-chairman, and five other directors were elected (see Appendix), and the regulations of the association were adopted. (These regulations were to be slightly revised in 1924.) The regulations provided that only banks with Chinese capital could become members of the new association (Article 1). Each member institution could be represented by one or several of its senior executives, but only one of them was entitled to vote (Articles 3 and 13). Before admission, the prospective member had to submit its accounting books kept during the last three years (Article 6). Admission was decided by a vote of the General Assembly; a two-thirds majority was required. The association was to be managed by a board of seven directors (in 1924 they would become nine). The entrance fee was very high at 1,000 Chinese dollars.[11]

Thus, the SBA was a selective club that in 1925 numbered twenty-four banks as members. These banks were represented by seventy-three managers and senior executives: twenty-four regular members and forty-nine consultative ones.[12] The high entrance fee, the examination of the accounting books, and the majority vote of two-thirds required for admission guaranteed that only the most prosperous and legitimate banking enterprises would enter the association.

At the same time, in 1917, the establishment of *Yinhang zhoubao* gave the association a means of spreading information and propagating

---

[11] Xu Cangshui, ed., *Shanghai yinhang gonghui shiye shi* [History of the Shanghai Bankers' Association] (Shanghai: Shanghai yinhang zhoubaoshe, 1925), *fulu*, pp. 1–9.

[12] Ibid., *fulu*, pp. 14–15.

opinions. Zhang Jia'ao was the main promoter of *Yinhang zhoubao*. His purpose was to address a professional audience, to dispense financial and economic information and statistics, and to survey foreign banking methods. The magazine inspired many reform projects and some official policies. It set an example soon to be followed by other institutions such as the Shanghai General Chamber of Commerce, the Shanghai Native Bankers' Guild, and the banking associations of Beijing and Hankou. Each of them started to publish its own journal in the early 1920s, but *Yinhang zhoubao* remained the most influential of them. Its readership had increased from seven or eight hundred in 1917 to ten thousand in the early 1920s. And its publication outlasted that of its rivals: It stopped only in 1950.[13]

At first, the office of *Yinhang zhoubao* was housed in the building of the Bank of China. The publication was directly supervised by Zhang Jia'ao, and it was funded by the eight banks that founded the SBA. In 1920 the association hired Xu Cangshui, a financial analyst who had just returned from Japan, to be chief editor. In 1925 an editorial committee was established; members of this first committee were Song Hanzhang, Sheng Zhushu, Xu Jijin, Ni Yuanfu, and Sun Yuanfang. Except for Xu Jijin, to whom Zhang Jia'ao had entrusted the magazine when he himself left for Beijing in July 1917, all the members of this editorial committee were or had been chairmen or vice-chairmen of the SBA. In fact, *Yinhang zhoubao* remained under the direct supervision of the SBA. However, those who contributed articles were not bankers but renowned specialists and academics.[14] This opening toward broader social circles, this appeal to public opinion (at least the opinion of wealthy and well-educated urbanites) was quite a departure from the closed world of the professional guilds.

Part of this successful performance can be explained by Zhang Jia'ao's capabilities as an organizer and promoter. Zhang also played a decisive role in the creation of the National Bankers' Association (Quanguo yinhang lianhehui) in 1920. The original idea came from the SBA, which was anxious at the prospect of the eventual bankruptcy and collapse of the Beijing government. The SBA was also afraid of the possible interference of the New International Consortium: There were rumors that foreign banks were considering taking over the control of Chinese

[13] Huang Hanmin, "'Yinhang zhoubao' jianshu" [Brief history of *Yinhang zhoubao*], in Zhongguo jindai jingji shi congshu weiyuanhui, ed., *Zhongguo jindai jingji shi yanjiu ziliao* [Research materials on Chinese modern economic history] (Shanghai: Shanghai shehui kexueyuan chubanshe, 1975), no. 4, pp. 161–71.

[14] Ibid., p. 164.

railways and other resources as a price for their financial assistance.

The SBA took the initiative of sending telegrams to other banking associations (of Beijing, Tianjin, Hankou, Suzhou, and Harbin), inviting their representatives to meet in Shanghai. A preparatory committee was established whose members were Chen Guangfu, Li Ming, Qian Yongming (all of them leaders of the SBA); Ma Yinchu, the already well known professor of economics at Beijing University who concurrently had been appointed to the research department of the Bank of China (at the request of Zhang Jia'ao) and who in 1920 was on leave from Beijing University and was investigating business activities in Shanghai; and Yao Zhongba (unidentified).[15]

The main rivals of the Shanghai modern bankers were those of Beijing and Tianjin. These northern bankers had close links with governmental circles: Most of their funds were provided by public institutions and officials. Among their shareholders and directors or managers one could count many former ministers. An example of this osmosis between political and banking circles was the combined activity of the communications clique and the Bank of Communications. But in Beijing also a new generation of bankers was asserting itself, represented by Zhou Zuomin, who founded the first private commercial bank in north China, the Kincheng Banking Corporation, thus setting a pattern for modern banking practice; and Wu Dingchang, who in 1912 had advocated the expansion of private capital in the recently reorganized Bank of China. In 1920 Wu was the chairman and general manager of the Gabelle Bank (Yanye yinhang). Both of these new-style bankers originally came from the lower Yangzi provinces. A native of Huai'an (Jiangsu), Zhou Zuomin had been trained at the Nanyang Academy (Shanghai) and Kyoto Imperial University from 1905 to 1914. The native place of Wu Dingchang's family was Wuxing (Zhejiang). When in 1917 Zhang Jia'ao was promoted to assistant general manager of the Bank of China and transferred to the head office of the bank, his arrival in Beijing stimulated local modernizing trends. For a while Beijing bankers went along with their Shanghai colleagues' struggle against official interference in banking operations and acted to protect what they considered the legitimate interests of their trade and the highest interests of their country.

The first meeting of the National Bankers' Association (Yinhang gonghui lianhehui) took place in Shanghai on December 5–8, 1920. There were twenty-three representatives, six of them from the SBA: Sheng Zhushu, Qian Yongming, Sun Yuanfang, Chen Guangfu, Song Hanzhang, and Li Ming. Thereafter there was a regular annual meeting of the

[15] Xu Cangshui, *Shanghai yinhang gonghui shiye shi,* pp. 129–31.

association plus extraordinary sessions when special circumstances required them.[16] Through the National Bankers' Association, Shanghai bankers, for a while, could lead a unified, national action to promote their views and policies.[17] One of their outstanding efforts was the organization of a Chinese Bankers' Consortium in January 1921. This consortium was headed by the Bank of China; Zhang Jia'ao was its main promoter. Although Beijing and Tianjin banks were the most numerous among the twenty-eight banks of the consortium, the new spirit was prevailing: Liang Shiyi's plan to take control of the banking group was efficiently countered.[18] The ambition of this powerful financial group was to extend loans to the Beijing government on the condition that the government would agree to reform public finances and work for the national interest.[19]

In the following weeks, several such governmental loans were granted by the consortium: the rolling stock loan (*cheliang jiekuan*) to the Ministry of Communications in January 1921, the Beijing octroi loan in February, the Shanghai mint loan (*Hu zaobichang jiekuan*) in March. We shall return later to the provisions of these contracts. Let us for now conclude that the group of young Shanghai bankers who lunched together in 1915 took only six years to provide themselves with a set of institutions and ad hoc organizations at both the local and national levels that enabled them to promote their policies and even at times to force them upon the government. They had made themselves into an autonomous force that the public authorities had to take into account.

But if the institutions they had created were instrumental in conveying their views and manifesting their will, the source of their power lay elsewhere: in the network of local solidarities and personal relations that was known as the Zhejiang clique.

It is not easy to identify the Zhejiang clique and to describe its operations. The type of interpersonal relations such cliques exhibited is poorly documented. They were part of a system of social intercourse whose prevailing patterns were implicit evidence of their existence among those who lived in a common social and cultural environment, but such evidence eludes the grasp of historians. Nor have the works of

[16] Ibid., p. 129.

[17] Zhang Yulan, *Zhongguo yinhangye fazhan shi* [History of the development of Chinese banking] (Shanghai: Shanghai renmin chubanshe, 1957), pp. 52, 56; Xu Cangshui, *Shanghai yinhang gonghui shiye shi*, pp. 4–5.

[18] Upton Close [pseud. for J. W. Hall], "Close-ups and China Money Josses," *China Review* (New York: China Trade Bureau), 2:4 (April 1922).

[19] Statement by Zhang Jia'ao as reported in "Formation of a Chinese Bankers' Consortium," *China Weekly Review,* January 29, 1921, p. 470ff.

anthropologists, which may throw light on the behavior and role of larger groups, been very helpful in the study of the individual reactions and initiatives taken by such groups of prominent personages. Still, we cannot be satisfied with the exclusive study of institutions. In China, perhaps more than elsewhere, the institutional interplay not only did not exclude personal relations but often merely reflected them. In this sense, Joseph Fewsmith's interpretation of Shanghai commercial organizations as *pouvoirs intermédiaires* should be accepted with some reservations.[20] Behind the institutional facade were motivating forces other than proclaimed principles or stated beliefs and convictions.

At the same time, attempting to reconstruct the network of personal relations and elucidate their interactions may well lead to a situation of no exit. Is history to be confused with the chronicles of some families or individuals and historians with social columnists? Relying on inadequate and scanty clues, I will nonetheless try to suggest what may have been the role of the Zhejiang clique at the center of which lay the SBA.

Although it originated with the rapid expansion of the native banks in the nineteenth century, the Zhejiang financial clique came of age in the early years of the Republican regime. According to a confidential report by the Shanghai Bureau of the South Manchurian Railway Company (SMRC) dated 1929,[21] the core of the Zhejiang financial clique consisted of six persons. Four of them were modern bankers: Yu Xiaqing, Li Ming, Zhang Jia'ao, and Qian Yongming. The fifth, Qin Runqing, belonged to a well-known family of native bankers from Ningbo.[22] The last one, Zhang Jingjiang (born in Wuxing, Zhejiang), was a wealthy businessman, an early supporter of Sun Yat-sen, and a well-respected figure in the Guomindang.

Around this core was an inner circle of twenty-six "very important" persons. A little more than half of them (fourteen) were natives of Zhejiang province, among them eight *qianzhuang* bankers and three modern ones: Hu Mengjia, Xu Jijin, and Song Hanzhang. In the same inner circle belonged twelve non-Zhejiangnese connected to the clique through personal and business relations. Among them were six modern bankers: Chen Guangfu, Zhou Zuomin, Tang Shoumin (all from Jinjiang, Jiangsu), Lin Kanghou and Zhao Xi'en (from Shanghai), and Bei Zuyi (born in Suzhou, Jiangsu).

---

[20] Joseph Fewsmith, *Party, State and Local Organizations in Republican China: Merchant Organizations and Politics in Shanghai, 1890–1930* (Honolulu: University of Hawaii Press, 1985), chap. 1.

[21] Nan Manshū Tetsudō Kabushiki, Shanhai Jimushō, ed., *Sakkō Zaibatsu* [The Zhejiang financial clique], Shanhai Mantetsu Chōsa shiryō, vol. 6 (1929; confidential).

[22] *Shanghai qianzhuang shiliao*, pp. 150, 647–65, 747–50.

Finally, an outer circle of "important persons" included a larger group of forty-four leaders (half of them natives of Zhejiang province). Among them were industrialists, large traders, compradors, and a few native modern bankers, such as Fang Jiaobo, the scion of a great family from Ningbo.

This Zhejiang clique of seventy-six "core leaders," "very important," and "important" persons controlled the main local professional associations: the General Chamber of Commerce, the Zhabei Chamber of Commerce, the district chambers of commerce, the Native Bankers' Guild, the SBA, the Shanghai Cotton Mill Owners' Association, and so on. In most of these institutions, members of the Zhejiang clique were elected president, vice-president, and director. For example, in 1922 Song Hanzhang and Fang Jiaobo, respectively, became president and vice-president of the General Chamber of Commerce. In 1924 they were succeeded by Yu Xiaqing and again Fang Jiaobo. After the controversial 1926 elections, another modern banker, Fu Xiao'en, took over as president. In 1927, when the chamber was reorganized, the new executive committee included two bankers—Zhao Xi'en and Lin Kanghou—along with industrialist Mu Ouchu and publicist Feng Shaoshan. The predominance of the Zhejiang clique was also strongly established in the board of directors of the General Chamber: in 1918 twelve (out of twenty-one identified directors) were affiliated with the clique; in 1924 that number increased to twenty-six (of thirty-five).[23]

Of course, the SBA was the stronghold of the Zhejiang group (see Appendix), which also controlled the Shanghai Native Bankers' Association, for many years presided over by Qin Runqing.[24]

The predominance of the Zhejiang clique in these professional associations can partly be explained by the funds invested by this clique in various branches of business. The survey made by the Shanghai Bureau of the SMRC gives a detailed description of the shares and positions held by members of the Zhejiang clique in twenty different branches of industrial, commercial, and financial activities from cotton mills to navigation companies, from silk factories to the grain trade.[25] But money and business were not the only sources of the group's power. Their political connections also accounted for their influence. Their relations with the Guomindang developed at an early date. Two men were instrumental in

---

[23] James S. Sanford, "Chinese Commercial Organization and Behavior in Shanghai of the Late Nineteenth and Early Twentieth Century," Ph.D. dissertation, Harvard University, 1976, pp. 238, 240, 277.

[24] *Shanghai qianzhuang shiliao*, pp. 647, 665.

[25] *Sakkō zaibatsu*, chap. 5, p. 19.

bringing together the Zhejiang clique and the Guomindang: Chen Qimei, military governor of Shanghai after the 1911 revolution, and Zhang Jingjiang, who after Chen Qimei's assassination in 1916 replaced him as Chiang Kai-shek's patron. Yu Xiaqing, Li Ming, Zhang Jia'ao, and Qian Yongming also had early and close connections with Chiang Kai-shek, and some of them had ties with Song Ziwen (T. V. Soong). These connections were to be of crucial importance in 1927, when Shanghai bankers supported Chiang Kai-shek's rise to power by raising a 30-million-dollar loan.[26]

But in the early 1920s, the Shanghai bankers were still looking toward Beijing and hoping for the reform of the national government. Their man in Beijing was Zhang Jia'ao. And, as already noted, they were related to the communications clique through a small group of Anhui and Jiangsu bankers such as Sun Yuanfang and Zhou Zuomin.

From this very fragmentary evidence, one can realize that the Zhejiang financial clique was a tightly knit elite group whose power was exerted through various institutions but did not really lie with any of them. Because of the economic and financial importance of Shanghai, the Zhejiang clique, which started as a local elite group, rapidly became a national elite group. That it still retained some of its earlier characteristics may be seen from the policies followed by the SBA bankers.

The SBA in Action: From Local Solidarities to National Modernization Drive

Modern bankers had in common with traditional merchants and bankers a sense of their responsibilities toward the local financial and business community. But from this start, modern bankers' conceptions evolved toward a more general goal-oriented policy. The SBA's policy developed along three main lines. It struggled to maintain the stability of the Shanghai market and to modernize monetary and financial systems. It also strove to be a political force to further the public and national interests.

The SBA and the Stability of the Shanghai Market

One of the first initiatives of the SBA after its formal establishment was the creation of a Joint Reserve Fund (*gonggong junbei jin*) of 300,000 Chinese dollars deposited with the Bank of China as protection against an emergency in any bank.[27] But in the spring of 1920 came the

---

[26] "Reminiscences of Ch'en Kuang-fu," chap. 5, "The National Revolution."
[27] Ibid.

signs of the business depression that set off a crisis of reconversion in Chinese treaty ports, especially in Shanghai and Tianjin. This was a crisis of external origin, and it reflected the difficulties of the major economic powers in the aftermath of World War I.[28] The crisis first reached China through foreign trade. By the summer of 1920, a heavy fall in exports, a concomitant decline in the value of silver, and a reduction in imports ushered in an era of domestic stagnation. The crisis rapidly spread to the banking sector. At first the banks most directly affected were the *qianzhuang* that financed the movement of merchandise between treaty ports and inland provinces and whose success depended on the swift turnover of stocks.

The situation was made worse by the failure of some foreign banks that had indulged in excessive speculation on the exchange rate. Such was the case of the Banque Industrielle de Chine (BIC), which moreover had also been hit by the growing deficit and the ultimate bankruptcy of one of its main customers, the Société Maritime et Commerciale du Pacifique. The collapse of the BIC in June 1920 created an upheaval in the Chinese financial market. It was a blow to the reputation of all foreign banks, and Chinese banks that previously had accepted foreign bank notes to keep as reserves now asked for silver. The unusual demand for silver that followed led to an extreme contraction of the market throughout the second half of 1921. The danger was increased by a series of extraordinary speculative waves known as the "stock exchanges storm" (*xinjiao fengchao*).

The idea of creating Chinese exchanges was first put forward by Sun Yat-sen. Yu Xiaqing took an interest, and in July 1919 he established the Shanghai Stock and Produce Exchange (Shanghai zhengzhuan wuping jiaoyisuo), which proved a success and brought forth many rival ventures, most of them purely speculative. Stimulated by a fictitious demand, commodity prices rose; but legitimate business was deprived of capital. In the autumn of 1921, money had become scarce, credit was tight, and inflation was strong. This crisis looked very much like the rubber crisis of 1910. In 1920–21, however, the Shanghai market did not collapse, thanks to the Chinese bankers themselves.

As early as May 1921, Shanghai bankers understood the danger brought about by the irrational expansion of the stock exchanges. The SBA joined the Native Bankers' Guild in asking the Ministry of

---

[28] For a detailed description of the 1921 commercial and financial crisis in Shanghai, see M. C. Bergère, "The Consequences of the Post–First World War Depression for the China Treaty Port Economy, 1921–1923," in *The Economy of Africa and Asia During the Interwar Depression,* ed. Ian Brown (London and New York: Routledge, 1989).

Agriculture and Commerce for the interdiction of stock exchanges.[29] Meanwhile, bankers maintained loans at a prohibitive rate. In September, to preserve their capital, the SBA ordered the banking staff, employees and managers alike, of their member institutions to refrain from investing in stock exchanges.[30] Some time later, the Native Bankers' Guild did the same.[31]

Confronted with the crash of the BIC, the SBA decided that Chinese interests should have unified representation. On July 3, 1921, the SBA called a meeting to discuss the matter, and the president and vice-president of the SBA, Sheng Zhushu and Qian Yongming, called on the French consul-general.

Thanks to the efforts of the Shanghai bankers and the coordinated action of the SBA and the Native Bankers' Guild, the worst was averted, and speculation gradually died down in 1922. But if the banking sector was sufficiently cohesive to dispel the immediate crisis, it still could not provide a solid and permanent link between capital and commercial enterprises. To improve this situation, the SBA called for the reform of monetary and financial institutions.

The Struggle for the Modernization of the Monetary and Financial Systems

Young Shanghai bankers rightly felt that archaic monetary and financial institutions were obstacles to the development of trade and industry. They led an arduous and permanent struggle at both local and national levels to reform these institutions. Their actions took many different forms. There were study groups to research various technical problems and suggest reforms. The results of their research were published in *Yinhang zhoubao*: quite often a series of articles dealing with a specific issue was brought together into a booklet. Suggestions were made to the government, and pressure was put on ministries. These actions were carried on through the SBA or the Federation of Banking Associations. Quite often the Shanghai General Chamber of Commerce or the Native Bankers' Guild was associated with the actions of the bankers, and they cosigned letters or telegrams addressed by the SBA.

One of the bankers' first efforts was to promote the adoption of a fixed terminology for new banking practices. On January 31, 1921, an ad hoc committee was set up, presided over by Xu Jijin, to select technical terms and spread their use among financial circles. A list of the

[29] *Yinhang zhoubao* 5:18 (April 17, 1921): 140.
[30] Xu Cangshui, *Shanghai yinhang gonghui shiye shi*, p. 8.
[31] *Shanghai qianzhuang shiliao*, pp. 120–21.

selected terms was published by the Yinhang zhoubao press in the form of a small book entitled *Yinhang kuaiji kemu mingci* (Handbook for the terminology of bank accounting).[32]

The SBA also insisted on the adoption of standard accounting based on the double-entry system, and they took part in the drafting of the banking regulation of 1921.[33] But they concentrated their action on three main points: organization of a modern stock exchange in Shanghai, currency reform, and consolidation of the internal debt.

Every Shanghai businessman felt the need for an institutional and regular link to make capital available to enterprises. This felt need was at the origin of the the "exchanges storm," which was to discredit the whole system for a long period. The SBA, however, did not see the institution of stock exchanges as just another means of earning easy money. It considered the exchange a legitimate way of regulating the market. In February 1922, when speculation was fading away, the SBA established a preparatory committee for the creation of a Chinese merchant stock exchange (*piaoju jiaohuansuo*). Xu Jijin, Yao Zhongba, and Xu Cangshui were in charge of the new committee, and they prepared for the future exchange a detailed draft regulation, which was published by the Yinhang zhoubao press as *Piaoju jiaohuansuo yanjiu* (Research on stock exchanges). Another special committee of the SBA, which met every Saturday during several months in late 1922, also drafted a law on shareholding (*piaojufa*).[34]

The chaotic condition of Chinese currency was another great worry of Shanghai bankers. The tael was still considered the unit of currency in foreign and Chinese commerce, but the tael was just a weight of silver, represented by no coin. The practice of trading and calculating in silver dollars had become general, although in large native transactions ingots of silver (sycees) were still very often used as a medium of exchange. But the taels used in the treaty ports varied in weight and fineness, and the silver dollars coined throughout the country were not standardized. The SBA, believing that unification of the currency (*tongyi bizhi*) would benefit trade and economic development, supported a reform policy that called for the abolition of the tael and the substitution of a uniform Chinese silver dollar. This idea was stated again and again at annual meetings of the Federation of Banking Associations: in December 1920

[32] Xu Cangshui, *Shanghai yinhang gonghui shiye shi,* p. 3.

[33] Frank M. Tamagna, *Banking and Finance in China* (New York: IPR, 1942), p. 43; see also F. E. Lee, *Currency, Banking and Finance in China* (Washington, D.C.: U.S. Government Printing Office, 1926), pp. 66, 82–84.

[34] Xu Cangshui, *Shanghai yinhang gonghui shiye shi,* pp. 9–10.

in Shanghai, in April 1923 in Hankou, in April 1924 in Beijing, and so on.[35] The Shanghai bankers did not stop at making recommendations. As they (rightly) considered it absolutely necessary that weight and fineness be invariable and reliable if a uniform Chinese dollar was to be adopted, they decided to make a loan to the Ministry of Finance for the erection of a modern mint, under central control, in Shanghai. The loan agreement was signed on March 3, 1921. The amount of the loan was 2.5 million Chinese dollars. The money was to be used exclusively for the purchase of the land, the construction of the building, and the purchase of the mint's equipment.[36]

Such a unification of the currency, however, would have deprived the *qianzhuang* banks of important profits derived from interport exchange and resulting from keeping banking accounts in taels whereas payments were made in dollars. In consideration of their own interests, *qianzhuang* bankers opposed the unification project; this opposition caused conflict between them and the SBA (as can be seen in numerous critical articles published in *Yinhang zhoubao*).[37] The solidarity that existed to protect the local market disappeared when the modernization drive threatened the vested interests of traditional bankers, and cooperation then gave way to conflict inside the Zhejiang clique itself.

Finally, Shanghai bankers were worried about the growing public finance deficit and the eventuality of governmental bankruptcy. One of the most important activities of official and semiofficial modern banks was the issuing and trade of government bonds. The Shanghai bankers were calling for the readjustment of China's domestic loans and the creation of a sinking fund: in this way they hoped that the interests of bond holders (the bankers themselves) could be protected and public credit could be restored. Their request was presented by the Federation of Banking Associations when it first met in December 1920. Both Shanghai and Beijing bankers decided to refrain from lending any money to the government pending its acceptance of this request. When in early 1921 the Beijing government attempted to go ahead and issue new bonds or to borrow fresh money, there was a general outcry from Chinese banking circles, and the government had to renounce its projects.[38] Finally, in March 1921, a presidential mandate approved the project that had been prepared by the Ministry of Finance, according to the plan laid by the

---

[35] Ibid., pp. 129–31.

[36] English summary of loan contract in H. G. Woodhead, ed., *The China Yearbook, 1923* (Tianjin: Tientsin Press Ltd., [1924]), p. 286.

[37] Huang Hanmin, "'Yinhang zhoubao' jianshu," p. 168.

[38] *China Weekly Review,* January 1, 1921. See also Upton Close, "The Chinese Bankers Assert Themselves," ibid., February 19, 1921, pp. 646–48.

Federation of Banking Associations, for the readjustment of China's domestic loans. To provide for the sinking fund, the government appropriated revenues from the surplus of maritime and native customs and from the salt tax and the wine and tobacco taxes. The inspector-general of Maritime Customs, Sir Francis Aglen, was to control the service of this sinking fund.

For a while banking circles tried to ensure the smooth working of this arrangement. They strongly opposed the Beijing government when it announced a new issue of bonds that were not properly guaranteed in July 1921[39] and again in spring 1923.[40] They also opposed Sun Yat-sen when, in late 1923 as the head of the southern (Nationalist) government, he asked for his share of the customs surplus.[41]

In pursuing their reformist policy, Shanghai bankers represented specific group interests, and that is why they came into conflict with the vested interests of traditional bankers, on the one hand, and the corrupt and powerless Beijing government, on the other hand. But at the same time, they were taking upon themselves responsibilities that in modernizing countries usually fall within the province of governmental policy. Because of the decline of state power, private managers thus were led to play a role usually assumed by state bureaucracies and to become the representatives of public and national interests as well as their own.

The SBA as a Political Force

What differentiated the SBA from the many cliques and factions struggling to influence or control the Beijing government in the early 1920s is that the SBA, while furthering the interests of its members, also strove toward more general goals of public and national interests. Chinese bankers broke the merchants' traditional rule that kept them away from what was seen as "dirty politics." What stimulated bankers' interests in politics was not theory. Their approach was a pragmatic one. They

---

[39] D. K. Lieu, "China Internal Loans," *China Weekly Review,* June 17, 1922.

[40] See the telegram addressed by the SBA to the Beijing Bankers' Association in *Shanghai zongshanghui yuebao* [Monthly journal of the Shanghai Chamber of Commerce], 3:3 (March 1923). See also Harold Fleming, "Chinese Bankers Attempt to Control Government Finance," *China Weekly Review,* September 29, 1923; and R. Gilbert, "Native Bankers and Domestic Bonds," *North China Herald,* November 3, 1923, p. 303.

[41] See the joint telegram of the Shanghai General Chamber of Commerce, the Native Bankers' Guild, and the SBA to Sun Yat-sen in *Shanghai zongshanghui yuebao* 3:12 (December 1923). It should be remembered that the revenues from maritime customs were earmarked for the service of foreign debts. What was left over after repayments to foreigners (i.e., the "surplus") had been appropriated in 1921 to service the consolidated internal debt.

perceived that militarism, financial chaos, bureaucratic despotism, and foreign interference were obstacles hampering China's development and that their struggle for economic modernization could not succeed without political reforms.

They were patriots. When the New International Consortium (Xin yinhang tuan) was organized in October 1920, foreign bankers invited Chinese participation. But the Chinese bankers firmly declined. At its first meeting, in December 1920, the Federation of Banking Associations decided to meet this challenge by organizing their own Chinese Consortium (Zhonghua yinhang tuan). The active opposition of Chinese bankers thus prevented the New International Consortium from taking any action, that is, granting loans to the Beijing government in exchange for the concession of revenues or control over administrative departments.

The Federation of Banking Associations also played an important part in the campaign of "people's diplomacy" (guomin waijiao) launched just before the Washington conference. The "people's delegates" (guomin daibiao) who had been mandated by the chambers of commerce and educational societies also had close connections with banking circles: Jiang Menglin was the grandson of a Shanghai qianzhuang banker, and Yu Rizhang was a friend of Song Hanzhang and Chen Guangfu.[42] Because of the declining legitimacy of the Beijing government, its envoys to the Washington conference (zhengfu daibiao) lacked representativeness and authority. The "people's diplomacy" was an attempt to bypass official procedure and to give a say to social forces at work in the treaty ports.

Bankers, however, did not deny the need for a state that would play its indispensable role in the modernizing process and at the same time would respect and protect the legitimate interests of social groups. The financial distress of the Beijing government gave the bankers a brief opportunity to put their ideas to the test. At its congress in December 1920, the Federation of Banking Associations warned the government that unless certain conditions were fulfilled, Chinese bankers would not agree to any new public loan. The bankers wanted the government to decrease military expenses, reform currency, and readjust internal loans. For Zhang Jia'ao, these demands were only expressing bankers' patriotism. The bankers were ready to lend money to a government that would work toward the country's progress.[43] To foreign observers, this

---

[42] W. S. A. Pott, "The People's Delegates to the Pacific Conference," China Weekly Review, October 22, 1921. On the Washington conference and the "people's diplomacy," see also M. C. Bergère, The Golden Age of the Chinese Bourgeoisie 1911–1937 (Cambridge: Cambridge University Press/Maison des Sciences de l'Homme, 1989), pp. 262–66.

[43] "Formation of a Chinese Bankers' Consortium," p. 470ff.

kind of censorship exercised by financial elites could be considered the beginnings of democracy.[44]

These social initiatives led to some success. Chinese interests were well represented and defended at the Washington conference (although the favorable outcome of the conference for China was due to complex international factors rather than to "people's diplomacy"). Moreover, for some months, in early 1921, Chinese bankers really imposed their control over the financial policy of the government. But as early as December 1920–January 1921, the Chinese Consortium relinquished the principles that it had itself posited, agreeing to make a $4-million loan to Liang Shiyi's cabinet. Contrary to what had been stated as imperative conditions for any loan to the government, there was no guarantee for the Liang Shiyi loan; furthermore, the money was to be spent for general administrative purposes, not on productive projects. This episode brought an end to the history of the Chinese Consortium. Thereafter Chinese banking associations (and especially the SBA) went on stating general principles, but they did not care to put them into practice. The Shanghai mint was not built; the rolling stock loan and the Beijing octroi loan did not serve any positive ends.

Conclusion

From the case of the SBA some tentative conclusions can be drawn. (1) The establishment of modern social institutions (with formal status and general goals) was facilitated rather than hindered by the existence of traditional associations. (2) However, the appearance of these modern institutions can hardly be considered an expansion of traditional institutions: It took leaders with new ideas and different (foreign) training to organize these institutions. (3) The new institutions did not displace the old associations. The two coexisted and, in spite of some divergent interests, generally cooperated. (4) Most of the power wielded by the new institutions should be traced to this cooperation. (5) The existence of such traditional associations can therefore be considered a favorable precondition in modernizing societies. But the transition from the archaic, particularistic stage to a modern open society, from the customary laws to the legal organization of social relations and economic production, cannot be completed without the intervention of state power, which remains the decisive factor in the modernizing process.

---

[44] Close, "Chinese Bankers Assert Themselves," pp. 646–48.

APPENDIX

Chairmen and Vice-Chairmen of the SBA, 1918–1926

	Chairmen	Vice-Chairmen
July 1918–Aug. 1920	Song Hanzhang	Chen Guangfu
Sept. 1920–Aug. 1922	Sheng Zhushu	Qian Yongming
Sept. 1922–Aug. 1924	Sheng Zhushu	Sun Yuanfang
Sept. 1924–Aug. 1926	Ni Yuanfu	Sun Yuanfang

SOURCE: *Shanghai yinhang gonghui shiye shi,* p. 12.

Members of the Board of Directors of the SBA, 1918–1926

July 1918–Aug. 1920	Song Hanzhang, Qian Yongming, Sheng Zhushu, Ni Yuanfu, Chen Guangfu, Sun Yuanfang, Li Ming
Sept. 1920–Aug. 1922	Sheng Zhushu, Qian Yongming, Ni Yuanfu, Sun Yuanfang, Ge Shengwu, Sun Hengfu, Jiang Shaofeng
Sept. 1922–Aug. 1924	Song Hanzhang, Qian Yongming, Sheng Zhushu, Li Ming, Ni Yuanfu, Sun Yuanfang, Tian Shaoying, Lin Kanghou, Ye Fuxiao
Sept. 1924–Aug. 1926	Ni Yuanfu, Sun Yuanfang, Song Hanzhang, Chen Guangfu, Wu Yunzhai, Wu Weiru, Ye Fuxiao, Zheng Lucheng, Li Ming

SOURCE: Ibid., p. 13.

CHAPTER TWO

Three Roads into Shanghai's Market

Japanese, Western, and Chinese Companies in the Match Trade, 1895–1937

SHERMAN COCHRAN

Between 1895 and 1937, Shanghai attracted sojourning capitalists from abroad and from all regions of China, and it served as headquarters for almost all China's foreign-owned long-distance trading firms as well as many Chinese-owned ones. The aim of this chapter is to characterize these sojourning big businesses and analyze their approaches to Shanghai's market. To achieve this aim, it focuses on firms marketing one commodity, matches, and in particular on three such businesses, all of them commercial giants: Japan's largest marketing firm, Mitsui Trading Company (Mitsui Bussan Kaisha); the West's and the world's largest match manufacturer, Swedish Match Company (Svenska Tändsticks Aktiebolaget); and China's leading match producer and distributor, China Match Company (Da Zhonghua huochai gongsi).

These three large corporations were alike in that they all set up headquarters for China in Shanghai and used Shanghai as a base for long-distance trade in the early twentieth century, but each adopted a different strategy to control the market in Shanghai and other Chinese cities. Was the approach used by each one illustrative of a national or cultural style of business behavior? That is, did Mitsui Bussan conform to a "Japanese model," Swedish Match to a "Western model," and China Match to a "Chinese model" of business organization and strategy? Or did these three companies depart from the usual patterns and behave in a manner reflecting the special character of Shanghai? Of the three, why did the Chinese firm have greater success in Shanghai than its larger and more internationally influential foreign rivals? This chapter explores these questions by characterizing each of the three businesses in relation to a different model.

Mitsui Bussan Kaisha in Shanghai: Creating the Japanese Model

The classic Japanese multinational firm, according to Japan specialists, has been the general trading company (sōgō shōsha). This type of
firm's primary objective has been to market goods abroad, or, in the
words of Japanese historian Yoshihara Hideki, to trade "all kinds of
goods with all nations of the world." To expand along these lines, it has
relied on a corps of Japanese sales representatives to travel overseas,
assume posts in foreign cities, and win cooperation from foreign nationals on the basis of face-to-face contact. Taking marketing and not
manufacturing as its specialty, it has invested heavily in the training of
these sales agents and has not generally built its own factories. At most
it has usually made indirect rather than direct investments in manufacturing; instead of constructing its own factories, it has encouraged independent Japanese industrialists to manufacture by making them loans that
obligate them, in turn, to export exclusively through it.[1]

The first Japanese company to fit this description was Mitsui Bussan
Kaisha, founded in 1876, and the first site for such a company's operations abroad was Shanghai, where Mitsui Bussan opened its first overseas
office in 1877. Prior to that time, even Japan's largest mercantile houses,
including Mitsui Bussan's parent firm, the house of Mitsui, had gained
little experience at trading abroad because of the seclusionist policies
imposed during the Tokugawa period between the seventeenth and
nineteenth centuries. Lacking experience, Mitsui Bussan at first imitated
practices used by Western firms in Shanghai, but before the end of the
century, as it added numerous other branches in China and other
countries, it introduced its own approach and made Shanghai the proving
ground for its two most innovative programs: overseas training and overseas marketing.

Training Japanese China Specialists

During its first two decades in Shanghai, 1877–98, Mitsui Bussan followed the Western companies' example by recruiting a team of Chinese
compradors (in its case led by Jin Yangsheng) and relying on them to
perform a variety of services: translations of Chinese dialects into foreign
languages, explanations of Chinese commercial practices, guarantees of

---

[1] The quotation is from Hideki Yoshihara, "Some Questions on Japan's Sōgō Shōsha," in
Shin'ichi Yonekawa and Hideki Yoshihara, eds., *Business History of General Trading Companies: The International Conference on Business History 13, Proceedings of the Fuji Conference* (Tokyo: University of Tokyo Press, 1987), p. 1. This and other essays in the same
volume provide useful references to the large number of studies available on *sōgō shōsha* and
greatly clarify the meaning of the "Japanese model." See also Mira Wilkins, "Japanese Multinational Enterprise before 1914," *Business History Review* 60:2 (Summer 1986): 199–231.

the personal integrity of other Chinese employees, recruitment of Chinese commission agents, and, in general, management of marketing for imported goods. In 1898, however, Mitsui Bussan became the first foreign company to seek an alternative to the comprador system. Complaining that it was paying compradors a full 1 percent of its transactions in China, Mitsui Bussan took the first step toward a distinctive marketing system by beginning to train Japanese replacements for its Chinese compradors.[2]

In 1898 Mitsui Bussan inaugurated a series of training programs in China, particularly at Shanghai. Under the first of these programs, which lasted from April 1898 to October 1915, Mitsui Bussan annually sent recent Japanese graduates of junior and senior high schools to Shanghai, Yingkou, Tianjin, Taibei, and Hong Kong for five years of full-time study. Aged fifteen to twenty, these young Japanese were known as "apprentices in Chinese commerce" (*Shinkoku shōgyō minaraisei*) and were groomed to become China "traders" (*boekijin*). When first introduced, this program drew complaints from Mitsui Bussan's branch managers, who doubted the value of investing in such inexperienced young people. In response, Mitsui Bussan's president, Masuda Takashi, made an inspection tour to observe firsthand the company's branches at Shanghai, Taibei, and Hong Kong in October 1898; in December 1898, at Masuda's urging, the company's board of directors in Tokyo introduced a second program.

Mitsui Bussan's second training program was for older and more experienced employees designated as "China trainees" (*Shina shūgyōsei*). Candidates for this program were selected on the basis of education, not age (with a junior high school diploma as the minimum requirement), willingness to participate, and "indomitability of spirit" (*fukutsu no tōshi*). Beginning in 1899, Mitsui Bussan annually selected ten employees, released them from their usual jobs, and sent them to China for three years of full-time study. The company arranged for them to study at branches in several cities—including Nanjing, Guangzhou, Hong Kong—with the largest number based at Shanghai.[3]

At Shanghai, Mitsui Bussan's headquarters for China provided the best Chinese language training in the company and perhaps in the entire

[2] Nihon Keieishi Kenkyūjo [Japanese Business History Research Institute], ed., "Kohon Mitsui Bussan Kabushiki Kaisha 100 nenshi" [A draft one-hundred-year history of the Mitsui Trading Company] (Tokyo: unpublished, 1978), vol. 1, p. 207. Masuda Takashi, president of Mitsui Bussan at the time, made the estimate of 1 percent.

[3] Ibid., pp. 213–14; Togai Yoshio, *Mitsui Bussan Kaisha no keiei shiteki kenkyū* [Historical studies of Mitsui Trading Company's management] (Tokyo: Tōyō Keizai Shinposha, 1974), p. 55.

country. As early as 1891, the Shanghai branch had begun to give its employees informal language training, and after Mitsui Bussan formally introduced training programs in 1898, the branch's program benefited from the leadership of Yamamoto Jōtarō, who had served Mitsui Bussan at Shanghai since 1888, had hosted and influenced President Masuda during his visit to Shanghai in 1898, and had risen to the position of branch manager in 1901.[4] As Yamamoto proudly reported at a meeting of all the company's branch managers in 1904, the graduates of Mitsui Bussan's Shanghai program spoke and read Chinese much better than people from other foreign language schools, including the Tōa Dōbun Shoin, Japan's best known foreign language institute in China. Other branch managers in China acknowledged Yamamoto's point, conceding the superiority of training given at Shanghai.[5]

Under Yamamoto's regimen, Japanese studying at Mitsui Bussan's branch in Shanghai became familiar with China's customs as well as its language. For example, according to Yamamoto, all Japanese apprentices and trainees had to dress in the clothes of common Chinese "coolies," wear their hair Chinese style (which, before the overthrow of the Manchu monarchy in 1911, was actually Manchu style with a bald pate and a queue down the back), and live with Chinese families. To encourage even more intimate contact, Mitsui Bussan offered Japanese apprentices and trainees bonuses if they would marry Chinese women, but reportedly no one took advantage of the offer. Through these activities, President Masuda noted, Mitsui Bussan taught Japanese trainees about "the mentality of the Chinese people, the basis for trust among Chinese merchants, and the flows of commercial goods [in China] in full detail."[6]

As Japanese graduated from Mitsui Bussan's training program, the company assigned them to replace Chinese compradors. In 1899, it pensioned off its comprador Jin Yangsheng and eight other Chinese at Shanghai, and it subsequently dismissed compradors at Tianjin in 1900,

---

[4] On Yamamoto's later role in Sino-Japanese relations as president of the South Manchurian Railway (Mantetsu) in the 1920s, see Akira Iriye, *After Imperialism: The Search for a New Order in the Far East, 1921–1931* (Cambridge, Mass.: Harvard University Press, 1965), chap. 5.

[5] *Kohon Mitsui Bussan Kabushiki Kaisha 100 nenshi*, pp. 215–16. On Tōa Dōbun Shoin, see Douglas R. Reynolds, "Japan Does It Better: Tōa Dōbun Shoin (1900–1945) and Its Mission," in *Essays in the History of the Chinese Republic* (Urbana, Ill.: University of Illinois Center for Asian Studies, 1983), pp. 30–37.

[6] *Yamamoto Jōtarō: denki* [Biography of Yamamoto Jōtarō] (Tokyo: Denki Hensankai, 1942), pp. 117–18; William D. Wray, "Japan's Big-Three Service Enterprises in China, 1896–1936," in Peter Duus, Ramon H. Myers, and Mark R. Peattie, eds., *The Japanese Informal Empire in China, 1895–1937* (Princeton, N.J.: Princeton University Press, 1989), p. 46.

Taibei in 1901, and Hong Kong in 1902. During these years, Mitsui Bussan's profits on trade in China tripled (from 114,381 yen for 1897–99 to 353,623 yen for 1900–2), and its profit rate doubled (from 10.0 percent to 20.3 percent in the same three-year periods).[7] Thereafter, the company never again hired another Chinese comprador.

Experience at Marketing

Once Mitsui Bussan completed the process of phasing out compradors and phasing in Japanese replacements, it began using graduates of its training program to expand its marketing system in China. During the first two decades of the twentieth century, the largest number in any one city was stationed at Shanghai, the site of Mitsui Bussan's headquarters for China, and the rest were spread over no less than seven of China's nine "macroregions."[8]

At Shanghai, Mitsui Bussan's branch at first grew steadily, and it mushroomed after the company's Tokyo headquarters reorganized its worldwide marketing system into departments in 1912. In 1909, on the eve of this reorganization, the Shanghai office was already the company's best staffed branch (with 48 employees) and best financed branch (with 18.2 percent of Mitsui Bussan's total operating capital) in the world.[9] During the following decade, the Shanghai office grew still faster, tripling its employees (who numbered 173 in 1919) and retaining its position as Mitsui Bussan's largest branch (table 1). This staff was needed to handle Shanghai's volume of transactions, which between 1910 and 1919 was consistently the highest of any branch in China and second (to New York) of all branches worldwide (table 2).

With Shanghai as its ever-growing beachhead, Mitsui Bussan extended its reach outward to other regions. As shown in table 3, Mitsui Bussan confined these offices to metropolitan centers in the cores of five of China's regions and reached down the urban hierarchy to smaller cities and towns in two regions, the Northeast (where the Japanese government had a sphere of influence) and the Southeast (which included Taiwan, a

---

[7] *Kohon Mitsui Bussan Kabushiki Kaisha 100 nenshi*, p. 208; Ishii Kanji, "Nisshin sengo keiei" [Business after the Sino-Japanese war], *Iwanami Kōza, Nihon rekishi,* vol. 16, Kindai 3 (Tokyo: Iwanami Shoten, 1976), p. 68, table 7.

[8] On the basis for viewing China as nine macroregions, see G. William Skinner, "Regional Urbanization in Nineteenth-Century China," in Skinner, ed., *The City in Late Imperial China* (Stanford, Calif.: Stanford University Press, 1977), pp. 211–49.

[9] William D. Wray, "China's Function in Japanese Business, 1898–1937: Banking, Shipping, and Trading," paper presented at the Conference on Japanese Imperialism in China, Stanford University, August 20–25, 1985, p. 25A, table 7.

Table 1
Number of Japanese Personnel in Mitsui Bussan's
Overseas Branches, 1909 and 1919

Overseas Branch	1909	1919
Northeast China		
Dalian	16	127
Andong	4	7
Niuzhuang (Yingkou)	13	11
Hanyang	5	10
Tieling	6	11
Changchun	8	14
Harbin	11	22
Vladivostok (Russia)	4	8
North China		
Tianjin	18	66
Beijing	—	5
Qingdao	3	52
Jinan	—	9
Lower Yangzi in China		
Shanghai	48	173
Wuhu	—	2
Zhefu	5	9
Middle Yangzi in China		
Hankou	19	62
Changsha	—	2
Changde	—	1
Chongqing	—	2
South and Southeast China		
Hong Kong	41	90
Haifang (Vietnam)	—	5
Saigon (Vietnam)	—	6
Shantou	—	6
Guangzhou	5	16
Fuzhou	3	7
Xiamen	3	8
Taibei	25	55
Jilong	—	2

(continued)

(Table 1, continued)

Overseas Branches	1909	1919
Tainan	21	36
Taizhong	—	4
Dagou	—	12
China trainees	9	33
Apprentices in trade	1	—
Outside China and Japan		
Seoul	16	61
Pusan	2	22
Jinseng	5	4
Sydney	2	21
Melbourne	—	4
Manila	5	15
Singapore	10	42
Bangkok	1	7
Medan	—	1
Java	3	—
Surabaya	—	32
Samarang	—	7
Batavia	—	15
Bombay	22	63
Karachi	—	1
Colombo	—	3
Calcutta	1	41
Rangoon	—	11
London	18	41
Lyons	3	13
Marseilles	—	7
Hamburg	7	—
New York	28	105
Dallas	—	19
San Francisco	4	20
Seattle	—	19
Portland	1	2
Buenos Aires	—	3

SOURCE: *Kohon Mitsui Bussan Kabushiki Kaisha 100 nenshi,* p. 339, table 6, and p. 340, table 7.

Table 2
Value of Transactions by Mitsui Bussan's
Leading Overseas Branches, 1910–1919
(in thousand yen)

Branch	1910	1912	1916	1919
Dalian	6,298	7,162	15,983	40,403
Shanghai	22,137	4,742	37,968	81,087
Hankou	5,973	2,623	7,839	19,635
Taibei	9,081	4,898	5,992	13,378
Hong Kong	7,677	943	18,292	52,116
New York	35,740	36,912	165,801	219,835
London	26,237	11,907	31,485	65,127
Calcutta	—	—	30,323	67,718
Bombay	2,597	1,676	26,190	55,574

SOURCE: *Kohon Mitsui Bussan Kabushiki Kaisha 100 nenshi*, p. 343, table 9.

Japanese colony since 1895). Thus Mitsui Bussan stationed its Japanese representatives in China mainly in cities at the pinnacles of China's regional and local urban hierarchies. In the nomenclature of central place theory, Mitsui Bussan took Shanghai as its "central metropolis," fanned out from Shanghai to "regional metropolises," reached below regional metropolises to "regional cities" only in regions under Japanese political influence, and did not otherwise extend its formal marketing hierarchy down to "greater cities," "local cities," or smaller towns in China.[10]

By training more foreign employees and setting up more offices than any other foreign company, Mitsui Bussan developed more expertise at marketing than any other foreign trading company in early twentieth-century China. Nonetheless, even its heavy investment in this elaborate marketing system did not automatically allow it to dominate Sino-Japanese trade. As illustrated by the match trade, it had to contend with Chinese rivals whose experience surpassed its own.

Sino-Japanese Competition in Japan and China

In the match trade, Mitsui Bussan had difficulty surmounting barriers to entry erected by its Chinese rivals. According to Mitsui Bussan's

---

[10] On this classification of cities, see G. William Skinner, "Cities and the Hierarchy of Local Systems," in Skinner, ed., *The City in Late Imperial China*, pp. 275–351.

Table 3

Locations of Match Companies' Salaried Representatives in China

	Mitsui Bussan Kaisha, 1910s	Swedish Match Company, 1930s	China Match Company, 1930s
Headquarters for China	Shanghai	Shanghai	Shanghai
Divisional offices at regional level	NE (7 cities) No (4 cities) LY (3 cities) MY (3 cities) SE, including Taiwan (10 cities) So (2 cities)	NE (2 cities) LY (1 city) MY (1 city) So (1 city)	LY (5 cities) MY (4 cities) SE (3 cities)
Subdivisional offices at county level			LY (24 counties)

Abbreviations: NE: Northeast; No: North; LY: Lower Yangzi; MY: Middle Yangzi; SE: Southeast; So: South
SOURCES: Yamashita, "Matchi Kōgyo to Mitsui Bussan," p. 155, table 27; *Liu Hongsheng qiye shiliao*, 1:153, 2:149, 3:65; *Zhongguo minzu huochai gongye*, pp. 71–72.

own secret study in 1899, it had never captured more than a meager 1.2 percent of the Sino-Japanese match trade during the 1890s because Chinese trading companies had monopolized the trade in Japanese-made exported matches. Before Mitsui Bussan had begun handling matches, Chinese trading companies—some based in Osaka or Kobe with offices in Shanghai and others based in Shanghai with offices in Japan—had formed binding agreements with Japanese match manufacturers. These Chinese companies assisted Japanese manufacturers in every phase of production and marketing by offering loans secured against factories, supplying transportation for matches shipped abroad, and handling distribution of matches within China. In return, Japanese manufacturers signed exclusive-dealing agreements, which precluded working with any other trading company, including Mitsui Bussan. To discourage Japanese manufacturers from beginning to market abroad on their own, Chinese trading companies retained full control over trademarks on all matches exported from Japan, affixing to match boxes their own labels, which made no reference to the names of Japanese manufacturers.[11]

In trying to break this Chinese hold on Japanese manufacturers, Mitsui Bussan resorted to extraordinary tactics. To appeal to Japanese match manufacturers, it offered them "joint trademarks" (kyōyū shōhyō), which featured the producer's trademark as well as Mitsui's own on match labels used in China. Still not content with its supply of matches, Mitsui Bussan went beyond its usual concentration on marketing to invest in manufacturing. In January 1907, it joined two Japanese match manufacturers, Naoki Masanosuke and Honda Yoshitomo, in founding the Nippon Match Company, which at the time had the highest production capacity of any Japanese factory making matches for export.[12]

While seeking supplies of matches in Japan, Mitsui Bussan aggressively underpriced its competitors in Shanghai. In 1902 and again in 1908 Mitsui Bussan's board of directors in Tokyo sanctioned this policy, targeting matches as one of the company's "most important commodities" and setting aside a reserve fund to cover all of its branches' losses on match sales. When the board expressed disappointment that the company's matches had encountered in Shanghai "the most severe

[11] On Chinese trading companies based in Osaka and Kobe, see Yamashita Naotō, "Keiseiki Nihon shihonshugi ni okeru matchi kōgyō to Mitsui Bussan" [The match industry and Mitsui Trading Company in the formative period of Japanese capitalism], Mitsui bunko ronso 6 (1972): 95–100. On Chinese trading companies based in Shanghai with offices in Osaka, see Zhang Zhongli et al., eds., Shanghai jindai baihuo shangye shi [History of modern Shanghai's trade in consumer goods] (Shanghai: Shanghai shehui kexue yuan chubanshe, 1988), pp. 180–85.

[12] Yamashita, "Matchi kōgyō to Mitsui Bussan," pp. 136–37, 162–64.

competition in China," Shanghai branch manager Yamamoto Jōtarō replied, "In Shanghai although matches are not profitable, we have not become demoralized, so our match business is growing little by little."[13]

Despite Mitsui Bussan's efforts, "little by little" was the most that could be said for the growth rate of Mitsui Bussan's share of Shanghai's match market. It captured 15–16 percent of the city's imported match trade between 1903 and 1904 and showed less profit there than in Dalian, Hong Kong, or Singapore. Subsequently, in 1910–12, its sales and revenue from matches remained consistently lower in Shanghai than in Taibei or Singapore. Even outside Shanghai, Mitsui Bussan's success was not overwhelming, bringing it an average of 18.2 percent of Japan's match exports between 1907 and 1915. Never rising above tenth in value among Mitsui Bussan's exports from Japan in the 1910s, matches slipped below twentieth in 1925 and ceased thereafter to be designated and promoted by the company as one of its "most important commodities."[14]

In light of Mitsui Bussan's elaborate marketing system, its sales in China and especially Shanghai were surprisingly small. Fortunately for the company, it depended on matches for only a tiny share of its total sales revenue—an average of a mere 2.1 percent per year between 1898 and 1916. As early as 1908 it distributed no fewer than 120 commodities abroad, and by the early 1920s, it began to handle an even wider variety including heavy as well as light industrial goods.[15] Mitsui Bussan thus protected itself against losses in a single commodity like matches by carrying numerous goods and distributing them in widespread locations. In the process, it developed a feature of its operation that has retrospectively become regarded as central to the Japanese model for international businesses.

Mitsui Bussan Kaisha and the Japanese Model

As this characterization suggests, Mitsui Bussan introduced at Shanghai all the basic elements that constitute the Japanese model for overseas business. Its investments at Shanghai were the first of their kind ever made by a Japanese firm abroad, and its performance as Japan's premier overseas business has helped to secure its reputation as the original "prototype" for Japanese-style international trading companies.[16]

---

[13] Ibid., pp. 141, 155–56, 160. Quotation from p. 141.

[14] Ibid., p. 130, table 18, and p. 152, table 25; *Kohon Mitsui Bussan Kabushiki Kaisha 100 nenshi*, pp. 419 and 444.

[15] Togai, *Mitsui Bussan Kaisha no keiei shiteki kenkyū*, p. 44; Yamashita, "Matchi kōgyō to Mitsui Bussan," p. 152, table 26.

[16] In historical analyses of Mitsui Bussan's internal business practices, "prototype" is a

While following no known Japanese precedents, Mitsui Bussan also consciously avoided Western models in the early twentieth century. In this respect it differed from some of Japan's other large enterprises such as the Japan Mail Steamship Company (Nippon Yusen Kaisha or N.Y.K.), which was modeled after the British-owned Peninsula and Oriental Steam Navigation Company (P. & O. Line), and the Japanese Yokohama Specie Bank, which was modeled after the British-owned Hongkong and Shanghai Bank.[17] Ironically, if Mitsui Bussan adopted any model in the match trade, the model was Chinese, not Japanese or Western. As shown here, Mitsui Bussan offered Japanese match manufacturers commercial and financial services almost identical to those that had already been provided by Chinese trading companies, and it competed with its Chinese rivals by introducing new services (such as "joint trademarks") in response to preexisting Chinese practices (such as retention of control over trademarks on export matches.)

If breaking all precedents for Japanese companies abroad, why did Mitsui Bussan choose Shanghai for its heaviest investment in marketing? If match sales yielded less profit in Shanghai than in cities elsewhere in the world, why should a non-Chinese company make an extra effort to promote matches as an "important commodity" in Shanghai? This latter question was raised by a Western business, Swedish Match Company.

Swedish Match Company in Shanghai: Conforming with the Western Model

If the watchword in the Japanese historical model for multinational firms is "marketing," then the watchword in the Western model is "manufacturing." Whereas the Japanese model distinguishes sharply between marketing (done by general trading companies like Mitsui Bussan) and manufacturing (done separately by independent industrial producers), the Western model highlights the integration of manufacturing with marketing as a central feature of Western multinational firms in the early twentieth century. According to this model, large Western manufacturing companies were motivated to enter overseas markets because of their domestic production—or, more accurately, overproduction. Once abroad, they continued to follow patterns established at home by specializing in particular products (rather than distributing a

term used by Togai, *Mitsui Bussan Kaisha no keiei shiteki kenkyu*, p. 13, and by Seiichiro Yonekura, "The Emergence of the Prototype of Enterprise Group Capitalism—The Case of Mitsui," *Hitotsubashi Journal of Commerce and Management* 20:1 (December 1985): 63–104.

[17] Wray, "Japan's Big-three Service Enterprises," pp. 63–64.

wide variety of goods as Mitsui Bussan did) and by buying and often closing foreign-built factories (rather than investing heavily in training and
salaries for sales representatives as Mitsui Bussan did).[18]

Founded in 1919, Swedish Match Company conformed closely to this
Western model. As its name implies, this firm specialized in a single
product; and in the 1920s, it invested heavily in manufacturing, forging a
worldwide chain of factories that by 1930 gave it direct or indirect control over no less than 62 percent of all the match production in the
world.[19] In fact, it failed to dominate only one major market in the non-
socialist world, China—the single largest match market of all—where its
market share never exceeded 7 percent; and within China, it fell short of
capturing the match market even of the city chosen for its nationwide
headquarters, Shanghai, where its market share never surpassed 15 percent.[20]

Why were China in general and Shanghai in particular exceptional?
If able to capture markets elsewhere in the world, why did Swedish
Match not have greater success in China and Shanghai? Perhaps answers
may be found in Swedish Match's conformity with the Western model.

Controlling Manufacturing and Dumping Matches

As the Western model would predict, Swedish industrialist Ivar
Kreuger, founder and head of Swedish Match, extended his company's
operations to East Asia and particularly China in the 1920s to solve the

---

[18] On the historical process whereby distribution was integrated with production, see the
classic study by Alfred D. Chandler, Jr., *The Visible Hand: The Managerial Revolution in
American Business* (Cambridge, Mass.: Harvard University Press, 1977). On economic
theories of multinational enterprise, see Richard E. Caves, *Multinational Enterprise and
Economic Analysis* (New York: Cambridge University Press, 1983), which reviews the scholarship of Stephen Hymer, Raymond Vernon, and other leading specialists. On historical
differences between the "American model" and the "European model" of multinational enterprises see Mira Wilkins, "The History of European Multinationals: A New Look," *The
Journal of European Economic History* 15:3 (Winter 1986): 483–510.

[19] Håkan Lindgren, *Corporate Growth: The Swedish Match Industry in Its Global Setting*
(Stockholm: Liber Förlag, 1979), pt. 3, and pp. 352–57, tables 20–22; idem, "The Kreuger
Crash of 1932: In Memory of a Financial Genius, or Was He a Simple Swindler?" *Scandi-
navian Economic History Review* 30:3 (1982): 202.

[20] The estimate of 7 percent is based on Qingdao gong shang xingzheng guanli zhu shiliao zhu [Committee on historical materials concerning the administration and management
of industry and commerce in Qingdao], ed., *Zhongguo minzu huochai gongye* [China's national match industry] (Beijing: Zhonghua shuju, 1963), pp. 26–27, 36, 42–43; Shanghai
shehui kexue yuan jingji yanjiu suo [Shanghai Academy of Social Sciences Institute of
Economics], ed., *Liu Hongsheng qiye shiliao* [Historical materials on Liu Hongsheng's enter-
prises] (Shanghai: Shanghai renmin chubanshe, 1981), vol. 1, pp. 153–54; vol. 2, pp. 147,
153, 161–62, 171, 187, 202, 222, 226; vol. 3, pp. 245, 248.

problem of overproduction. His plan was to achieve maximum profits by selling expensive Swedish-made matches in the lucrative markets of Western Europe and by channeling cheap Eastern European–made matches into the less profitable markets of East Asia. On the one hand, this arrangement was expected to yield high profits for his home manufacturers in Sweden, and on the other hand, it would meet the demand of his Eastern European manufacturers for a share of the world's export market. To transform this vision into reality, Kreuger took action in Europe and Asia during the mid-1920s. In Europe, he formed monopoly agreements with the Baltic states, Poland, Czechoslovakia, Austria, and Italy, specifying that matches manufactured in these countries for export be sent exclusively to Siam, French Indo-China, and above all, China. Meanwhile, in East Asia, he tried to reserve China's market for Swedish Match's Eastern European affiliates by buying out China's Japanese suppliers and reducing their output in both Japan and China. Since Swedish historians have fully documented his company's actions in Europe,[21] the following account concentrates on its actions in East Asia.

Swedish Match captured the Sino-Japanese match trade by buying out Japanese match manufacturers and taking over production in the Japanese match industry. Whereas Japanese-owned Mitsui Bussan and Chinese-owned trading companies in Japan had confined themselves largely to indirect investments before the 1920s, the Western-owned Swedish Match Company made large direct investments in the mid-1920s. Between September 1924 and October 1927, Swedish Match took over all of the leading Japanese match mills. In 1924, it bought outright Mitsui Bussan's only match factory, the Nippon Match Company, which was then Japan's second-largest manufacturer in the industry; in 1925, it gained controlling interest in Kobayashi Match Manufacturing Company; and in 1927, it purchased a majority of the shares in Daido Match Company, a firm created in the same year as a result of the merger of Swedish Match with Toyo Match Company, Japan's largest manufacturer of matches. By the end of 1927, investments in these and twenty smaller Japanese firms gave Swedish Match control over 73 per-

---

[21] On Kreuger's scheme, see Lindgren, *Corporate Growth*, pp. 104–5, 337–40. On other aspects of Kreuger's career, see this and the five volumes in the series *The Swedish Match Company, 1917–1939: Studies in Business Internationalization* (Stockholm: Liber Förlag, 1979, 1985): Karl-Gustaf Hildebrand, *Expansion Crisis Reconstruction, 1917–1939* (1985); Lars Hassbring, *The International Development of the Swedish Match Company, 1917–1924* (1979); Hans Modig, *Swedish Match Interests in British India During the Interwar Years* (1979); and Ulla Wikander, *Kreuger's Match Monopolies, 1925–1930, Case Studies in Market Control through Public Monopolies* (1979).

cent of Japan's match exports worldwide, not to mention 81 percent of the matches made for Japan's domestic market.[22]

With this overwhelming control of production, Swedish Match began in 1928 to cut drastically the volume of matches sent from Japan's factories to China and other markets abroad. Between 1928 and 1931 exports from Swedish-controlled companies in Japan were reduced by three-quarters. To be sure, Swedish Match's export strategy was not the sole determinant of this collapse; the effects of the worldwide depression and general weakness of the industry were evident in the simultaneous decline of exports from match firms in Japan not controlled by Swedish Match. But the Western company's determination to cut production is reflected in the rates of decline. While exports from factories in Japan not under its control fell by half, exports from its factories there fell by a full three-quarters.[23]

In Shanghai, as in Japan, Swedish Match gained control over Japanese-owned manufacturing. From Toyo Match Company, it bought the Lower Yangzi region's only two Japanese-owned match factories, a large one at Shanghai for 631,399.23 yen and a smaller one at Zhenjiang, both of which had operated under the name Sui Sung (Sui Sheng) Match Company. In 1928 at the time of purchase, according to Swedish Match's Torsten Hultman, the Shanghai factory "was very badly fitted with machinery of old and inefficient types"; Swedish Match left both factories unimproved until 1931.[24]

By cutting back production in Japan and Shanghai, Swedish Match cleared the way in China for the sale of matches made in Eastern Europe. Calling these brands "Cheap European" in its internal correspondence, Swedish Match set prices on them that lived up to this designation. Compared with the matches it exported to other parts of the world in 1929 and 1930, the ones sent to China had by far the lowest prices: an average of 34.25 Swedish kronas per case compared with 105 kronas per case to Great Britain, 74.45 to the United States, 69.35 to the Dutch East Indies, and 43.50 to Siam and Indo-China.[25]

In line with this low f.o.b. price, Swedish Match's matches sold cheaply in the streets of Shanghai. According to a survey conducted at Shanghai in 1929 by the Jiangsu Match Manufacturer's Association

---

[22] Lindgren, *Corporate Growth*, p. 338; Hildebrand, *Expansion Crisis Reconstruction*, p. 96; *Zhongguo minzu huochai gongye*, p. 25.

[23] Lindgren, *Corporate Growth*, p. 338.

[24] REM to Swedish-Chinese Export and Import Co., October 1, 1928, File D-3769, Shanghai Municipal Police Archives (Washington, D.C.: U.S. National Archives); Hultman to Kiang, August 10, 1932, ibid.

[25] Lindgren, *Corporate Growth*, p. 340.

(Jiangsu huochai tongye lianhehui), Swedish Match's brands retailed at the time for less than locally made matches, selling at 29.50 yuan per case for first-class matches compared with Chinese-made first-class matches at 34 yuan and 26.50 yuan per case for second-class matches compared with Chinese-made second-class for 26–30 yuan and Chinese-made third class at 25–28 yuan.[26]

By this kind of dumping on China, Kreuger achieved his goals in Europe. As he expected, Swedish Match's Eastern European branches absorbed large losses on the China trade, which constituted fully one-third of the company's worldwide exports between 1929 and 1931, and, as he hoped, the company's profits on matches manufactured in Sweden rose steadily during these years.[27]

Manufacturing in Shanghai for Distribution in China

On January 1, 1931, Ivar Kreuger's policy of dumping in China ceased to be tenable because on that day the Guomindang government regained tariff autonomy (which had been denied to China under treaties with the West since the mid-nineteenth century) and raised China's tariff on imported matches from 7.5 percent to 40 percent ad valorem. Finding this tariff prohibitive, Swedish Match sharply curtailed its exports to China, but it did not withdraw from the country.[28] On the contrary, once Swedish Match ceased to regard China as a special dumping ground, it began to approach China's market exactly as it did profitable markets elsewhere in the world: first, by seeking a match monopoly under the sponsorship of the local government and second, by manufacturing in the country's central metropolis (in China's case, Shanghai) for nationwide distribution. Unfortunately for the company, the strategy that it had used elsewhere in the world during the 1920s encountered special obstacles in China during the early 1930s.

In seeking a match monopoly, Swedish Match tried in vain to win sponsorship from the Guomindang. In 1929 and 1930, upon hearing news of the Guomindang's plans for a higher tariff, the company proposed a monopoly in China comparable to the ones it enjoyed in several other countries. Its negotiator, a specialist on East Asia named Jerome

---

[26] *Liu Hongsheng qiye shiliao*, vol. 1, p. 107; *Zhongguo minzu huochai gongye*, p. 28.

[27] Hildebrand, *Expansion Crisis Reconstruction*, pp. 197–99.

[28] Exports fell from 1,040,000 cases in 1931 to 310,000 cases in 1932 according to *STAB's Deliveries of Matches, 1932–40*, Swedish Match Central Archives, Vadstena Landsarchiv (Regional Archives, Vadstena), Sweden (hereafter cited as Swedish Match Archives). Slightly lower figures, a drop from 960,000 to 180,000 cases, are given in *Zhongguo minzu huochai gongye*, pp. 303–4.

Greene, who was affiliated with Lee Higginson & Co., met several times with the Guomindang government's minister of finance, Song Ziwen (T. V. Soong), and Song's later successor as minister of finance, Kong Xiangxi (H. H. Kung). In the course of these negotiations, Swedish Match offered the Guomindang government a large loan rumored to be between five million and twenty million yuan for exclusive rights to China's match market for fifty years; but in China, unlike the Baltic states, Poland, Czechoslovakia, Austria, and Italy, Swedish Match never received official approval for a match monopoly.[29]

Lacking official support from the Guomindang government, Swedish Match decided in 1931 to jump the government's tariff wall by refurbishing its factory at Shanghai and manufacturing within China on a large scale. As the company's Torsten Hultman observed at the time, the factory was "in every detail rebuilt and refitted with the best machinery made, imported by us direct from Sweden ... making it the best factory in the Far East." The company installed six fully automatic machines—the only ones in China—and raised the factory's production capacity to 130 cases (almost a million boxes) of matches per day. With this capacity, it could have produced 30–40 percent of all the matches eventually made in Shanghai between 1932 and 1936. Swedish Match also refurbished its other factory, a smaller one at Zhenjiang, which acquired a capacity of one-half million boxes of matches per day.[30]

Unfortunately for the company, at the very moment that it cleared the tariff barrier and started to sell domestically manufactured matches at a profit in China, it ran into a second hurdle: the anti-Japanese boycott of 1931–34. Swedish Match was targeted for the boycott on the grounds that its Shanghai factories were still Japanese-owned. The Western company insisted that "not one penny" of Japanese capital was any longer invested in these mills, and it purged the remaining signs of Japanese influence, changing registration from Japanese to American, the name from Sui Sung (Sui Sheng) to American Far Eastern Match Company (Mei guang huochai gongsi), the foremen from Japanese to Swedish, and the labels from old to new ones. It even jettisoned some of the Japanese-made equipment, but it retained its six hundred factory workers, all of whom were Chinese.[31]

---

[29] Hildebrand, *Expansion Crisis Reconstruction,* pp. 161–62. On the rumors, see *Liu Hongsheng qiye shiliao,* vol. 1, pp. 124–26; and *Zhongguo minzu huochai gongye,* p. 34.

[30] Hultman to Kiang, August 10, 1932, Shanghai Police Archives, D-3769; enclosure in letter from Amfeaco (China branch of Swedish Match) to Swedish Match, July 24, 1937, *STAB Statistical Dept., Marknadsanalyser (1935),* Swedish Match Archives; *Zhongguo minzu huochai gongye,* pp. 40, 73–74; Eurén, "The Swedish Match Company's Interests in China," March 31, 1944, "*S.Y.E.,*" *Hongkong, Shanghai 1941–45,* Swedish Match Archives.

[31] Hultman to Kiang, August 10, 1932, and Hultman, "Report of Conferences," August

Despite the changes, Swedish Match felt the boycott's effects for almost three years between mid-1931 and early 1934. Its lost sales are difficult to show quantitatively because it did not begin to produce on a large scale in China for domestic consumption until early 1931, only a few months before the boycott began in July 1931; accordingly, there is no pre-1931 baseline with which to compare 1931–34 sales figures. There are, however, other indications, all of which suggest that the company suffered from the boycott. In reviewing its Shanghai factory's first year of production at the end of 1931, for example, Swedish Match's accountants noted that the boycott caused the factory to cut its production of half-finished goods 25 percent below the amount originally planned. They also blamed the boycott for 25 percent of the 26,109 yen in bad debts that they wrote off for the year. According to Swedish Match's Shanghai manager, Sigvard Eurén, the boycott against its goods was strong in the Lower and Middle Yangzi and Southeast regions and cut into sales substantially from mid-1931 to the end of 1932 and sporadically in 1933 and 1934. Not until mid-1934 did the company cease to be troubled by this longest and most intense of all Chinese boycotts.[32]

Thus, characteristically, Swedish Match responded to the higher tariff and intense boycotts of the 1930s by adjusting its manufacturing system, not its marketing system. To clear the tariff barrier, it geared up factories in Shanghai and Zhenjiang, and to cope with the boycott, it slowed their rate of production; but in China it never fundamentally altered its marketing approach, which remained unchanged throughout the 1920s and 1930s.

Marketing in the Western Way

Swedish Match, like many other Western firms before it, depended on Chinese compradors to market its goods. By the time it reached China in 1919, it had available to it an alternate marketing trail blazed in China's match market by its foreign predecessor, Mitsui Bussan, which, as noted earlier, had replaced its Chinese compradors with 173 Japanese sales representatives stationed in Shanghai and another 656 Japanese employees working in twenty-nine other Chinese cities. But Swedish

---

17, 1932, both in Shanghai Police Archives, D-3769.

[32] Financial statement of December 31, 1931 in Ing F. Dahl, *Kina Bokslutshandl Stat mm., Reorg: 1931–33,* vol. 10, no. 40, Swedish Match Archives; Eurén to Tse Tsok Kai, April 10, 1934, and Eurén to Swedish Match, March 28, 1934, in *China Manschuriet 1934,* Swedish Match Archives; F0371/16173/F5242/1/10 Brenan to Lampson, May 13, 1932, Public Records Office, Kew Gardens, England.

Match took the more commonly trod Western path, retaining its Chinese compradors and never employing more than one foreigner in the sales department at Shanghai or at any of its branch offices in the Northeast at Dalian and Changchun, the Middle Yangzi at Hankou, or the South at Hong Kong.

How could each Western sales manager supervise his Chinese staff and cover a vast region? In China, as elsewhere in the world outside Europe, each of Swedish Match's Western managers relied on direct correspondence to exercise control over all employees and commission agents. In each regional office only the Western manager was authorized to sign letters on the company's stationery, and only he was supposed to receive correspondence from Chinese agents. He was to keep all copies of this correspondence in a locked file and all confidential letters in a safe.

Since each manager was a Westerner illiterate in the Chinese language, he had his Chinese sales manager translate his correspondence to and from Chinese agents whose letters, Shanghai manager Eurén observed, were "practically all...in Chinese." With every letter to a Chinese agent the Western sales manager enclosed a translation, but he signed only the English version of the letter—not the Chinese translation—and he used on each letter a chop saying in Chinese that letters were invalid unless they bore the Western manager's own signature. As a further precaution, he was instructed to check on the accuracy of his Chinese sales manager's translations by periodically having independent translations done.[33]

To ensure adequate surveillance, Swedish Match used this system of direct correspondence in tandem with a system of cash deposits. Under the latter, Swedish Match extended no unsecured credit to its Chinese commission agents. Before the Western sales manager authorized any delivery of goods, he was supposed to have in hand the commission agent's cash deposits in amounts of silver equivalent to the full value of the goods. If the Western sales manager did not receive payment from an agent within thirty days, then he was supposed to cover the cost of the goods by drawing funds from the agent's cash deposit.[34]

If studies of Swedish Match in other countries are any indication,[35]

---

[33] Eurén to Wulfsberg, January 5, 1934, and Eurén, "Memorandum Re: Hankow," March 10, 1934, both in *China Manschuriet 1934*, Swedish Match Archives; enclosure in Amfeaco to Swedish Match, July 24, 1937, *STAB, Statistical Dept., Marknadsanalyser (1935)*, Swedish Match Archives.

[34] Eurén, "Memorandum Re: Hankow," March 10, 1934, *China Manschuriet 1934*, Swedish Match Archives.

[35] The closest available analogy to Swedish Match's marketing system in China is found in Hans Modig's study of Swedish Match's marketing system in India. See his *Swedish*

this system of direct correspondence and cash deposits kept Swedish Match's local agents in check elsewhere in the world and prevented cheating, shirking, and violations of company policies. But in China the company had great difficulty preventing Chinese employees' financial manipulations. For example, prior to price rises, a Number One in Swedish Match's Shanghai factory secretly retained large quantities of matches, which he claimed were purchased by Chinese commission agents; then, after prices rose, he sold the goods to the agents at the new higher prices and pocketed the difference. In the most flagrant case discovered by the company, its Chinese comprador at Hankou systematically manipulated its cash deposits for no fewer than eight years, 1926 to 1934.[36]

Throughout the 1930s Swedish Match's highest officials were aware of their marketing system's failures in China. In 1931 Gunnar Ekstrom, head of Swedish Match for Asia, reported the problem to Fred Ljungberg, who at the time was second only to Ivar Kreuger at the Swedish headquarters of the company's worldwide operations. "We have left our sales too much in the hands of Chinese dealers," Ekstrom lamented. "[W]e have very little knowledge of the ultimate destination of our matches sold."[37]

In response to complaints from headquarters in Sweden, Eurén in Shanghai acknowledged in 1934 that the company's policy of requiring cash deposits put it at a disadvantage vis-à-vis its rivals in China, but he saw no alternative to this policy. According to Eurén's premise, "To use shop guarantees or other securities than cash or to give unsecured credit would for us, as a foreign concern, mean to give away matches to any dealer who for some reason or other does not wish to pay." Exasperated, Eurén insisted that "no Chinese of the class with whom we deal can be given any credit whatsoever. Giving credit would be the same as to give the money away." As a result, "We have been forced to do our business on a cash basis or against a cash deposit which amounts to the same thing. This naturally reduces possibilities of sales as against our Chinese competition but . . . this cannot be helped."[38]

Match Interests in British India During the Interwar Years, pp. 72–75, 91–92, 166–67, 192–95, 219–20.

[36] Eurén to Wulfsberg, February 20, 1934, *China Manschuriet 1934,* Swedish Match Archives. On the case in Hankou, see Sherman Cochran, "Losing Money Abroad: The Swedish Match Company in China during the 1930s," *Business and Economic History,* 2d series, 16 (1987): 83–91.

[37] Ekstrom to Fr. Ljungberg, May 19, 1931, Fr. Ljungberg's Confidential Letters, Swedish Match Archives. On Ekstrom's and Ljungberg's careers as leading executives, see Hildebrand, *Expansion Crisis Reconstruction,* pp. 220, 387, and passim.

[38] Eurén to Swedish Match, December 27, 1934, *China Manschuriet 1934,* Swedish

Retaining this premise, Swedish Match never made heavy investments in marketing, never expanded its sales staff, and never granted credit to Chinese commission agents on terms as favorable as those provided by Mitsui Bussan, or, as shown below, by Swedish Match's Chinese rivals. Its unwillingness to adopt these policies (as exceptions to policies that it used in other countries) limited its control over distribution, weakened its appeal to Chinese distributors, and left it with a share of China's market well below its worldwide standards.

In light of Mitsui Bussan's record, Eurén was clearly wrong about a foreign company having no alternative in China. If, like Mitsui Bussan, Swedish Match had recruited and trained a large marketing staff, then it could have built up rapport between its foreign salaried representatives and its Chinese commission agents; and on the basis of that rapport, it could have granted credit and sold on consignment as Mitsui Bussan did.[39] But Eurén and Swedish Match did not depart from the Western model.

Swedish Match Company and the Western Model

This comparison with Mitsui Bussan underscores Swedish Match's lack of adaptability (or obliviousness to the need for adaptability) in its marketing system in Shanghai and elsewhere in China. The Western company failed to capture a share of China's market as large as its share of the world's market because its management responded to each successive challenge—to reserve China as a dumping ground, vault over protective tariffs, overcome antiforeign boycotts, appeal to local commission agents—by adjusting its manufacturing system without fundamentally changing its marketing system. Limited by its orientation to manufacturing elsewhere in the world, Swedish Match envisioned no possibilities beyond the Western model in China.

Such a stark contrast between Japanese and Western approaches should not imply that the Japanese approach was economically rational and the Western approach economically irrational. On the contrary, each approach had its own rationale and ran its own risks. Mitsui Bussan justified its investment in marketing by having its numerous and highly trained staff members handle a wide variety of goods and thus achieved (in the rhetoric of economic theorists) economies of scope;[40] and it ran

---

Match Archives.

[39] On Mitsui Bussan's granting of credit, see Yamashita, "Matchi kōgyō to Mitsui Bussan," pp. 111–13 and passim.

[40] On this concept, see Scott J. Moss, *An Economic Theory of Business Strategy: An Essay in Dynamics without Equilibrium* (New York: Wiley, 1981), pp. 110–11.

the risk, as illustrated in the Sino-Japanese match trade, of not recruiting enough manufacturers to keep its marketing system adequately supplied. Swedish Match, by contrast, with its heavy investment in manufacturing, coordinated production and supply under a single ownership and had less justification for investing in marketing because it specialized in only one product.

Was there a better way? If the roads taken into Shanghai's match market by Mitsui Bussan and Swedish Match both led to performances well below these foreign giants' usual standards, then what other path was open? In this industry, as it turned out, the route to the top was followed by a Chinese firm, China Match Company.

China Match Company in Shanghai: Building upon the Chinese Model

Models for multinational corporations are not worth testing against the history of China Match Company because it, unlike Mitsui Bussan and Swedish Match, conducted almost all its business at home rather than abroad. More appropriate in this case is a model for Chinese long-distance trading organizations, and, fortunately, G. William Skinner has derived such a model from central place theory. According to Skinner's scheme, enterprising Chinese moved up a "merchant-financier track," and they advanced most readily if they hailed from localities that produced "the great trading groups of traditional China." As a result, they "proceeded in a framework of same-native-place particularism," and with help from their cohorts they rose through markets in an urban hierarchy. "It is clear," Skinner has observed, "that in building up a commercial hegemony, regionally based entrepreneurs often moved up the hierarchy to a strategically situated commercial city and then consolidated their position throughout its trading system by expanding their operation to lower-level dependent central places."[41]

Skinner's model, designed to describe late imperial China, raises issues for the postimperial period of the 1920s and 1930s. Did Chinese businesses continue to rely on particularistic native-place ties to conduct trade in the twentieth century? And, as those businesses expanded, did they continue to move up an urban hierarchy to bigger and more central cities so that they could consolidate control over markets in smaller and less central cities? Skinner's model has already generated important research on such questions,[42] and these questions are worth asking in the

---

[41] G. William Skinner, "Mobility Strategies in Late Imperial China: A Regional Systems Analysis," in Carol A. Smith, ed., *Regional Analysis* (New York: Academic Press, 1976), pp. 327–64 (quotations are from pp. 354 and 358).

[42] For examples, see Yoshinobu Shiba, "Ningpo and Its Hinterland," in Skinner, ed., *The*

case of Liu Hongsheng, a Chinese businessman who in 1920 entered the match industry, in 1930 founded China Match Company, and by 1937 secured 55 percent of the match market in the Lower and Middle Yangzi and Southeast—three times more than his closest rival, Swedish Match Company. To analyze Liu's climb to the top, it is worth exploring the questions derived from Skinner's model with reference first to Liu's Hongsheng Match Mills outside Shanghai in the 1920s, then to his China Match Company in Shanghai during the early 1930s, and finally to his match cartel, which was formed in the mid-1930s.

Moving "Down" from Shanghai, 1920–1930

Before entering the match industry in 1920, Liu Hongsheng's business practices had closely conformed to Skinner's model. Born and raised in Shanghai, Liu, like his father before him, had maintained strong particularistic ties with associates from his native place of Dinghai county, which was 150 kilometers southeast of Shanghai in Ningbo prefecture, and in 1920 he had become head of the Association of Ningbo Sojourners in Shanghai (Shanghai Ningbo tongxianghui). By then, at age thirty-two, Liu had come to fit Skinner's description of a "regionally-based entrepreneur." Liu had landed his first job (through native-place connections) only a decade earlier in 1909 with the British-owned Kaiping Mining Company, and he had become a millionaire during World War I by using Shanghai as a base to market this firm's coal throughout the Lower Yangzi region.[43] But contrary to Skinner's model, in the 1920s Liu did not locate his match business in the most central place available to him, Shanghai, or reach down from Shanghai to consolidate control over lower-level cities. Instead, he selected lower-level cities outside Shanghai as sites for all elements of his match business: manufacturing, personnel, and marketing.

For manufacturing, Liu chose the city of Suzhou, where in 1920 he built the Hongsheng Match Mills. As Liu was well aware, in the course of the nineteenth century Suzhou had become an economic backwater; at the time Liu decided to build there, it had, according to the *China*

City in Late Imperial China, pp. 391–439; Susan Mann Jones, "The Ningpo *Pang* and Financial Power at Shanghai," in Mark Elvin and G. William Skinner, eds., *The Chinese City Between Two Worlds* (Stanford, Calif.: Stanford University Press, 1974), pp. 73–96; and William T. Rowe, *Hankow: Commerce and Society in a Chinese City, 1796–1889* (Stanford, Calif.: Stanford University Press, 1984).

[43] Liu Nianzhi, *Shiyejia Liu Hongsheng chuanlü—huiyi wode fuqin* [A biography of the industrialist Liu Hongsheng—reminiscences of my father] (Beijing: Wenshi ziliao chubanshe, 1982), chaps. 1–2.

Commercial Atlas, "only two minor silk filatures and one modern cotton mill,"[44] making it an industrial midget compared to Shanghai. In this seemingly inauspicious setting, Liu invested 90,000 yuan of his own money and raised another 30,000 yuan to construct his first match factory.[45]

To recruit marketing personnel, Liu also reached outside Shanghai. For this purpose, he adapted particularistic ties (in conformity with Skinner's model) by turning to his native place. In 1920, the same year that he entered the match industry, he donated funds to establish a school, the Dinghai County Middle School (Dinghai zhongxue), in his home county in Ningbo prefecture. Following customary practice, the school admitted only residents of his home county and charged no tuition. Once the school began producing graduates in the 1920s, Liu turned the graduates to his own advantage by offering them positions with his company as trainees (*lianxisheng*) and subsequently, upon their successful completion of the training course, appointments as salaried representatives (*zhiyuan*).[46] In other words, Dinghai County Middle School formed one end of a pipeline that channeled into Liu's personnel pool a steady flow of young Ningbo native-place associates all beholden to Liu for their educations and their jobs.

Manufacturing his matches in Suzhou and recruiting his staff in Ningbo, Liu consolidated his control over cities at lower levels than these two in the urban hierarchy (as would be expected according to Skinner's model). Before 1927, as one of Liu's former managers observed in a 1961 interview, Liu's marketing avoided the "great cities" (*da chengshi*) and concentrated on the "middle- and small-sized cities" (*zhong xiao chengshi*).[47] Meanwhile, Liu followed a similar strategy in the Middle Yangzi region, constructing in 1920 his second factory at Jiujiang (rather than the region's central metropolis of Hankou) and marketing in lower-level cities.

In this way Liu steadily built up his sales. By 1925 his success attracted attention from Swedish Match, which tried, without success, to buy him out.[48] By the late 1920s, his Suzhou factory ranked third highest in production and sales of any Chinese-owned match manufacturer in the

---

[44] Quoted by Linda Cooke Johnson, "The Decline of Soochow and the Rise of Shanghai: A Study in the Economic Morphology of Urban Change (1756–1894)," Ph.D. dissertation, University of California at Santa Cruz, 1986, p. 423.

[45] *Liu Hongsheng qiye shiliao*, vol. 1, p. 76.

[46] *Zhongguo minzu huochai gongye*, p. 82.

[47] Interview with Wang Xingyao, September 1961; *Liu Hongsheng qiye shiliao*, vol. 1, p. 109.

[48] *Liu Hongsheng qiye shiliao*, vol. 1, pp. 84–92.

Lower Yangzi region, and his Jiujiang factory, although smaller than the one at Suzhou, ranked first in the Middle Yangzi region (table 4).

Not until 1930, after he had manufactured and marketed matches for a decade in relatively peripheral settings, did he move his business up to the city where he had resided all his life, Shanghai.

Moving "Up" to Shanghai, 1930–1932

In 1930, from his subregional platform, Liu launched his business into the more competitive markets at Shanghai and metropolises in other regions, and between 1930 and 1932 he vindicated his approach by achieving a series of stunning industrial and commercial successes.

In manufacturing, Liu took his first steps toward greater productive capacity by persuading two other Chinese match manufacturers, Yingchang Match Company and Zhonghua Match Company, to join him in forming a combine. Ironically, his plan benefited from Swedish Match's policy of dumping. In 1928, when the dumping began, Liu immediately tried to capitalize on other Chinese match manufacturers' panic by proposing a merger. Although his Hongsheng Match Mills had smaller production capacity than Shanghai's largest Chinese-owned match factory (see table 4), Liu urged its owner and the owner of the third-largest factory to merge their factories with his and make him the head of the combine. Initially rebuffed, he wore down these Chinese manufacturers' resistance as Swedish Match's dumping took its toll during the following two years, especially during the first half of 1930 when Yingchang (capitalized at 716,811 yuan) lost 93,000 yuan and Zhonghua (capitalized at 300,062 yuan) lost 17,000 yuan while Liu's Hongsheng Mills, firmly anchored in less competitive markets outside Shanghai (and capitalized at 579,245) lost only 3,000 yuan. In July 1930, the three companies finally came to terms, forming China Match Company with Liu as general manager. Capitalized at 1,910,000 yuan (of which 29.57 percent was held by Liu and his brother), it permitted Liu to quadruple production from 31,000 to 120,000 cases per year. With the leading Lower Yangzi firms under control, Liu then bought at the end of 1930 the two largest match companies in the Middle Yangzi region and several smaller ones there.[49]

In marketing, upon entering Shanghai Liu not only enlarged but also reorganized his system of distribution. Although not abandoning his particularistic network of Ningbo distributors, he incorporated them into an impersonal administrative organization. This marketing system

[49] *Zhongguo minzu huochai gongye,* pp. 60–65; *Liu Hongsheng qiye shiliao,* vol. 1, p. 137.

Table 4

Production and Sales for Leading Chinese-owned Match Companies
1927–1929 (in cases)

Company	Founder or Manager	Location	1927 Production	1927 Sales	1928 Production	1928 Sales	1929 Production	1929 Sales
Hongsheng	Liu Hongsheng	Suzhou	27,300	25,600	31,200	28,200	26,900	28,000
Yusheng	Liu Hongsheng	Jiujiang	18,000	16,900	19,900	17,300	20,100	19,600
Yinchang	Shao Erkang	Shanghai						
Yinchang	Shao Erkang	Shanghai	64,500	64,900	71,000	66,900	71,800	70,000
Yinchang	Shao Erkang	Zhenjiang						
Guanghua	Zhao Zhicheng	Hangzhou	45,000	45,000	45,000	45,000	45,000	45,000
Danhua	Xiang Zhengang	Tianjin	56,000	56,000	52,000	52,000	48,000	48,000
Danhua	Xiang Zhengang	Beijing	42,000	33,800	33,800	33,800	37,700	37,000
Zhenye	Cong Liangbi	Jinan	33,000	33,000	28,400	28,400	20,200	20,200
Zhenye	Cong Liangbi	Jining	18,400	18,400	19,600	19,600	16,000	16,000
Zhenye	Cong Liangbi	Qingdao	—	—	14,400	14,400	20,000	20,000
TOTAL			304,200	293,600	315,300	305,600	305,700	303,800
Others			343,800	315,100	487,900	410,400	413,400	346,400
TOTAL			648,000	608,700	803,200	716,000	719,100	650,200

SOURCE: Survey conducted by the Chinese Match Union, Liu Hongsheng Archives, file 02-063, pp. 002–010 at Shanghai Academy of Social Sciences.

resembled its counterparts at Mitsui Bussan and Swedish Match in that it was staffed by salaried employees who were responsible for recruiting local Chinese commission agents and monitoring the agents' activities. It differed from the marketing systems in foreign firms in that it consisted entirely of Chinese, and it reached several cities and towns too low in the urban hierarchy to have been touched by Mitsui Bussan or Swedish Match.

China Match's commitment to marketing in cities in the Lower Yangzi region not reached by its foreign rivals was evident at every level of its marketing organization. At the top, unlike the foreign firms, it divided its sales department (*yingye ke*) in two. One part was responsible for "distant points" (*yuan qu*) in the same metropolises of the Middle Yangzi and Southeast where Mitsui Bussan and Swedish Match had their offices; the other part (for which the foreign firms had no corresponding organization) was responsible for "nearby points" (*jin qu*) within the Lower Yangzi region outside Shanghai. As shown in table 3, China Match thus extended its marketing reach not only to its "divisional offices" (*fen shiwusuo*) at the level reached by Mitsui Bussan and Swedish Match but also to subdivisional offices or "marketing outlets" (*jingxiao dian*) in twenty-four counties at lower-level cities than the ones reached by Mitsui Bussan and Swedish Match. At this local level, China Match's Chinese salaried representatives dealt with Chinese commission agents who, in turn, distributed through small Chinese wholesale merchants and retail stores.[50]

This finely articulated marketing system gave China Match's headquarters in Shanghai the means for gathering commercial information, regulating prices, and achieving control in local markets. When the company was formed in 1930, its management immediately had all its local representatives conduct surveys to determine which of its more than sixty brands were most popular around each divisional office. On the basis of this information, its management designated each division's "important trademark," which generally reflected a feature of the locality (e.g., in Suzhou "Bao Ta," named after a local pagoda, was the important trademark). To deepen consumers' loyalties to an "important trademark" wherever possible, the company eliminated forty of its brands and began lowering the price of its "important trademark" in each locality, making the amounts of the decrease proportionate to the strength of the local competition in each place.

Once the local market was cornered, China Match raised prices and took high profits. In 1930, for example, it drove out the competition

---

[50] *Zhongguo minzu huochai gongye*, pp. 71–72.

between Shanghai and Nanjing by selling one brand at the low price of 34.17 yuan per case; in 1931, after cornering the market, it raised the price to 48.94 yuan per case. The net gain from this one area was an increase in revenue of 1.8 million yuan. By 1932 several divisional offices had their "important trademarks" fully established, and they were instructed by directives from Shanghai to resort again to these same tactics of "first lower prices, then raise prices" if any newcomer tried to break into the local market.[51]

To retain managerial authority on all levels, Liu adopted an organizational philosophy summarized in the slogan "Generous benefits, strict control." "Generous benefits" in the form of salaries and bonuses were paid according to rank in the sales organization's hierarchy. In China Match's central headquarters at Shanghai, heads and deputy heads of the sales department received 300 yuan per month, standard bonuses (given to all staff members according to their seniority, attendance, and supervisors' evaluations), and special bonuses given at Liu Hongsheng's personal discretion. At the middle level, heads of divisional offices made 100–120 yuan per month plus standard bonuses. At the lowest level, subordinates to divisional heads earned 50–100 yuan per month plus standard bonuses.[52]

"Strict control" was exercised through a "guarantee system," which required employees to have guarantors post bond on their behalf. Executives at the high and middle levels were exempted from this process, but bond for each employee below the rank of divisional head had to be posted in amounts that varied according to the volume of goods and cash the employee handled: a bond of 20,000 yuan for a head cashier; 10,000 yuan for a bill collector; 5,000 yuan for a clerk, a stock keeper, or a canvasser; and 500–2,000 yuan for a staff member holding a lesser position.[53]

Introduced between 1930 and 1932, this administrative organization gave China Match Company a distributing system in China superior to the one at Swedish Match. On the basis of close rapport with its local commission agents, its salaried representatives released goods on consignment without requiring cash deposits—a practice that gave China Match a distinct advantage over Swedish Match in attracting commission agents. As Sigvard Eurén of Swedish Match observed, China Match's "sales system is different from ours. They stock up their dealers with one to two months' supply held by the dealers in consignment."[54]

[51] Ibid., pp. 72–73.
[52] Ibid., pp. 78–79.
[53] Ibid., pp. 80–81.
[54] Eurén to Fr. Ljungberg, March 3, 1934, *China Manschuriet 1934,* Swedish Match

Relying on its manufacturing and marketing systems, China Match made a spectacular entrance into the market between 1930 and 1932. At the height of the anti-Japanese boycott between July 1931 and June 1932, China Match supplied 46.2 percent (100,753 cases) of the matches sold in the Lower Yangzi and 72.7 percent (20,045 cases) of those sold in the Middle Yangzi. As it gained control over markets, its marketing system followed the strategy of "first lower prices, then raise prices" to reap high profits. Between its opening in July 1930 and the end of 1931 it quadrupled its average prices (from 14.47 yuan per case to 43.33 yuan per case).[55] As table 5 shows, in 1931 its total profits correspondingly quadrupled (from 125,535 yuan to 545,823 yuan), and its profit rate rose to 23.06 percent—higher than ever before or ever again in its history. In 1932, its profits slipped slightly (to 415,186 yuan at a profit rate of 15.98 percent), but it still seemed to have attained almost complete control over the match markets of China's richest and most populous regions—until, suddenly, its march toward monopoly was interrupted.

Surviving Chinese Competition in Shanghai, 1933–1935

Ironically, after subduing his major competitors, Liu Hongsheng had difficulty overcoming his minor ones. His merger of 1930 had induced the two largest Chinese match manufacturers in Shanghai to join him in forming China Match Company, and his success at capitalizing on the tariff and boycott had enabled him to outsell his one large Western rival. But between 1933 and 1935 he suffered from price wars with small Chinese match companies that gained access to this industry with relative ease because match-making machinery was cheap and technologically simple compared to machinery in other industries. As a result, China Match's profits came crashing down. As shown in table 5, the company's high prices of 1931 and 1932 were driven down between 1933 and 1935, transforming its great gains of 1930–33 into equally great losses in 1934 and 1935. As also shown in table 5, China Match succeeded in cutting its costs annually between 1933 and 1935, but its savings were far outweighed by falling prices.

To end his losses, Liu tried to obliterate his opposition. As part of this combative approach, he attempted in March 1933 to underprice the smaller Chinese firms in the Lower Yangzi region, seven of which had been attracted into the booming market within the preceding year. To

---

Archives.
   [55] *Liu Hongsheng qiye shiliao*, vol. 1, p. 147; vol. 2, p. 171.

Table 5

China Match Company's
Prices, Costs, Profits, Rates of Profit, Production, and Capital,
1930–1944

Year	Price per average case (yuan)	Production costs per average case (yuan)	Profits (yuan)	Profit rate (percent)	Production (cases)	Capital (yuan)
1930 (Jy–Dec)	34.17	28.27	125,535	6.57	64,500	1,910,080
1931	48.94	31.17	545,823	23.06	140,410	2,367,300
1932	48.97	31.89	415,186	15.98	120,549	2,598,480
1933	41.88	30.51	62,197	2.07	129,254	3,000,000
1934	34.06	26.93	−423,793	−11.61	147,596	3,650,000
1935	30.92	24.05	−506,579	−13.88	150,093	3,650,000
1936	40.55	26.01	838,062	22.96	146,950	3,650,000
1937	41.94	26.68	333,056	9.12	96,711	3,650,000
1938	—	—	1,770,092		33,230	
1939	—	—	1,021,925		67,128	
1940	—	—	2,354,515		54,956	
1941	387.00	236.00	2,862,660		40,766	
1942	733.00	503.00	6,731,927		16,779	
1943	2,752.00	1,635.00	16,542,783		10,812	
1944	41,979.00	22,440.00	111,712,667		13,831	

NOTE: Currency for 1937–1941 is in *fabi* and for 1942–1944 is in the Wang Jingwei government's *chu zhuan*.
SOURCES: *Liu Hongsheng qiye shiliao* 2:170–71, 248, and 3:96–97; *Zhongguo minzu huochai gongye*, pp. 75, 82.

strengthen his attack, he formed an alliance with Swedish Match, which agreed to help him try to drive the other Chinese firms out of business. Against their common enemies, the two big companies—one Chinese, one Western—joined forces, exchanged price lists, discussed market conditions, and took joint action. As Eurén secretly reported to his superiors in Sweden, "We are still in close contact with the China Match Co.," which wanted to lower prices because "the smaller factories not affiliated with the China Match Co. were cutting into the China Match Co.'s market.... The price reduction [by Swedish Match] was therefore made in full agreement with the China Match Co."[56]

While Liu's alliance with Swedish Match broadened his war against small Chinese firms, he launched a new marketing offensive to strengthen his attack. To mobilize China Match's salaried staff in divisional offices, he introduced the Sales Bonus System (Xiaohuo jiangli zhidu) in 1934. This system provided new incentives for raising sales because it permitted local divisional offices to retain a percentage of annual sales revenue for over-quota sales on an incremental scale: 1 percent on sales 1–10 percent above quota, 1.2 percent on sales 11–20 percent above quota, 1.4 percent on sales 21–30 percent above quota, 1.6 percent on sales 31–40 percent above quota, and 1.8 percent on sales 41–50 percent or more above quota. Conversely, this system withheld portions of regular annual bonuses from divisional offices that failed either to sell their full quota or to collect all their unpaid debts.[57]

To win over local commission agents during price wars, Liu's China Match Company formed the Marketing Association (Jingxiao tongye lianhehui) in 1934. The company induced Chinese sales agents to join this organization by offering them not only the usual commissions but also monthly bonuses at 0.3 yuan per case and annual bonuses set at the discretion of salaried supervisors in divisional offices. In return, China Match insisted that the agents pledge their allegiance exclusively to it, sell only its brands, and operate at prices and in territories according to its specifications. To check on loyalty, the Marketing Association also gave bonuses to members for making secret reports on other members' violations of the rules.[58]

Although aggressive, this marketing offensive failed to stop the kind of commercial guerrilla warfare that small Chinese firms were waging. Repeatedly Liu signed price agreements with his fellow Chinese

---

[56] Eurén to Swedish Match, March 20, 1933, *STAB Korr China 1933,* Swedish Match Archives.

[57] *Liu Hongsheng qiye shiliao,* vol. 2, pp. 153–54; *Zhongguo minzu huochai gongye,* p. 76.

[58] *Liu Hongsheng qiye shiliao,* vol. 2, pp. 149–50.

industrialists only to see the signers ignore the agreements and cut prices. As China Match's losses mounted, Swedish Match's management began to take Liu Hongsheng's complaints seriously. "On this occasion," Eurén noted in May 1933, "the China Match Co. were perfectly frank with us. They informed us of the difficulties in making the smaller factories adhere to the price agreement and their own failure to put into effect the new prices agreed upon." Within the one year of 1933, according to Eurén's reckoning, China Match's prices fell by 25 percent (even more than indicated in table 5).[59]

Liu failed to persuade small companies to lower production and raise prices because the match manufacturers in Shanghai made these decisions based on the expectation that a cartel would soon be formed. On this premise, every match manufacturer had reason to keep production high between 1933 and 1935 whatever his losses on low prices in the short run so that later, once the cartel was formed, he would receive high quotas which would earn him high profits in the long run. As Eurén of Swedish Match wrote to his superiors in Stockholm in 1933, "In view of the possibility that quotas are planned, we have delayed as long as possible . . . reducing our output as it is probable that the ultimate quota figure will be based upon previous production figures." The same rationale seems to have guided China Match's planning. Despite its losses, it increased its production between 1933 and 1935 and manufactured more in each of these unprofitable years than it had made in each of the preceding profitable years (see table 5). Eurén accused the small companies of overproducing because of short-sightedness and incompetence; in his contemptuous assessment, they were nothing more than "small mosquito factories who do not keep check on their costs." But they too probably produced at or near capacity in hopes that a cartel would eventually award them high production quotas.[60]

If match manufacturers anticipated that a cartel would be formed, they also anticipated who would form it. "Nobody now suspects us of attempting to control the industry," Eurén wrote to Sweden in March 1934, because Swedish Match's dominance "would obviously be impossible at present." The only possible candidate for organizing the cartel was Liu Hongsheng who, Eurén feared, might in early 1934 have already begun "getting control for himself." In reply, Eurén's superiors in Sweden resigned themselves to this eventuality. Kreuger's successor as

<hr />

[59] Eurén to Swedish Match, May 20, 1933, and November 24, 1933, *STAB Korr China 1933,* Swedish Match Archives.

[60] Eurén to Swedish Match, November 24, 1933, *STAB Korr China 1933,* Swedish Match Archives.

chairman of Swedish Match's board and head of its worldwide operations, Fred Ljungberg, wrote Eurén in 1934, "As he [Liu] is evidently entirely unscrupulous in the methods he uses to fight his opponents, he is, of course, a hard nut to crack." Unwilling to vie with China Match for control of China's match industry, Ljungberg instructed Eurén that he should "frankly tell him [Liu] that our aim is not to obtain any kind of control or predominant position in the market but merely to secure a reasonable yield on our investment in the Shanghai factory." To avoid further losses, "we wish to be guided by the principle 'live and let live' in China," Ljungberg told Eurén. In fact, he left Eurén with no alternative to this policy, concluding that "co-operation with Chinese manufacturers still appears to be the only remedy to the present situation."[61]

Like Ljungberg, Liu Hongsheng began to call for match manufacturers to live and let live in the mid-1930s. Fierce competition had first given him a commanding share of the market in 1931–32 and then suddenly taken it away in 1933–35. In search of more stable market control, he switched his strategy in the mid-1930s from competition to cooperation.

Forming a Shanghai-based Interregional Cartel

As match manufacturers had anticipated, Liu Hongsheng began to form a match cartel in the mid-1930s. After broken price agreements and vicious price wars, no one in the industry trusted anyone else to perform a cartel's most fundamental tasks—setting quotas on production, specifying prices, establishing sales territories—because each industrialist feared his competitors would exceed their quotas, cut their prices, and sell across territorial boundaries at his expense. In this atmosphere of distrust, Liu's prospects for a cooperative venture might have seemed bleak, but with surprising speed he inaugurated a Shanghai-based match cartel for the Lower and Middle Yangzi and Southeast.

In July 1934 under the auspices of the National Match Manufacturers' Association (Quanguo huochai tongye lianhehui), Liu established the Joint Sales Office (Lianhe banshichu) with its headquarters at Shanghai. By September, only two months later, he recruited nine smaller Chinese firms into the office almost entirely on his own terms. He offered them the chance to raise profits by setting quotas on production and sales, and he based the quotas on the Guomindang's tax records, July 1931–June 1934, rather than on the number of machines per factory, which would have given smaller firms higher quotas. To the smaller firms, he made

---

[61] Eurén to Swedish Match, March 2, 1934, and Fr. Ljungberg to Eurén, July 13, 1934, *China Manschuriet 1934*, Swedish Match Archives.

one minor concession—the right to manufacture 40 percent above quota if a factory's production fell as low as twenty cases per day—but he retained authority to make all future decisions by insisting that China Match's staff members be assigned to the majority of the Joint Sales Office's top positions: six of the eleven seats on the office's board of directors, three of the five positions on the office's standing committee, and all of the office's most important administrative posts including general manager (which Liu held), assistant general manager, and heads of general affairs, accounting, and business affairs.[62]

While winning cooperation from smaller Chinese firms, Liu Hongsheng also convinced Swedish Match to work with the Joint Sales Office. On February 24, 1934, six months before the office opened, he showed a proposal for it to Swedish Match and found Eurén wary but interested. "Our experience in the past when we have made price agreements," Eurén reminded Liu, "has not been such as would encourage us to relinquish control of our sales. On the other hand, you know that we have strictly kept the price agreements until broken by others." As negotiations proceeded, Liu allayed Eurén's fears by conceding more administrative authority to Swedish Match than he had surrendered to the Chinese members of the Joint Sales Office. To give Swedish Match a role in decision making, he authorized the creation of a "Control Committee" consisting of three members, two from the Chinese members of the office and one from Swedish Match. This committee had the power to consider all major issues that came before the office—quotas, prices, sales territories—and its members had to reach unanimous decisions for its actions to be binding. With the addition of this committee, Liu induced Swedish Match to sign an agreement with the Joint Sales Office on July 27, 1935, one year after the office had opened.[63]

Liu's predominance over his Chinese and Western rivals in the Joint Sales Office was most clearly manifest in its quotas. Under these quotas, his China Match Company was guaranteed more than half the match sales in the Lower and Middle Yangzi and the Southeast. More precisely, the quotas set in late 1935 for eight provinces (Jiangsu, Zhejiang, Fujian, Anhui, Jiangxi, Henan, Hubei, Hunan) allocated 54.87 percent of the market to China Match, 29.31 percent to the other nine Chinese firms, and 15.82 percent to Swedish Match. [64]

---

[62] *Zhongguo minzu huochai gongye,* p. 101. A copy of the agreement establishing the Joint Sales Office appears in *Liu Hongsheng qiye shiliao,* vol. 2, pp. 177–82.

[63] Eurén to Lieu [Liu], February 27, 1934, *China Manschuriet 1934,* Swedish Match Archives; a copy of the agreement between the Joint Sales Office and Swedish Match dated July 27, 1935, appears in Ing F. Dahl, *Kina Div Avtal 1935–39,* vol. 10, no. 47, Swedish Match Archives; *Liu Hongsheng qiye shiliao,* vol. 2, pp. 189–94.

[64] Agreement dated July 27, 1935, in Ing F. Dahl, *Kina Div Avtal 1935–39,* vol. 10, no. 47, Swedish Match Archives; *Zhongguo minzu huochai gongye,* p. 104.

Almost immediately the cartel, consisting of the members of the Joint Sales Office plus Swedish Match, had dramatic effects on production, prices, and profits. As early as July 1935 its members cut production by 20 percent; and during October, November, and December of 1935, they raised prices once per month, with increases ranging from 3 to 3.6 yuan per case on large cases and 2.4 to 3 yuan per case on small cases each time. Over the next two years between April 1935 and April 1937 within the Lower and Middle Yangzi and Southeast the cartel raised average match prices by a total of 50 percent.[65] As a result, some members of the cartel profited handsomely.

The chief beneficiary of the cartel was Liu Hongsheng's China Match Company. As table 5 shows, China Match, after having accumulated the biggest debts in its history between 1934 and 1935, then made the highest profits in its history between 1936 and 1937.[66] This dramatic reversal of its fortunes was largely attributable to the effectiveness of the cartel.

Swedish Match was pleased with the cartel too. Writing to his superiors in Sweden, the usually dour Eurén predicted optimistically in February 1937 that the cartel "will furnish a working basis and a fairly satisfactory one considering that we are working in China," and in July 1937 his office jubilantly confirmed that his forecast had been borne out: "Since the 1st of February 1937, competition has been largely eliminated by allotting tax stamps on an agreed quota basis."[67]

The remaining Chinese match companies in the Lower and Middle Yangzi belonging to the Joint Sales Office seem to have benefited from membership in it according to each one's size. Middle-sized firms such as Zhongguo Mills of Shanghai, Zheng Da Mills of Ningbo, and Chusheng Mills of Hankou were profitable in 1936 and 1937. Some small member firms such as Zhongnan Mills in Shanghai and Minsheng Mills in Suzhou suffered losses in 1936 and 1937, but not enough to deter other small firms from joining the cartel. When Liu agreed to take new members in February 1937, no fewer than eleven Chinese firms responded, raising the number of participating Chinese companies from ten to twenty-one.[68]

---

no. 47, Swedish Match Archives; *Zhongguo minzu huochai gongye,* p. 104.

[65] *Zhongguo minzu huochai gongye,* pp. 104–5 and 119–20.

[66] Ibid., pp. 82–83 and 104–5.

[67] Eurén to Swedish Match, February 19, 1937, Ing F. Dahl, *Kina Div. 1935–39,* vol. 10, no. 47; enclosure in letter from Amfeaco to Swedish Match, July 24, 1937, *STAB, Statistical Dept., Marknadsanalyser (1935),* both in Swedish Match Archives.

[68] *Zhongguo minzu huochai gongye,* pp. 120–21; Eurén to Swedish Match, February 19, 1937, Ing F. Dahl, *Kina Div Avtal 1935–39,* vol. 10, no. 47, Swedish Match Archives.

Between 1935 and 1937, Liu Hongsheng tried to go beyond his interregional cartel and create a national one. His proposal for a nationwide match monopoly, the Chinese National Joint Production and Sales Union for Matches (Zhonghua quanguo huochai chanxiao lianyingshe), won tacit support from Japanese and Chinese match manufacturers in North China between 1935 and 1937 and received official sanction from the Guomindang on February 1, 1936. But despite official backing, he failed to recruit more than a few companies elsewhere in China, and even in the North he was not consistently effective at enforcing quotas or reducing production.[69] Thus, in terms of Skinner's hierarchy of places, once Liu took as his base the central metropolis of Shanghai in the 1930s, he raised his control over the match market from the regional to the interregional level and tried without success to reach the national level.

China Match Company and the Chinese Model

This account of Liu Hongsheng's rise to the top of China's match industry shows that he conformed with Skinner's model in some respects and departed from it in others. Liu's recruitment of staff members for his marketing system from Dinghai County Middle School in his native place indicates that "a framework of native-place particularism," as Skinner calls it, persisted in Chinese businesses of the twentieth century. Similarly, Liu's use of first Suzhou and later Shanghai as bases from which to consolidate markets in smaller cities follows the pattern that had been established in late imperial China, according to Skinner. By the same token, even as this account of Liu's career provides examples of conformity with Skinner's model, it also reveals three striking departures from the model: in the 1920s, Liu avoided the city of greatest economic centrality, Shanghai, in favor of lower-level Suzhou as the initial base for his match business; in the early 1930s, he supplemented his particularistic network of Ningbo associates with an impersonal administrative organization for managing his marketing system; and in the late 1930s, he went beyond his regional base to exercise control over interregional (albeit not national) markets.

If, as Skinner's model suggests, these three steps were extraordinary, then why did Liu take them? In each case, the explanation is traceable to the competitiveness of the Shanghai market. In the 1920s, Liu started his match business outside Shanghai to avoid competition with Mitsui

---

[69] *Zhongguo minzu huochai gongye,* pp. 106–22; *Liu Hongsheng qiye shiliao,* vol. 2, pp. 226–42.

Bussan, Swedish Match, and Chinese companies. In the early 1930s, he supplemented his particularistic Ningbo sales network with an impersonal administrative organization to maintain control over noncompetitive markets in lower-level cities where his rivals' marketing systems did not reach. And in the late 1930s, he formed a cartel as a response to devastating competition from smaller Chinese match companies.

Of these responses to competition in Shanghai, the formation of the interregional cartel was the most innovative. To be sure, within Liu's own experience, it was not wholly unprecedented. After all, he had taken a step toward the cartel by forming China Match Company as a combine in 1930. In addition, he had negotiated cooperative arrangements for his firms in other industries: for his Huashang Cement Company (Huashang shuili gongsi), he signed with two other Shanghai-based cement companies interregional market-sharing agreements covering thirteen provinces in the mid-1920s and early 1930s; and for his China Briquette Company (Zhonghua meiqiu gongsi) he made local price-setting agreements with four other Shanghai manufacturers of briquettes (which were made of coal dust and clay) in 1930.[70] Nonetheless, the Joint Sales Office for matches went far beyond these earlier efforts because it encompassed many more firms, formed a cartel that included a foreign company,[71] and cast a marketing net both widely across regions and deeply down a hierarchy of sales representatives and Chinese commission agents responsible for distributing consumer goods to a mass market. Indeed, Liu's Joint Sales Office was probably the largest and most effective private cartel ever formed in Chinese history.

Conclusion

The commercial successes and failures of big businesses owned by Shanghai sojourners depended on the distinctive strengths and capacities for adaptation of those businesses. Upon reaching Shanghai, each faced the problem of how to adapt to local circumstances without compromising its own culture—its values, organization, and patterns of behavior—and each one's record at solving this managerial problem helps to explain the outcome of the battle for China's match market. To clarify the concepts of "culture" and "adaptability," it is worth restating the models of Japanese, Western, and Chinese businesses, evaluating the

---

[70] *Liu Hongsheng qiye shiliao*, vol. 1, pp. 190, 199–201, 210, 216, 224, 233, 243–45.

[71] In 1931, Liu tried but failed to persuade Japanese rivals in Shanghai to sign his market-sharing agreement with Chinese cement companies. See *Liu Hongsheng qiye shiliao*, vol. 1, p. 226.

extent to which the three companies in question conformed to their respective models, and assessing the historical validity of the models themselves.

As characterized by their originators, each model differs sharply from the other two. The model for overseas Japanese business is the general trading company (sōgō shōsha), which owns an international marketing operation, leaves manufacturing largely to independently owned factories, and invests heavily in training and employing Japanese marketing agents abroad. By contrast, the model for overseas Western business is the vertically integrated corporation, which owns international marketing and manufacturing operations, leaves marketing largely to locally based indigenous compradors and commission agents, and invests heavily in factories abroad. Unlike both of these models for big overseas businesses, the Chinese model for big domestic business is the native-place association, which owns regional or interregional marketing and manufacturing operations, assigns administrative responsibility for marketing and manufacturing to trustworthy employees from the owner's native place, and uses profits from long-distance marketing to invest in manufacturing.

The Chinese model, by drawing upon central place theory and focusing on geographical locations within China, implicitly highlights another difference—this one between foreign and domestic firms' points of entry into a market. Whereas the Japanese and Western models for overseas business assume that a sojourning foreign firm generally initiates trade abroad at the host country's largest port and city of greatest economic centrality, the Chinese model for domestic business contends that successful sojourning Chinese entrepreneurs commonly enter their country's market in smaller cities and consolidate commercial control over local and regional markets in nearby cities and towns before moving "up" the urban hierarchy to the country's biggest and most economically central city. In other words, while foreign firms almost invariably enter a market at the "top" city in a host country's nationwide trading system, domestic firms often reach this same city only after climbing "up" from a smaller place.

Taking these models as representations of Japanese, Western, and Chinese businesses' cultures, it is possible to evaluate the extent to which each business in this case followed or departed from existing cultural norms while adapting to Shanghai. In relation to the Japanese model, Mitsui Bussan became the most "Japanese" of all general trading companies in China. It was the first Japanese firm to own and operate a marketing system in the country's central metropolis, Shanghai; it left manufacturing of matches for China's market largely in the hands of independently owned Japanese factories in Japan; and it trained more foreign employees and set up more offices throughout the country than were introduced by any other Japanese company (or, for that matter, by a foreign company of any nationality) before the end of World War II.

In relation to the Western model, Swedish Match was no less exemplary. In China, as in much of the rest of the world, it was very "Western" in concentrating on manufacturing, leaving marketing to indigenous compradors and commission agents, and investing heavily in factories at the country's central metropolis, Shanghai, while spending little on a distributing network there or in other Chinese cities. Repeatedly its management responded to challenges by adjusting its manufacturing system in Shanghai without reforming its marketing system there or elsewhere in China.

Compared to these two foreign firms, China Match Company deviated more decisively from cultural norms. Its manager, Liu Hongsheng, was very "Chinese" in owning regional and interregional marketing and manufacturing operations, relying on staff members from his native place, and consolidating control over markets in cities and towns smaller than his initial urban base, Suzhou, before he moved "up" to the largest and most economically central of twentieth-century China's cities, Shanghai. But he also departed from the model first by opening his business in a smaller city than the city of his residence and later by expanding his marketing system and his cartel to include Chinese employees and cartel members who were subordinated under his authority by impersonal administrative devices rather than particularistic native-place ties.

In deviating from Chinese norms, Liu Hongsheng creatively solved his sojourning business' problem of adapting without compromising his culture. On the one hand, he showed adaptability by following a circuitous route up China' marketing hierarchy and forming organizations not based on native-place ties, and on the other hand, he continued to benefit from having followed the usual practices of retaining control over lower-level markets (which remained beyond the reach of foreign firms) and keeping trustworthy native-place compatriots in key administrative positions. In Shanghai, he thus gained a competitive edge over his larger foreign rivals by retaining his "Chinese" marketing techniques while supplementing them with "un-Chinese" ones.

By comparison, Liu's foreign rivals did not adapt as readily within the confines of their cultures, and their adaptation or nonadaptation helps to explain why they proved unable to dominate China's and especially Shanghai's match market as fully as they dominated other markets. Mitsui Bussan recognized early that Liu and other Chinese match producers were able to acquire technology cheaply and exploit local advantages effectively. Rather than alter the culture of its overall approach, Mitsui

Bussan ceased to designate and promote matches as one of its "most important commodities" in 1925 and thereafter gave priority to goods that its Chinese rivals marketed less competitively. Swedish Match, a specialist in matches, did not have within the culture of its overall approach the luxury of simply shifting its attention to the promotion of other products. Far from contemplating this drastic step, its management did not take even the small step of investing more heavily in marketing at Shanghai than in other cities abroad. Rather than adapt, Swedish Match settled for a smaller share of Shanghai's market than it was accustomed to holding elsewhere in the world.

It is worth noting that this historical case raises questions that might guide theorists in reassessing the historical validity of the models used here. For example, while Mitsui Bussan's record aptly exemplifies the Japanese model, the absence of any known Japanese precedent for its approach to China's market raises questions about the origins of the Japanese model and Mitsui Bussan's influence on its successors. According to available research, Mitsui Bussan set an example that was followed to the fullest by very few companies before World War II, and it did not become a model for a large number of Japanese firms until the 1950s. In fact, it was long regarded as so original and uncharacteristic of Japanese companies that the term used to describe its form of business, *sōgō shōsha*, was not coined until after World War II.[72] So perhaps more needs to be known about the history of Mitsui Bussan and other Japanese general trading companies (not to mention overseas Japanese manufacturers) before *sōgō shōsha* or any other model can be considered historically valid for overseas Japanese businesses in general.[73]

Swedish Match Company's close adherence to the Western model raises a different question about typicality. If as suggested here Swedish Match's rigid conformity to the Western model left it with a smaller market share in China than elsewhere in the world, did Western firms that departed from the Western model have any greater success in China? The few case studies currently available give an affirmative answer,[74] which, in turn, raises the possibility that the Western model

[72] See Nakayama Ichiro and Shinohara Miyohei, eds., *Nihon deizai jiten* (Tokyo: Kodansha, 1973), pp. 618 and 640–42.

[73] For recent and thoughtful reflections on questions for future research on *sōgō shōsha* (including the question of how the first *sōgō shōsha* came into existence), see Hideki Yoshihara, "The Business History of the Sōgō Shōsha in International Perspective," in Yonekawa and Yoshihara, eds., *Business History of General Trading Companies,* pp. 337–53.

[74] My preliminary findings on this subject are in "Chinese Cultural Barriers to Foreign Control over Trade," paper delivered at the annual meeting of the Association for Asian Studies, Washington, D.C., 1989.

used here applies less well to the behavior of Western firms in China than to the behavior of Western firms elsewhere in the world. Not until more historical research is done will it be known whether Swedish Match was representative of Western business in presocialist China.

Liu Hongsheng's conformity to some features of the Chinese model and deviations from others once again raise the issue of representativeness. Did other Chinese entrepreneurs follow Liu's example, and, whatever example they followed, did they outmaneuver foreign rivals as successfully as he did? Or was the rise of Chinese industrialists generally blocked in China by their foreign rivals? A lively debate over the outcome of Sino-foreign commercial rivalries is already under way,[75] but it will not be settled until additional studies have been done on other businesses in Chinese history.

For these additional studies of sojourning Western, Japanese, and Chinese businesses, it is difficult to imagine a more promising historical setting than Shanghai in the late nineteenth and early twentieth centuries. It was there that almost all big Western sojourning businesses in China made their entry into the country's market. It was there that almost all big Japanese sojourning businesses made their entry into any foreign market. And it was there that almost all big Chinese sojourning businesses completed their climb from smaller Chinese cities and towns to the top of China's urban hierarchy.

How models of businesses' behavior will be refined by future research on Shanghai's business history is difficult to predict, but if this study of the match trade is any indication, it seems safe to venture this generalization: whatever approach a sojourning business had previously used elsewhere, it invariably needed to adapt to Shanghai's market. Even a Japanese, Western, or Chinese firm that had captured a large share some other market was not likely to capture an equally large share of Shanghai's market if, upon reaching Shanghai, it doggedly continued to carry on business as usual.

---

[75] For a fuller comment (with references to the various debaters) on Sino-foreign commercial rivalries, see Sherman Cochran, *Big Business in China: Sino-Foreign Rivalry in the Cigarette Industry, 1890–1930* (Cambridge, Mass.: Harvard University Press, 1980), chap. 1 and passim.

CHAPTER THREE

New Culture, Old Habits
Native-Place Organization and the May Fourth Movement

BRYNA GOODMAN

Studies of the May Fourth Movement in Shanghai have not stressed native-place organization, and it would be surprising if they did, since the period is celebrated for its themes of iconoclasm, enlightenment, nationalism, and modernity, themes that are understood to constitute a rupture with old, "particularistic" social ties. The nationalism of the May Fourth Movement and the self-proclaimed cultural radicalism of the associated New Culture Movement have led the sympathetic historian to seek out expressions of new cultural and political forms and to relegate cultural continuities to the status of remnants. In the process, we have lost track of some of the social networks and organizations that underlay and facilitated the movement.[1] In examining the relation between native-place associations in Shanghai and the May Fourth Movement, this chapter seeks to regain a balance.

While May Fourth historiography has not stressed the role native-place associations played in providing organizational forms for the patriotic activities of students, businessmen, and workers, some notice of several of the most influential of such organizations—the Ningbo, Shandong, and Guangzhao *huiguan;* associations of Zhejiang and Shandong students; and seamen's associations of Ningbo and Guangdong, for instance—has been unavoidable.[2] Moreover, the persistence and

This chapter is based on a larger study of native-place sentiment and organization in Shanghai, "The Native-Place and the City: Immigrant Consciousness and Social Organization in Shanghai, 1853–1927" (Ph.D. dissertation, Stanford University, June 1990). For critical comments and suggestions on this paper or on issues discussed here, I would like to thank Andrew Char, Prasenjit Duara, Harold Kahn, Michael Meranze, Elizabeth Perry, David Sacks, Ernst Schwintzer, Lyman Van Slyke, Jeffrey Wasserstrom, and Zhang Jishun.

[1] See, for example, issues raised in Arif Dirlik, "Ideology and Organization in the May Fourth Movement: Some Problems in the Intellectual Historiography of the May Fourth Period," *Republican China* 12:1 (November 1986): 5.

[2] See, for example, Joseph Chen, *The May Fourth Movement in Shanghai* (Leiden, 1971).

adaptability of native-place ties throughout this period and extending into the 1920s have been a focus in other contexts—notably in studies of the Shanghai bourgeoisie by Marie-Claire Bergère and Susan Mann.[3] Nonetheless, neither the full role of native-place organizations nor the ways in which these "traditionalistic" organizations changed over this period have been recognized.

Native-place ties did not merely persist into the Republican era. In the midst of the political and social upheavals surrounding the May Fourth Incident of 1919, native-place sentiment experienced both rebirth and "modernization," if such a term may be applied to an old cultural tradition. The forms of native-place association changed as Shanghai changed. Native-place sentiment acquired a new vocabulary and new organizations, which took on new social, economic, and political projects. It is precisely this reformulation of an old sentiment that makes the study of traditionalistic social forms important for an understanding of the development of Chinese modernity.

In the early Republican period, new forms of native-place associations (*tongxianghui*) appeared; these rejected the elitist outlook of the older *huiguan*. Spurning the traditionalistic rituals of the *huiguan,* these new associations noisily adopted rituals of democratic populism and openness, publishing notes of meetings, correspondence, and financial accounts and vying with the Beijing government for the numbers of times they revised their constitutions. Rejecting the traditional *huiguan* architecture, with its central altar, stage, and courtyard, the new native-place organizations chose for themselves secular high-rise Western-style buildings with lecture halls, product display rooms, newspaper-reading rooms, recreation rooms, and offices built over shopping arcades, the whole topped with flags (see figures 1 and 2).

While these more modern associations rejected traditionalistic aspects of older native-place associations, and in particular, their elitist leadership and customary procedures of governance, they did not reject the principle of organization according to native-place origin. Contrary to the presuppositions about the withering of particularistic and traditionalistic ties we have imposed on our understanding of this period,

---

[3] Marie-Claire Bergère, *L'âge d'or de la bourgeoisie chinoise* (Paris, 1986), pp. 148–159; Susan Mann Jones, "The Ningbo *Pang* and Financial Power at Shanghai," in Mark Elvin and G.W. Skinner, eds., *The Chinese City Between Two Worlds* (Stanford, Calif.: Stanford University Press, 1974). See also Marie-Claire Bergère, Noël Castelino, Christian Henriot, and Pu-yin Ho, "Essai de prosopographie des Elites Shanghaïennes a l'époque républicaine, 1911–1949," *Annales* (July–August 1985), pp. 901–929, which concludes that regional solidarities were possibly the most relevant factor in the organization of both commercial and governmental elites in Shanghai throughout the Republican era.

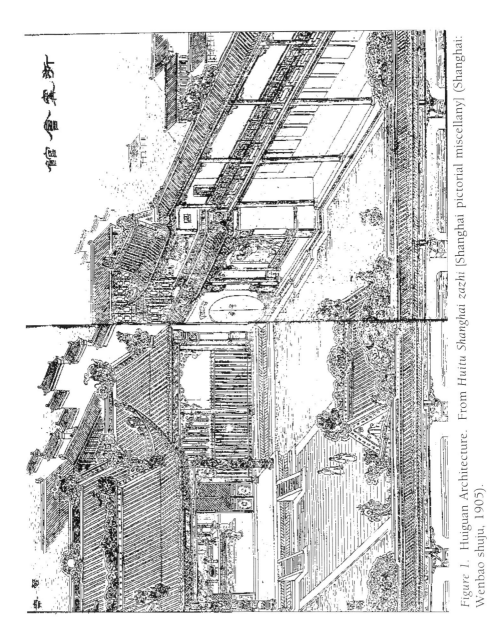

Figure 1. Huiguan Architecture. From *Huitu Shanghai zazhi* [Shanghai pictorial miscellany] (Shanghai: Wenbao shuju, 1905).

Figure 2. Pudong Tongxianghui (1937). From *Pudong tongxianghui huisuo luocheng jinian tekan* (Shanghai, 1937).

contemporaries did not view native-place ties as an obstacle to the strengthening of China as a modern nation. Rather, they reaffirmed the importance of native-place ties by fashioning their image of modernity out of the unquestioned raw material of native-place community.[4]

Native-place organization underlay many of the social coalitions that staged the Shanghai student, commercial, and worker strikes following the news of the May 4 arrests of students in Beijing. In this process, both old and new native-place groups were crucial to nationalistic social mobilization. Moreover, they formed the component elements of the more celebrated, more "modern" organizations of the period—those overarching organizations formed along occupational lines, such as the Shanghai Student Union (Shanghai xuesheng lianhehui), the Shanghai General Chamber of Commerce (Shanghai zong shanghui), and the more politically activist Shanghai Federation of Commercial Groups (Shanghai shangye gongtuan lianhehui).

The decade after the Revolution of 1911 witnessed enormous growth in social organizations of all sorts. New groups formed, some traditional in form, composition, and function and some not. Not only did the overall number of native-place associations (*huiguan* and *tongxianghui*) increase, but the numbers of members also increased. In the process, native-place sentiment became identified with the goals of nationalism and modernization believed necessary to save China.

The Proliferation of Native-Place Organizations in the Early Republican Period

A convenient index of social organizations in the early Republican period may be found in the successive detailed editions of *Shanghai*

---

[4] The meeting notes, accounts, and constitutions of these new associations were published in yearly reports and sometimes in the newspapers as well. See, for example, *Shaoxing qixian lühu tongxianghui ge gong zhangcheng* (Shanghai, 1920); *Shaoxing lühu tongxianghui tonggao* (Shanghai, editions of 1911, 1912, 1913, 1914); *Shenbao*, May 14, 1919. See also Oya Kotaro, "Shanhai ni okeru dōkyō dantai oyobi dōgyō dantai" [Regional groups and trade groups in Shanghai], *Shina kenkyū* [China research], 19 (1929): 145–156; and Negishi Tadeshi, *Chūgoku no girudo* [The guilds of China] (Toyko, 1953), pp. 199–200; and idem, *Shanhai no girudo* [The guilds of Shanghai] (Tokyo, 1951), pp. 42–43. This automatic reliance on native-place ties may also be observed in the lives of prominent Shanghai capitalists like Yu Xiaqing, who first relied on native-place ties to establish himself in business in Shanghai and then went on to serve the sojourning Ningbo community in Shanghai as a leader of both the Ningbo *huiguan* and *tongxianghui*. Yu's biographer, Chen Laixin, notes that Yu's life confirms the Chinese proverb "yu ren tian xia shi; bi zi ben xiang shi" (if you want to take on the matters of the world, you must begin with your native place). *Yu Xiaqing ni tsuite* [Regarding Yu Xiaqing] (Kyoto, 1983), pp. 11–15.

zhinan (Guide to Shanghai), published by Shanghai shangwu yinshuguan (Shanghai commercial press).[5] In a section entitled "public enterprises" (*gonggong shiye*), the guidebook listed the names and addresses of Shanghai charitable associations, educational associations, religious associations, hospitals, museums, mortuaries and burial grounds, *huiguan, gongsuo* (trade associations), and many institutions less easily categorized. As new forms of association developed over the course of the Republican period, they appeared in this publication. While comparison of these listings with other sources suggests that the guidebook was not complete and that it sometimes delayed several years before listing new types of organizations, it nonetheless includes the major associations of each type and indicates trends in the formation of associations.

While the guidebook reveals the intense organizational activity of the period generally and the overall proliferation of social organizations of all sorts, a comparison of the 1910, 1914, 1916, 1922, and 1930 editions demonstrates that much of this growth was expressed in native-place organization. Increase in the number of native-place associations is indicated by the entries in the guidebook: in 1910, twenty-six *huiguan* and no *tongxianghui* were listed; in 1914, thirty-four and none; by 1916 the numbers were forty-four and twenty-one; in 1922 the numbers increased to fifty-three and thirty-one, in 1930 to sixty-two and fifty-seven.

The numbers not only demonstrate an increase in native-place organizations but reveal that *traditional* native-place associations, *huiguan,* grew continuously over the course of this period, as did the newer, more modern, and somewhat more broadly based native-place associations, called *lühu tongxianghui* (literally, "associations of fellow-provincials sojourning in Shanghai"). *Tongxianghui,* which numbered fewer than ten in 1911, do not appear in the guidebook until 1916, when twenty-one such organizations are listed. Their numbers increased steadily along with *huiguan* in the years that followed.

This pattern of dual growth continued into the 1930s. Although *tongxianghui* represented greater numbers of people, the number of *huiguan* continued to exceed the number of *tongxianghui.* The *Shanghai shangye minglu* (Commercial directory of Shanghai) of 1931, for example, lists sixty-eight *huiguan* and fifty-four *tongxianghui.*[6] These numbers reflect the growth of sojourning populations over this period, the increasing

---

[5] *Shanghai zhinan* (Shanghai: Shanghai shangwu yinshuguan, editions of 1910, 1914, 1916, 1919, 1922, 1930). This guidebook seems most reliable for formal associations of commercial and professional groups. It does not appear reliable, unfortunately, for worker organizations. The figures from the 1919 edition do not appear to reflect updating from the 1916 edition and therefore are not included here.

[6] *Shanghai shangye minglu* (Shanghai: Shanghai shangwu yinshuguan, 1931).

subdivision of the geographic native-place units, and the persistent importance of *huiguan*.[7] In fact, several communities that did not formally organize until this period first established *tongxianghui*, then went on to crown their efforts by constructing *huiguan*.[8]

The Origins and Character of Tongxianghui

Tongxianghui were a distinct organizational trend of the Republican era, emerging roughly at the time of the Revolution and multiplying over the next three decades. Different native-place communities gave birth to *tongxianghui* at different times, in response to differing circumstances. The first *tongxianghui* were born in the atmosphere of the late Qing reforms and the local self-government movement surrounding the Republican revolution. Among these early *tongxianghui* were those of Huzhou, Haining, Ningbo, and Shaoxing (all Zhejiang prefectures) and Anhui and Gansu provinces. Each of these associations was established before 1912. *Tongxianghui* continued to increase in number throughout the Republican period, growth spurts often coinciding with periods of popular social mobilization. In May and June of 1919, for example, notices in the *Shenbao* announced the formation of at least ten new native-place organizations. Many of these added the goal of resisting foreign aggression to their statements of purpose.[9]

A history of the Jiangning *tongxianghui* presents a typical contemporary view of the development of *tongxianghui*:

The functions of *huiguan*...are to store coffins or ship them back to the

---

[7] Although figures for all of Shanghai are not available, some indication of population growth in this period is available from statistics for the International Settlement (see Appendix). The first population figures available for the areas of Shanghai under Chinese jurisdiction are for 1929: Jiangsu, 1,046,622; Zhejiang, 283,995; Guangdong, 36,947; Anhui, 51,099; Shandong, 20,395; Hubei, 19,681; Hunan, 5,282; Jiangxi, 5,926; Fujian, 9,654; for a total of 1,500,500, including figures from provinces with smaller sojourning populations. Zou Yiren, *Jiu Shanghai renkou bianqian de yanjiu* [Research on the evolution of population in old Shanghai] (Shanghai, 1980), pp. 114–115.

[8] For example, on May 3, 1919, the Wenzhou tongxianghui printed a notice in *Shenbao* of a meeting to collect money to build a Wenzhou *huiguan*. A similar notice for Changzhou people appeared on May 8. Other *tongxianghui* repaired, expanded, or refurbished preexisting *huiguan*. See, for example, a notice of the Hubei tongxianghui, *Shenbao*, May 18, 1919.

[9] *Shenbao*, May 1919. These were the Jiangning lühu tongxianghui, Anhui lühu xiehui, Suzhou tongxianghui, Anhui xuesheng tongxianghui (of Shangda), Hangzhou tongxianghui, Jiangbei lühu tongxianghui, Qingpu lühu tongxianghui, Jiading lühu tongxianghui, Haiyan lühu tongxianghui, and Sichuan lühu xuehui. Because the life of many associations was brief, these spurts of growth are not clearly indicated by the listings of solidly established associations in the editions of *Shanghai zhinan*.

native place, as well as worship gods and perform *jiao* rituals. As for modern spirit... certainly they were insufficient as organizations. In this century, thinking about popular government increased, and the spirit of organization also became more common. People with some modern knowledge also desired to participate in social organizations, solidify native-place sentiment, and perform necessary acts to benefit the public.... Therefore the Jiangning tongxianghui was formed in 1913.[10]

This account reflects the contemporary perception of *tongxianghui* as an explicitly modern form of association, suitable, indeed essential, to modern civic participation.

Often *tongxianghui* were formed after a period of conflict between *huiguan* elders and competing groups within the larger native-place community. In some communities the impetus for the formation of more democratic and popular *tongxianghui* came from *tongxiang* workers. This was the case for the Ningbo tongxianghui, which was founded as a result of agitation by Shen Honglai, a cook and the leader of an association of Ningbo menial servants. Shen succeeded both in creating a new and broader-based native-place association as well as instituting a measure of reform and greater accountability into traditional *huiguan* procedures. In other cases, students and intellectuals demanded new, more modern, and more accessible forms of association. An example of the latter type was the Chaozhou tongxianghui, which was formed as an eventual result of agitation led by Zhang Jingsheng, a notorious fringe figure of the New Culture Movement. In this instance, students clashed with *huiguan* elders over the use of *huiguan* funds, demanding an organization that would better serve student needs and interests.[11]

Although the impetus for *tongxianghui* formation could come from students or worker groups within the native-place community, it would be inaccurate to describe the *tongxianghui* as associations of students or workers. Despite their origins, because the new associations usually depended on *huiguan* for funding or for meeting rooms or both, they commonly came to be dominated by the more wealthy and powerful members of the sojourning community. Moreover, while *tongxianghui* were significantly more open and democratic than the more traditional *huiguan,* they still generally excluded poor members of the native-place community by requiring both letters of introduction from current members and yearly membership fees. *Huiguan* meeting notes generally

---

[10] *Jiangning liuxian luhu tongxianghui huikan* (Shanghai, 1935).

[11] Zhang was the editor of *Xin wenhua yuekan* [New culture monthly] and an ardent advocate of sexual enlightenment. The development of the Ningbo and Chaozhou *tongxianghui* as well as their activities in the Republican era are described in Goodman, ''Native Place and the City,'' chap. 5.

record from ten to sixty members present at meetings and do not refer to
a larger regular membership. *Tongxianghui* publications list from several
hundred to as many as ten thousand members, with thousands present at
annual all-member meetings. Here we see that *tongxianghui* represent a
substantial increase in membership, but clearly still a small proportion of
their larger sojourning communities.

As the Republican period wore on, sojourning communities with both
huiguan and *tongxianghui* tended to develop a loose division of labor
governing the activities of their native-place associations. *Huiguan*
retained their ritual, burial, and charitable functions and continued to be
controlled by a small group of businessmen who met every few weeks to
discuss the upkeep and disposal of (often considerable) *huiguan* urban
property holdings. As associations, *tongxianghui* tended to reflect
middle-class concerns and were more involved in the day-to-day affairs
of this middle sector of the sojourning community. *Tongxianghui* records
reflect substantial involvement in commercial arrangements, commercial
and family disputes, education, charity, and political organizing.

Student and Worker Native-Place Associations

While *huiguan* and *tongxianghui* were the major institutional forms of
native-place associations, they were not the only kinds of native-place
organization. Both *huiguan* and *tongxianghui* were general native-place
associations; they subscribed to the rhetoric of an all-inclusive native-
place community, regardless of class or social group. They were,
nonetheless, understood to have a primarily merchant constituency, with
the relatively small membership of the *huiguan* representing the business
elite and the *tongxianghui* including a larger commercial community as
well as journalists, educators, and intelligentsia.[12] The growth of these
native-place institutions associated with commercial circles (*shangjie*) was
accompanied by the development and growth of associations of sojourning students (*lühu xueshenghui*) and coexisted with a variety of trade and
worker associations (most commonly *bang, bangkou, gonghui, gongsuo,* or
she), which were also formed on the basis of native place. Unfortunately,
it is considerably more difficult to describe the numbers and trends of
formation of these associations. Since their native-place composition is
often not revealed by their name, many of these associations escape
detection.[13]

---

[12] In practice, there was some overlap between the members of each association. *Huiguan* leaders often served as directors of *tongxianghui.*

[13] While this is also a problem in studying *huiguan* and *tongxianghui,* these types of associations left considerably more records.

STUDENT ASSOCIATIONS. Student native-place associations followed roughly the same pattern of development as *tongxianghui,* finding their origins in the early-twentieth-century reforms and the development of new educational institutions. Twenty-four student associations, among them associations of sojourning students, appear in the 1916 edition of *Shanghai zhinan.* Often student associations are listed according to school. While such associations undoubtedly included coalitions of students from different communities, this type of listing masks the fact that many schools (particularly trade and business schools) were sponsored by native-place associations (both *huiguan* and *tongxianghui*) or dominated by students from one or two regions. Moreover, students often belonged both to school-level organizations, which are listed in guides and directories, and to native-place student associations, which are often not listed. In addition to a Fudan University Students' Association, for instance, there was also a Fudan Chaozhou Students' Association. There were also overarching native-place student associations that transcended school boundaries, for instance, the Association of Fujian Students, which met at the Fuzhou huiguan (San shan huiguan), and the Association of Zhejiang Students Sojourning in Shanghai.[14]

While students may have criticized *huiguan* as superstitious and traditionalistic, the fact that they did not find native-place organization in itself objectionable is evident in the prevalence of native-place organizations at the radical Shanghai University (Shanghai daxue, hereafter Shangda), several years after the May Fourth Movement. Materials on the "revolutionary martyrs" of Shangda amply demonstrate that the most radical students participated in Shangda *tongxianghui* as a matter of course and as a matter of necessity.[15] The memoir of one former Shangda student, Zhong Fuguang, a student of the Communist labor organizer and Party historian Deng Zhongxia, recalled the Sichuan tongxianghui as meeting both political and personal needs:

> This was a form resulting from the party's method of organizing everyone into groups. At the time, if you didn't belong to an organization, there was no way to be politically active. Therefore there were many provincial *tong-xianghui* at Shanghai University. Other schools were the same. The main activities of the *tongxianghui* were to bring together people's feelings and

---

[14] *Shenbao,* May 5, 9, and 13, 1919.

[15] Zhang Chongde (1903–1937) and He Weisheng (1902–1926), both from Zhejiang province, were activist students at Shangda. Both participated in the Shangda Zhejiang tongxianghui, which was the largest native-place organization at the school. Together with their fellow-provincial students, they studied social and economic conditions in Zhejiang in order to participate in revolutionary struggles in their native place. Shanghai shiwei dangshi ziliao zhengji weiyuanhui, ed., *Shanghai daxue* (Shanghai, 1986), pp. 67–68.

unite people. Everyone was studying outside his or her native place. If something came up it could be taken to the *tongxianghui*.[16]

Zhong's suggestion that the *tongxianghui* form resulted from Party initiatives is mistaken, of course, but it confirms the sense that there was no perceived contradiction between native-place organizations and social revolutionary goals and suggests the importance of using native-place sentiment and the vehicle of native-place organizations to pursue effective social mobilization.[17]

WORKER ORGANIZATIONS. Native-place organization developed among Shanghai workers from the moment they immigrated or were recruited to work in the city. A variety of native-place *bang*[18]—among the most prominent in Shanghai, the Guangdong *bang*, Ningbo *bang*, Subei *bang*, Hubei *bang*, Shaoxing *bang*, Wuxi *bang*, and local Shanghai (*ben*) *bang* — characterized Shanghai labor from the opening of the port in 1843 through the Republican era.[19]

---

[16] Ibid., pp. 106–107.

[17] See also Shanghai shehui kexueyuan lishi yanjiusuo, ed., *Wusi yundong shiliao* [Historical materials on the May Thirtieth Movement], vol. 1 (Shanghai, 1981), p. 416.

[18] The term *bang* appears in a variety of contexts and can apply to a range of associations, formal and informal, from business to worker associations. It is the most common term used to describe native-place organization of labor. It is important to note that it does not necessarily imply a formal organization. The mere presence of Ningbo workers permits the use of the term "Ningbo *bang*." That people from one native place will act as a group is assumed within the terminology.

[19] In the late nineteenth century certain trades were dominated at first by Guangdong people on whom the British relied as they moved enterprises from Guangdong to Shanghai. This was the case, for example, with the first group of machine workers in Shanghai, who were employed in shipyards. Guangdong people initially monopolized a number of other trades for similar reasons. Guangdong sojourners dominated the early wood-working business associated with ship repair, though the community was divided into two *bang*—workers from the Taishan area and woodworkers from all other areas of Guangdong. The foreman who led the Taishan *bang* recruited new workers himself from his native place. Guangdong people coming to Shanghai had first to join their *bang* (paying a small fee) before they could work. In return, these *bang* provided a degree of security, guaranteeing some assistance in the event of old age, sickness, and burial. Guangdong people did not have advantages in all enterprises, however. Because many of the directors of the Jiangnan Bureau of Manufacturing were from Xiangtan (in Hunan province), the first group of workers and craftsmen were also from Hunan, recruited through *tongxiang* connections. Knife and metal-tools workers were divided between the Shaoxing *bang* and the local Shanghai *bang*. Iron-workers in ship-repair were divided among the local *bang* and the Wuxi bang, which gradually dominated. Wuxi workers also dominated the blacksmith trade, which they shared with local Shanghai and Ningbo craftsmen. See Zhongguo shehui kexueyuan, Jingji yanjiusuo, ed., *Shanghai minzu jiqi gongye* [Shanghai's national machine industry] (Beijing, 1979), pp. 7, 9, 13, 30, 50–54, 58–63, and 68.

Just as the contributions of *tongxiang* merchants in support of education strengthened (though by no means explains) student organization by native place, patterns of recruitment, deployment, and labor control strengthened worker organization by native place. Prominent Chinese capitalists in the early Republican period—men such as Liu Hongsheng (of Dinghai county, Zhejiang), Yu Xiaqing (of Zhenhai county, Zhejiang), Zheng Bozhao (of Zhongshan County, Guangdong), and the Rong brothers (of Wuxi county, Jiangsu)—established themselves in Shanghai with the help of native-place networks and recruited their *tongxiang* as managers and foremen in their enterprises. These people in turn recruited *tongxiang* workers. Foreign owners of Shanghai enterprises relied on Chinese foremen and labor recruiters, who similarly recruited among their *tongxiang*.[20]

Whereas regional groups had monopolized specific trades in the late nineteenth century, by the early Republican period the shifting fortunes and populations of different groups led to a more complex situation of shared participation in specific trades and enterprises.[21] That specific *bang* ceased to monopolize specific occupational niches did not mean that the various regional groups mixed or that the importance of the *bang* diminished. Instead, labor and industry in the 1920s and 1930s was characterized by *bang* subdivision within the multi-*bang* work unit.

Shanghai textile mills were dominated by Shaoxing, Ningbo, and Jiangbei *bang*, although there were also groups from Nanjing, Anhui, and the Shanghai countryside.[22] Workers at the British-owned Shanghai

---

[20] See Chen Laixin, *Yu Xiaqing*, pp. 12–15; Cheng Renjie, "Yingmei yan gongsi maiban Zheng Bozhao" [British-American Tobacco Company comprador Zheng Bozhao], *Wenshi ziliao xuanji* (Shanghai, 1978), no. 1, pp. 130–135; Shanghai shehui kexueyuan jingji yanjiusuo, ed., *Rongjia qiye shiliao* [Historical materials on the Rong family enterprises], vol. 1 (Shanghai, 1980), p. 118; Marie-Claire Bergère, *L'âge d'or*, pp. 148–159; Emily Honig, *Sisters and Strangers* (Stanford, Calif.: Stanford University Press, 1986), pp. 57–78. See also the chapters in this volume by Elizabeth Perry and Emily Honig.

[21] Monopolization was possible only in certain types of trade. The post–Opium War cotton trade in Shanghai was much more complex and could not be dominated by one native-place group. It comprised instead ten major *bang* and numerous smaller ones. See Shanghai shi gongshang xingzheng guanli ju, *Shanghai shi mianbu shangye* [Shanghai's cotton trade] (Beijing, 1979), p. 193. The continuity of the names of such organizations (*bang, bangkou*) as well as a variety of terms with religious associations (*tang* and *she*) suggests a certain continuity in the character of these worker associations at least through the May Fourth period. Materials from the mid-1920s, however, suggest the growth of more secular types of native-place worker associations, often called *lühu gonghui* (sojourners' union) or *zhuhu laogonghui* (association of laborers staying in Shanghai), reflecting both labor organizing efforts and the increasing radicalization of the Shanghai proletariat. See, for example, Shanghai shehui kexueyuan, *Wusi yundong*, vol. 1, pp. 398, 401.

[22] Zhu Bangxing, Hu Lingge, and Xu Sheng, eds., *Shanghai chanye yu Shanghai zhigong* [Shanghai industry and workers], 1939, reprinted by Shanghai renmin chubanshe (Shanghai,

Tramway Company were divided between the Ningbo and Subei *bang,*
which dominated separate divisions within the company.[23] Shaoxing
tongxiang, introduced by Shaoxing relatives and recruited by a Shaoxing
forewoman, predominated in the leaf-packing department at the British-
American Tobacco Company. Women from Yangzhou (Subei) predominated in the more strenuous rolling department.[24] Flour mill workers at
the Fuxin mills were divided among the Hubei bang and Wuxi bang,
each of which dominated different sectors of the machine room.[25] Among
those who worked on the riverfront, the dockworkers were mainly from
Subei; those who worked in warehouses were mainly from Ningbo; and
those on the ships watching the holds were mainly from Guangdong.[26]

As with student associations, it is important to assess the social and
political character of worker native-place *bang. Bang* divisions could
mean competition and rivalry, interethnic tensions, harassment, and
fighting.[27] In the same manner as student native-place organization,
worker native-place organization occurred at levels that both subdivided
and transcended their institutions of work. In other important respects,
however, the omnipresent native-place organization of workers differed
from that of students. The leaders of worker *bang* tended not to be ordinary workers themselves, but instead were foremen, labor contractors,
and even merchants and minor officials.[28] Moreover, membership and
allegiance were more automatic than voluntary.

1984), p. 202. See also Honig, *Sisters and Strangers,* pp. 57–78.

[23] Zhu, Hu, and Xu, *Shanghai chanye,* pp. 264–265. See also Elizabeth Perry's chapter
in this volume.

[24] Shanghai shehui kexueyuan, Jingji yanjiusuo, ed., *Yingmei yan gongsi zai hua qiye ziliao
huibian* [Collected materials on the British and American Tobacco enterprise in China]
(Beijing, 1983), vol. 3, pp. 1027–1028.

[25] Zhu, Hu, and Xu, *Shanghai chanye,* pp. 625–662. It is interesting to note that as gang
organization of labor grew during the 1930s, native-place ties influenced workers' entrance
into gangs. In the case of the Fuxin mill, Hubei workers tended to join the Red Gang
(Hongbang), whereas Wuxi workers tended to join the Green Gang (Qingbang). Nonetheless, it would seem that gang membership did lead to a certain weakening of native-place
ties, as the gangs displaced many of the functions of *tongxianghui.* See also Cai Xiaoqing,
Zhongguo jindai huidang shi yanjiu [Research on secret societies and gangs in modern
Chinese history] (Beijing, 1987), p. 333.

[26] Zhu, Hu, and Xu, *Shanghai chanye,* p. 647.

[27] For references to fights between workers escalating to melees between their respective
native-place *bang,* see ibid., pp. 264–265; *Shenbao,* May 3 and 16, 1919; June 2, 1919; and
Cai Xiaoqing, *Zhongguo jindai huidang,* p. 332. For a discussion of the particular prejudice
of Jiangnan workers against workers from poverty-stricken Subei (who often performed the
most laborious, ill-paid, and demeaning tasks), see Honig, *Sisters and Strangers,* pp. 70–78,
as well as her chapter in this volume.

[28] Cai Xiaoqing, *Zhongguo jindai huidang,* pp. 331–332.

Communist labor organizers surveying Shanghai in 1921 noted that preexisting organic associations among workers—both regional *bang* and gang-type organizations—posed a major obstacle to the formation of worker unions. Nonetheless, although they viewed native-place *bang* as a kind of feudal tie that subjected workers to the manipulation of officials and compradors (not to mention retrograde gang bosses and contract brokers), Party organizers learned that to organize labor effectively they had to work with the preexisting *bang*, make friends with their leaders and, through the leaders, attempt to radicalize the members.[29]

The Subdivision of the Native-Place Community

Some idea of the plethora of native-place associations coexisting in 1919 may be provided by the following partial listings of associations of Guangdong and Zhejiang fellow-provincials.[30] These lists are by no means comprehensive and are merely meant to suggest the range of associations within each native-place community.

Guangdong Associations in Shanghai (1919)

Huiguan

Guangzhao gongsuo
Shunde huiguan
Nanhai huiguan
Chaozhou huiguan
Chaohui huiguan
Jiepufeng huiguan

Tongxianghui

Zhaoqing tongxianghui
Jiaying wushu lühu tongxianghui
Lühu dapu tongxianghui

---

[29] *Deng Zhongxia wenji* [Collected writings of Deng Zhongxia] (Beijing, 1983), p. 425; and "Shanghai gongzuo jihua jueyi'an" (1926) in *Zhongguo zhongyang wenjian xuanji* [Collected central party documents] (Zhongyang danganguan, 1982), vol. 2, pp. 182–183; Cai Xiaoqing, *Zhongguo jindai huidang*, pp. 331–334.

[30] These lists are compiled on the basis of organizations mentioned in Shanghai shehui kexueyuan lishi yanjiusuo, ed., *Wusi yundong zai Shanghai shiliao xuanji* [Collected historical materials on the May Fourth Movement in Shanghai] (Shanghai, 1980); also mentioned in *Shenbao*, 1919, and in the publications and meeting notes of Guangdong and Zhejiang organizations in Shanghai: *Chaozhou huiguan yi'an beicha; Siming gongsuo yi'an lu; Ningbo lühu tongxianghui yuebao.*

Other

Guangdong Club (Guangdong julebu)
Guangdong Sojourners' Reconstruction Association
Guangdong Sojourners' Commercial Association
Chaozhou Sugar and Miscellaneous Goods Association
[Chaohui] Third-Class Pawnshop Association
Fudan Chaozhou Students' Association
Association of Guangdong Seamen

Zhejiang Associations in Shanghai (1919)

Huiguan

Siming gongsuo (Ningbo huiguan)
Zheshao huiguan
Zheyan huiguan
Shaoxing huiguan
Haichang gongsuo (Haining huiguan)
Huzhou huiguan
Dinghai huiguan
Dinghai shanchang huiguan

Tongxianghui

Ningbo lühu tongxianghui
Shaoxing lühu tongxianghui
Quanzhe lühu tongxianghui
Haiyan lühu tongxianghui
Hangzhou lühu tongxianghui
Wenzhou tongxianghui
Haichang lühu tongxianghui

Other

Shaoxing International Improvement Society
Huzhou Student and Commercial Fellow-Sojourners' Association
Ningbo Student Association
Association of Zhejiang Sojourning Students
Fudan Zhejiang Student Association
Fudan Shaoxing Student Association
Ningshao Cotton Trade Welfare Association
Ningshao Lacquerers' Association
Siming Long Life Society (Ningbo workers in foreign homes and
    restaurants)
Jun'an she (Ningbo seamen)

This long and varied list of associations indicates several important developments of the early Republican period. First, it demonstrates a growing articulation of "social circles" (*jie*), that is, the separation, both in language and in organizational identity, of layers of businessmen and merchants, students, workers, and sometimes journalists. Whereas several decades earlier, general appeals to the *tongxiang* community did not normally specify groups within the community, now appeals to fellow-sojourners "of all circles" (*lühu tongxiang gejie*) or to *tongxiang* "of commercial, student, worker, and journalist circles" (*shang-xue-gong-bao jie*) expressed the differentiation of separate interest, status, or economic groups. Although appeals to greater *tongxiang* community were still possible in the May Fourth period, they no longer carried the suggestions of brotherhood or ritual equality that characterized the nineteenth-century *tongxiang* community.[31]

Second, while the formation of new associations certainly meant a splitting off from the old *huiguan,* this splitting was not necessarily antagonistic. New associations lacking their own buildings (as was especially the case when these associations were not commercial associations) commonly met at the building of the older association (*huiguan* or *gongsuo*). For instance, the Chaohui pawnshop association met at the Chaohui huiguan; the Hangzhou tongxianghui met at the Qianjiang huiguan; the Suzhou tongxianghui met at the Pingjiang gongsuo; the Jiading tongxianghui met at the Cake and Bean Trade Gongsuo; the Fujian Student Association met at the San shan huiguan; Ningbo workers' associations held important meetings at the Siming gongsuo.

Third, the proliferation of groups reflects increasing geographical fragmentation. As the populations of fellow-provincials in Shanghai increased, there was increasing subdivision within the Shanghai community according to smaller geographical units of native-place origin. The question is how to interpret this fragmentation. The interaction of these groups, viewed through the meeting notes of the Ningbo and Chaozhou *huiguan,* suggests that this type of division did not mean competition or antagonism among newly subdivided units. Geographic subdivision of the native-place community resulted, rather, from the enormous growth in Shanghai's immigrant populations over the course of this period and each group's attainment of a sort of "critical mass" resulting from a combination of numbers and wealth. In practice, on all major issues, groups from the same province combined their forces and worked together, issuing joint telegrams and meeting together in the largest of the *tongxiang* meeting places.[32]

---

[31] Goodman, "Native-Place and the City," chap. 3.

[32] *Chaozhou huiguan yi'an beicha; Siming gongsuo yi'an lu.* Consulted for the period

Finally, the formation of new native-place groups often coincided with political ferment. New associations were founded with explicitly political purposes, in addition to the generally expressed goals of contributing to native-place sentiment and facilitating contact between fellow sojourners. The birth of *tongxianghui* coincided, significantly, with the period of Republican revolution.[33] A second major spurt of growth occurred in the May Fourth period, as noted above.[34]

The Role of Native-Place Organizations in the May Fourth Period

Native-place organizations were crucial actors in the patriotic upsurge of 1919. The patriotic activities of merchant-led native-place associations preceded the surge of student activism in Shanghai and sustained the political mobilization that followed the news of the arrests of students in Beijing.[35] Less obviously, but no less importantly, native-place associations provided models of new and "modern" types of social organization.

Major merchant-dominated native-place associations organized for patriotic political activity early in 1919, well before the development of student activism in Shanghai.[36] On February 6, 1919, seven associations jointly signed a telegram asking the Beijing government to resist Japanese demands and preserve China's sovereignty in the Paris conference. Four of these associations were the Guangzhao gongsuo and the associations of Zhejiang, Ningbo, and Shaoxing sojourners in Shanghai.[37] Concern over the disruption of the north-south peace negotiations in Shanghai

---

1913–1937.

[33] See Negishi, *Chūgoku*, pp. 199–202. In an analysis in which the motive force of change appears to be "the spirit of the times," Negishi suggests *tongxianghui* were a product of nationalist and republican sentiment. See also *Shanghai yanjiu ziliao xuji* [Shanghai research materials, continuation], reprint of 1939 edition (Shanghai, 1984), p. 303. The stated purpose of the Ningbo tongxianghui, founded in 1909, was "to unite the *tongxiang* group and develop the spirit of self-government." If the precise connections between association formation and political ferment remain elusive, there is no question about their coincidence or the prominent Nationalist and Republican rhetoric of the new associations.

[34] See n. 9.

[35] I am not suggesting that merchants advocated the same kind of social mobilization or tactics as the students.

[36] Materials in Shanghai shehui kexueyuan, *Wusi yundong zai Shanghai*, demonstrate this persuasively. On this point see also Chen, *May Fourth Movement*, pp. 194–195. Chen argues that the May Fourth Movement in Shanghai differed from that of Beijing in that the leadership, in the initial stages, was not the students, but rather was drawn from intellectual and business circles.

[37] The other three associations were the Foreign Goods Trade Association, the Export Trade Association, and the World Peace Federation. Shanghai shehui kexueyuan, *Wusi yundong zai Shanghai*, pp. 144–145.

prompted the urgent formation of the Shanghai Federation of Commercial Groups (Shanghai shangye gongtuan lianhehui).[38] This association was formed on March 3, 1919, in the Ningbo tongxianghui building, with the purpose of exerting pressure to end the north-south civil war, resume the peace talks, and otherwise bring a return of the political stability needed to foster business.[39] This federation of fifty-three groups was composed primarily of native-place associations and trade associations (many of which represented merchants from a single native place). The native-place associations involved were

Ningbo lühu tongxianghui
Guangzhao gongsuo
Chaohui huiguan
Zhaoqing lühu tongxianghui
Danyang lühu tongxianghui
Jianghuai lühu tongxianghui
Wenzhou lühu tongxianghui
Jiaying lühu tongxianghui
Guangdong Sojourners' Commercial Association
Dapu lühu tongxianghui
Sichuan lühu tongxianghui
Jiangning lühu tongxianghui
Jiangsu Pottery Trade Association
Shaoxing lühu tongxianghui
Zhejiang lühu tongxianghui
Pinghu lühu tongxianghui
Jiepufeng huiguan
Hubei lühu tongxianghui
Jiangxi lühu tongxianghui

This group was active throughout April, agitating both for peace within China and for a favorable resolution of the Qingdao question, internationally, sending telegrams to the Paris conference as well as to Chinese representatives in Europe, voicing its concern.[40]

---

[38] At this time, two separate governments, the Beijing government and the Guangzhou Military Government, both claimed legitimacy and were engaged in a north-south civil war.

[39] Chen Laixin, *Yu Xiaqing,* p. 44. The leaders of this organization were Yu Xiaqing, Zou Jingzhai, Chen Liangyu, Ye Huijun, Fang Jiaobo, Feng Shaoshan, and Tang Jiezhi. Yu, Chen, and Fang were prominent leaders of the Ningbo huiguan; Feng and Tang were leaders of the Guangzhao gongsuo.

[40] Shanghai shehui kexueyuan, *Wusi yundong zai Shanghai,* pp. 648–654. At the Paris conference the powers decided on April 30 to accept Japan's demands for the transfer of all previously German interests in Shandong and to reject China's position. Knowledge of this decision touched off the Beijing University student protests on May 4.

On May 6, the first day of activity after the news of the events of May 4 reached Shanghai, the Association of Shandong Sojourners in Shanghai sent a telegram to the Beijing government protesting the failure to protect Qingdao. The Federation of Commercial Groups urged businesses to participate in an urgent upcoming "Citizens' Assembly" (Guomin dahui) to discuss the situation. On May 7 and 8, the federation sent urgent telegrams to the president, the cabinet, and the Ministry of Education in Beijing urging the release of the students and the calming of the angered public. The federation also sent a telegram to the Chinese delegates to the Paris peace conference, urging them to refuse to sign the treaty.[41] Finally, the federation served as a watchdog organization for the more reluctant Shanghai General Chamber of Commerce, admonishing it for its less radical stance.[42]

Following meetings held by educators at Fudan University on May 6 and a preparatory meeting at the Jiangsu Provincial Education Association, a "Citizens' Assembly" was held on May 7 to protest the loss of Qingdao, the arrests of the students in Beijing, and the actions of the "traitorous" officials. This mass meeting brought together fifty-seven associations, including representatives of twenty-four schools (a number of which, like the Shaoxing Sojourners' School, were sponsored by native-place associations) and eleven native-place associations. These included a number of associations not included in the Shanghai Federation of Commercial Groups, among them

> Henan tongxianghui
> Jiangbei Sojourners Preservation Society
> Anhui Consultative Committee
> Sichuan lühu tongxianghui
> Shandong lühu tongxianghui
> Fujian Reconstruction Committee
> Hunan Affairs Preservation Society
> Quanzhe [All-Zhejiang] lühu tongxianghui
> Hubei Reconstruction Committee
> Shaoxing International Improvement Society
> Wenzhou tongxianghui

On May 9, merchants began a boycott of Japanese goods. The newspapers announced the closing of numerous schools and businesses to observe the fourth anniversary of China's acquiescence to Japan's Twenty-one Demands. Prominent among the private schools that closed

---

[41] Ibid., pp. 158, 171–173.
[42] Ibid., p. 233.

in protest were those of Guangdong, Ningbo, and Huzhou sojourners in Shanghai. All of this activity occurred before the formal establishment of the Shanghai Student Union on May 11.[43] In the next week, groups of workers and craftsmen, organized by trade and native place, joined in the protest and boycott. One such group, the association of local Shanghai and sojourning Shaoxing construction workers (Hu-Shao shuimuye gongsuo) printed several notices in the *Shenbao*. In language both traditionally deferential and also borrowing terms from a more modern political vocabulary, the workers expressed their concern, outrage, and determination to act:

> All those with blood and breath are profoundly affected. We who belong to worker circles [*jie*] are also a sector of the citizenry. Witnessing the tragedies of national subjugation, past and present, is like being flayed. Accordingly, in conscience we advocate following the manner of the gentlemen of each *jie* who prepare meetings [of resistance], and ourselves suggest a means of resistance. All of those in our trade belong to worker circles, but we should not, because of that, speak only of labor.[44]

The workers announced that where they formerly used Japanese wood, metal, glass, and cement, they would no longer do so. Declaring that "for the purpose of saving the nation from extinction" all the workers must obey the boycott and "exhibit the determination of citizens," the workers also enjoined their foremen and the owners of the enterprises for which they worked to obey. In a notice printed in the *Shenbao* on May 17, the workers addressed the directors of their trade (*yedong*) as follows:

> [I]n the importing of Japanese goods you could say our trade is at the top of the list...all of our people are united...and from this day on will not use Japanese goods. If you meet with foreign-organized engineering projects that have already arranged the purchase of Japanese goods, you must find a way not to use them...If it is a Chinese project that has arranged to use Japanese materials, the materials should be immediately replaced by Chinese materials...and the proprietor of the enterprise should compensate [the relevant parties]. If the proprietor does not consent, there is only one suitable approach—we will stop work. Although there are many fools and dimwits among our worker *jie,* our blood is warm and honest. We will do our utmost hoping to protect our nation's territory.[45]

In the course of these weeks of agitation, *tongxianghui* throughout the city held numerous urgent meetings to discuss the political situation with their fellow-provincials and to send repeated telegrams to the authorities

---

[43] Ibid., pp. 181–183, 186–188, 192, 195–196.
[44] Ibid., p. 212.
[45] Ibid., pp. 226–227.

in Beijing and to authorities in their native provinces. Networks of
fellow-provincials served as conduits for information. The telegrams of
these groups to their fellow-provincials in Beijing and to the authorities of
their native provinces fill the pages of the *Shenbao,* as paid advertisements and as news items. Jiangsu fellow-provincials sojourning in other
provinces similarly sent telegrams to the Shanghai General Chamber of
Commerce to exert pressure and exhort the chamber to defend China's
national sovereignty. Native-place associations printed repeated declarations of their unity and resolve to boycott Japanese goods, urging all
Chinese (in their own respective groups) to do the same.[46]

Shanghai students declared a strike on May 26 and began actively to
encourage merchants and industrialists to maintain their boycott. When
news arrived of the June 2 mass arrests of students in Beijing, the students began to exert pressure for a general strike. Merchants announced
this move on June 5 in a meeting that included students, educational
leaders, leaders of native-place and trade associations, and journalists.
The meeting featured impassioned speeches by merchants as well as students and educational leaders. Among the speakers identified as belonging to "merchant circles" was Cao Muguan, school principal and also
delegate of the Association of Shaoxing Sojourners. Cao announced that
all the Shaoxing merchants had met at the association and resolved to
strike in unity, demanding the punishment of the traitorous officials, the
recovery of citizens' rights, and the release of the students. Cao was followed by Zhou Xisan, delegate of the Guangzhao gongsuo, who expressed
the same resolutions. These speeches and resolutions were echoed by
the Jiangning huiguan representative and by Chen Liangyu, who
represented both the Association of Ningbo Sojourners and the Tobacco
and Wine Federation. Chen was also a director of the Ningbo huiguan.[47]

At a second meeting, of "student, commercial, industrial, and newspaper circles" at the General Chamber on June 7, participants resolved
to maintain the strike until the national traitors had been punished and
dismissed. According to the *Shishi xinbao,* among the merchants, the
three *bang* of Shandong, Ningbo, and Guangdong were the most
determined.[48]

Native-place networks were vital links in the extraordinary merging of
student, business, and worker concerns and in the formation of the

---

[46] *Shenbao,* May 1919.

[47] Shanghai shehui kexueyuan, *Wusi yundong zai Shanghai,* pp. 300–305. The general
strike had already begun by the time of this meeting, which may be read as a moment in
which association leaders acted belatedly to support and coordinate actions already taken
by their consitutencies.

[48] Ibid., pp. 324–325.

"united front" effort that characterized this period of the movement. In the organization of strike activity, native-place associations performed a number of critical tasks, disseminating information, organizing political activity, and maintaining order. On the day of the strike announcement, the Ningbo tongxianghui, after an urgent meeting, published a notice attesting to the fervent patriotism of Ningbo fellow-provincials and urging the unified action of the Ningbo community.[49] The notice also stressed the need to maintain order, resolve disputes, and refrain from incidents involving foreigners. The Siming gongsuo (Ningbo huiguan) sent the following telegram to the Beijing government, expressing a fear for the maintenance of public order:

> Shanghai's commercial, student, worker circles indignantly rise in fervor and strike. People's hearts beat wildly; danger extreme. If situation not immediately resolved, fear social structure will collapse. Humbly ask release students in prison. Dismiss three officials to ease people's indignation and stabilize situation. Presented on behalf of Shanghai Siming gongsuo's full body of 400,000 people.[50]

The *gongsuo* also disseminated urgent public notices to maintain order, presumably intended for the 400,000 Ningbo residents it claimed to represent in the telegram just quoted:

> Urgent Announcement of the Shanghai Siming gongsuo:
> Compatriots, you have patriotically stopped work. In your actions be civilized. Shanghai's population is great and order is critical. If we can be organized and unified we can show our spirit more strongly. On no account assemble in the streets. On no account take part in demonstrations. If you encounter foreigners be calm. Maintain mutual respect and they will respect us. We pray everyone will pay attention and be careful.[51]

The Guangzhao gongsuo similarly sent telegrams to the Beijing government exhorting the officials to listen to public opinion. On June 7, the *gongsuo* also printed an urgent appeal to all Guangdong fellow-provincials to maintain public order and avoid fights with foreigners.[52] Other *huiguan* and *tongxianghui* disseminated similar notices exhorting both unified patriotic activity and the maintenance of strict order among their fellow-provincials.

Native-place organizations were also responsible both for spreading the merchant strike to other areas and for the strict enforcement of the boycott. The Ningbo Chamber of Commerce decided to join the strike

---

[49] *Shenbao*, June 6, 1919.
[50] *Siming gongsuo yi'an lu,* June 1919.
[51] Ibid.
[52] *Shenbao*, June 7, 1919.

when it received a telegram from the Shanghai Ningbo tongxianghui expressing its resolve to strike. Once the Ningbo strike went into effect, both the Ningbo Chamber and the Ningbo Labor Union (Qiyi gonghui), in addition to a variety of other Ningbo associations, kept in close contact with the Shanghai Ningbo tongxianghui, requesting both news and direction. *Huiguan* and *tongxianghui* alike investigated reports of individuals who conducted business with Japanese. In cases of traitorous behavior, full meetings of *tongxiang* were held to proclaim individuals guilty and henceforth excluded from the native-place community. One such offender, Lu Zongyu, was denounced by the Lühu Haichang (Haining) gongsuo, which printed a notice in the *Shenbao* announcing that Lu would no longer be recognized as a Haining *tongxiang*.[53]

Communication between the Shanghai Chamber of Commerce and Shanghai businesses went through the intermediary of the native-place associations,[54] to which the chamber appealed but on which it was unable to exert its will. When, after a secret meeting with the Chinese authorities the chamber urged *tongxianghui* on June 10 to counsel their communities to stop the strike, the request was rebuffed.[55] Guangdong, Ningbo, and Shandong shopkeepers met immediately with their native-place groups and repudiated the action of the chamber. The powerful Ningbo tongxianghui printed a notice in the *Shenbao* the next day stating that its directors had considered and rejected the chamber's appeal, stressing that contrary to the chamber's wishes Ningbo merchants in Shanghai would not resume business. The Shandong merchants printed a similar notice in the *Shishi xinbao*.[56]

When the Beijing government finally responded to the strike demands and dismissed the "national traitors" Cao Rulin, Lu Zongyu, and Zhang Zongxiang, powerful native-place associations announced the decision to

---

[53] For example, see *Shenbao*, June 9, 10, 12, and 14, 1919; Shanghai shehui kexueyuan, *Wusi yundong zai Shanghai*, p. 391.

[54] It should be pointed out that many of the leaders of the Shanghai General Chamber of Commerce, like Yu Xiaqing and Zhu Baosan, were also directors of their native-place associations. Yu, at the time, was a director of the General Chamber, a director of the Siming gongsuo, and a leader of the radical Shanghai Federation of Commercial Groups. Tension between the somewhat conservative chamber and the more radical federation was awkward for him, and he responded by ceremonially resigning from all three roles. He did not resign, however, as a director of the Ningbo tongxianghui. *Shenbao*, June 15, 1919.

[55] A heated meeting of the Commercial Federation, called in response to the action of the chamber and held at the Shaoxing tongxianghui, voiced protest but was unable to resolve the matter in unity. Unfortunately the lines of division are not clear. Shanghai shehui kexueyuan, *Wusi yundong zai Shanghai*, p. 389–391.

[56] *Shenbao*, June 10 and 11, 1919; Shanghai shehui kexueyuan, *Wusi yundong zai Shanghai*, pp. 389–391.

end the strike. The Ningbo tongxianghui exhorted all Ningbo people to return to business but to use only Chinese products. It also sent a telegram to Ningbo residents in Hankou advising them to return to work, saying, "The Ningbo market in Shanghai has re-opened" (*hu yongshi kai*).[57] These instances suggest that native-place *bang*, rather than the Chamber of Commerce or the Commercial Federation or any other overarching organization, were crucial in determining the opening and closing of businesses. This was particularly evident in cities in which the general strike was partial. In Hankou, for instance, the businesses of sojourning Guangdong and Ningbo merchants closed, initiating the strike, while many other shops remained open.[58]

Huiguan and *tongxianghui* throughout this period also exerted themselves on behalf of arrested *tongxiang*. The Shanghai Sojourning Anhui Consultative Committee expressed concern over the arrest of Chen Duxiu and contacted the Beijing Anhui huiguan for assistance in securing his release. Similarly, the Shanghai Fujian Reconstruction Committee urged the release of arrested Fujianese students.[59]

In the activities of native-place associations in the May Fourth period, we see the articulation of "modern" values and practices that have been attributed, in their origins, to May Fourth student activism. These included the organization of workers for educational and patriotic purposes. For example, at the end of April or in the first days of May, the Jiangbei Fellow-Provincials' Preservation Committee (Jiangbei lühu weichihui), which was composed of yarn and coal workers, established a private lecture hall in Zhabei "to organize Jiangbei manual and commercial workers to hear educational classes in their leisure time." Lectures were designed to enlighten and improve the morality of the many coolies and "unlearned country bumpkins" among the Jiangbei fellow-provincials, as well as to encourage patriotism, lawfulness, and sanitation.[60] If such activities may have expressed an old-fashioned paternalism, both the mechanism—organized classes for workers—and the content—patriotism and sanitation—were new.

It is also critical to note the strategic uses of traditional institutions and practices in the organization of modern political activity. Though less important in this period than in the late nineteenth century, *huiguan* still staged popular ritual events for the larger native-place community.

---

[57] *Shenbao*, June 13, 1919. The Chinese term here is striking, since the *tongxianghui* could have simply said that the Shanghai market had reopened. Clearly, Ningbo people saw it as *their* market, which was simply situated in Shanghai.

[58] Ibid., June 15, 1919.

[59] Ibid., June 16, 20, 21, and 24, 1919.

[60] Ibid., May 5, 1919.

Such events provided the occasion for mass propagandizing. While most native-place associations held meetings to discuss the political situation and write telegrams, some associations, like the Jiangyin huiguan, met political necessities with religious ceremonies. Gathered together for a feast, the Jiangyin fellow provincials prayed before the altar of the god Guangong to ask for his assistance and protection and for the strength and unity to "wipe away China's shame" in a time of national danger. Other traditional practices could be put to similar uses. For instance, on the occasion of the gathering of fellow-provincials for the *huiguan*-sponsored Ghost Festival (Zhongyuan jie) in the summer of 1919, the Ningbo huiguan printed and distributed special notices urging the use of national products.[61]

Native Place, Class, and Nation

The events of 1919, as we have seen, reveal not only the appearance of new groups, but also their interactions. An examination of the rhetoric of native-place sentiment and a sketch of some of the interactions of native-place associations at different levels throughout this period offer clues to the contributions of native-place associations to emerging nationalist and class identities.

The Native Place and the Nation

The urgent need for existing social organizations and specifically native-place associations (partly because of a lack of other effective forms of popular association) to form a foundation for nationalist mobilization was perceived by *tongxianghui* and echoed in their statements throughout the 1920s, 1930s, and 1940s. The Ningbo tongxianghui, for example, organized lectures on the benefits of native-place organization and the promotion of national products. The Ningbo and Suzhou tongxianghui stressed the interconnectedness of native-place organization and the project of national salvation, coining slogans such as "In unity against the outside, love the native place, love the country" (*yizhi duiwai aixiang aiguo*) and "Business and enterprise cannot afford not to unite in groups. The nation is but one big group encompassing and bringing together

---

[61] *Shenbao,* June 11, 1919. This article, entitled, "Jiangyin Tongxiang Do Things in an Unusual Way," concludes with a marvelous combination of May Fourth secularism and pragmatism that, "while this type of activity borders on the superstitious, it may also be seen as a sincere expression of will." See also *Siming gongsuo yi'an lu,* July 1919. For a description of late-nineteenth-century *huiguan* ritual, see Goodman, "Native Place and the City," chap. 3.

many small groups. For the wealth and strength of the country, it is imperative to unite in groups."[62] As the following statements suggest, *tongxianghui* throughout the Republican era were conceived explicitly as instruments of nationalist mobilization:

> There is not a day we do not suffer the incursions of economic imperialism. If we do not intensively organize and strengthen our spirit of unity, we will not avoid defeat and elimination. [We must] assemble many people with similar language and customs who can conform to and communicate with each other and together organize in a group to plan for public welfare. This provides a basis for struggles against the outside and also gives the struggle for internal reform something to rely on. It also helps to prevent oppression and insults. This is the essential idea behind *tongxianghui.*[63]

and:

> [In order to establish] nationalism it is necessary to have organizations. But seeking strong groups, we must first mutually and effectively unite. Our people's ability to organize is weak. But "love one's home, love one's native-place" sentiment is very strong. For instance [this is expressed in] *huiguan* and *tongxianghui,* etc. Using this as a base, it is possible for our people to make use of this, going from the small to the great and from weakness to strength. Nationalism becomes gradually possible. Our Henan tongxianghui serves people of all *jie,* represents a large population and moreover has a long history.[64]

Such statements illuminate an interesting paradox: universal identity (nationalism) depended on the further articulation of specific identity. Public spirit was to be developed through the strengthening of loyalties to one's native place, and the mobilization of the native place was to serve the nation. In this fashion, native-place strength contributed to national strength. Through a kind of metonymy, the native place could stand for the nation.[65] In this fashion, abstract ties were personalized and concretized through local relationships and community.

In any event, throughout the May Fourth period in Shanghai, division of the Shanghai populace into native-place groups proved no obstacle to jointly organized expressions of nationalism. Despite the increasing

---

[62] The Suzhou tongxianghui was formed in the midst of May Fourth agitation. *Shenbao,* May 25 and 26, 1919.

[63] *Chaozhou lühu tongxianghui niankan* (Shanghai, 1934), introduction.

[64] *Henan lühu tongxianghui gongzuo baogao* (Shanghai, 1936), pp. 1–3.

[65] An explicit statement of this principle may be found in *Jiangsu* magazine, a journal of radical sojourning Jiangsu students in Japan at the beginning of the twentieth century: "Those who love China cry out: China has nothing but corruption! Those who love Jiangsu cry out: Jiangsu has nothing but corruption! It can be plainly said that Jiangsu is a microcosm of China...[therefore] discussing corruption is the appointed duty of Jiangsu." *Jiangsu* (reprint of 1903 Tokyo edition, Taipei, 1969), 1:3.

geographic subdivision of provincial native-place communities, the different associations routinely combined and worked together in coherent and well-organized fashion. Many small groups (*xiao tuanti*) were perceived as organic constituents of the large group (*da tuanti*), the nation.[66] In the May Fourth Movement in Shanghai, native-place groups clearly acted as units for the organization, expression, and dissemination of nationalist ideology. Without these groups, it is difficult to imagine how such effective social mobilization could have occurred.

Native-Place Sentiment and Class Consciousness

We have seen divisions within the native-place community according to *jie*, or circles of interest, occupation, age, or class. We have also seen the formation of new, more popularly based groups with more open and democratic structures of government. The divisions by *jie* within the native-place community reflect a certain consciousness of the need to organize according to one's interests, rather than submit to organization by native-place elites. It is therefore critical to ask (1) if we may still speak of an overarching native-place community in this period and (2) whether class tensions precluded identity with and cooperation within the larger group.

It is possible to speak of the larger native-place community as an idea that could be evoked effectively, for specific purposes, throughout the Republican period. Underlying this idea, in their ritual, charitable, and educational functions, *huiguan* and *tongxianghui* served larger communities than their predominantly merchant elite and middling merchant or intellectual directors and constituency. The Ningbo huiguan served not only the large community of Ningbo residents in Shanghai, but also sojourning fellow-provincials nationally, by coordinating a national system of shipment, storage, and burial of the coffins of Ningbo fellow-provincials. As part of this complex enterprise, the 1910s and 1920s saw the building of north, south, east, and Pudong branch coffin repositories. *Huiguan* also continued ritually to serve a large religious community, although the increased numbers of sojourners now rendered the

---

[66] See *Shenbao*, May 25 and 26, 1919. Such slogans from the May Fourth period echoed throughout the 1920s, 1930s, and even into the 1940s. For example, in 1944 a special commemorative issue of the association of Jiangsu sojourners explained *tongxianghui* as follows: "All these various *bangpai* divisions are organizational units for individuals, and each group forms a circle of life. The different circles knit together to form an extremely long interlocking mechanism." *Dongting dongshan lühu tongxianghui sanshizhou jinian tekan* (Shanghai, 1944), introduction.

sorts of community gatherings that took place in the nineteenth century impossible.[67]

Huiguan and *tongxianghui* served as important charitable and welfare institutions, maintaining increasing numbers of schools and hospitals over the course of the Republican period. The presence of *huiguan* resources to some extent ensured that their *tongxiang* would have an interest in maintaining some degree of community and identity, in order to partake of *huiguan* services and support.

The egalitarian language of native-place sentiment, by which both wealthy and poor could share equally in the *tongxiang* bond as fellow-provincials, could be exploited by both high and low. When dissenting groups came to demand a piece of *huiguan* property, they would argue that it was, in effect, already their own, since it was *tongxiang* property. *Huiguan* leaders were then forced either to maintain the rhetoric of brotherhood and community or breach it by pointing out—as did the Chaozhou huiguan directors in 1926 when confronted with demanding students—that it was in fact their property, not the property of the *tongxiang*.[68] In general, *huiguan* leaders chose to preserve the rhetoric of community in order to gain the allegiance of the community. For this reason *huiguan* changed organizationally as the new organizational form of the *tongxianghui* gained legitimacy. *Huiguan* as well as *tongxianghui* began to adopt public constitutions, formal voting procedures, more representative assembly, and at least the appearance of openness and more democratic rule.

Evidence that the larger community could be effectively mobilized by the old institutions may be found in *huiguan* ability to tap the larger community for funds for community projects. In the course of large-scale mortuary and hospital construction in 1918, for example, the Siming gongsuo decided to engrave the names of contributors on stone and wood. It counted 320 contributors of more than 50 yuan; 17,320 contributors of 1–50 yuan; and 2,770 contributors of "a few coins." Here we find a total of 20,470 people "fervently contributing out of love for the native place." While far shy of the community of 400,000 claimed by the *gongsuo* in the May Fourth agitation of the next year, it is nonetheless an impressive number. This pool was increased in January of 1919, moreover, when the *huiguan* decided to increase the effectiveness of its money-raising campaign by bringing the leaders of

---

[67] See *Shanghai siming gongsuo si da jianzhu zhengxinlu* (Shanghai, 1925); and *Siming gongsuo yi'an lu,* 1917–1921. Forty-one native-place cemeteries or coffin repositories are listed in the *Shanghai shangye minglu,* 1931.

[68] *Chaozhou huiguan yi'an beicha,* 1926.

"each Ningbo trade and *bang*" (more than a hundred representatives in all) to the *gongsuo* to combine their efforts. In the course of this meeting, it was decided that all those "in commercial circles" would deduct pay from all their *tongxiang* workers at the rate of five fen from each yuan of salary for one month.[69]

At the end of May 1919, when the French consul asked the Ningbo *huiguan* to move a children's burial ground, the *huiguan* called a mass meeting and vowed to use the full strength of the Ningbo community to oppose the French. Through this manifestation of mass unity (or at least the persuasiveness of the threat), the *gongsuo* managed to secure from the French a promise to preserve the integrity of their graveyard in perpetuity.[70]

Despite such demonstrations of the existence of effective community for certain purposes and in certain contexts, it is evident that by the May Fourth period there was also considerable tension within native-place communities, particularly between workers and their *tongxiang* employers.[71] While native-place associations still occasionally resolved strikes and labor disputes, by the May Fourth period and in the early 1920s such resolution was more the exception than the rule. The French authorities noted in 1921 that whereas worker-employer negotiations through the intermediary of "guilds" had been possible until that moment, those days had given way to a preference for intimidation and direct action.[72]

One example of this new preference for intimidation and even violence may be found in the strike of Ningbo seamen and stokers that followed the May Fourth commercial strike, announced on June 5, 1919. Interestingly, nationalism here appears to have propelled the workers into their struggle. In a reminiscence of the strike, a worker who was the leader of the Association of Ningbo Seamen (Jun'an she) describes how workers heard the slogans of the May Fourth period and "could not stifle [their] patriotic sentiment." Feeling the seamen should strike in support of the movement, this man and other organizers went among their co-workers to spread propaganda, with the result that more than five thousand workers struck and effectively stopped sea-going traffic.[73]

---

[69] *Siming gongsuo yi'an lu,* 1918–1919.

[70] Ibid., 1919.

[71] This tension might be compared to that which developed earlier (in the nineteenth century) in south China, between rich and poor branches within lineages.

[72] Ministère des Relations Exterieures, archives, Serie Asie: Chine 31, Shanghai (1918–1922), Report of June 13, 1921.

[73] Shanghai shehui kexueyuan, *Wusi yundong zai Shanghai,* pp. 343–344, 358.

Concerned by the crippling effects of the stoppage of traffic, Ningbo huiguan officials decided to negotiate with the strikers. The striking seamen, in a group of more than a thousand, agreed to meet at the Siming gongsuo to discuss their actions. This much was possible. But when gongsuo director Fang Jiaobo, who was also a leader of the General Chamber of Commerce, began to lecture the seamen on their duty to return to work, his *tongxiang* seamen refused to listen. A large worker jumped behind Fang, grabbed his collar from behind, and ripped his shirt. According to several accounts, the other seamen applauded and yelled, "Beat him, beat him." Fang fled, and the workers declared a victory. Here we see the failure of greater *tongxiang* community and evidence of independent class organization and solidarity in opposition among the *tongxiang* worker *jie*.

In this strike the separate native-place organizations of workers did not prevent their cooperation across lines of regional identity. The different native-place organizations to which Ningbo and Guangdong seamen belonged were able effectively to coordinate their efforts.[74] This incident parallels the actions taken by the Shanghai and Shaoxing construction workers' association as they expressed their determination to enforce the anti-Japanese boycott. Worker subdivision into Shanghai and Shaoxing *bang* did not prevent joint organization. Moreover, the workers appear to have been radicalized by their organized assertion of nationalism, threatening to strike if their foremen and the chiefs of the enterprises that employed them did not adhere to the boycott.

Other evidence also points to the breakdown of vertical native-place ties that formerly transcended class, binding together a greater *tongxiang* community. In this period, for example, *huiguan* and *tongxianghui* for the first time contemplated and in certain cases instituted badges of membership.[75] This sort of practice would have been entirely unnecessary in the nineteenth century when the relevant communities were not only smaller, but better ordered by structures of deference. At that earlier time, unlike in the May Fourth period, artificial means were not necessary to decide which *tongxiang* could enter the building and which would do best to remain outside.

While suggesting these important tensions in the larger native-place community, research on native-place associations in the May Fourth period makes two points clear. We cannot understand social organization and social movements in the early Republican period without recognizing the crucial role of native-place associations, old and new.

---

[74] Ibid., pp. 358–361; *Siming gongsuo yi'an lu*, June and July 1919.
[75] *Siming gongsuo yi'an lu*, April 1920.

Nonetheless, we cannot understand native-place communities without recognizing the emergence of class ties and consciousness. While native-place organizations persisted and indeed expanded in this period, their "particularism" did not preclude integration into larger wholes. Just as native-place organization did not subvert nationalism, native-place ties complicated but did not preclude class consciousness. A study of the growth of native-place associations in the May Fourth period suggests the possible ironies of an unexpected fit: how apparent anachronisms—*huiguan* and *tongxianghui*—accommodated themselves to (and even promoted) the community-transcending imperatives of national mobilization and class formation.

APPENDIX: Population Growth Statistics for the
International Settlement

	1910	1915	1920	1925	1930
Jiangsu	180,331	230,402	292,599	308,096	500,000
Zhejiang	168,791	201,206	235,779	229,059	304,544
Guangdong	39,336	44,811	54,016	51,365	44,502
Anhui	5,263	15,471	29,077,	26,500	20,537
Shandong	2,197	5,158	10,228	12,169	8,759
Hubei	3,353	7,997	11,253	14,894	8,267
Hunan	680	2,798	2,944	7,049	4,978
Jiangxi	1,488	5,353	7,221	10,506	4,406
Fujian	2,134	5,165	9,970	12,464	3,057
Total*	413,314	539,215	682,476	723,086	910,876

*Total also includes figures for Henan, Hebei, Sichuan, Guangxi, and other provinces with
relatively small numbers of sojourners in Shanghai.
SOURCE: Zou Yiren, *Jiu Shanghai renkou bianqian de yanjiu* [Research on the evolution of
population in old Shanghai] (Shanghai, 1980), pp. 114–115.

CHAPTER FOUR

The Evolution of the Shanghai Student Protest Repertoire; or,

Where Do Correct Tactics Come From?

JEFFREY N. WASSERSTROM

Student protests involving educated youths were a central feature of Shanghai life during the Republican era, particularly after the events of 1919 (discussed in the previous chapter) convinced foreign and domestic elites (as well as students themselves) of the potency such actions could have. Throughout the 1920s, 1930s, and 1940s, educated youths continually took to the streets to protest new foreign threats to their nation's sovereignty, the continuing lack of political freedom at home, and abuses of power by Chinese officials. With the exception of the years of the Japanese occupation, in fact, a year never went by in which Shanghai students did not stage some kind of demonstration or rally. At least once a decade, moreover, educated youths played central roles in a multiclass struggle that, like the May Fourth Movement, brought the city's ordinary economic and political life to a virtual standstill. Sometimes, as in the May Thirtieth Movement of 1925 and the Three Workers' Uprisings of 1927, students either played a secondary role to or at least had to share the vanguard position with workers during these new struggles. More often, however, they took the lead in staging demonstrations and

For reading and commenting upon earlier versions of this chapter, I would like to thank Tom Gold, David Keightley, Frederic Wakeman, Elizabeth Perry, John Israel, the Chinese and Western participants in the Shanghai symposium, the members of the Berkeley dissertation group, Dan Letwin, Tim Weston, and David Johnson. Finally, I am grateful to Joseph Esherick and Liu Xinyong, collaborators on related projects whose views on student protest have influenced my own for the better. I would also like to thank Stanford University Press for allowing me to use material from my book *Student Protests in Twentieth-Century China: The View from Shanghai* (Stanford, Calif.: Stanford University Press, 1991) here; the chapter here is adapted from chapter 3 of that work.

mobilizing popular support; and nearly all the most dramatic events of the Resist Japan Movement of 1931, the December Ninth Movement of 1935, and the Anti-Hunger, Anti–Civil War Movement of 1947 were student-led mass actions.

Scholars interested in the history of Shanghai student movements have asked a wide range of questions about these upsurges. They have analyzed the issues that drove students to take to the streets between 1919 and 1949 and the ways political parties tried to help shape or put an end to the youth protests of these years.[1] Some have also drawn attention to such topics as the role of intergenerational conflicts in spurring youths to action,[2] the connections between student unrest and broad intellectual trends,[3] and the part economic considerations played in precipitating certain protests.[4] These scholars, working in China, Taiwan, Japan, and the West, have all tended to ignore, however, two basic questions: Why did Shanghai students use the particular methods they did to express their anger and try to gain redress for their grievances? And how were large groups of the city's youths so frequently able to carry out hastily arranged mass actions in such an orderly fashion that it seemed as though everyone involved was following a carefully rehearsed plan?

Existing works have, in fact, generally taken student tactics for granted, as if students just naturally take certain actions when protesting or as if certain kinds of grievances naturally lead protesters to behave in certain ways. The first of these assumptions is problematic because student protesters in different times and places have found it "natural" to take very different kinds of actions. Shanghai students, for example, have almost never employed some of the protest techniques upon which Western youths relied most heavily during the student movements of the 1960s, such as occupying school buildings. Conversely, European and American youths have seldom involved themselves in boycotts or

---

[1] Some examples of works by scholars who emphasize such topics are John Israel, *Student Nationalism in China, 1927–1937* (Stanford, Calif.: Stanford University Press, 1966); Suzanne Pepper, "The Student Anti-war Movement" in her *Civil War in China* (Berkeley: University of California Press, 1978), pp. 42–94; Wu Mu et al., *Zhongguo qingnian yundong shi* [A history of the Chinese youth movement] (Beijing: Zhongguo qingnian chubanshe, 1984); and the identically titled but very different Bao Zunpeng, *Zhongguo qingnian yundong shi* [A history of the Chinese youth movement] (Taibei: Zhengzhong shuju, 1954).

[2] Jessie Lutz, "The Chinese Student Movement of 1945–1949," *Journal of Asian Studies* 31:1 (1971): 89–110.

[3] See, for example, Vera Schwarcz, *The Chinese Enlightenment* (Berkeley: University of California Press, 1986).

[4] Saito Tetsuro, "Neizhan shiqi Shanghai xuesheng de yishi, shenghuo he yundong" [The ideology, lives, and activities of Shanghai students during the Civil War], *Fudan xuebao* [Fudan journal], no. 6 (1986), pp. 89–95.

publicized their anger by biting their fingers and writing out slogans in blood, two activities favored by Chinese protesters during the first decades of this century.[5]

Furthermore, even in the case of tactics that students in very different cultural settings have all found effective, youths in different times and places often find it most "natural" to carry these events out in very dissimilar ways. The case of parades illustrates this point nicely, since marches have accompanied almost all modern student movements. The typical Shanghai youth demonstration of the Republican era, however, was very different in terms of style and structure from, say, the violent processions that accompanied the Argentinian campus unrest of 1918[6] or the equally rowdy student marches that occurred periodically in Tsarist Russia.[7] In other words, students may tend to use tactics that come "naturally" to them, but differing cultural and historical contexts determine (or at least affect) what is "natural."

The second assumption alluded to above, that there is likely to be an organic connection between the grievance that triggers a protest and the tactics protesters use, is more appealing at first glance. That workers angered by the introduction of a new technology often smash machines, for example, seems an obvious case of the dovetailing of intent and form. Similarly, when Chinese student beat up school cooks and broke pots to show their displeasure with the quality of campus food during the "strikes at the dining hall" of the first years of the century, there were clear links between the grievance and the tactic.[8] The connections were equally clear when, in 1902, the students of Shanghai's Nanyang College (which later evolved into Jiaotong University) expressed their anger at the disciplinary actions of a specific teacher and school policies limiting their access to reformist and revolutionary publications by staging a classroom strike.[9] That educated youths in cities throughout China

---

[5] See, for example, the report in the *Shanghai Municipal Police [SMP] Files*, reel 65, I.D. 6691, which describes two people writing out anti-Japanese slogans in their own blood during a Shanghai meeting connected with the 1915 boycott in response to the "Twenty-one Demands." For basic background on the tactics used by Western youths during the 1960s, see George Katsiaficas, *The Imagination of the New Left* (Boston: South End, 1987); and William Friedland and Irving Horowitz, *The Knowledge Factory* (Chicago: Aldine, 1970), pp. 66–88.

[6] See Richard Walter, *Student Politics in Argentina* (Boston: Basic Books, 1968), pp. 44–45.

[7] See Daniel Brower, *Training the Nihilists* (Ithaca, N.Y.: Cornell University Press, 1975), p. 135.

[8] Chiang Mon-lin, *Tides from the West* (New Haven, Conn.: Yale University Press, 1947), p. 64.

[9] *North China Herald*, November 19, 1902; Wang Min, "Wusi xuqu—Zhongguo de caoqi xuesheng yundong" [May Fourth overture—the early period of the Chinese student

demonstrated their hatred of Japanese imperialism by organizing boycotts of goods from that country in 1915, 1919, and other years is yet another example of a tactic organically linked to the grievance in question.[10]

This kind of appeal to nature, although it certainly explains some tactical choices, nonetheless becomes problematic on closer inspection. First, there is always more than one possible tactic that has a natural link to a grievance. Early-twentieth-century Chinese students dissatisfied with cafeteria meals might just as "naturally" have staged hunger strikes to bring attention to their complaint, but they did not. Second, tactics organically connected to one grievance often reappear in protests triggered by quite different, unrelated causes. In both the West and China, for example, though at some points workers have indeed broken machines because they disliked a particular technology or objected to the way management was using that technology, at other points they have broken machines simply because they have discovered that such action is an effective form of "collective bargaining by riot."[11] In addition, while Shanghai students often used classroom strikes to show their displeasure with specific teachers and school policies (e.g., in the 1905 struggle at Aurora University over how much voice students should be accorded in matters of school governance), strikes of this sort were equally central parts of protests (such as the Anti–U.S. Brutality Movement of December 1946) attacking national political figures, state policies, or foreign governments.[12]

A third problem with emphasizing the organic links between grievances and tactics is that such an approach does not explain the special twists specific populations give to standard techniques. The case of

---

movement] in Wang Min et al., *Shanghai xuesheng yundong dashiji, 1919–1949* [Major events in the Shanghai student movement, 1919–1949—hereafter *Dashiji*] (Shanghai: Xuelin, 1981), pp. 1–17.

[10] For a general overview of these boycotts, which highlights the role of students, see Kikuchi Takaharu, *Chūgoku minzoku undō no kihon kōzō: taigi boikotto no kenkyū* [The structure and base of Chinese national movements: Research on antiforeign boycotts] (Tokyo: Dainan, 1966).

[11] This term is from Eric Hobsbawm's classic essay on British Luddism, "The Machine Breakers," in Hobsbawm, *Labouring Men* (London: Weidenfeld and Nicolson, 1964), pp. 5–22. For examples of Chinese machine breaking in which the technology in question was the source of the grievance, see David Strand, *Rickshaw Beijing* (Berkeley: University of California Press, 1989), pp. 155, 254–256 and passim; for comparable acts unrelated to technological innovation, see Jean Chesneaux, *The Chinese Labor Movement 1919–1927* (Stanford, Calif.: Stanford University Press, 1968), pp. 255, 257 and passim.

[12] The 1905 strike is described in Ruth Hayhoe, "Towards the Forging of a Chinese University Ethos: Zhendan and Fudan, 1903–1919," *China Quarterly* 94 (1983): 323–341; and Zhao Shaoquan et al., *Fudan daxuezhi* [Fudan university gazetteer] (Shanghai: Fudan daxue, 1985), vol. 1, 1905–1949, pp. 30–31 and 47–48.

boycotts illustrates this point. Although it may have been "natural" for Shanghai students to try to stop the sale of Japanese products in 1919, appeals to nature do not help us to understand why May Fourth activists formed *shirentuan* (groups of ten) to enforce this boycott. These groups were mutual responsibility units, whose members pledged to refuse to buy Japanese products, ensure that their fellow group members refrained from buying Japanese products, and do publicity work to spread word of the boycott among the population at large. Each of these *shirentuan* had a designated leader who served as the group's representative to larger collectivities, such as the "groups of one hundred" composed of ten *shirentuan*.[13] That Shanghai students found it "natural" to form groups of this sort had much to do with the historical and cultural context in which they operated, but little to do with the specific grievance behind their protest.

Those who do not see student tactics as "natural" often see them as conspiratorial. In the case of Shanghai youth movements, such an approach often means one that uses the activities of Chinese Communist Party (CCP) campus organizers to account for the types of methods students employed, as well as for the general coherence of youth actions.[14] Both pro- and anti-Communist Chinese historians often give CCP organizers much of the credit for deciding on the proper actions to be used during various student movements, although scholars working in the PRC differ markedly (for obvious reasons) from their counterparts working in Taiwan on the issue of whether these underground activists used simple persuasion or trickery and deceit to get other students to go along with the Party's plans.[15] But while this kind of explanation is popular with

---

[13] *Shirentuan* are described in various sources, including Joseph Chen, *The May Fourth Movement in Shanghai* (Leiden: E. J. Brill, 1971); Chow Tse-tsung, *The May 4th Movement* (Cambridge, Mass.: Harvard University Press, 1960); and *Far Eastern Review* 15:6 (June 1919): 441. For a fuller discussion of "groups of ten" and additional documentation, see Wasserstrom, *Student Protests*.

[14] Other kinds of conspiracy theories have also been used to explain Shanghai student protests: most notably, in 1919 the Japanese tried to discredit the May Fourth Movement by claiming that Chinese youths were being used as "puppets" by American missionaries. For an example of this kind of interpretation, see Shanhai Nihon Shoko Kaigisho, *Santō mondai ni kansuru Nikka haiseki no eikyō* [The effects of the boycott of Japanese goods connected with the Shandong question] (Shanghai: Shanhai Nihon Shoko Kaigisho, n.d., probably 1919), pp. 430–459.

[15] See, for example, the analysis of the use of traveling propaganda brigades that accompanied the December Ninth Movement in Bao Zunpeng, *Zhongguo qingnian yundong shi*, pp. 165–166, and the same author's *Zhongguo gongchandang qingnian yundong shilun* [A discussion of the history of the Chinese Communist Party's youth movement] (Nanjing, 1947). The pro-CCP version of this kind of explanation appears in countless works published in the People's Republic—see, for examples, virtually any issue of journals such as *Shanghai qingyunshi ziliao* [Historical materials on the Shanghai youth movement] or Wu Mu, *Zhong-*

critics and defenders of the CCP alike, it is ultimately problematic for several reasons. The first is that even PRC memoirs by former student activists, which begin with the claim that CCP members guided the youth movement, often admit in passing that underground activists frequently had to follow the lead of other students to avoid "alienating themselves from the masses."[16] Still more damning to any theory based on the role of the CCP are two simple facts: many of the same tactics used in Party-led (or supposedly Party-led) upsurges were also used during the May Fourth Movement, which occurred before the founding of the Party; and such a theory does not adequately explain how, precisely, it was possible for small groups of underground organizers to communicate to their fellow students their visions of what given protest actions should be like.

A third possible approach to tactics, which can for convenience be called an "ideological" one, stresses the connection between tactical choices and the political philosophies of the protesters involved. At the most general level, this kind of approach certainly has some validity: militant revolutionaries, who consider the use of certain forms of violence appropriate, for example, will obviously be drawn to different tactics than will protesters influenced by Gandhian ideas of nonviolent resistance. Debates within protest groups, furthermore, often revolve around the fit between ideology and tactics. In the early 1930s, for instance, some Communist organizers refused to participate in petition drives aimed at convincing the Guomindang (GMD) to take a stronger stance toward Japanese aggression because they felt that this particular form of protest granted too much legitimacy to the GMD regime and hence contradicted the basic tenets of the CCP. These organizers were subsequently criticized for their actions. This criticism, however, was not based on the claim that ideology was irrelevant, but rather on the assertion that the "leftists" in question had misinterpreted Marxism: they had forgotten that at certain stages in the revolution Marxists should use a mixture of legal and extralegal techniques to further their goals.[17]

---

guo qingnian.

[16] See, for example, Wu Cengliang, "Kangzhan shengli qianhou jiaoda xuesheng yundong duanpian" [Fragments on the student movement at Jiaotong University before and after the victory in the War of Resistance], *Dangshi ziliao* [Materials on Party history], 15 (1983): 44–54, which describes this happening in relation to a 1947 event.

[17] See Wen Jizhe, "Sanshi niandai chu 'zuo' qing cuowu dui Shanghai xueyun de yingxiang" [The influence of "left wing" errors of the early 1930s on the Shanghai youth movement], *Shanghai qingyunshi ziliao* [Materials on the Shanghai student movement—hereafter, *SQZ*], no. 4 (1983), pp. 7–10; and idem, " 'Jiu-yiba' hou Shanghai xuesheng yundong yiji 'Gong wutai shijian' " [The Shanghai student movement after "September 18th" and the "Public Arena Incident"], *SQZ*, no. 2, (1985), pp. 9–12.

This said, there are two major problems with an ideological approach to protest actions. First, like the conspiratorial approach, it does not fully account for the fact that protesters often have a shared understanding of how to behave during a mass action, even when many of them have never attended a planning meeting and when many of them, though they share a common grievance, subscribe to differing political philosophies. Second, it does not explain why groups with radically different political agendas and ideologies often stage almost identical protests. For example, if ideology determines tactics, it is hard to see why the radical and loyalist youth groups that struggled for control of the Shanghai student movement during the first years of the Civil War era (1945–1949) frequently staged marches almost indistinguishable in form.[18] It is also revealing that May Fourth students, who espoused an ideology that rejected the hierarchical tradition they associated with Confucianism, organized *shirentuan* that stuck closely to the basic principles of the traditional *baojia* (household registration) system, which made similar uses of groups of ten.

Although each of the three approaches outlined above has something to offer, none satisfactorily explains the particular forms and general coherence of Shanghai student protests. I will argue here that a more fruitful way to approach the issue is to view these protests as acts of political theater structured by what Charles Tilly refers to as a distinctive protest "repertoire" made up of a set of familiar "scripts" for collective action.[19] This approach does not deny the relevance of the factors treated thus far: the nature of a grievance could indeed make local youths favor particular scripts; CCP activists often tried to work themselves into leading roles so they could make an act of street theater serve the Party's ends; and ideological concerns, as well as still less tangible forces such as individual inspiration and whimsy, led students to add to or modify their repertoire in countless subtle ways. Nonetheless, interpreting Shanghai student actions in theatrical terms demands a set of assumptions (e.g., that protest is a genre of learned and practiced behavior) and leads to exploration of topics (e.g., the connections between protests and nonpolitical gatherings) different from the three approaches criticized above.

Treating theater and politics as analogous or overlapping activities is not unusual.[20] Western philosophers have always been interested in the

---

[18] For details on these marches, see Wasserstrom, *Student Protests,* chap. 9.

[19] Tilly, *From Mobilization to Revolution* (Reading, Mass.: Addison and Wesley, 1978), pp. 151–159.

[20] The following paragraphs present a condensed version of the discussion of political theater in Joseph W. Esherick and Jeffrey N. Wasserstrom, "Acting Out Democracy: Political Theater in Modern China," *Journal of Asian Studies* 49:4 (November 1990):835–865. For more detail on the concepts discussed and additional citations, please see that piece.

links between tragedy and politics, and Western dramatists have always used the stage to make political points.[21] Anthropologists such as Victor Turner and Clifford Geertz have recently used dramatic metaphors to explain the ways in which power is exercised and contested in various cultures.[22] Historians and journalists, meanwhile, have used theatrical metaphors to describe mass actions as diverse as eighteenth-century English riots and American student protests of the 1960s.[23] Linkages between theater and politics are even embedded in the English language itself, in phrases such as "staging a demonstration."

The tendency to take seriously the performative aspects of politics is not, however, a uniquely Western phenomenon. Classical Chinese philosophers were as deeply interested in this topic as their Western counterparts, although they focused on the political implications of a more tightly circumscribed genre of performance, *li* (orthodox ritual), rather than aesthetic theater.[24] Furthermore, long before CCP authors penned operas glorifying the land reform campaigns of the 1940s and dissident intellectuals criticized Communist leaders by writing plays filled with historical allusions, Chinese writers and political figures were well aware of the part theatrical performances could play in buttressing or undermining ruling regimes, as the early Qing bans on certain kinds of dramatic performances and late Qing arrests of leading radical actors attest.[25] The links between the vocabularies of theater and politics are, furthermore, as clear in Chinese as they are in English: in one of his most important essays, Mao described the 1920s as the time the proletariat mounted the "stage" of history; and in 1989, protesters called for Li Peng and Deng Xiaoping to *xiatai* (get off the stage).[26]

---

[21] Karen Hermassi, *Polity and Theater in Historical Perspective* (Berkeley: University of California Press, 1977).

[22] Turner, *From Ritual to Theater* (New York: Performing Arts Press, 1982); Geertz, *Negara: The Theatre State in Nineteenth-Century Bali* (Princeton, N.J.: Princeton University Press, 1980).

[23] See, for example, E. P. Thompson, "Patrician Society, Plebian Culture," *Journal of Social History* 7:4 (1974): 383–405; and Theodore White, *The Making of the President, 1968* (New York: Atheneum, 1969), pp. 257–313.

[24] For further discussion of the links and differences between *li* and theater, see Esherick and Wasserstrom, "Acting Out Democracy," which is reprinted with some additional comments on ritual in Jeffrey N. Wasserstrom and Elizabeth J. Perry, eds., *Popular Protest and Political Culture in Modern China: Learning from 1989* (Boulder, Colo.: Westview, 1992), pp. 28–66.

[25] Colin Mackerras, *The Chinese Theater in Modern Times* (Amherst: University of Massachusetts Press, 1975), pp. 48–49, 202–203 and passim; Evelyn Rawski and Susan Naquin, *Chinese Society in the Eighteenth Century* (New Haven, Conn.: Yale University Press, 1987), pp. 61–62.

[26] Mao Zedong, "Xin minzhu zhuyi lin" [On new democracy], in *Mao Zedong xuanji* [Collected works of Chairman Mao] (Beijing: People's Publishing House, 1952) vol. 2; Wu

Although theorists such as Victor Turner argue that all political events can be treated as social dramas of a sort, it seems especially appropriate to treat highly symbolic forms of mass action, such as the student demonstrations of the Republican era, in theatrical terms. By this I do not mean to trivialize the events or to imply that participants in struggles such as the May Fourth Movement were merely playacting. Student demonstrations of the Republican era were often serious acts indeed, inspired by deeply held convictions, and they had some important consequences for both the protesters themselves (some of whom paid for their convictions with their lives) and the authorities they challenged (some of whom fell from power as a result of campus unrest). Treating these actions in dramatic terms remains appropriate, nevertheless, because their ability to move an audience is what made student protesters so threatening to government officials. Generally unarmed and lacking in economic clout, Shanghai students became a potent force through their ability to stage public performances that inspired shows of support from members of other social classes and symbolically challenged the legitimacy of ruling elites.

The performances Shanghai students staged during mass movements were not carefully rehearsed dramas, but improvisational pieces of street theater. It may thus seem inappropriate to talk of either "scripts" or a "repertoire" structuring their actions. However, as performance theorist Richard Schechner persuasively argues, it is wrong to think of even the most experimental forms of theater as completely unstructured.[27] Improvisational theater troupes do not hold formal "rehearsals" that "set an exact sequence of events," he writes, but they depend on "preparations" (equivalent to the training exercises of sports teams) that teach members of the group basic skills, give them a sense of how to work together, and make them ready to "do something appropriate" at a given moment.[28] When they take the stage, these "preparations"—as well as their previous experiences on stage and their time spent watching other groups of actors perform—provide the members of a skilled improvisation group with a repertoire of familiar gestures, movements, and lines. This set of familiar "scripts" from which to improvise gives coherence to even the most novel skits. Similarly, if an unplanned mass action is to be

Mouren et al., eds. *Bajiu Zhongguo minyun jishi* [English title: *Daily Reports on the Movement for Democracy in China*] (New York: privately published, 1989), pp. 262 and 267. For additional examples, see Esherick and Wasserstrom, "Acting Out Democracy."

[27] Schechner, "From Ritual to Theater and Back," in Richard Schechner and Mady Schuman, eds., *Ritual, Play, and Performance* (New York: Seabury Press, 1976), pp. 196–222.

[28] Ibid., p. 222.

coherent, the participants must be working from the same set of scripts; they must have learned how to protest by taking part in preparations that readied them to "do something appropriate" during the event.

What kinds of routines prepare protesters for action, and where do the scripts that form a collective action repertoire come from? The most obvious place to look for answers to these questions is the past: the easiest actions for protesters to take are variations upon mass actions they have staged successfully during previous struggles. Studies by scholars interested in Western popular movements suggest, however, that protesters are also often prepared to carry out and are attracted by actions that are familiar for other reasons. The collective strategies used by other groups can, for instance, have a significant impact upon the tactics a set of protesters uses. As Todd Gitlin and others have noted, for example, American student protesters of the 1960s often adapted tactics associated with the Civil Rights movement, contemporaneous French campus struggles, and Third World guerrilla insurrections.[29]

Events that have nothing at all to do with protest or the expression of grievance can also help introduce new scripts into a group's repertoire, as Charles Tilly's study *The Contentious French* illustrates. Tilly argues that most of the tactics seventeenth-century French protesters used were simply variations upon familiar, everyday routines, rituals, and ceremonies.[30] Works by other European social historians, such as Michelle Perrot, similarly point to connections between protest marches and riots, on the one hand, and such routine events as annual festivals, parades marking the birthdays of monarchs, and weekly religious rites, on the other.[31]

Recent work on Chinese unrest highlights one other kind of activity that can provide groups with collective action scripts: theatrical performances themselves. Historical dramas can help keep a collective action repertoire fresh simply by reminding people of what protesters have done in the past. Joseph Esherick has shown, moreover, that in China operas have sometimes done more than this: the portrayals of legendary heroes

---

[29] Gitlin, *The Sixties: Years of Hope, Days of Rage* (New York: Bantam, 1987), pp. 250, 263 and passim; see also Katsiaficas, *Imagination of the New Left*.

[30] Tilly, *The Contentious French* (Cambridge, Mass.: Harvard University Press, 1986), pp. 116–118 and passim.

[31] See, for example, Perrot, *Workers on Strike, France 1870–1891* (New Haven, Conn.: Yale University Press, 1987); Natalie Davis, *Society and Culture in Early Modern France* (Stanford, Calif.: Stanford University Press, 1975); E. P. Thompson, "Eighteenth-Century English Society: Class Struggle without Class?" *Social History* 3:2 (1978): 71–133; and Nicholas Rogers, "Popular Protest in Early Hanovarian London," *Past and Present* 79 (1978): 70–100.

by actors at village temple fairs provided some participants in the Boxer Uprising with important cues for their own behavior.[32] In a related vein, a recent Cultural Revolution memoir describes a Red Guard rally at which, as a part of their effort to humiliate a local Communist official, a group of rebels forced their victim to don the hat of an imperial official (borrowed from an opera company) so they could ritually decap him (in the manner of Beijing opera performances) to symbolize his dismissal from office.[33]

Working from the premise that various protests can be seen as acts of political theater, this chapter examines some of the "scripts" from which Shanghai students worked, the familiar events and activities that "taught" youths how to protest and lent an aura of coherence to mass actions that might otherwise have dissolved into chaotic gatherings. I will not try to prove that students self-consciously modeled their behavior during a given protest upon, say, a particular past event or a certain ceremony. This would be impossible, because for many events the only sources we have are newspaper accounts; even where we have memoirs by former participants, few of these accounts directly address the issue of why a particular type of action was chosen.[34] Instead, in an effort to show how the city's youth created a unique protest tradition by putting already acquired skills to new kinds of uses and improvising upon familiar patterns of activity, I will highlight similarities between Shanghai student protests and other events and pinpoint some of the people who (often unintentionally) helped teach youths how to carry out these protests.

It is fairly easy to show that the various mass movements that followed the May Fourth struggle of 1919 relied heavily upon familiar scripts, since this first great modern student upsurge served as a model for much that would come after it. Many of the participants in the May Fourth Movement remained on university campuses—first as students and then as professors—to pass on their protest tradition to later generations, and many of those who took part in subsequent movements self-

---

[32] Esherick, *The Origins of the Boxer Uprising* (Berkeley: University of California Press, 1987).

[33] Gao Yuan, *Born Red: A Chronicle of the Cultural Revolution* (Stanford, Calif.: Stanford University Press, 1987), p. 183.

[34] While I was in Shanghai in 1986 and 1987, I interviewed a number of people who had taken part in student protests during the Republican era. When I asked them why they had staged a specific kind of protest on a specific date, they generally either dismissed the question as irrelevant or gave me their own variations upon the naturalistic ("that was just what students did"), conspiratorial ("we were following the orders of underground CCP activists"), or ideological ("as Marxists we needed to adopt that kind of tactic") explanations described and criticized above.

consciously claimed to be trying to reenact the events of 1919. The real challenge for anyone trying to understand the evolution of Shanghai student strategies thus lies in figuring out where the tactics used in the May Fourth Movement itself came from. This chapter will concentrate, therefore, on this first great *xuechao* (student tide), because even in 1919 students already had a number of useful scripts with which to work and hence seldom took wholly new actions.

One can get a good sense of this by looking closely at the first major event in the Shanghai May Fourth Movement in which students played the dominant role—the May 26 rally and parade marking the start of the great classroom strike of 1919, which was attended by at least some twelve thousand students.[35] The day began with a mass rally at the Recreation Ground outside the West Gate, during which youths of each participating school stood together and listened to a brief opening speech by the president of the Shanghai Student Union (SSU). A musical interlude followed, after which a Boy Scout raised the national flag, to which the assembled youths bowed. These preliminaries completed, the students swore a solemn oath to persevere until they achieved their patriotic goals, then filed out of the park in an orderly fashion to march through the city. The demonstration ended with the youths returning to the Recreation Ground to hear more speeches, after which they shouted out "Long Live the Republic!" three times and dispersed.

Shanghai's students had never before staged anything comparable to this protest, in terms of size, scope, or elaborateness, but every step in the ceremony had roots in familiar activities. To begin with, some of the youths who took part in the May 26 gathering had taken part in a very similar event nineteen days earlier: the Guomin dahui (Citizens' Assembly) of May 7 organized by some of the city's leading educators and merchant groups to protest the May Fourth Incident. Then too people had gathered at the Recreation Ground to listen to speeches by representatives of organizations; then too marchers (many of whom were students who divided themselves up into brigades based on school affiliation) had paraded through the city. Holding a meeting at the Recreation Ground was also nothing new even to those students who had never before taken part in a political gathering of any kind, since this was the site of regular citywide sporting competitions (which often began with educators giving

---

[35] My reconstruction of the day's events is based primarily on Shanghai shehui kexueyuan lishi yanjiusuo, ed., *Wusi yundong zai Shanghai shiliao xuanji* [Selected historical materials on the May Fourth Movement in Shanghai] (Shanghai: Shanghai renmin, 1960), pp. 256–257, and *Minguo ribao*, May 27, 1919, p. 10. Press estimates of attendance ranged from 12,000 (*China Press*, May 27, 1919, p. 1) to 25,000 (see the *Shenbao* article in *Wusi yundong zai Shanghai*, p. 257).

opening speeches to youths arrayed in school teams) and Boy Scout reviews.

If gatherings such as sports meets provided potential models for part of the day's program, other phases of the May 26 protest were more similar to quite different events. The swearing of sacred oaths, for example, had long been used by Chinese rebels and revolutionaries as a way of demonstrating a group's solidarity and seriousness of purpose. Thus the youths who gathered on May 26 would all have been familiar with the ritualized "script" involved. Many would have seen dramatic recreations of such events in popular operas such as *The Three Kingdoms,* and at least some would also have read about a much more recent performance of a similar rite by a group of Shanghai tobacco workers in 1918.[36] This worker oath taking is particularly interesting, because like the student one, it too was used to mark the beginning of a strike, though in this case a *bagong* (labor strike) rather than a *bake* (classroom strike).

In contrast, the raising of the national flag was reminiscent not of earlier Chinese protests but rather of the civic rituals carried out by Shanghai's British community on holidays such as the recently celebrated Empire Day, which always began with a Western Boy Scout hoisting the Union Jack.[37] Thus when the May 26 rally began with a Chinese Boy Scout raising a flag, the only novelty was that the flag was a Chinese one. With the musical interlude, however, we are back within the confines of the protest tradition, since such songs had been a standard part of patriotic rallies involving students since at least as far back as the anti-Russian agitation of 1903.[38] Finally, much of the day's program when taken as a whole, from the initial gathering at the Recreation Ground to the final three cheers for the Republic, would have seemed very familiar to at least some youths, since a much smaller but otherwise very similar demonstration had taken place on May 31, 1918, in response to rumors that Chinese officials had signed secret agreements with Japan.[39]

The preceding paragraphs have not exhausted the topic of familiar elements in the May 26 program—one could, for example, also draw

[36] For details on this event, see Elizabeth Perry, "Shanghai on Strike," paper delivered at the International Symposium on Shanghai History, Shanghai, September 1988.

[37] See *Shanghai Times,* May 24, 1919, p. 7, for a description of how this day was celebrated in 1919.

[38] See *North China Herald,* April 30, 1903, p. 832, and May 7, 1903, p. 885. For details on this movement, see Yue Zhi, *Shanghai ju E yundong shulun* [On the Resistance Against Russia Movement in Shanghai], *Dangan yu lishi* [Archives and history], no. 1 (1986), pp. 58–64.

[39] See the "Chinese Press" section of *North China Herald,* June 8, 1918, pp. 571–572; and *Minguo ribao,* June 1 and 2, 1918, p. 10.

links between the bowing to the flag and the bowing to Confucius that began the traditional school day and so forth—but they should suffice to indicate the types of people and events that helped teach youths how to protest and the kinds of scripts from which May Fourth students worked. We have seen that youths could learn from educators and folk heroes, as well as from earlier generations of student protesters. Similarly, we have seen that while some scenes in the day's drama were much like those that had accompanied past *xuechao,* others were improvisations upon official ceremonial forms, such as Empire Day rituals, that seem at first glance as far removed from protest activities as anything can be.

This last point is worth examining in some detail, because while it requires nothing more than common sense to assume that protesters will model their behavior upon actions other protesters have taken in the past, neither those in positions of authority nor those who take part in radical mass actions often think of protests as having anything much in common with such matters as officially sponsored gatherings or governmental procedures. Recent work on the history of popular unrest in England and France, however, shows that very strong connections between these seemingly disparate types of events often do exist. Studies by Natalie Davis, E. P. Thompson, and others suggest that many (if not most) of the basic tactics used by European protesters—ranging from effigy burnings to grain stoppages to religious riots—are best treated as inverted versions of authorized rituals, rearrangements of official scripts in which ordinary people take the radical step of temporarily usurping roles normally played by powerholders.[40]

The events of May 31 and June 12, 1919, show clearly that this same tendency toward inversion and usurpation helped shape May Fourth protests.[41] The parades of both these days grew out of student anger over the behavior of domestic officials and imperialist encroachments on Chinese territory: the former followed a mass memorial service called to honor a Beijing youth who had died as a result of injuries he received

---

[40] This point is brought out most explicitly in Tilly, *The Contentious French* pp. 116–117; and Davis, *Society and Culture,* pp. 161–164. See also Thompson, "Patrician Society, Plebian Culture," and "The Moral Economy of the English Crowd in the 18th Century," *Past and Present* 50 (1971): 76–136, as well as Rogers, "Popular Protest in Early Hanovarian London." As far as I know, no sinologist has hitherto specifically looked, as I will here, at similarities between the scripts used in official procedures and those used in protest events. Philip Kuhn's analysis of "orthodox" and "heterodox" military hierarchies, in *Rebellion and Its Enemies in Late Imperial China* (Cambridge, Mass.: Harvard University Press, 1971), however, does draw attention to a comparable kind script sharing in regard to organization as opposed to tactics.

[41] See Chen, *May Fourth,* pp. 101–103 and 166–174 for basic descriptions of the two events.

during the protest of May Fourth itself; the latter was held to celebrate
the fact that Cao Rulin and the other "traitorous" officials (whom the
students had criticized for taking too weak a stance toward Japan) had
finally been dismissed from the government. Ironically, however, in
terms of style these two radical processions owed a great deal to events
organized by just the type of authorities whose actions the students con-
demned.

The parade following the martyr's memorial meeting, for example,
was strikingly like the public processions that traditionally followed funeral services for high Chinese officials, such as that held in late 1917 to
honor Sheng Xuanhuai, the famous comprador and founder of Nanyang
College. According to the *North China Herald,* Sheng's enormous funeral
procession—in which Nanyang students and "children carrying banners"
as well as other youths took part—comprised seventeen different sections of marchers (each headed by its own band) and cost an estimated
$300,000.[42] The May 31 memorial march in honor of the student protes-
ter Guo Qinguang was not nearly as elaborate as Sheng's, but in many
other basic ways the two events were much alike, the main difference
being that in the protest march the crowd elevated one of its own to a
position of public respect.[43]

The memorial services for the official and the protest martyr both
involved all the following elements: music (school bands played and
groups of students sang before and during the May 31 march); banners
(made of silk and peacock feathers in the one case, cloth in the other);
mourners who wore distinctive clothing (various costumes were worn in
the 1917 procession, while in 1919 students wore special black armbands and white hats); and a representation of the deceased (a statue of
Sheng in the one case, a picture of Guo in the other). In a very real
sense, events like Sheng's funeral, as well as the much smaller services
for deceased family members in which individual students took part,
were bound to serve (whether consciously or not) as scripts for action
when students decided to honor their own dead.[44]

---

[42] *North China Herald,* November 24, 1917, pp. 467–468. My comments on Sheng's
funeral are all based on this source.

[43] The service for Guo is described in Shanghai shehui kexueyuan, *Wusi yundong zai
Shanghai,* pp. 272–278; and Zhongguo shehui kexueyuan, eds., *Wusi aiguo yundong* [The patriotic May Fourth Movement], vol. 2, pp. 265–266.

[44] At least one other specific event may well have served as a model for the mass
memorial service of 1919: the mourning ceremonies cum protests that Shanghai students
and professors held in 1913 to honor Song Jiaoren. I am grateful to Don Price for pointing
this out to me.

The victory marches of June 12 were inspired by a much more joyous event than the memorial parade of May 31, so it is not surprising to find that they were quite different in style. Like the procession honoring Guo, however, they too can be read as protest variations upon official scripts, though in this case the dramaturgy was that of celebratory rather than funereal parades. Joseph Chen has already noted the similarities between the events of June 12 and those that normally occurred at Chinese New Year, with fireworks being set off throughout Shanghai as an accompaniment to the parades that filled the city's streets.[45] The victory parades that greeted news of the traitors' dismissal were also a good deal like those that took place each year on October 10 to honor the 1911 Revolution, as the following quotations from articles in the *Shanghai Times,* describing the 1918 "Double Ten" celebrations and the events of June 12, 1919, respectively, indicate:

> In the Settlement the Chinese flag was profusely displayed....Chinese school children took part in a procession in Nantao....Chinese bands livened up the procession and as the children went along they either sang or shouted cheers for the Republic. (October 11, 1918, p. 7)

> There was a procession of about 4,000 students in the native city....The procession which included 1,000 girls paraded all the streets, with flying banners....The Lungwha Orphanage Band discoursed the usual "patriotic" airs we are accustomed to hear, while the national flag was displayed from many shops. (June 13, 1919, p. 7)

Annual holiday displays were not the only potential celebratory models with which students were familiar, however, for just a little more than six months before the June 12 processions Shanghai had been the scene of a whole series of special victory parades honoring the end of World War I.[46] Youth groups had played a vital part in some of these ceremonies, which can be treated as dress rehearsals of a sort for mass actions of the May Fourth era. The celebrations in honor of the armistice, like those in honor of the dismissal of the "traitorous" officials, included mass meetings, fireworks, and parades by troops of school children, Boy Scouts, college students and others.[47] The 1918 parades were different from those of the following June in certain key ways—most notably, the earlier ones were much more elaborate, and the Western

[45] Chen, *May Fourth,* p. 166.

[46] See *Shanghai Times,* November 20 and 25, 1918; and *Shenbao,* November 23, 1918, for descriptions.

[47] Along with Chen's description of the June 12 events, see *North China Herald,* June 14, 1919, p. 725; *Shanghai Times,* June 13, 1919, p. 7; Zhongguo shehui kexueyuan, *Wusi aiguo yundong,* pp. 286–287; and the June 21 report (dossier no. 238) from Mr. Phillips, the acting consul-general, in British Foreign Office (hereafter F.O.) 371/3695.

authorities were the main organizers of the former whereas they tried to stop the latter from taking place—but the basic similarities in form remain striking.

This theme of foreigners inadvertently teaching Chinese students protest techniques and providing scripts for antiimperialist gatherings becomes even more apparent if we focus on one youth group that played a particularly important role in the May Fourth Movement: the Chinese Boy Scouts. This organization, which was originally directly affiliated with local foreign Boy Scout troops, was founded in 1913 and by 1919 included thirteen troops in Shanghai proper.[48] These Boy Scouts, like their counterparts in other countries, took part in a variety of activities, some of which were purely recreational while others were geared toward public service. At first glance, no less likely training ground for participants in radical movements seems imaginable, since this organization expressly claimed that scouting was "not intended to lead youths to interfere in the government of the country," but rather simply to encourage boys to be "honorable, useful and pure," "live a healthy open air life," and fill "every moment with useful and health giving hobbies."[49] In fact, however, when the May Fourth Movement broke out, Boy Scouts immediately began to use the techniques they had learned in the new cause of protest.[50] Since troop leaders were often students or teachers at local schools, this transition from being part of a Western-run organization to being an anti-imperialist vanguard was actually quite logical.[51]

---

[48] I have not yet found any comprehensive source on the founding and early years of the Chinese Boy Scouts, other than a brief piece by one G. S. F. Kemp, "Boy Scouts Association of China," *Xin qingnian* 2:5 (1917): 455–457. Most of what I know about them therefore is based on piecing together bits and pieces from the English language press—see, for example, *North China Herald,* March 15, 1919, p. 712, and November 24, 1917, p. 469.

[49] Kemp, "Boy Scouts."

[50] This phenomenon was not limited to Shanghai, since other cities also had Boy Scout troops. For examples of Boy Scouts taking part in protest activities in other parts of China, see the press clippings in the British Foreign Office dispatches from Tianjin (September 1, 1919) and Hankow (December 17, 1919) in F.O. 228/3527.

[51] *North China Herald,* March 15, 1919, p. 712, lists the organizational sponsors of several troops, which presumably provided the troop leaders. Interestingly, this list includes the names of two of the Shanghai colleges (Fudan and Nanyang) most active in the May Fourth Movement, as well as mentioning troops belonging to two other bodies (the Y.M.C.A. and the World Students' Federation) that were also centers of radical student activity during the struggle. The local head of the Chinese Boy Scout Association expressly directed troop leaders to mobilize their scouts for action to aid the May Fourth Movement (see Zhongguo shehui kexueyuan, *Wusi aiguo yundong,* vol. 2, p. 136). For information on the role of the World Students' Organization, see Xin Gonglin et al., "Wusi shiqi de huanqiu Zhongguo xuesheng hui" [The World Students' Organization during the May Fourth era], *Shanghai qingyunshi ziliao* 12 (1984): 91–95.

What specifically did Boy Scouts do during the May Fourth Movement that can be traced back to their earlier troop activities? Forming ranks and marching is the first thing that comes to mind; this skill, which they practiced and carried out as part of regular reviews, was obviously applicable during the May Fourth Movement.[52] Along with simply marching in antiimperialist parades, however, the Boy Scouts often performed important functions as monitors during marches, assemblies, and strikes, taking charge of keeping order among the protesters themselves and between protesters and outsiders.[53] Scout training had made them familiar with this policing function, too. Just the previous March, in fact, troops of Chinese Boy Scouts had helped the Shanghai Municipal Police (SMP) keep order when the latter were arranging for the deportation of German subjects.[54] Two months later, instead of simply assisting the SMP, the Boy Scouts were taking the skills they had learned and setting themselves up as a kind of mirror police force.[55]

These, then, are some of the ways in which official ceremonies, by training youths in routines and providing them with scripts that could be easily adapted to suit radical purposes, could inadvertently teach them how to protest. Many other related ideas could be explored here, such as the connections between campus military training and the style of protest marches.[56] Much more could also be said about some of the issues brought up in passing: topics such as the connections between yearly festivals and protest behavior could themselves be the focus of entire papers.[57] I will return to some of these themes later, but now it is

---

[52] For examples of Chinese Boy Scout drills, see *North China Herald,* November 24, 1917, p. 469.

[53] See, for example, Chen, *May Fourth,* pp. 118 n.3 and 127–128; and Zhongguo shehui kexueyuan, *Wusi aiguo yundong,* vol. 2, pp. 136, 167, and the pictures before pp. 207, 215, and 242.

[54] See *North China Herald,* March 15, 1919, p. 712.

[55] It is worth noting that even before the May Fourth Movement imperialists had played an important role in "teaching" youths how to carry out antiimperialist struggles: a *North China Herald* editorial called attention to this irony in 1905, in fact—see the August 11 edition, p. 332—by remarking that the anti-American agitation of that year was being conducted in a "characteristically American manner." According to this article, the Shanghai protesters of 1905 learned most of the techniques they were using from American missionaries. The editors went on to say that "Americans cannot, therefore, but feel gratified with the aptitude manifested by their pupils, even if they are perhaps the first victims of the weapons they have placed in [these pupils'] hands."

[56] See "Chinese Cadets at Drill," *North China Herald,* June 2, 1917, pp. 505–506, for a description of the military training program at one local college just before the May Fourth Movement.

[57] There is a rapidly growing literature on the connections between festivals and protest in various contexts; see, for example, Davis, *Society and Culture;* Perrot, *Workers on Strike;* Gail Hershatter, *The Workers of Tianjin, 1919–1949* (Stanford, Calif.: Stanford University

worth moving on to look in some detail at another set of activities that provided youths with scripts for action and trained them in the skills they would use during the May Fourth Movement: ordinary campus life.

An obvious link exists between classroom activities and such student protest techniques used in 1919 as streetside lecturing drives and the writing of pamphlets and petitions. Whereas in the previous examples we saw the municipal authorities and even the police inadvertently play-ing the role of "teachers," here we see professors and middle school instructors training students (again often inadvertently, of course) in pro-test tactics. Youths interested in publicizing the arrest of Beijing students for protesting the terms of the Versailles Treaty and in convincing members of other social groups to join the patriotic movement began by simply turning to actions they either did or watched their instructors do in the classroom. Whether or not they had ever given a speech before, all members of the student propaganda teams that swarmed through Shanghai in the wake of the May Fourth incident were intimately familiar with what went into a lecture.[58] It was likewise a short jump from com-posing essays to composing pamphlets, from reading memorials to writ-ing petitions, and from acting in school pageants to performing patriotic plays on the streets.[59]

Teachers were by no means the only ones who provided Shanghai students with "scripts" for lecturing and performing on the streets, for these same youths had all been exposed to a wide variety of other poten-tial role models, from storytellers to itinerant Daoist preachers to Confu-cian lecturers who came to villages to expound upon the sacred edicts.[60]

Press, 1986); and Esherick, *The Boxer Uprising.*

[58] On the lecture teams, see Shanghai shehui kexueyuan lishi yanjiusuo, *Wusi yundong zai Shanghai,* pp. 294–297, 399, and passim; and Fudan University, *Xiaoshi tongxun* [Com-munications on school history], 8 (1984): 19 and passim. The classroom was not the only context in which student protesters were exposed to lecturers—since they listened to speeches at various public events, such as the Guomin dahui discussed above—nor were professors the only ones who could serve as their mentors. This latter point is illustrated by an anecdote in Zhang Guotao's memoir, *The Rise of the Chinese Communist Party* (Lawrence, Kan.: Kansas University Press, 1971), 60, which describes a meeting between a group of Beijing student lecturers and an "elderly Christian pastor." According to Zhang, who was a member of the student lecture team, the pastor had been moved by the youths' "patriotic fervor" when he had listened to them on the street, but had said that their "speeches were not colloquial enough" and gave them pointers on how better to reach "the average man."

[59] See *China Weekly Review,* June 1, 1918, p. 29, for an account of sample school pageants of the era; for the role of dramatic performances in student propaganda drives, see Chen, *May Fourth,* p. 65.

[60] The influence of some of these performers on student propagandists is treated in Wasserstrom, *Student Protests,* chap. 8.

The streetside lectures students gave also drew from operatic scripts: youths often gave their speeches from atop makeshift stages and used rhetoric reminiscent of that of the loyal heroes of Chinese drama. Nonetheless, campus activities probably played the most important role in preparing students to be effective publicists for their political causes. Not only did classroom drills train May Fourth activists in literary techniques, but the organizational and oratorical experiences these youths had gained from participating in campus debating clubs, literary societies, and student councils proved invaluable when it came time to take to the streets. The student clubs and societies around which Shanghai campus life revolved in fact gave May Fourth activists ready-made blueprints for setting up protest leagues in 1919. It is hardly surprising, therefore, that the heads of these leagues were often people who had already become familiar with playing leadership roles in other kinds of student associations. Zhu Zhonghua, the first temporary president of the SSU, for instance, had been a leading figure in the Fudan Self-Governing Association before the outbreak of the May Fourth Movement; thus even when the May Fourth Movement first began, Zhou was no novice at holding meetings and giving public addresses. Zhu had also had ample opportunity to practice these skills as a founding member of the Fudan Traveling Lecture Corps, which had been established in March 1919 to spread information on scientific topics and current affairs to the masses and which included several other early leaders of the SSU among its members.[61]

The preceding pages have focused on ways in which activities essentially unrelated to protest helped prepare students for collective action, but in some cases May Fourth students found models for action in tactics other groups had used effectively in the past. The most important tactic students borrowed from another class was, of course, the boycott, a form of protest merchants used long before the May Fourth Movement to achieve economic and political ends.[62] Perhaps the most important local

---

[61] See *Xiaoshi tongxun* [School history bulletin] (Fudan), 8 (1984): 15 and 32–38, for details on this corps and a memoir by Zhu, respectively. The Beida Speech Corps played a very similar role to the Fudan Traveling Lecture Corps, in both providing the local youth movement with leaders and training those leaders in public speaking and organizing, a point brought out in Arif Dirlik's recent study, "Ideology and Organization in the May Fourth Movement," *Republican China* 12:1 (1986): 3–19. For a full discussion of the ways in which even the most seemingly nonpolitical of campus clubs and associations contributed to student movements by providing youths with leadership skills and forging between individuals connections that facilitated mass mobilization, see Jeffrey Wasserstrom and Liu Xinyong, "Student Life and Student Politics: Shanghai, 1919–1949," *Social History,* 14:1 (1989): 1–30.

[62] For background on Chinese boycotts both before and after May Fourth, see C. F. Remer, *A Study of Chinese Boycotts* (Baltimore: Johns Hopkins University Press, 1933).

precedent for the anti-Japanese boycott of 1919 was the anti-French boycott of 1898. Triggered by French attempts to build on land the Ningbo
Native-Place Guild was using as a cemetery, this boycott lasted six
months. Like the May Fourth boycott, it was accompanied by a general
strike of sorts: many merchants from Ningbo closed their shops, and
Ningbo laborers working for French employers refused to work until the
matter was settled.[63]

Other tactics that students had watched members of differing social
classes employ during the period immediately preceding May 1919 may
also have served as scripts for some May Fourth actions. For example,
although one cannot trace any kind of direct link between the Hongkou
Riots of 1918 and May Fourth activities, there was at least a tenuous connection. Youth leaders took great pains to deny the claim that the May
Fourth Movement was just another series of "antiforeign" outbursts, but
the fact remains that some students did harass Japanese (and Chinese
who were considered "pro-Japanese" or bought Japanese products) in
1919. If such harassment can qualify as a protest "tactic," it is one that
should be understood as related to previous anti-Japanese riots in which
students generally played little part.[64]

Students, while occasionally looking to scripts provided by members
of other social classes, more frequently simply looked to their own tradition of mass action, which even in 1919 was already a rich one.[65] When
May Fourth students drafted petitions of complaint, for example, they
were using a protest tactic that members of the intelligentsia had been
using for millennia,[66] and when they pasted up posters denigrating hated
officials they were replicating an action performed by exam candidates of
the early Qing.[67] Even the May Fourth Beijing protest itself was very
similar in form to a pre-twentieth-century intelligentsia protest: the mass

[63] See Susan Mann Jones, "The Ningpo Pang and Financial Power at Shanghai," in Mark
Elvin and G. William Skinner, eds., The Chinese City Between Two Worlds (Stanford, Calif.:
Stanford University Press, 1974), pp. 73–96.

[64] For relevant citations and information on the antiforeign violence that accompanied
Shanghai's May Fourth Movement, which is generally played down or ignored in both
Chinese and Western accounts of the events of 1919, see chapter 1 of my dissertation,
"Taking It to the Streets: Shanghai Students and Political Protest, 1919–1949" (University
of California, Berkeley, 1989).

[65] For basic background on pre-twentieth-century student movements, see Lin Yutang, A
History of the Press and Public Opinion in China (New York: Greenwood, 1968), and Bao
Zunpeng, Zhongguo qingnian.

[66] Such petitions had in fact been used as early as A.D. 153. See Lin, Press and Public,
p. 35.

[67] See Tsing Yuan, "Urban Riots and Disturbances," in Jonathan Spence and John Wills,
From Ming to Ch'ing (New Haven, Conn.: Yale University Press, 1979): 301.

petition drive criticizing capitulation to the Japanese staged at Tiananmen in 1895.[68]

Returning to Shanghai and moving forward in time, we see precursors of many May Fourth tactics in the student upsurges of the preceding two decades. Student strikes, which played so vital a role in the May Fourth Movement, for example, had grown increasingly common since the Nanyang College strike of 1902. Dozens of similar incidents took place on other campuses during the following years, precipitated by causes as disparate as anger over the way youths were being disciplined to disgust with the poor quality of school food.[69] Students and progressive teachers from various schools also joined together to hold mass rallies to protest imperialist encroachments on Chinese territory several times during the pre–May Fourth period: along with the previously mentioned anti-Russian protests of 1903 and the anti-Japanese struggles of 1915 and 1918, local youths had participated in patriotic assemblies during the anti-American agitation of 1905.[70] Thus, while the May Fourth Incident is rightly treated as a great point of origin in Chinese youth movement history, the protesters of 1919 also must be seen as but the newest inheritors of a longstanding tradition. The May Fourth student leader Duan Xipeng directly acknowledged this "inheritance" in his speech at the inaugural meeting of the National Student Union in 1919, when he held up Chen Dong—an exam candidate whom Song Dynasty officials eventually sentenced to death for his activities in campaigns against government corruption—as a model for union members to emulate.[71]

The influence student movement history had upon campus activists increased dramatically after 1919 because of the high regard successive generations of educated youths had for the participants in the May Fourth Movement. Viewing their predecessors of 1919 as selfless heroes and successful protesters—since they had forced the "three traitorous officials" from office—new cohorts of campus activists spoke of the need to continue on in the "May Fourth spirit." Looking to the past for

---

[68] See Andrew Nathan, *Chinese Democracy* (New York: Knopf, 1985), p. 8.

[69] The best general treatment of Shanghai student protests of the early twentieth century is Wang Min, "Wusi xuqu." On these strikes, see also Mary Rankin, *Early Chinese Revolutionaries: Radical Intellectuals in Shanghai and Chekiang, 1902–1911* (Cambridge, Mass.: Harvard University Press, 1971), pp. 61–64; and Chiang Monlin, *Tides from the West* (New Haven, Conn.: Yale, 1947), pp. 48 and 64.

[70] For student participation in the 1905 protests, see *North China Herald,* June 30, 1905, p. 724; and the August 8, 1905, dispatch by British Consul-General Pelham Warren in F.O. 228/2155.

[71] For details on Chen Dong's life history, see Lin, *Press and Public Opinion,* pp. 48–50; Duan's speech is quoted in Zhongguo shehui kexueyuan, *Wusi aiguo yundong,* vol. 1, p. 473.

inspiration, they kept the May Fourth repertoire alive in new struggles they sometimes referred to as *Xin Wusi yundong* (New May Fourth movements).

During the 1920s through 1940s Shanghai youth movements generally followed May Fourth patterns closely, with protesters working from many of the scripts that had proved successful in 1919. First, students angered by a new incident held mass meetings, drafted telegrams of complaint, and pasted up wall posters. Next, they called classroom strikes, mounted streetside lecture campaigns to publicize their cause, and petitioned the authorities to release youths arrested during the initial stage of the unrest. Finally, they promoted labor strikes and boycotts of foreign goods, marched on police stations to demand an end to police interference with the popular movement, staged parades similar to those described above, and when there were martyrs (as there usually were) held mass memorial services to honor the dead.

Although this pattern was not unique to Shanghai, the peculiarities of the city's social, political, and cultural environment highlighted in other chapters gave unique twists to many aspects of the local student movement in 1919. The division of the city into different administrative districts, for example, allowed activists simply to move their base of operations to a new part of town when a police force got too interested in their activities. In addition, as Bryna Goodman has indicated (see Chapter 3), the unusually prominent role of native-place groups in Shanghai influenced local mass movements in a variety of ways. In terms of the specific tactics they employed, however, local May Fourth student activists were much like their counterparts in other cities, who also held memorial services for Guo Qinguang, formed *shirentuan* to enforce the anti-Japanese boycott, gave streetside lectures, staged victory parades when the "three traitorous officials" were dismissed, and so forth.[72]

This similarity is hardly surprising, since students in other parts of the country were exposed to many of the same kinds of scripts that influenced Shanghai's campus activists, and campus activists in different parts of the country were in contact with each other both before and during the May Fourth Movement. (Because not all youths had as much contact with foreigners and with Western types of political rituals, local

---

[72] For a sense of the tactical similarities between Shanghai's May Fourth protesters and those of two other cities, see Strand, *Rickshaw Beijing,* pp. 173–177; and David Buck's comments on 1919 protests in Jinan in *Urban Change in China* (Madison: University of Wisconsin Press, 1978), pp. 116–117. Comparable events in other cities are discussed in Peng Ming, *Wusi yundongshi* (Beijing: Renmin chubanshe, 1984), to date the most comprehensive Chinese-language study of the struggle, and Zhongguo shehui kexueyuan, *Wusi aiguo yundong.*

protest actions sometimes differed [e.g., not all students performed flag-raising ceremonies at the start of their May Fourth strike]). Shanghai's past also affected the course of events in 1919: local youths were more successful than their counterparts in other cities at organizing and mobilizing support for a general strike of workers and merchants as well as students, for example, in part because the events of 1898 provided a precedent for this kind of protest. Nonetheless, despite local variations of this sort, the student protest repertoire was already basically a national one in 1919, and it became even more standardized during the decades that followed, as campus activists from differing regions met in national unions to trade information concerning the tactics they had found most effective.

As regular as the May Fourth pattern of student activism outlined above became, however, Republican protesters of the 1920s through 1940s did not content themselves with simply trying to reenact the events of 1919. These youths continually refined and adapted the protest techniques they inherited from the May Fourth era. In addition, they occasionally introduced their own new tactics into the repertoire. As a result, the street theater of later years often differed from that of 1919 in subtle but important ways.

Differences between the student petition drives of 1931 and those that accompanied the May Fourth Movement illustrate this point. The petition drives of 1931, like those of 1919, were intended both to put pressure on the government to take a stronger stance against Japan and to be more lenient toward student protesters, but they were in other ways quite dissimilar. The first contrast simply has to do with how far the petitioners involved traveled. Shanghai's May Fourth students were content to present their demands to local government authorities and merely send telegrams of complaint to Beijing. Their counterparts in the Resist Japan Movement that followed the Manchurian Incident of September 18, 1931, in contrast, were determined to travel to the capital city of Nanjing to present their case in person to the central authorities.

Travel introduced a new element into a familiar script, giving some group petition drives a quasi-religious air. The protest petition has always had religious overtones of a sort in China. Throughout imperial times, petitioning the gods for favors was an important part of many forms of both official and folk worship. And because orthodox theology drew close parallels between the natural and supernatural worlds, equating the roles of officials to those of deities, this religious petitioning could serve naturally as a mode for political remonstrance. As Emily Martin Ahern writes, it could become a "learning game" that taught ordinary

Chinese "how to analyze (and so manipulate) the political system that governed them."[73]

If petitioning officials was linked to petitioning the gods, traveling to present the remonstrance connected students to another kind of religious script: the pilgrimage. Religious pilgrims were a familiar part of the landscape in late imperial and Republican China.[74] Journeying to sacred spots to meet with special priests and present petitions to special deities, these pilgrims traveled in groups, carrying banners identifying them by their village of origin. Similarly, Chinese student petitioners of 1931 descended upon Nanjing from all over the nation, carrying comparable banners that identified the cities from which they came. Like their religious counterparts, these political pilgrims gathered to listen to speeches (in this case by Guomindang officials) and visit sacred sites (in this case Sun Yat-sen's tomb). Many then returned home to await the results of their petitions.[75]

Pilgrimage scripts were not the only ones from which the traveling petitioners of 1931 worked, however: some, influenced in part by the rising importance of military exercises in ordinary school life, saw their protests in martial rather than religious terms. As memoirs make clear, Shanghai students often treated their trips to Nanjing like military campaigns: they formed brigades, selected "generals" to lead them, and generally enforced a militaristic discipline among themselves.[76] When the authorities at Shanghai's North Station—acting on orders from Nanjing to prevent further petitioners from traveling—tried to stop students from setting off for the capital, youths quite literally put their military training to use by taking over the station by force. Youths from Jiaotong University then put a different sort of school training to use by starting up a train themselves and setting off for Nanjing.[77] If the 1931 campaigns

---

[73] Ahern, *Chinese Ritual and Politics* (Cambridge: Cambridge University Press, 1981), p. 92.

[74] For background on religious pilgrimages, see Rawski and Naquin, *Chinese Society,* pp. 85–86; and C. K. Yang, *Religion in Chinese Society* (Berkeley: University of California Press, 1961), pp. 87–88.

[75] The best discussion of 1931 petition drives of this sort remains that in Israel, *Student Nationalism,* pp. 47–86.

[76] Ren Jianshu, "'Jiu-yi-ba' shibian houde Shanghai xuesheng yundong" [The Shanghai Student Movement after the September Eighteenth Incident], *Shanghai qingyunshi ziliao* 4 (1982): 6–11, mentions the increasing *junduihua* (militarization) of the petition drives of 1931; see also the firsthand accounts in *Shenghuo* 6:43 (November 17, 1931): 793–796; and *Fan-Ri jiuguo* [Resist Japan and save the nation (published by a Fudan anti-Japanese league)], 2 (1931): 12–16. There were militaristic overtones to various earlier protests, but none quite so extreme as in these petition drives.

[77] Huang Lin, "Wo zai Shanghai dixia douzheng shenghuo de duanpian" [Fragments on my life fighting in the Shanghai underground], *Shanghai dangshi ziliao tongxun* [Communica-

revealed the effects changes in campus routines could have on the way traditional techniques were carried out, the petition presentation students organized to greet General George C. Marshall's arrival in Shanghai (in December 1945) showed that official ceremonial forms could also lead to variations in the performance of protest scripts. This petition, like many that preceded it, was aimed at removing a foreign power's troops (in this case American ones) from Chinese soil; it also called for an increase in domestic freedom. The mass gathering that was planned to accompany its presentation was also not unusual, since it was to be a parade along one of Shanghai's main streets. The style of this parade, however, was not typical in at least one regard: students marched along behind standard bearers carrying American and Chinese flags. This and other details indicate that there was more to the event than simply a reenactment of a traditional student protest technique. It was also an imitation of the official reception local Guomindang leaders had organized to mark Marshall's arrival, which included marching bands playing the two countries' national anthems and prominent displays of both nations' flags.[78]

As these two examples indicate, although the May Fourth Movement may have set a pattern that later youth movements followed closely, the pattern was continually being modified by student exposure to other kinds of scripts. Nor did student idealization of the May Fourth Movement preclude genuine innovation, since a few novel tactics did work their way into the student protest tradition after 1919, though these again were less pure innovations than improvisations upon familiar scripts. The "popular tribunals" of 1931 and 1936 are clear cases in point. These public "trials," organized by students to punish officials who interfered with the youth movement, were in an obvious sense mockeries of the official ritual of the courtroom, which students turned into a protest tactic by usurping the role of magistrate. It is interesting to note, however, that school training also played an important part in the first and most famous of these "tribunals" (that which took place on December 10, 1931): most of those who played the roles of "lawyers" and "judges" were law students.[79]

tions on materials on Shanghai Party history], no. 9 (1986), pp. 14–22. Train commandeering itself entered the protest repertoire after this time, with similar events happening in both 1935 and 1947. See Wang, *Dashiji*, pp. 178–179 and 269.

[78] For a full treatment of the "Welcome Marshall" demonstration, see my "Popular Protest and Public Spectacle in Post–World War II Shanghai," paper presented at the 1988 annual meeting of the Association for Asian Studies. See also Wang, *Dashiji*, pp. 252–253.

[79] On this event, see Wen Jizhe, "Sanshi niandai chu 'zuo' ying cuowu dui Shanghai xueyun de yingxiang"; *Le Journal de Shanghai*, December 12, 1931; and Wang, *Dashiji*, p. 143. A less dramatic 1936 popular tribunal is described in Shanghai Party History Study

My main intent so far has been to try to suggest why Shanghai students used the particular kinds of tactics they did and why youths so
often seemed to have a shared vision of how to carry out a given mass
action. Tracing the connections between student tactics and other forms
of social activity is, however, important for a variety of other reasons
besides answering the questions posed at the beginning of this chapter.
One reason is that paying close attention to the scripts from which student protesters worked can also help account for some of the tactical
differences between youth movements occurring in different times and
places. For example, both Shanghai youths of the Republican era and
American students of the 1960s found imitating their professors a useful
method for drawing attention to their causes. However, thanks to
differences in the basic scripts for classroom behavior from which these
two groups worked, the typical Chinese streetside lecture drive is quite
unlike the "teach-in," which is its closest American counterpart. Shanghai student propaganda campaigns of the Republican era, like Republican
classrooms themselves, were structured around one person imparting
knowledge and moral dicta to a group; American "teach-ins" of the
1960s, in contrast, for which seminars and discussion groups rather than
lectures served as models, more often took the form of debates or dia-
logues. Many other examples could be used to illustrate this same
point—for example, differences in festive and ritual traditions go a long
way toward accounting for the fact that student demonstrations in some
cultures involve orderly arrangements of brigades with specially designated group leaders, while in others they are much more anarchic
affairs—but for now the case of lecture campaigns and "teach-ins" will
suffice.[80]

Another reason it is worth taking the time to isolate collective action
scripts is that similarities between student protests and other kinds of
events could have implications for the efficaciousness of the tactics
youths employed. Students' reliance upon a tactic with which another
group was also familiar, for example, could make members of that group
more sympathetic to the youth movement in question. The linguistic and
other points of commonality (e.g., the similar uses of oaths noted above)
between student strikes (bake) and labor strikes (bagong) could, for
instance, help bridge the large cultural gap that separated educated
youths from factory workers. And bridging this gap was crucial, since

Group, *Shanghai kang-Ri jiuwang yundong ziliao xuanbian* [Selected materials on the anti-
Japanese movement] (Shanghai: Party History Study Group, 1985), pp. 342–345.

[80] For additional discussion of comparative issues, see Wasserstrom, *Student Protests,*
chap. 3.

students were most powerful when they allied with workers in actions such as the *sanba* (literally, "triple stoppages," the third "ba" standing for cessations of market activity) of 1919 and 1925.

Basing a protest in some way upon an authorized activity or a script favored by those in power could also increase a youth movement's chances for success, though for a different reason: because it could make the event harder to suppress. Charles Tilly argues it was mainly for this reason, in fact, that protesters in seventeenth-century France so frequently modeled their actions on officially approved ceremonies.[81] Through mimicry, protesters were able either to disguise (for a time at least) that their actions threatened the government or, even when the challenge was explicit, to give their actions an air of legality through the appearance of following official patterns, thus making interference more difficult than it otherwise would have been.

These observations concerning preindustrial France have direct relevance for Republican Shanghai, where disguise and apparent legality also made imitative protest particularly troublesome for those in positions of authority. The "Welcome Marshall" petition march mentioned earlier is a clear case in point. Even though the local police were aware that the march was meant to embarrass GMD officials, interference with the event could have created serious problems for the Chinese government, since in outward appearance it looked like a simple attempt by Shanghai students to greet a foreign dignitary. Overt steps to interfere could have created a diplomatic incident, with Marshall wondering why his hosts had stopped a group of youths from presenting their own equivalent to the official welcoming parade he had received.

Even when international issues were not involved, however, student protests of the Civil War era (1945–1949) often placed the authorities in the awkward position of trying to justify suppressing events that looked a great deal like gatherings the GMD itself sponsored. Throughout these years radical youths continually staged protests on political anniversaries, such as March 8 (International Women's Day) and May 4 itself, which the government claimed should be celebrated with mass gatherings. These protests, which despite their radical intent of challenging the government were often similar to the official ceremonies marking these days, presented the authorities with a dilemma: they could either allow the events to take place (and take the chance that letting protesters shout antigovernment slogans would bring new converts to the opposition) or take repressive action and risk appearing hypocritical (a stance that also could alienate popular support). Either way the students could come out

---

[81] Tilly, *The Contentious French*, pp. 116–118.

ahead, since, whether or not they were allowed to carry their protest through to the end, they had a good chance of winning sympathy for their cause.

Foreigners faced the same dilemma during earlier decades, since banning events that looked like official or routine gatherings could also make them appear hypocritical. This point is brought out clearly in a memoir by a former St. John's middle school student who participated in the May Fourth Movement; the memoir argues that his school's authorities were hypocritical in claiming in the spring of 1919 that *bake youxing* (stop[ping] classes and demonstrat[ing]) was against campus rules. Less than six months previously, the author points out, the authorities had in fact *required* students to *bake youxing* when they suspended classes and ordered youths to participate in the World War I victory parades sponsored by the Shanghai Municipal Council (SMC).[82] Similarly, if the SMC had taken active measures to disrupt the memorial service for the May Fourth martyr Guo Qinguang, it would have run the risk of angering not only students, but also many other Chinese who viewed the event less as a protest than as an accepted form of honoring the dead.

There was yet another reason, besides familiarity and the fact that such events were hard to suppress, why students may have found improvising upon official scripts particularly attractive, and I will end my discussion of protest tactics by looking briefly at this point. This third reason, which is again suggested by Charles Tilly's work on French protesters, is that mimicking an official procedure can be a very powerful way of criticizing the officials who normally take charge of this procedure. When crowds improvise upon official scripts and act out roles normally played by powerholders, such actions can not only the give an air of legality but can also suggest that those in charge of running the system are not doing the job properly. Mockeries of official rites, in which ordinary people usurp positions of authority, thus challenge the legitimacy of those in power.

This point was not missed by those whom Shanghai student protests challenged: we have clear evidence that at least some foreigners viewed the tendency of youthful protesters to usurp official duties as a direct threat to the whole Concession system. Particularly disturbing to the foreigners were the actions of the Boy Scouts and specially organized student *baoandui* (order-keeping brigades), groups whose members wore

---

[82] Zhou Peiyuan, "Zai jiaohui xuejiao de aiguo douzheng" [Patriotic struggles at a missionary school], in Zhongguo shehui kexueyuan, eds., *Wusi yundong huiyilu* [Remembering the May Fourth Movement] (Beijing: CASS [Chinese Academy of Social Sciences], 1979), vol. 2, pp. 639–644.

special uniforms and acted like a shadow police force—only in this case the law they were upholding was the law of the boycott and the anti-imperialist movement generally. The following quotations, taken from reports by foreign journalists and officials, illustrate the degree to which student actions were viewed as posing a very real threat to the status quo:

> [W]e may say at the outset that we were pleased at the sight of Chinese Boy Scouts and others doing what they could to maintain order. . . . But the question came into our mind at the time:—By whose authority was that aid given? (*The Celestial Empire,* June 14, 1919, p. 518)

> **Lawlessness in Shanghai**
> On Sunday evening the students who had constituted themselves a special police force practically assumed charge of Nanking Road . . . bands of Chinese paraded the Settlement wearing uniforms and badges, functioning generally as if they had been armed by the authorities with full powers. (*North China Herald,* June 14, 1919, p. 685)

> [B]ut it must not be forgotten that had not some counter-demonstration been made on their [the Shanghai Municipal Council's] part, they would have had to sit by and watch the Students Union usurp the duties of the police of the Settlement. [The SSU headquarters was closed to show] that students would not be allowed to usurp the duties of the regular administration by patrolling the streets. (Acting Consul-General Phillips dispatch no. 236, June 21, 1919, F.O. 371/3695)

One of the most radical details of May Fourth protests, therefore, was the implication inherent in some tactics that ordinary people might be able to perform official functions better and more justly than the foreign authorities; later protests would pose comparable threats to the legitimacy of those who ruled Shanghai. The popular tribunal of 1931 mentioned above, for example, directly challenged the GMD's judicial system, while in the same year foreigners again accused students involved in an anti-Japanese boycott of acting "as if they were police enforcing the laws of the country."[83] More abstractly, even less militant events—such as the "Welcome Marshall" parade—could serve to undercut the position of current powerholders. Parodies of official GMD ceremonies were, in fact, one of the most powerful weapons students had in their struggle to raise doubts concerning the right of Jiang Jieshi (Chiang Kai-shek) to rule the nation during the Civil War.[84]

---

[83] "Police Report for November," *Municipal Gazette,* December 25, 1931, pp. 558.

[84] This topic is examined at much greater length in Wasserstrom, "Popular Protest and Public Spectacle in Post–World War II Shanghai."

I have tried in this chapter to call attention to the various types of scripts from which Shanghai student protesters worked and to some reasons why it is important to understand the connections between youth movement tactics and other kinds of actions. Because this topic is large and complex, it is impossible to deal with all aspects of it in a single chapter. Some topics only touched upon here, such as the role of religious rituals in shaping the style of political protests, and others ignored completely, such as the possible influence Japanese and Korean protests of the May Fourth era had on Shanghai events of 1919, deserve much fuller discussion.[85]

I hope that, despite these limitations, I have at least been able to give a sense of how crucial it is for students of Chinese youth movements to start paying as much attention to what students did when angered as they have in the past devoted to understanding the causes of student dissatisfaction. It is obviously important to know what triggered waves of student unrest. But it is equally clear that, if we want to understand fully the meaning of these upsurges, we must know much more about how participants chose their tactics and the significance those choices had for those who observed or were challenged by youth movements. If this chapter has succeeded in being an exploratory step in that direction, it has shown that, to paraphrase Chairman Mao, correct tactics (like "correct ideas") do not simply "drop from the sky."[86]

Epilogue

When I presented an earlier version of this chapter in China in 1988 as part of the International Symposium on Modern Shanghai, I intentionally omitted all references to events that occurred after 1949. I did this because drawing connections between youth movements of the Republican and Communist eras would have placed Chinese participants in the

---

[85] Japanese events—such as the student rally described in the *Japan Advertiser*, February 12, 1918, p. 1—are worth taking into consideration as possible models for May Fourth protests because many of the Chinese youths who led the anti-Japanese marches of the late 1910s were exchange students in Tokyo before May 1918. While few May Fourth protesters were likely to have witnessed Korean student actions firsthand, almost all of them would have read about these events, since newspapers such as *Minguo ribao* were filled with stories about the Korean uprising during the spring of 1919. Many of the actions Korean students took, moreover—for example, having one school's students walk in front as a special vanguard brigade during parades and marching en masse to police stations to demand the release of their arrested comrades—were similar in basic ways to May Fourth actions, as the report in *Shanghai Times*, March 15, 1919, p. 7, illustrates.

[86] Mao Zedong, "Where Do Correct Ideas Come From?" in *Four Essays on Philosophy* (Beijing: Foreign Languages Press, 1968), pp. 134–136.

conference in an awkward position, since Party line insists that the student protests of the two periods have nothing in common. Stopping the story of Shanghai student activism at 1949 seemed unnatural, however, because events of the earlier decades had shown that Chinese students had not stopped improvising upon May Fourth scripts. As different as the Red Guards—with their anti-intellectual stance and devotional loyalty to Chairman Mao—were from the protesters of 1919 and 1935, even a casual reading of Cultural Revolution memoirs had made it clear that along with borrowing scripts from other struggles (such as Land Reform campaigns) youths of that era turned at times to May Fourth–style tactics.[87] While conducting research in Shanghai two years before the conference, moreover, I had seen even more convincing proof of the continuing vitality of the May Fourth repertoire. Throughout mid-December 1986, I had divided my time between reading about pre-1949 May Fourth–style demonstrations in the archives and watching contemporary youths stage mass actions that were almost identical in form.[88]

While it already seemed unnatural in 1988 to end a paper on the May Fourth repertoire with the CCP's rise to power, the events of 1989 make it impossible for me to conclude without briefly surveying the kinds of scripts from which contemporary students work, beginning with those they have inherited from earlier generations of protesters. Various scholars have noted the debt the students of 1989 owed to history. Frank Pieke, one of the most insightful observers of events in Beijing, for example, has emphasized the influence the April Fifth Movement of 1976, during which enormous crowds descended upon Tiananmen Square to mourn Zhou Enlai and attack the Gang of Four, had upon the protesters of 1989.[89] Vera Schwarcz, Jonathan Unger, and Anita Chan, meanwhile, have noted that, despite their attempts to distance their movement from the stigma of Red Guardism, the students of 1989 resurrected some techniques associated with the early years of the Cultural Revolution.[90] David

---

[87] For the influence of Land Reform tactics on Red Guards, see Gao Yuan, *Born Red;* for a description of Red Guard tactics in Shanghai, see Neale Hunter, *Shanghai Journal* (New York: Praeger, 1969).

[88] I discuss the 1986 movement in much greater detail in the epilogue to *Student Protests.*

[89] Pieke, "Observations During the People's Movement in Beijing, Spring 1989," paper presented at the International Institute of Social History, Amsterdam, July 7, 1989; and "A Ritualized Rebellion: Beijing, Spring 1989," unpublished paper cited with the author's permission.

[90] Schwarcz, "Memory, Commemoration, and the Plight of Chinese Intellectuals," *Wilson Quarterly* (Autumn 1989), pp. 120–129; Anita Chan and Jonathan Unger, "Voices From the Protest Movement, Chongqing, Sichuan," *Australian Journal of Chinese Affairs* 24 (1990): 259–279.

Strand, in an essay on Beijing protests of the last seventy years, has gone back still further in time to argue that the protests in the capital in 1989 were often reminiscent of those of the May Fourth era in terms of the destinations marchers chose, the underlying organizational principles involved in demonstrations, and the role traditions of remonstrance played in structuring student actions.[91]

Participants in the 1989 protests and the Chinese audiences they sought to influence were themselves keenly aware of the historical precedents for many of their actions. When a group of youths knelt before the Great Hall of the People to present a petition to China's rulers, for example, militant students criticized the petitioners for using a technique "tainted with the stains of feudalism" in the fight for democracy.[92] Although this tactic may not have conformed to the ideology of the movement, however, it proved a powerful one: in part because the act of kneeling helped locate the act within a long-standing tradition of patriotic remonstrance, the petition in question gained the students a great deal of popular support and sympathy, especially when the CCP refused to perform the ritually correct response of coming out to accept the petition.[93]

While many students were uncomfortable with the idea that their protests were similar to those of imperial officials or Red Guards, they were proud of the links between their actions and those of participants in the May Fourth and April Fifth movements. In part to counter official attempts to label new protests acts of *luan* ("chaos" or "turmoil," a code word for the anarchy of the Cultural Revolution era), the students of 1989 went to great lengths to present their struggle as a continuation of those of 1919 and 1976. They wrote wall posters that stressed their attachment to the May Fourth and April Fifth traditions and argued that the only ones creating *luan* were the leaders of the CCP. They reinforced the idea that they were direct descendants of the heroes of 1919 in symbolic terms by resurrecting the New Culture Movement slogan "Science and Democracy" and by staging one of their most important demonstrations on the seventieth anniversary of the May Fourth Movement.[94] Ironically, much of the credit for familiarizing contemporary

[91] Strand, "Protest in Beijing: Civil Society and Public Sphere in China," *Problems of Communism,* May–June 1990, pp. 1–19.

[92] Han Minzhu, ed., *Cries for Democracy* (Princeton, N.J.: Princeton University Press, 1990), p. 64.

[93] Ibid., p. 63; Esherick and Wasserstrom, "Acting Out Democracy."

[94] For examples of official attempts to raise the specter of Red Guardism, as well as student responses to this charge and uses of May Fourth and April Fifth imagery, see Han, *Cries for Democracy,* pp. 83–85, 131–136, 269–271, 305, and 321; and Yu Mok Chiu and Frank Harrison, *Voices from Tiananmen Square* (New York: Black Rose Books, 1990), pp.

youths with the May Fourth tradition and repertoire, as well as for teaching them to think of the April Fifth Movement in heroic terms, must go to the current CCP leadership itself: through lectures, textbooks, speeches at anniversary celebrations, rituals honoring school martyrs and the like, Party officials and historians provided the students of 1989 with detailed information concerning the tactics that earlier generations of disaffected students had found most effective.

As in the case of Republican youth movements, however, historical precedent does not explain all the tactics students employed in 1989. Along with resurrecting standard May Fourth–style forms of actions, contemporary students also improvised upon scripts familiar to them for other reasons. As in the past, student awareness of the techniques used by other groups of protesters served as one source of inspiration. There were various native precedents for the hunger strikes students staged in May 1989, for example, including a 1980 group fast in Hunan as well as refusals to eat by individual dissidents during imperial times.[95] There were also distinctly Chinese features of the way the strike was carried out (e.g., participants grouped themselves together on the basis of school affiliation, and some youths' testaments were appeals to their parents to understand the protest as more than an unfilial act).[96] The strikers made it clear, nonetheless, that their act was in large measure an improvisation upon an imported script, and foreign equivalents to the protest profoundly affected the way international audiences responded to the fast.[97]

Daily life experiences also helped prepare the students of 1989 for action, much as they had done in the Republican era. Craig Calhoun, an astute observer of the Beijing events of 1989, has argued that in organizing for action protesters frequently "borrowed templates from other settings": class monitors, for example, went from taking charge of circulating course materials to using their skills to "organize food for hunger strikers."[98] In a similar vein, Corinna-Barbara Francis notes that "the students' ability to organize themselves so effectively... and to maneuver

---

91–93. For further general discussion of the issue of historical symbolism, see Ernest Young, "Imagining the Ancien Régime in the Deng Era," in Wasserstrom and Perry, *Popular Protest,* pp. 14–27.

[95] James Watson, "The Renegotiation of Chinese Cultural Identity," in Wasserstrom and Perry, *Popular Protest,* pp. 67–84; Yi Mu and Mark Thompson, *Crisis at Tiananmen* (San Francisco: China Books, 1989), pp. 42–44; Pieke, "Ritualized Rebellion."

[96] Han, *Cries for Democracy,* pp. 199–203.

[97] Yi and Thompson, *Crisis at Tiananmen,* p. 172; *Newsweek,* May 29, 1989, p. 21.

[98] Calhoun, "The Beijing Spring, 1989," *Dissent,* Fall 1989, pp. 435–447, esp. pp. 436 and 442; see also Pieke's discussions in "Observations" and "A Ritualized Rebellion" of the importance of *danwei* (work units) and *danwei* leaders in the 1989 protests.

politically with the government owes a great deal to the training and skill developed by students in school," where they are taught to "organize and be organized, lead and be led." Just as I haved argued that May Fourth activists created their own version of the *baojia* system to serve a radical cause, Francis writes that the students of 1989 were "able to turn communist political culture to their own democratic ends."[99] To cite a case in point, before helping to form an independent student association, Wu'er Kaixi had honed his leadership skills by serving on his middle school's official student council.[100]

Still another irony of the 1989 events was that, as in the past, some of the most dramatic and threatening student actions were usurpations of or variations upon official ceremonies. Joseph Esherick's eyewitness account of the 1989 protests in Xi'an describes the way in which students in that city manipulated official ritual forms and capitalized on the inability of the authorities to interfere with an action that borrowed heavily from official scripts to turn Hu Yaobang's funeral into an occasion for effective protest.[101] And, as Dru Gladney has noted, the placement of the Goddess of Democracy in Tiananmen Square also needs to be seen in part at least as a reworking of a CCP ritual, since large white statues of Mao were carried through the same area during National Day celebrations of the late 1960s.[102]

Shanghai students, who took many of their tactical cues from Beijing, joined their counterparts in other cities in turning the mourning rites for Hu Yaobang and the anniversary of the May Fourth Movement into occasions for protest.[103] They added a local twist to this pattern on May 27, however, by turning a Shanghai holiday into an attack on the CCP.

---

[99] Francis, "The Progress of Protest in China: The Spring of 1989," *Asian Survey* 29:9 (1989): 898–915, esp. p. 915.

[100] Yu Mok Chiu and Harrison, *Voices from Tiananmen Square,* p. 155.

[101] Esherick, "Xi'an Spring," *Australian Journal of Chinese Affairs* 24 (1990).

[102] Gladney, "Bodily Positions and Social Dispositions: Sexuality, Nationality, and Tiananmen Square," paper presented at the Institute for Advanced Study, Princeton University, April 26, 1990, cited with author's permission.

[103] Provincial protests have received much less attention than those in the capital, but several useful eyewitness accounts on Shanghai have already appeared in the *Australian Journal of Chinese Affairs:* Shelley Warner, "Shanghai's Response to the Deluge," 24 (1990): 299–314; Kate Wright, "The Political Fortunes of Shanghai's *World Economic Herald*" 23 (1990): 121–132; and Roy Forward, "Letter from Shanghai" 24 (1990): 281–298. John Maier's "'Tian'anmen 1989': The View from Shanghai," *China Information* 5:1 (1990): 1–13, which makes good use of an important *neibu* (for internal circulation only) report on unrest in the provinces, contains a good analysis of local events, and the press reports and other materials on Shanghai in Wu, *Baijiu Zhongguo,* help fill in the picture. My own understanding of Shanghai protests has been aided by reading Deborah Pellow's unpublished memoir, "A Choreography of Dissent: Shanghai 1989."

Local officials usually mark May 27, the date set aside for Shanghai's citizens to celebrate their "liberation" from Guomindang rule, by covering buildings throughout the city with banners extolling the virtues of the CCP. Sometimes they also convene assemblies at People's Square where speakers remind their listeners of the various ways in which life in the city has improved since 1949. On the fortieth anniversary of Shanghai's "liberation," however, the only rally held at People's Square was a student demonstration of some ten thousand youths demanding more democracy.[104]

Theatrical and religious performances, the final genres of collective action isolated above as sources for student protest scripts, also helped shape the events of 1989. According to Perry Link, the arrival of successive waves of petitioners at Tiananmen Square in April and May had a distinctly theatrical feel. When he watched the events, he writes, they reminded him most strongly of "morally charged Beijing Opera"; other scholars have likewise described the protests of 1989 as having an operatic quality.[105] Some commentators have drawn attention to the cinema rather than the stage as a source of inspiration, arguing that the dissident film *He shang* (River elegy)—which was extremely popular in intellectual circles before being banned early in 1989—helped remind students of what protesters had done in the past and provided them with new scripts from which to improvise.[106]

The significance of religious models for action has received less attention, but the use students made of goddess figures opens up some interesting avenues for exploration. For example, several days before Beijing students erected their now famous Goddess of Democracy, Shanghai students paraded along the Bund carrying a replica of the Statue of Liberty. This act, like its Beijing counterpart, was reminiscent of state rituals; along with the use of Mao figures in National Day celebrations alluded to above, the Guomindang staged a parade in honor of Jiang Jieshi's birthday in 1945 in which a large statue of the Generalissimo was carried through the streets of Shanghai. This said, it is important to remember that both the state rituals and student demonstrations in question had roots in an older religious tradition of carrying representations of gods through the streets at New Year's and on the birthdays of the deities in question.

---

[104] Wu, *Bajiu Zhongguo,* p. 479.

[105] Link's comments are quoted in Strand, "Protest in Beijing," p. 16; see ibid., p. 8, for further discussion of operatic motifs in relation to Republican mass movements.

[106] See, for example, Gladney, "Bodily Positions."

I have not tried in the preceding sketch to give a comprehensive overview of the tactics involved in the complex protests of 1989. My goal has simply been to draw attention to the ways in which contemporary students continue to refine, improvise from, and introduce new scripts into the May Fourth repertoire. Perhaps the most important continuity between past and present, however, has less to do with the persistence of certain culturally specific forms of action (such as mass petition drives, streetside lecture campaigns, parades involving youths marching under school pennants, and the like) than with the continued potency of student performances. The events of 1989 showed that educated youths have lost neither the ability to win the support of large segments of the urban populace nor the ability to undermine the legitimacy of ruling elites with powerful pieces of street theater.

CHAPTER FIVE

Regulating Sex in Shanghai
The Reform of Prostitution
in 1920 and 1951

GAIL HERSHATTER

In Shanghai, the sale of female sexual services was big business in the first half of the twentieth century. Contemporary estimates of the number of women involved ranged as high as a hundred thousand, which would make prostitution the largest single employer of female labor, outnumbering even cotton spinners in China's largest industrial city.[1] If the

---

[1] The fragmentary statistics available indicate the secular growth of prostitution. A 1920 report of the Special Vice Commission counted 4,522 Chinese prostitutes in the International Settlement alone, or one out of every 147 Chinese residents of the Settlement. If the greater population of Shanghai was taken as 1.5 million, the report added, and if prostitutes in the French Concession were figured in, then 1 in 300 Chinese residents of Shanghai sold her sexual services for a living. Special Vice Committee, "Vice Conditions in Shanghai," *Municipal Gazette* 13:681 (March 19, 1920): 84. These figures did not include what the report referred to as "sly" prostitutes, and in fact another set of statistics collected at around the same time found more than 60,000 prostitutes at work in the two foreign areas, most of them streetwalkers known as "pheasants." James Hundley Wiley, "A Study of Chinese Prostitution" (M.A. thesis, University of Chicago, 1929), p. 45; Yi Feng, "Changji wenti yanjiu" [Research on the problem of prostitution], *Funü gongming yuekan*, February 1933, p. 39. By 1935, combined estimates of licensed and unlicensed prostitutes ran to 100,000, with much of the increase attributed to rural disaster and Depression-related factory closings. Luo Qiong, "Changji zai Zhongguo" [Prostitution in China], *Funü shenghuo* 1:6 (December 1935): 37. A postwar study put the number of full-time prostitutes at 50,000, but suggested that the figure should be doubled to take account of women "whose activities approach those of prostitutes." Yu Wei, "Shanghai changji wubaige an diaocha" [An investigation of five hundred cases of prostitution in Shanghai], *Shizeng pinglun* 10:9/10 (October 15, 1948): 10. If the Shanghai population at that time is taken as 4.2 million, then one in every 42 city residents was directly involved in prostitution. Compare the highest estimates of 100,000 prostitutes to the number of female industrial workers in Shanghai: 173,432 women. The largest subgroup of these, about 84,000, were in cotton spinning. So there were arguably more prostitutes than cotton spinners in Shanghai, China's largest industrial city. (Emily Honig, *Sisters and Strangers: Women in the Shanghai Cotton Mills* [Stanford, Calif.: Stanford University Press, 1986] pp. 24–25, gives the total number of female industrial workers in Shanghai as 173,432 in 1929. Of these, the largest number [84,270] were em-

population of Shanghai is taken as about three million million in the early 1930s, then one of every thirty residents sold sex for a living.

The hierarchy of prostitution in the city was complex, ranging from courtesans called *shuyu* and *changsan,* who sold dining companionship and singing more often than sexual services, to streetwalkers called "pheasants" (*yeji*) who might service many customers a night.[2] The women of this hierarchy, whose experiences varied significantly according to native place and class of brothel, operated in a city that was itself fragmented among several different municipal administrations. Until 1951, none of these administrations declared prostitution illegal, but all sought to regulate it through licensing, taxation, and ordinances against streetwalking.

At several points in the history of treaty-port Shanghai, members of the foreign and Chinese communities initiated intense campaigns to regulate or ban prostitution. Some, including health officers of the International Settlement government, were concerned primarily with the spread of venereal disease among the foreign population. Others, chiefly foreign missionaries and women reformers, deplored the spread of "commercialized vice" and its effect upon prostitutes, customers, and foreign children growing up in Shanghai. In the 1920s and 1930s, groups of Chinese activists sought to abolish prostitution as part of their drive to modernize China and improve the status of Chinese women. Finally, in the late 1940s the Guomindang-run municipal government of Shanghai undertook the registration of prostitutes with an eye to eventual abolition.

Although these groups of reformers differed in their aims and methods, they had one thing in common: they all failed significantly to affect prostitution in Shanghai. Not until the establishment of the People's Republic did any municipal government succeed in closing brothels, punishing traffickers, and reeducating prostitutes. A comprehensive discussion of attempts at abolition is beyond the scope of this chapter. But an examination of two attempts to regulate prostitution—one in the International Settlement in 1920, the other in post-Liberation Shanghai—reveals the extent to which the state could wield authority over contested social terrain.

In comparing these two campaigns, it must be remembered that "the state" was not a steady entity. The Shanghai Municipal Council of the 1920s was merely a local authority, albeit one with ties to powerful

ployed in cotton spinning. Of 54,508 women workers counted in 1946, 35,306 were cotton spinners.)

[2] For a full discussion of the hierarchy of prostitution in Shanghai and its changes over the first half of the twentieth century, see Gail Hershatter, "The Hierarchy of Shanghai Prostitution, 1870–1949," *Modern China* 15:4 (October 1989): 463–498.

foreign powers. The People's Government of the 1950s, in contrast, was closely integrated with the national government, carrying out policy directives that were at least partially coordinated with other cities in China. The 1920s reformers were foreigners, and their governing body made little attempt to alter Chinese institutions except as they impinged on foreign life in Shanghai. The 1950s reformers were Chinese, and they explicitly identified themselves as agents of nationalistic renewal through the cleansing of Chinese social institutions. The 1920s government acted reluctantly to ban prostitution, reacting to pressure from reformers who were peripheral to state authority. The 1950s government, in contrast, controlled the timing, nature, and extent of reform, with no visible input from nonstate groups.

In spite of these significant differences, however, the two governments are comparable: each reached down into local society to regulate and alter the working conditions of prostitutes, and each made an attempt to regulate commercial sexuality in ways that had not been attempted by any earlier state authority. The two campaigns also evidence a similar concern, often implicit but always discernible, with the pernicious effect that prostitutes—loose women who were also women on the loose, detached from the control of families—had on public health and morality. The account that follows looks closely at two aspects of the reform campaigns: their relationship with governmental authority and their analysis of the nature of prostitution.

Legal Regulation: The 1920 Campaign

Almost from the beginning of their tenure in Shanghai, public health authorities in the International Settlement expressed their concern about the growth of prostitution and its effect on the health of the European population. In 1869, when Dr. Alex Jamieson conducted a survey of public health problems in the International Settlement, his list of health hazards included the city sewage system, the condition of the river, the water supply, vaccination, and brothels.[3] Foreigners subsumed the sale of sexual services under the general category of dirt and disease threatening the white population in a colonial environment. Edward Henderson, official surgeon to the foreign municipality, repeatedly referred in his 1871 report on prostitution to the lack of cleanliness among native prostitutes; his comments were consonant with the foreign representation of

---

[3] R. Alex Jamieson, "Memorandum on the Sanitary Condition of the Yang-King-Pang and Hongque Settlements at Shanghai, September 23, 1869," *North-China Herald*, March 22, 1870, p. 211.

China and Chinese as filthy, disease-ridden, and potentially dangerous to Europeans. The discourse on dirt was not confined to Chinese, but was extended to other people of color; Henderson denounced as "the worst in every way" those Shanghai brothels "where Malays, negroes, &c. are the principal visitors." He recommended that prostitutes be inspected and certified healthy.[4]

In 1877 a lock hospital (one containing facilities for the treatment of venereal disease) was opened for the examination and certification of Cantonese prostitutes who serviced foreign sailors. (Henderson proposed to confine his inspection efforts to the 223 women in 62 houses that serviced foreigners, since he felt that including the 1,385 other known prostitutes whose clientele was Chinese would be "impossible, as it would be impolitic.") Effective inspection required an elaborate procedure in which prostitutes were registered by the Shanghai Municipal Council (SMC), issued cards with their photographs attached, and required to appear weekly to undergo examination and have their ticket validated by the doctor. Diseased women were to have their cards and photographs impounded until they were cured. Treatment was voluntary, but brothels whose employees failed to appear were to be contacted by the police and closed down by the Mixed Court if the inmates resisted treatment. Foreign prostitutes were exempt, since they were regarded as more apt to seek medical advice and therefore cleaner than their Chinese sisters.[5]

The allocation of public funds for the lock hospital and the involvement of municipal organizations like the police and the courts made some residents of the International Settlement profoundly uneasy. In terms that anticipated the debate half a century later, one unhappy taxpayer objected that government regulation of prostitution condoned immorality, asking: "There was always one test for a Christian man by which he could tell whether he ought to support an undertaking and that was, Could he ask the blessing of God on it?... Could any one ask that blessing on a scheme countenancing and protecting fornication, in fact making provision for the flesh to fulfill the lusts thereof?"[6] Nevertheless, the hospital went into operation. Initially reluctant to appear for inspection, the women eventually turned the examinations, which were intended to control them, to good advantage by using their registration cards as advertisements for their services.[7] The registration and

---

[4] Edward Henderson, *A Report on Prostitution in Shanghai* (Shanghai: North-China Herald, 1871), pp. 16, 27–28 and passim.

[5] *China Medical Journal* 38:1 (January 1924), supplement, pp. 8–11. The French Council agreed to cooperate in these efforts.

[6] Ibid., p. 11.

[7] Special Vice Committee, "Vice Conditions in Shanghai," pp. 83–84.

inspection of some prostitutes continued until 1920.[8] Although the cost of operating the hospital was partially defrayed by fees and fines collected from the brothel keepers,[9] these covered only about one-third of the total, leaving the Municipal Council in 1920 with a net annual outlay of almost 5,000 taels.[10] The SMC thus drew no direct tax revenue from prostitution; in fact, the costs of running the lock hospital made prostitution a net drain on the municipal budget.

In spite of the problems involved in inspecting prostitutes, municipal authorities before World War I apparently rejected the alternative of abolition. Jamieson, while denouncing the "baneful" effects of prostitution on families, women, and public health, felt that it would exist as long as human nature "is constituted as at present." He argued that "attempts to abolish this form of vice can never prove successful, and therefore that rational men will direct their energies towards limiting the extent and lessening the severity of the inevitable effects."[11] Through the second decade of the twentieth century, the official approach to prostitution remained confined to medical inspection and to a clause in the 1898 licensing bylaw (never enforced) that required brothels to obtain a license.[12]

---

[8] The debate over the efficacy of the lock hospital continued among medical personnel into the 1880s, with Henderson himself calling it a failure in 1886 and proposing that it be either improved or closed. In 1900 it was closed and inspections transferred to a new isolation hospital. *China Medical Journal* 38:1 (January 1924), supplement, pp. 13–15.

[9] *China Medical Journal* 38:1 (January 1924), supplement, p. 3.

[10] Special Vice Committee, "Vice Conditions in Shanghai," p. 83.

[11] Jamieson, "Memorandum on the Sanitary Condition," p. 211.

[12] Special Vice Committee, "Vice Conditions in Shanghai," p. 83. The licensing bylaw was so inclusive that it rivaled the better-known warlord attempts to tax everything that moved. It read in full:

"No person shall keep a fair, market, Chinese Club, lodging house, music hall, theatre, circus, cinematograph, eating house, or other place of refreshment or public entertainment, hotel, tavern, billiard, bowling or dancing saloon, brothel, pawnshop, Chinese money exchange or cash shop, Chinese gold-smith's or silversmith's shop, dairy, laundry, bakery, slaughterhouse, livery stable, public garage, pen for cattle, pigs, sheep or goats; or sell or keep a shop, store, stall or place for the sale of clothing, wines, spirits, beer or other alcoholic beverages, or any noxious drugs and poisons, proprietary or patent medicines, butcher's meat, poultry, game, fish, fruit, ice, vegetables or other foodstuffs, tobacco, lottery tickets or chances in lotteries, or hawk any goods; or keep for private or public use, or let ply or use for hire any launch, sampan, ferry or other boat, any horse, pony, mule or donkey, any motor car, motor bicycle, or other motor vehicle or, [sic] carriage, cart, handcart, ricsha [sic], sedan-chair, wheelbarrow or other vehicle or drive any tramcar, motor vehicle or horse drawn vehicle; or pull any ricsha or keep or have in his possession any dog, within such limits without a licence first obtained from the Council and in the case of foreigners countersigned by the Consul of the nationality to which such person belongs. In respect of such licenses the Council may impose such condi-

While prostitution as an institution was relatively unregulated, prostitutes as individuals encountered municipal authority in several types of situations. Streetwalkers or "pheasants" were apprehended daily for violating the municipal ordinance against soliciting.[13] The women were usually fined three to five yuan and released; they were detained only when they could not pay the fine.[14] The Mixed Court heard a dozen or more cases each year in which Chinese were accused of allowing children under sixteen in brothels; in such cases, the madams were usually fined several dozen yuan.[15] Sex workers of every rank, from courtesans to pheasants, could and did bring civil suits in the Mixed Court, which would grant them declarations of freedom.[16] Prostitutes who fled the brothels outright were picked up by the police and also taken to the Mixed Court, which frequently remanded them to a group of refuge homes collectively known as the Door of Hope.[17]

As World War I drew to a close, Shanghai prostitution became the subject of sustained public debate among foreigners and some of the Shanghai elite. The worldwide movement of troops during the war was

tions and exact such security as the nature of the particular case may require and charge such fees in respect therefore as may be authorized at the Annual General Meeting of Ratepayers. And any person offending against or infringing any provision of this Bye-law shall be liable for every offence to a fine not exceeding one hundred dollars and a further fine for every twenty-four hours' continuance of such offending or infringing not exceeding twenty-five dollars or to any such other penalty as shall be prescribed by the law to which such person is amenable."

Anatol M. Kotenev, *Shanghai: Its Mixed Court and Council* (Taipei: Ch'eng-wen, 1968; reprint of 1925 edition), p. 574. Clearly the council had to be highly selective in the application of this bylaw, and until the furor of 1920, brothels were not a high priority.

[13] The number of women charged reached a high of 1,234 in 1917, but from 1912 to 1924 was typically a half to a third of that number. Kotenev, *Shanghai: Its Mixed Court and Council,* p. 315.

[14] See, for example, *Shenbao,* March 14, 20, April 7, November 17 and 18, 1919, p. 11.

[15] Kotenev, *Shanghai: Its Mixed Court and Council,* p. 314; *Shenbao,* May 7, 1919, p. 11, and December 8, 1920, p. 11.

[16] Civil suits were apparently more common than criminal charges against brothel keepers, even though trafficking in women was against the law of the Republic of China. Prosecutions for trafficking heard in the Mixed Court dropped off sharply after 1917, for reasons not explained in the sources. Kotenev, *Shanghai: Its Mixed Court and Council,* pp. 295, 315–316. For one such case, see *Shenbao,* May 7, 1920, p. 11.

[17] Founded in 1900 by a group of foreign missionary women, by 1920 the Door of Hope homes—partially funded by the Municipal Council, depended upon by the police, and used by the Mixed Court—were regarded as "almost public institution[s]." C. E. Darwent, *Shanghai: A Handbook for Travellers and Residents* (Shanghai: Kelly and Walsh, 1920), p. 154. They provided a safe house, taught literacy and handicraft skills, and ultimately helped to arrange marriages for most inmates. For typical cases in which prostitutes were sent to the Door of Hope, see *Shenbao,* May 7, July 17, 1919, p. 11.

accompanied by the spread of venereal disease; this diffusion became a frequent subject of discussion in Chinese medical journals, as well as in what the *North-China Herald* called "newspapers and periodicals of the highest possible class."[18] Many of these articles explicitly linked venereal disease to prostitution.[19] In the International Settlement of Shanghai particularly, the menace of venereal disease was heightened by the visible expansion of prostitution: the number of brothels rose from 463 in 1871 to 633 in 1920, an increase of nearly a third, while the number of known prostitutes almost tripled, jumping from 1,612 to 4,575. Estimated figures for the French Concession pushed the totals still higher.[20]

The dual concern with increases in disease and commercialized sex dovetailed with the agenda of foreign Christians, many of them missionaries by profession, who were increasingly turning their attention to medical, educational, and industrial reform in China.[21] In 1916, Mary Ninde Gamewell published a heartfelt description of the nightly traffic in women that took place in teahouses along Nanjing and Fuzhou Roads:

> In and out among the square tables, filling the brilliantly lighted rooms, trail slowly little processions of young girls. Nearly all are pretty and very young. Clad in silk or satin, adorned with jewelry, their faces unnatural with paint and powder, they follow the lead of the woman in charge of each group. She stops often to draw attention ingratiatingly to her charges and expatiate on their good points. When one is chosen she leaves her to her fate and passes on to dispose of others. Multitudes of victims, innocent of any voluntary wrong, having been sold into this slavery when too young to resist and not uncommonly in babyhood, are kept up hour after hour in the close atmosphere of the tea-room awaiting the pleasure of their prospective seducers. Out on the street, by ricsha [sic] and on foot, women continue to hurry to the tea-houses with their living merchandise, and still they keep

---

[18] *North-China Herald*, November 3, 1917, 259; also see *China Medical Journal*, especially 1917–1930.

[19] It would be interesting to determine whether the actual incidence of venereal disease in Shanghai was increasing during this time or whether we are talking about a panic based on perceptions. Statistics in the *China Medical Journal*, 38:1 (January 1924), supplement, p. 19, on cases treated at the General Hospital, show no clear rise (1910–1914: 599 cases; 1915–1919: 507 cases; 1920–1922: 591 cases, which is an increase, but by 1920 the debate was already well under way). The same statistics show an actual decline in venereal disease cases as a percentage of all patients treated at the hospital between 1910–1914 and 1915–1919, and then a rise in the 1920–1922 period (7.5, 6.6, and 8.2 for the three periods respectively).

[20] Special Vice Committee, "Vice Conditions in Shanghai," pp. 83–84.

[21] For contemporary statements of their social agenda see, for example, Tyler Dennett, "New Codes for Old," *Asia*, August 1918, pp. 657–664; "Child Labour in China," *China Medical Journal* 38:11 (November 1924): 923–929.

arriving till the night is far advanced and business at a stand-still.[22]

Perhaps because of the religious impulse behind much social reform, the discussion of prostitution among the foreign community in Shanghai from the beginning had a moralistic tone. The Women's Christian Temperance Union in late 1916 appealed to the Shanghai Municipal Council to deal more forcefully with street solicitation. When the council demurred, saying that brothels were "as a rule restricted to definite areas," the *North-China Herald* asked sarcastically:

> For example, is the region of the Nanking Road all about the Town Hall "a definite area" such as ought to be tolerated? From an early hour in the evening immoral women appear quite openly in this part of our main street. There is an alleyway next door to the entrance to Louza police station which nightly sends forth a number of them,...If the community likes its daughters to push their way by these women in going to the Town Hall dances, there is no more to be said.[23]

Writing to the *North-China Herald* in 1917, a reader who signed him or herself "Pride's Purge" asserted that Shanghai had no right to call itself a model settlement as long as "palaces of vice and extravagance" continued to exist there. "What might give food to whole families in devastated countries or should have gone to the help of our defenders goes to help in swelling an immoral woman's revenue to enable her to have motor cars and bedeck her unfortunate carcase [sic] with jewels," s/he exclaimed.[24] Among many missionaries and female Christian activists, the moral argument was combined with an appeal for women's rights. The Reverend Isaac Mason, for instance, argued that "commercialized vice" should be abolished "to make women free, and give them a chance to choose their own moral path, and not be thrust down as slaves to men's lusts and harpies' greed, without any regard to their own wishes."[25] Miss Laura White, an activist in the Women's Christian Temperance Union, was quoted as saying that "the matter was such as to demand the attention of the whole of the women of Shanghai....[T]he women could handle the matter better than did the men."[26]

Chinese Christians who joined the public discussion on prostitution emphasized a different set of concerns, positing a connection between the habit of frequenting brothels and the weakness of China as a nation.

---

[22] Mary Ninde Gamewell, *The Gateway to China* (New York: Fleming H. Revell, 1916), p. 48.

[23] *North-China Herald,* December 16, 1916, p. 571.

[24] Ibid., September 8, 1917, pp. 557–558.

[25] Ibid., December 21, 1918, p. 748.

[26] Ibid., February 10, 1917, p. 284; for similar assertions by other women, see ibid., April 12, 1919, p. 101, and July 5, 1919, p. 49.

In a Chinese-language guide to Shanghai, which bore the didactic English subtitle "What the Chinese in Shanghai Ought to Know," Huang Renjing commented:

> Famous persons from all over the country go to brothels. They are the leaders of our people. When leaders are like this, one can imagine the situation among industrialists and businessmen.... The development of the West is due to the skill of the craftsmen and the diligence of the merchants. They are not like the degenerates of our country, who make use of brothels to reach their goal. I hope that our people will learn from the Westerners, not go to brothels, and forbid prostitution. It is possible to catch up with the Westerners. The reason they developed from barbarism to civilization at this speed is that most of them do not go to brothels. They have virtue; we Chinese should learn from them.[27]

Chinese Christians, like their secular May Fourth counterparts, linked prostitution to China's political vulnerability in the international arena. "The amount of money wasted in Shanghai on prostitution in half a year," observed one Chinese Christian acerbically, "is enough to redeem the railroads which have been mortgaged to the Japanese."[28]

Both foreign and Chinese Christian commentators located the ultimate cause of prostitution in individual moral weakness. Male and female sexual desire, economic need, and social custom were powerful but secondary factors; the problem could be solved if only all the parties involved could be guided to make correct moral choices. One Chinese Christian essayist argued that women became prostitutes not only because they were poor but because their parents, preferring money to virtue, were willing to sell them into prostitution. Traffickers preyed on women who were not only economically vulnerable, but morally deficient: "Anywhere there are weak, helpless, poor, stupid, or licentious women who might be caught, the agents of prostitution will be ready to go." Commercialized sex was facilitated by all those "local evil elements" who were willing to sacrifice their scruples for the sake of profits: traffickers and madams, certainly, but also "the landlords who ask a high price for the brothel's rent, the doctors who give prostitutes papers to prove that they are healthy, the lawyers who use clever arguments to defend the business, the pharmacy salesmen who sell forbidden drugs to prostitutes, the local officials and policemen who accept bribes, the tax collectors who have the right to reduce their tax, and some other institutions they deal with who are in charge of trade and transportation." In

---

[27] Huang Renjing, *Huren baojian* [Precious mirror of Shanghai; English title: *What the Chinese in Shanghai Ought to Know*] (Shanghai: Huamei shuju, 1913), pp. 134–135.

[28] *Chinese Recorder*, August 1920, pp. 579–580.

this analysis, men's patronage of brothels could not be explained by reference to ineluctable sexual desire; the essay cited French and American medical authorities who held that men could live perfectly well without sex. Therefore, prostitution could not be justified by arguing that it sacrificed a few women to protect womankind from uncontrollable male sexuality. In this rendering, prostitutes were both victims and morally deficient; customers went to the brothels because of their moral failings and ultimately became victims both of further moral decay and venereal disease.[29]

Non-Christian Chinese placed less emphasis on the primacy of morality, though they also criticized individual character flaws. An anonymous writer for the newspaper *Shenbao* attributed its development not to economic privation or to male lust, but to female vanity and the desire to move up the social ladder. He wrote:

> Colorful carriages, huge buildings, rich decorations and beautiful clothes—all these are admired by society, aren't they? A person from a common family or poor family doesn't even dream of having all these. But once she becomes a prostitute, she can enjoy them. If she is lucky, she can be promoted and compare with famous and rich ladies. People are amazed by her luxurious life. They don't ask where her money comes from. The prostitute is not shamed, but rather honored for this. When there is no other way to satisfy her vanity, what should she fear? Why shouldn't she become a prostitute? Then how can the numbers of prostitutes decrease? Therefore, I would say, it is not women's fault that they become prostitutes. The power to eliminate prostitution is in the hands of men. If prostitutes cannot get what they admire, the number of prostitutes will be fewer and fewer. This is not a matter of law, but rather is a problem we have made ourselves.[30]

Writing in the "mosquito newspaper" *Crystal* (which regaled the Chinese community with political and entertainment gossip and devoted close to an entire page of each issue to courtesans), another Chinese author took a more systemic approach, summarizing three common explanations for prostitution: that women lacked other employment opportunities, that prostitutes were victims of madams and male brothel keepers, and that prostitution was often a route up the social ladder, allowing a poor woman to become a wealthy concubine. Each of these explanations mandated a different solution: more jobs for women in the first case, abolition of madams in the second, and a lifelong ban on marriage for prostitutes in the third. Yet the author concluded that all three approaches shared a common theme; prostitution was a product of the

---

[29] *Shenbao*, May 19, 1919, p. 11.
[30] Ibid., April 9, 1919, p. 11.

social system, and any measure that tried to eliminate it without larger social change in the status of women was of necessity superficial.[31]

The largely foreign movement that emerged, however, opted for a narrowly focused approach to the problem. In May 1918, missionaries, doctors, and women activists representing seventeen philanthropic and religious organizations met to form the Committee on Moral Improvements, later known as the Shanghai Moral Welfare Committee and still later as the Moral Welfare League. The committee's express purpose was to investigate ways of eliminating prostitution in the International Settlement.[32]

The newly formed committee was soon at loggerheads with the Shanghai Municipal Council (SMC), criticizing its patchwork approach to control and remediation of prostitution. The Moral Welfare Committee opposed medical examination of prostitutes because it gave clients a false sense of security, encouraged vice, and involved the ratepayers in a system of approved prostitution. Furthermore, the committee criticized the fact that inspection was limited to prostitutes who serviced foreigners: "Are the Chinese of our community not worth taking equal care about...? We take equal care about the whole community with regard to other contagious diseases; why not with these...?"[33] The Moral Welfare Committee asked that the SMC remove the word "brothel" from the general licensing bylaw (Bylaw 34).[34] Supervision, argued the Committee, "implied official sanction,"[35] and government licensing of prostitution was "a positive hindrance to any progressive policy in the interests of the moral welfare of Shanghai."[36] The committee ridiculed the argument that if prostitution were eliminated in the Settlement it would just move elsewhere in Shanghai: "Strange that we do not hear the argument that it is no use trying to put down robberies in the Settlement, as they would still go on just over the borders; or that it is useless to practise hygiene on our side of the line as the other side is still insanitary!"[37] Finally, the committee accused the SMC of being willing "to leave conditions as they are, to cover things up and to preserve a prudery which ill-becomes the practical gentlemen who form the governing body of this Settlement."[38]

---

[31] *Jingbao,* March 27, 1920, p. 2.

[32] *North-China Herald,* May 25, 1918, p. 469, and December 14, 1918, p. 644; Wiley, "Chinese Prostitution," pp. 94–96.

[33] *North-China Herald,* December 21, 1918, p. 748.

[34] Ibid., April 5, 1919, p. 7; Kotenev, *Shanghai: Its Mixed Court and Council,* p. 574.

[35] *North-China Herald,* April 12, 1919, p. 114.

[36] Ibid., December 14, 1918, p. 645.

[37] Ibid., December 21, 1918, p. 748.

[38] Ibid., April 5, 1919, p. 7.

The SMC, for its part, opposed the Moral Welfare Committee's publicity campaign and defended Bylaw 34. It argued that the bylaw had "proved a means whereby such houses can be shepherded into certain areas and generally kept under better control than would otherwise be possible."[39] But the SMC's argument was weakened by the fact that licenses had never actually been granted to brothels under this bylaw.[40]

After a year of agitation by the Moral Welfare Committee, the Ratepayers' Meeting of 1919 voted to establish a committee to investigate "vice conditions" in the International Settlement.[41] The final report of this Special Vice Committee, submitted in March 1920, was considerably more moderate than the initial positions espoused by the Moral Welfare Committee. Although it advocated the ultimate elimination of brothels, it concluded that immediate suppression was impossible. Instead, it recommended that Bylaw 34 be strictly enforced so that every brothel had to obtain a municipal license. Licensing, however, would be an interim measure. Each license would be assigned a number, and every year one-fifth of the numbers would be selected at random and the licenses withdrawn. In that way, prostitution could be eliminated from the International Settlement within five years. During the five-year period, brothels were to be subject to a number of other restrictions: they had to submit to police and health inspections, they were forbidden to sell opium or alcohol, and they could not not allow their prostitutes to solicit customers. Every brothel would be required to exhibit the address of the nearest police station and of other places where prostitutes could get help and free medical assistance and to display a statement that no woman could be detained against her will. Medical examinations of prostitutes were to be discontinued. In addition, the Vice Committee recommended strengthening institutions like the Door of Hope.[42]

Modified though this report might be from the original agenda of the Moral Welfare Committee, it was still too radically interventionist for the municipal government. The SMC continued to favor regulation rather than elimination of brothels. Council members argued that if licenses were withdrawn from the brothels, they would just move outside the

---

[39] Ibid., December 14, 1918, p. 645.

[40] Ibid., April 5, 1919, p. 45.

[41] The Special Vice Committee (SVC), as it was called, had nine members: three appointed by the SMC, three by the Moral Welfare Committee, and three by the first six. In the course of its existence the Vice Committee held twenty-two meetings, examined twenty-five witnesses, consulted municipal records, and solicited Chinese views through the Chinese General Chamber of Commerce. Special Vice Committee, "Vice Conditions in Shanghai," p. 83.

[42] Ibid., pp. 84–86.

Settlement and beyond the reach of regulation; unlicensed brothels would proliferate in the Settlement and require more police to suppress them; and street soliciting would increase. Aside from this major caveat, though, the SMC endorsed many of the report's provisions and added a few of its own.[43]

Undaunted by the SMC opposition, the Special Vice Committee brought a resolution to accept the report before a Ratepayers' Meeting in April, where it passed over the objections of SMC members.[44] Once the resolution was carried, the SMC was obliged to carry it out, and in May 1920 it took steps to license brothels. Brothels of every rank, from courtesan establishments to houses for streetwalkers, were to go to the International Settlement's tax bureau to register and pay for their licenses. The police were placed in charge of ascertaining where the brothels were and how many prostitutes resided in each one.[45] Licensing fees were modest, one dollar per half-year. No licenses were to be issued to any brothel near a school, a provision that made several of the city's most eminent courtesan houses ineligible for licensing. If a brothel violated any of the stipulations in the Vice Committee report (solicitation, serving alcohol, etc.), its license could be revoked.[46] In any case, all licenses were to be withdrawn permanently within five years. Although it was a far stronger measure than that initially favored by the SMC, it remained a compromise resolution that fell short of a serious effort at abolition. It contented itself with gradually rendering commercial sex invisible by withdrawing brothel licenses, rather than undertaking a comprehensive campaign to eliminate trafficking, provide for displaced prostitutes, or penalize customers.

The abolition plan was supported by some sectors of the Chinese elite. Letters from individuals, from educational and student associations,

---

[43] For instance, it recommended that health officials take on increased responsibility for treatment of venereal disease, as well as for education and record keeping. It approved the idea of funding the Door of Hope and enforcing laws against soliciting, indecent advertisements, and sale of alcohol in unlicensed premises. As with prostitution itself, however, the SMC felt that licensing rather than prohibition was the practical approach to alcohol consumption in brothels. Finally, the SMC maintained that the medical examination of prostitutes should continue. *Municipal Gazette,* April 1, 1920, p. 124.

[44] Ibid., April 9, 1920, p. 164. Supporters of the SMC approach apparently were not well prepared for this meeting. Several years later, when debate over the policy broke out again, the *North-China Herald* would note that the vote was taken "when the room contained practically nobody but those who were for that vote, in defiance of the urgently expressed opinion of the Council." *North-China Herald,* August 26, 1922, p. 571.

[45] *Shenbao,* July 2, 1920, p. 11.

[46] *Municipal Gazette,* May 13, 1920, pp. 192–193; on ineligible courtesan houses, see *Shenbao,* July 2, 1920, p. 11.

and from Chinese Christian groups endorsed the findings of the Special
Vice Committee and called for an end to prostitution.[47] But those who
wrote for the city's burgeoning "mosquito" press were more critical.
One essayist in the *Crystal* wryly observed that in abolishing licensed
prostitution, municipal authorities were limiting their own revenues in
what amounted to an act of social charity. But the writer implied that
this self-sacrificing act would be wasted if social relief was not provided
for the unemployed prostitutes. They certainly did not want to become
industrial workers or peasants, he noted in a revealing commentary on
social hierarchy. Though they would be happy to become concubines,
new social conventions called for monogamy.[48] Another *Crystal* commentator noted that banning prostitutes without banning customers amounted
to abolishing selling while continuing to permit buying. It was the opposite of the Chinese campaign to boycott Japanese goods, in which buying
was to be eliminated. The provisions of the law reflected the fact that
men had power relative to women, just as Japan did relative to China.
Thus it was impossible to ban whoring (*piao*) in the one case and sale of
Japanese goods in the other.[49]

As the licensing regulations began to take effect, another reaction
emerged among Chinese residents of Shanghai: panic in the commercial
sector of the population that made its living providing services to upper-
class brothels. A group of shopkeepers wrote to the Chinese General
Chamber of Commerce, arguing "that 1st class brothels serve as places of
meeting and entertainment of prominent merchants and gentry, these
houses are very different from the 2nd and/or low class bawdy houses,
and that 1st class brothels have a great deal to do in the matter of promoting the prosperity and development of local commerce." If these
brothels were closed, argued the merchants, "the writers [of the note]
[would] suffer greatly." They asked that licensing of first-class brothels be
canceled and some other measures be adopted instead. The Chinese
General Chamber of Commerce forwarded their letter to the SMC with

---

[47] One such letter, signed by ten individuals, commented: "We view with alarm the
unprecedented growth of prostitution within the foreign settlement during the last few
years, and believe that stringent action should at once be taken in order to check it." A
similar letter was signed by the Kiangsu (Jiangsu) Education Association, the Shanghai Education Association, the National Vocational Education Association, the Overseas Chinese Association, the Western Returned Students' Union of Shanghai, the World's Chinese Students' Federation, and the Shanghai Chinese YMCA. *North-China Herald,* April 10, 1920,
p. 85.

[48] In the future, mused the author, when concubinage was abolished, perhaps prostitutes
would become "common wives" (*gong qi*) under socialism. *Jingbao,* March 27, 1920, p. 2.

[49] Ibid., June 15, 1920, p. 2.

an endorsement.[50]

At the same time, the sing-song girls or *shuyu* joined the chorus of opposition to licensing. Though they did not approach the SMC directly, they apparently asked a local French resident, J. E. Lemière, to speak on their behalf. Sing-song girls, explained Lemière in a June 23 missive to the SMC, were not prostitutes: "The singing girls are really artists; they earn their living by entertaining guests, receiving a regular fee for each attendance. They may be likened to actresses.... [T]hey never considered themselves to be prostitutes and as a matter of fact a great number never departed from the path of morality." Like the Chinese merchants, Lemière made a strong case for the commercial importance of the sing-song houses and their connections to the larger urban economy:

> [I]t is customary for the Chinese of the best classes to meet daily in those houses of entertainment, where they receive their friends and discuss business matters. To oblige the singing girls to register as prostitutes, to oblige a house of entertainment to register as a house of prostitution, will compel both of them either to close their houses in this settlement or emigrate somewhere else, a measure which will not only cause strong disaffection amongst the best Chinese classes, but will also cause a lot of shop-keepers, like tailors, shoe-makers, embroiderers, Jewellers [sic], piece good retailers, musical instrument merchants, restaurant keepers, etc., to follow those girls where they will decide to fix their new abode, thus causing a very serious loss to the Revenue Department and it appears to me that both loss of revenue and the annoyance caused to the Chinese Ratepayers can be and ought to be avoided.[51]

To these commercial cries of distress, the SMC could only reply that the resolution adopted by the Ratepayers' Meeting obliged them to license all brothels. The council did leave a loophole, however: sing-song houses that did not operate as brothels would not be required to conform to the regulations.[52] Here legal necessity reinforced tradition in forcing the *shuyu* to downplay the sale of their sexual services.

The licensing procedure generated a new set of encounters between brothels and the police. A detective team of one Chinese and one Westerner patrolled the brothels to make sure that each had obtained a license and was displaying it prominently. Unlicensed operators were taken to the Mixed Court, where they could be fined as much as 50 yuan or jailed for six weeks; those who failed to display their licenses were assessed smaller penalties. Since licenses were supposed to be

[50] *Municipal Gazette,* July 8, 1920, p. 259.
[51] Ibid., July 8, 1920, pp. 259–260.
[52] Ibid., July 8, 1920, p. 260.

nontransferable, owners who obtained them improperly were fined and had their licenses revoked. Brothel owners who employed unlicensed prostitutes were penalized, as were the individual women. Violations of multiple regulations sometimes led to jail sentences for owners of as long as one year. Frightened, some brothel owners took pains to conceal evidence of license violations, such as keeping young girls or opium implements on the premises.[53] Others moved their establishments to the French Concession or to the Zhabei district in the Chinese territory, where they made it known to municipal authorities that they were willing to pay taxes if allowed to operate.[54] Individual prostitutes whose houses had been closed developed their own subterfuges, as a Chinese guide to the brothels explained in 1922:

> Even though there is only one name on the sign [outside a brothel], inside there is not just one prostitute. Those whose licenses have been drawn still operate, writing their names on a piece of red paper which is stuck on the door at dusk so that seekers can find it. It is taken down during the night and put up again the next day. Also, guests do not stay in the brothel; instead they rent a room. So although the police strictly inspect, they cannot easily discover the secret.[55]

In December 1920, after the brothels had been duly licensed, their phased closing began with the first drawing of licenses. The brothels whose numbers were drawn, 174 in all, were required to close their doors by the end of March 1921.[56] Similar drawings took place every year until 1923.[57] In April 1924, it was announced that the remainder of licensed brothels were to be closed on December 31, 1924.[58]

The advocates of suppression thus triumphed, but the controversy did not end there. The Moral Welfare Committee continued to act as a self-appointed watchdog over the implementation of the resolution[59] and to quarrel publicly with the formulations of the SMC about the success of the new policy. In the Municipal Report for 1921, for instance, the

---

[53] *Shenbao*, October 4, 8, 30; November 19, 24; December 12, 13, 1920, p. 11.

[54] On the French Concession see *Shenbao*, July 2, 1920, p. 11; and Wang Liaoweng, *Shanghai liushinian huajie shi* [A sixty-year history of the Shanghai flower world] (Shanghai: Shixin shuju, 1922), p. 13; on Zhabei, see *Jingbao*, March 27, 1920, p. 2.

[55] Wang Liaoweng, *Shanghai liushinian huajie shi*, p. 214.

[56] *Municipal Gazette*, December 23, 1920, p. 434. The drawing, commented the *North-China Herald*, was accomplished with only one slight hitch: "After three numbers had been drawn, something went wrong with the drum, and instead of the fourth number tinkling into the receiver, the whole 881 tumbled out. The only thing to be done...was to begin the draw de novo." *North-China Herald*, December 25, 1920, p. 876.

[57] *Municipal Gazette*, December 15, 1921, p. 407; December 13, 1923, p. 435.

[58] Ibid., April 3, 1924, p. 138.

[59] See, for example, *North-China Herald*, March 26, 1921, pp. 813–814.

Commissioner of Police stated that the SMC's predictions about the failure of the policy had become fact: "[W]hile 218 brothels have been closed officially, prostitution and its attendant evils have in no way decreased, but have merely spread over a much wider area with the consequent impossibility of any effective police control." When questioned by an indignant Frank Rawlinson of the Moral Welfare League, an SMC official wearily replied that "police reports show that while brothels officially closed, remain closed, it is nevertheless a fact that the former occupants, having no other means of earning a living, continue a life of prostitution in private houses, where they are in no sense subject to police control." He added that police were unable to prevent prostitution, since "prostitution is not an offence under the national laws having jurisdiction over the concerned." True, police had given the ratepayers what they wanted; licensed brothels were being gradually suppressed. But, he added, police control of brothels consisted only in their ability to enforce the license conditions. "The fewer the licenses, therefore, the less control there must be of prostitution and its attendant evils."[60]

This exchange was the beginning of another acrimonious round of public debate. After repeated inquiries by Rawlinson as to what the police were doing to enforce a rigorous policy of suppression, an SMC official finally chided him publicly. Police could not take action against unlicensed prostitutes, he said, unless they were practicing in an unlicensed brothel, since prostitution itself was not illegal. "Much as the Council is in sympathy with the aims of your League, as with every other effort to promote the moral welfare of the Settlement," he continued testily,

> it is of opinion [sic] that, easy as it is for the Moral Welfare League and others to advocate a more rigorous policy of suppression, it is in fact practically impossible to do more than is being done at present. That your League should hold a contrary view and consider more effective suppression possible, can, in the Council's opinion, be only attributed to your League's refusal to face the real facts of the case, and to the apparent confusion existing in the minds of its members regarding brothel-keeping, which, if not under license, is an offense under a Municipal By-law, as distinguished from prostitution, which is no offence.[61]

Angry letters continued throughout the summer of 1922, with some citizens expressing approval of the Moral Welfare League's approach to prostitution and others criticizing its inadequacies. The *North-China Herald* was generally unsympathetic to the methods of the league, if not

[60] *Municipal Gazette,* April 13, 1922, p. 120.
[61] Ibid., June 22, 1922, p. 223.

its aims. In August it commented:

> [W]hat end can Dr. Rawlinson hope to achieve by shutting up the houses and driving their inmates over the borders of the Settlement?... [I]t must be remembered that Shanghai is a town chiefly filled by Asiatics whose view of these questions is quite different to [sic] ours, with the further complication of a large influx of unhappy Russian girls, who have but the one alternative to starvation.... [A] very comprehensive, liberal and merciful scheme of rescue work would seem indispensable before we set the terrors of the law in motion against them.[62]

In another editorial it added that the league approach, in addition to being narrow and inhumane, was ineffective: "[T]he plain fact of the matter is that the women are to be found in all sorts of streets where they were previously unknown.... So far from these women being made more inaccessible, they are more easily found than before. There is the less distance to go to find them from any residential district."[63]

Although some members of the league began to express doubts about the policy's effectiveness, the leadership of the league continued to defend its approach and to dispute the assumption underlying much of the criticism: that prostitution was a necessary evil, bolstered by economic necessity and male desire. When one *North-China Herald* reporter argued as much, Isaac Mason retorted:

> Does your correspondent really believe that a large number of girls are of necessity doomed by a beneficent God to be sacrificed to the ungoverned lust of men in return for money to maintain an existence? That such girls, through no fault of their own, are born into a wheel of fate, and their sacrifice is necessary because of men's desire?...And if such a thing is thinkable, how are these girls—this maiden tribute—to be provided?... To call passion an "unconquerable" physical requirement is to forget the great numbers of both men and women who daily conquer, and who live chaste lives; such language only serves to encourage those who are glad of an excuse to take the easier path.... These diseases are the consequence of wrong-doing, and are not to be charged to those who wish to preserve a moral conscience and the decencies of civilization.[64]

Impassioned as Mason's rhetoric on this subject was, it paled beside that of one of his supporters, who wrote from the upriver town of Jiujiang:

> For good and righteous cause did the Creator put the barbed wire of abominable disease around the whole neighborhood of sexual crime, and so firmly secure it there that no device of regulation, registration, inspection, or medical treatment can pull out the stakes, and secure immunity to the

---

[62] *North-China Herald,* August 26, 1922, p. 571.

[63] Ibid., p. 574.

[64] Ibid., January 6, 1923, pp. 32–33.

trespasser. . . .

The averment of your correspondent that prostitution is a necessary evil is a public insult to all decent men and women; and men who practise it are a shame and a stinking cancer on the British name in the East. The dogma is pestilential, and ought to be stamped out like the plague.[65]

In spite of the fervent sentiments of these gentlemen, prostitution, both licensed and unlicensed, persisted long after its official demise. Chinese-language guidebooks and memoirs confirm that, just as the critics had predicted, many brothels moved to the French Concession.[66] In the International Settlement, the government declared an end to brothels when the last licenses were withdrawn in 1924—but collected vastly increased revenues from licensing fees in a new category, "sing-song houses."[67] Arrests for street soliciting varied from year to year, but showed no pattern of decrease after 1920. (Nor was there a massive increase, as some critics had predicted.) And to these arrests of individual prostitutes were added the cases of brothels that failed to obtain licenses or continued to operate after they were withdrawn.[68]

Though the league and the licensing controversy eventually faded from view, later observers judged the league approach ineffective in either controlling venereal disease or eliminating prostitution. In 1923,

[65] Ibid., January 13, 1923, p. 103.

[66] Hu Jifan, *Shanghai xiaozhi* [Small records of Shanghai] (Shanghai: Chuanjing tang shudian, 1930), juan 8, n.p.

[67] Licensing fees for 1920–1926 were as follows:

Year	No. of licenses	Amount (taels)
1920		1,281
1921		977
1922		634
1923	547	392.64
1924	283	201.02
1925	3,744	27,029.04
1926	4,717	33,700.46

Through 1924 these were known as brothel licensing fees, after 1924 as sing-song house licensing fees. *Shanghai Municipal Council Report and Budget, 1925* (Shanghai: Kelly and Walsh, 1926), pp. 43A–44A; ibid., 1926, p. 412.

[68] The figures for the two types of cases heard by the Mixed Court were:

Year	Brothels charged	Prostitutes charged
1920	103	246
1921	296	452
1922	181	377
1923	89	672
1924	154	398

Kotenev, *Shanghai: Its Mixed Court and Council,* pp. 315–316.

the Shanghai Medical Society urged that venereal disease be approached primarily as a public health problem. Although they preferred regulated districts to "indiscriminate promiscuity," a survey of the local situation convinced them that regulation had failed and that "no appreciable good would be got by a superintendence of prostitution even with a much larger and more expensive organization than heretofore, particularly as the local circumstances are entirely unfavourable for success." A comprehensive approach to prostitution, they asserted, would have to involve preventive and rescue work, improvement of employment opportunities and working conditions for women, and efforts to make prostitution less profitable. Furthermore, the physicians were intent on establishing the authority of the medical profession over the control of venereal disease. This meant not only that unorthodox medical treatments by "chemists," "quacks," and "nostrums" should be prohibited, but also that government officials should remove themselves from involvement: "[t]he medical profession and not the administration authorities should be in charge of general prophylaxis." In short, the doctors argued that it was high time to delink the issues of public health and public morality and to redefine venereal disease as a problem best left to one set of professionals—themselves.[69] (Predictably, the activists of the Moral Welfare League were unconvinced of the superiority of this approach. Where Jesus said "Go, and sin no more," commented Isaac Mason, "the voice of today seem [sic] disposed to say 'go, and be more hygienic next time, and patronize a well-conducted place'.")[70]

A more blunt critique of the license-and-eliminate scheme was proffered by A. Hilton Johnson, Deputy Commissioner of Police. "Brothels in the strictly legal sense" were fast disappearing, he said, "[b]ut if the aim of the Council was the abolition of *prostitutes* or the suppression of *prostitution* or the improvement of *public morality,* then, of course, the measures adopted by them at the instance of the Rate-payers have been a failure." Twenty of his senior police officers reported that prostitution had spread out of the former brothel districts over a wider area of the International Settlement. Solicitation in public parks and amusement places had greatly increased, with former "crudely aggressive tactics" replaced by "the 'glad-eye' method of attraction." Hotels, lodging houses, and secret houses of assignation had largely replaced the brothels, while "chauffeurs, ricksha coolies, hotel boys, lodging house employes [sic], professional pimps and others" now enjoyed the profits formerly collected by brothel keepers. From a police point of view, he concluded,

---

[69] *China Medical Journal,* 38:1 (January 1924), supplement, pp. 16–17, 26–29.

[70] *North-China Herald,* February 2, 1924, p. 179.

conditions were both better and worse: better because the decline of brothel districts meant less "street rowdyism," worse because no brothels meant the disappearance of news centers where police could get information.[71]

Foreign residents of Shanghai added their voices to the chorus of criticism, noting that the demise of the brothels and the increase in unlicensed prostitution presented both police and citizens with a problem. One letter to the *North-China Herald* complained, "The serio-comical situation in the International Settlement of Shanghai to-day is that prostitution cannot be driven from the streets, because the police are afraid of making a mistake and insulting a decent woman, while decent women avoid being out after dark fearing to be taken for prostitutes."[72] Continuing the rhetorical linkage of prostitution with dirt, another dissatisfied writer declared about the league, "[T]he moral turpitude that was confined and so more under control, has been by their efforts, released from control, and now pollutes the atmosphere. They have done their sweeping with a dirty broom where they should have used the latest scientific method, a suction sweeper."[73] A third writer accused the league of "trying to drain a ditch with a sieve," while a Chinese observer preferred a metaphor rooted in local geography, saying that the league's chances of success were "equal to that of anyone who might try to mop up the Huangpu river with a bath sponge."[74]

In his 1931 report on Shanghai municipal governance prepared for the SMC, South African jurist R. C. Feetham noted that he had "received communications from Chinese correspondents referring in strong terms to the prevalence of prostitution in the Settlement, and to the evils resulting therefrom, and complaining of the failure of the Police to take any effective action to deal with this problem." After reviewing the history of licensing and the withdrawal of all licenses by 1925, he commented:

> But the plan did not prove effective for the purpose of eliminating brothels, or restricting prostitution. The problem as to how to secure effective control of an evil which cannot be eliminated remains unsolved, and, under the law as it at present stands, the decision against continuance of any licensing system has imposed on the police an extremely difficult task. Police efforts are at present limited to taking measures to confine prostitutes within certain areas, and to keeping some check on soliciting in the streets. Special demands made on the Police in recent years by the general crime situation

[71] *Municipal Gazette,* March 6, 1924, pp. 92–93.
[72] *North-China Herald,* February 9, 1924, p. 218.
[73] Ibid., October 18, 1924, p. 115.
[74] Ibid., January 19, 1924, p. 98, and October 20, 1923, p. 187.

have, however, made it difficult for the Commissioner to spare sufficient men for such work.[75]

Chinese critics, more openly nationalistic and vocal than a decade before, and now committed to the elimination of prostitution, assumed that Settlement authorities were indifferent to the welfare of the Chinese population. Feetham concluded, however, that the law and the absence of a licensing system left the Settlement government no effective means of coping with the problem. Yet by the late 1930s, a veteran of the police force, looking back at the 1920s campaign, concluded that while it had been a mistake to abandon licensing, it was no longer practical to restore it, "for prostitution has increased to such an extent that it is no longer a question of unlicensed brothels, but rather of a deliberate commercial enterprise."[76] The proliferation of ancillary occupations such as masseuses, tour guides, and tea hostesses made regulation seem virtually impossible.[77]

Perhaps the most telling, and openly sardonic, commentary on the failure of the campaign came from a Chinese-authored guide to Shanghai slang published in 1935. Explaining the local term "to open a room," which meant to invite a prostitute to come to one's room at a hotel, author Wang Zhongxian noted that the custom had begun during the 1920s elimination campaign. In Wang's rendition, after several years of the ban on prostitution, the Settlement government realized that the policy was a failure and once again permitted brothels to operate. But to save face the government instituted two requirements: the brothels had to be renamed "sing-song houses" and guests were not permitted to stay overnight. (The attempt to exempt courtesans from licensing, so earnestly argued by Lemière and others in the 1920s, appeared to this author as just so much manipulation of names to disguise the resumption of business as usual.) The police had assiduously enforced the provision against overnight guests, Wang continued, capturing many "mandarin ducks" (a popular term for lovers). Hence the custom of summoning a prostitute off-premises to enjoy a night of social and sexual activity. Wang concluded:

> Brothels don't permit men and women to stay together, yet in a hotel one can "truly melt the soul" [a term generally used in guidebook literature to refer to sexual intercourse]. This is truly contradictory to the point of being

---

[75] R. C. Feetham, *Report to the Shanghai Municipal Council,* vol. 2 (Shanghai: North China Daily News and Herald, 1931), pp. 89–90.

[76] E. W. Peters (ed. Hugh Barnes), *Shanghai Policeman* (London: Rich and Cowan, 1937), p. 204.

[77] See Hershatter, "Hierarchy of Shanghai Prostitution," passim.

funny. Things that happen in the concessions are all according to foreign rationality. They cannot be explained using a Chinese mind. If the mode of organization were not special, it would not be a "Special Municipality" worthy of the name.[78]

Ultimately, this campaign to end prostitution, like every other campaign until 1949, fell victim to a combination of factors: a weak municipal government with limited jurisdiction, a refusal to acknowledge the many vested interests that benefited from prostitution, and an inability to develop a comprehensive welfare program that could address the social causes of prostitution. In addition, the 1920s campaign in particular was hampered by divisions in the foreign community over the most effective and the most moral strategy to pursue. While the debate generated a great deal of heat in the foreign press, its effect on the Chinese prostitute population and their clientele was minimal. And in spite of the Moral Welfare League's expressed concern about the status of women, the campaign certainly did nothing to increase the degree of control that Shanghai prostitutes exercised over their own lives. In fact, Chinese prostitutes remained virtually invisible in the reform discourse of the 1920s; the debate was not really about them, but about the intersection of "commercialized vice" and colonial "uncleanliness" that so threatened Victorians abroad.

Abolition: The 1950s Campaign

Preparation

Even before Cao Manzhi entered Shanghai with the People's Liberation Army, he knew that eliminating prostitution was one of the tasks that awaited him as head of the Civil Administration Department (Minzheng ju).[79] He had first encountered prostitutes seventeen years earlier,

---

[78] Wang Zhongxian, *Shanghai suyu tushuo* [An illustrated dictionary of Shanghai slang] (Hongkong: Shenzhou tushu gongsi, n.d.; reprint of Shanghai: Shanghai shehui chubanshe, 1935), pp. 28–29.

[79] Cao Manzhi was vice-chair of the political takeover committee of the Shanghai military management group (Shanghai junguan hui zhengwu jieguanhui fuzhuren), vice-secretary of the people's government, and head of the Civil Administration Department. He was primarily responsible for the 1950s reform campaign, from taking in (*shourong*) prostitutes to curing their venereal disease to providing job training. He calls the reform of prostitutes "the most complex and difficult" of the problems involved in the takeover of Shanghai. Cao Manzhi, "Introduction," in Yang Jiezeng and He Wannan, eds., *Shanghai changji gaizao shihua* [A history of the reform of Shanghai prostitutes] (Shanghai: Shanghai sanlian shudian, 1988), pp. 1–2. Unless otherwise noted, all subsequent references to Cao Manzhi's activities are based on interviews with him conducted in Shanghai, November 10 and 20, 1986.

as a young county secretary in the underground Party organization in Shandong. There he saw madams and prostitutes going to the Commerce Bureau (Gongshangju); he watched coastal families supplement their incomes by sending their wives and daughters aboard ships in port to sell sex to the sailors. Born in the 1910s, Cao was of the generation that grew up in the wake of the May Fourth movement, and he had been moved by May Fourth writings on the oppression of women in Chinese society. But it was the Chinese Communist Party (CCP) that decisively shaped his understanding of the nature of prostitution. He read Clara Zetkin's account of her conversation with Lenin; as he recalls it, Zetkin wanted to start a magazine about how to liberate prostitutes, but Lenin admonished her that prostitutes could not be liberated unless the world proletariat was liberated. For Cao, too, prostitution was inseparable from the larger social context of feudalism and imperialism. If ordinary women were oppressed by the social system, prostitutes were ruined (*cuican*) by it. "That is to say," he recalled in a 1986 interview,

> in terms of social relationships, prostitutes suffered the greatest pain.... Prostitutes suffered ruination not only from the harmful social relationships in China, but also from the ruination of imperialism, which was quite widespread. The ruination of imperialism was more brutal and cruel than [that caused by domestic Chinese factors].... If China had been a strong nation, if its people had been a people with high international standing, if we had not suffered the invasion of foreign power, then our women would not have suffered such great ruination.... The CCP made the liberation of prostitutes an important part of liberating women.

Since 1938, Cao had been involved in several campaigns to eliminate prostitution in Shandong, and he knew that prostitution in Shanghai could not be effectively banned until the urban social environment was decisively altered. This meant, among other things, that the power of the Qing Bang (Green Gang) and the Hong Bang (Red Gang), two gangs whose members ran many of the larger brothels, had to be broken.[80] It also meant that if the government forbade prostitutes to practice their trade, it had to be able to offer them an alternate means of support. So for almost two years after the city was taken over, Cao bided his time:

> When we had just entered Shanghai, we were not prepared. If we had

---

[80] The connection of Qing and Hong Bang members to the brothels is indisputable, but many of the details remain murky. Huang Jinrong, who was closely associated with both groups, reputedly "either protected or controlled all of the opium *hongs*, gambling joints, and brothels in the French Concession." See Brian G. Martin's chapter in this volume. For the brothel-related activities of other gang members, see Zhu Xuefan, *Jiu Shanghaide banghui* [The gangs of old Shanghai] (Shanghai: Shanghai renmin chubanshe, 1986), pp. 67, 98, 177–180, 209, 272, 343, 348, 353.

abolished [prostitution] immediately, how would we have fed them? Where would we have sent them? They had no homes to return to. So we had to harden our hearts. After Liberation, prostitutes were still on the street, so our cadres didn't like it, and the democratic parties didn't like it. They felt that in Shanghai, liberated by the CCP, women who had been ruthlessly and forcibly ruined should not be allowed to continue to suffer. At the time there was really nothing we could do. If you are going to use force, first of all you have to have a place to put her, a place for her to eat, and next you must prepare to treat her illnesses. And our methods for treating illness, our medicines, all had to be prepared in advance. We also had to prepare a group of cadres, but the number of cadres I had brought in was extremely limited. I had to take over all of Shanghai—the city government, the courts, the jails, the police stations, the GMD Administration Bureau (Xing-zheng yuan), all the administrative bodies of Shanghai. My organization took over altogether more than five hundred units, but I was given only twenty-eight cadres. How could we do everything? The PSB [Public Security Bureau] had brought in even fewer cadres than I, yet they had to take charge of every aspect of public order....So, we were very sad. At the time, when I lay down to sleep, some cadres criticized me: why do you still permit prostitution? Why doesn't the leadership solve the prostitution problem quickly? Why not arrest the hoodlums? Why not solve the problem of prostitution? I said, "You sleep well, right? I haven't been to sleep yet. Will you give me a building? I don't have a building yet, how I am going to take them in? If I take them in, for sure there will be nothing to eat on that day. Shall we make prostitutes into beggars on the street? What kind of policy is that?" So for a time we permitted them to continue, but it was because we had to, and absolutely not because we wanted to. We hardened our hearts and got through that period, and later took them in.

During the two years before the reform campaign began, the Public Security Bureau continued to license brothels and prostitutes, just as the Guomindang had done in the late 1940s. Yet the number of people involved in the trade shrank for several reasons. New government regulations in August 1949 put severe restrictions on the freedom of brothel owners to run their business. Brothels were forbidden to entertain government employees or minors, sell drugs or permit gambling, host large banquets, arrange assignations between prostitutes and clients outside the brothel walls, allow sick prostitutes to work, or force any woman to have sexual relations or remain in the brothel against her will. The newspapers publicized the fact that a prostitute could bring charges against any owner who tried to prevent her departure or marriage or who tried to charge her fees or keep her personal possessions.[81] If brothel owners still had any doubt that the environment was becoming

---

[81] Yang Jiezeng and He Wannan, *Shanghai changji gaizao shihua,* pp. 28–30.

inhospitable to prostitution, they could look to the fate of their compatriots in other cities: between 1947 and 1951, prostitution was successfully banned in Shijiazhuang, Jilin, Beijing, Tianjin, Nanjing, Suzhou, Yangzhou, Zhenjiang, and Hangzhou.

In response to these measures, many Shanghai brothel owners closed their establishments. Some of the biggest gang-connected operators, dubbed "brothel tyrants" in the press, fled the country at Liberation; others were arrested and executed in the April 1951 campaign to suppress counterrevolutionaries.[82] At the same time, women returned to their home districts as the rural economy began to recover from civil war, or found other jobs in Shanghai. In mid-1950, the newspaper *Dagongbao* reported that the number of licensed prostitutes in the city had declined from 1,897 (in early 1949) to 662 and the number of brothels from 518 to 158.[83] By November 1951, the numbers were down to 180 licensed prostitutes in 72 brothels.[84] Of course, licensed prostitutes were only a fraction of the women who sold sexual services, and they continued to be outnumbered by their clandestine sisters, the "secret" prostitutes (*anchang*). Nevertheless, by late 1951 the city government faced a much reduced prostitute population when it finally turned its attention to closing the brothels and clearing the streets.

On November 13, 1951, police gave brothel owners one last chance to go out of business without facing criminal sanctions. The Public Security Bureau called together owners of the city's remaining brothels and informed them that they were to close their establishments and personally arrange other means of support for their employees. Most owners ignored this order, and a week later the police held a meeting with licensed prostitutes and told them that the brothels would soon be closed down. Public Security officials then decided to go to the city government for a formal decision to close the brothels, which was issued on November 23.[85]

Even before police in the busy central districts of Shanghai began preparations to arrest the owners and take in the prostitutes, across town another drama was unfolding. In early November, women who were employed as teachers, social workers, or staff of the Women's Federation were quietly taken aside by their supervisors and told to report to a large building complex at 418 Tongzhou Road, in the Tilan qiao district. They were selected for having completed high school or college and for

---

[82] *Jiefang ribao* (Shanghai), November 23, 1951.

[83] *Dagongbao* (Shanghai), June 11, 1950, p. 4.

[84] *Jiefang ribao*, November 23, 1951.

[85] Ibid.; *Dagongbao*, November 27, 1951, p. 1.

experience working with people. But when they learned that the building was to be a labor and education center for former prostitutes and that their new job would be to reform these women, some of them resisted the assignment. Recalls Yang Xiuqin,

> I didn't want to go. I was only eighteen, and I felt that I couldn't do this work. At that time everyone had the impression that prostitutes were low-class people, prostitution was a low-class business, and asking us to have contact with those people wasn't easy to accept, so I didn't want to go. I cried. I sat on the stairs and cried. After that the leaders talked to me quite a bit. They said, "These people have also been oppressed. They didn't want to do it [become prostitutes]. After Liberation our New China does not permit the existence of the system of prostitution. The work we are going to do has not been done by anyone before, and is of far-reaching significance." They talked reason to me, persuaded me, so in the end I went.[86]

The reluctant recruits, who numbered more than fifty, were given three weeks of training. During this period they were not allowed to return home, write letters, or make phone calls, because the government did not want the timing of its planned raid on the brothels compromised.[87]

The classes, taught by a staff member of the Civil Administration Department, focused on what the government saw as the dual nature of prostitutes. On the one hand, they had been cruelly treated, and deserved the sympathy of the reformers:

> They themselves didn't want to engage in prostitution. They had suffered and been oppressed. We cadres were first of all to sympathize with them, and second to be warm to them, because they had not felt warmth. They had no parents, had left their own families, and they had a madam supervising them. They called her "mama," and the only others in their lives were customers. These were all economic relationships, without human warmth. So we wanted to show them some human warmth. We were not to use hitting or cursing as methods of reform, but rather were to try to persuade and educate them, to raise their consciousness.[88]

On the other hand, the reformers-in-training were told, prostitutes dwelled in a social environment that encouraged them to be parasites, and one purpose of reform was to ensure that they broke with their old habits:

> Because many of them had been in the brothels for many years, leading a life of luxury, or as we call it profiting by the labor of others (*bulao erhuo*), leading a life of debauchery (*huatian jiudi*). If you suddenly asked them to

---

[86] Yang Xiuqin and Xu Huiqing, personal interview, Shanghai, November 11, 1986.

[87] Ibid.; Yang Jiezeng and He Wannan, *Shanghai changji gaizao shihua*, pp. 34–36.

[88] Yang Xiuqin and Xu Huiqing, personal interview, Shanghai, November 11, 1986.

labor, they wouldn't be accustomed to it. We were to educate them to
labor, to live by the labor of their own hands, not to rely on prostitution.[89]

The program of reform was to address both sides of the prostitute's character, using three methods: education in everything from literacy to class
consciousness, cure of venereal and other diseases, and training in working habits and skills.[90] The work would be conducted at the Tongzhou
Road complex, which was formally dubbed the Women's Labor Training
Institute (Funü laodong jiaoyangsuo).

Between 8 P.M. on November 25 and 10 A.M. the next morning, police
moved swiftly to arrest brothel owners, round up prostitutes, and seal the
doors of the brothels. In all, 324 owners were arrested and subsequently
sentenced either to prison or to labor reform. Strictly separated from
them, and remanded by the police to the Women's Labor Training Institute, were 181 licensed prostitutes and 320 streetwalkers.[91]

The Subjects of Reform: Competing Discourses

When the prostitutes, transported by police trucks, arrived at the
main gate of the Women's Labor Training Institute, the staff was lined up
to welcome them. For the inexperienced reformers, their first sight of
prostitutes en masse was a shock:

> We had never seen prostitutes before and we always thought that prostitutes
> must be very beautiful—either their faces, or their makeup, or their clothes
> must be good-looking. But after they arrived, we saw that they were not
> good-looking at all. Because the day that they came they were not working.
> They had their bedrolls with them, and their luggage all packed up. Many
> were wearing no makeup. Others had been crying and their powder was
> smudged and not good-looking.... They seemed even less attractive than
> ordinary people.[92]

Why were the women so bedraggled and depressed? Newspaper articles written at the time of the roundup give no clues. According to the
accounts prepared for public consumption—stories that quickly became
the official mythology of reform—prostitutes had been brutally mis-
treated in their working lives. Virtually every account cited the grinding
poverty of their family of origin, the kidnap and forced sale of many
women into prostitution, the sadistic behavior of brothel owners and
madams, and the mistreatment and even murder of prostitutes who

---

[89] Ibid.
[90] Huang Shi, Shanghai Public Security Bureau, personal interview, November 15, 1986.
[91] *Xinwen ribao* (Shanghai), November 27, 1951, p. 1; *Jiefang ribao*, November 27,
1951, p. 1; *Dagongbao*, November 27, 1951, p. 1.
[92] Yang Xiuqin and Xu Huiqing, personal interview, Shanghai, November 11, 1986.

became too ill to work.[93] The women were portrayed as being acutely conscious of their oppression and its causes, and desperate for liberation. Reports published the day after the roundup virtually all cited the reactions of two prostitutes, Wu Caifeng and Wang Acai, who had made impromptu speeches in the police station while awaiting processing. Wu reportedly stood on a stool in the Laozha police station and declared, "Sisters, we are liberated, we are born anew [*women xin shengle*]! Sisters, why have our pure bodies been trampled on by others? We were all loved by our parents; why did we sink to this state? It was the Guomindang reactionaries who harmed us! Today we are excited and happy! The people's government, under the leadership of Chairman Mao, is helping us to turn over. Today is our most memorable day, our most glorious day." On their ride to the Women's Labor Training Institute, when one woman inadvertently used the word "prostitute," another was said to have replied, "If anyone uses the word 'prostitute' again, I won't answer to it!"[94]

Such was the representation of their state of mind in the press—an account that assumed a direct causal connection between suffering and class consciousness, between oppression and desire to be reformed. Though it made for inspiring reading, this story not only oversimplified the social relations of the prostitute's world, but also trivialized the problems faced by the reformers. The roundup sundered the only reliable relationship the prostitute knew—that with her madam and the madam's paramour, who were often adoptive parents as well as cruel employers. As exploitative as brothel life might be, it was all these women had to rely upon. Their fear was increased by the rumors that pervaded the city in the days before the brothel closings: that the women's heads would be shaved, that they would be distributed to the PLA as collective wives, that they would be used as live minesweepers in the military campaign to take Taiwan.[95] Given this atmosphere, the roundup scene lacked the picture-perfect class consciousness of the newspaper reports, as Cao Manzhi acknowledged many years later:

> We loaded them into cars. These people all cried. They didn't get in the cars. They all hung onto the madams, calling "Mama, daddy, the Communists are going to murder us, we don't want to go," "they're going to sell us again, we want to stay with mama and daddy," etc. They cried and carried on.

---

[93] See, for example, *Dagongbao*, November 26, 1951, p. 6, and December 14, 1951, p. 4; *Xinwen ribao*, November 25, 1951, p. 4, and November 27, 1951, p. 4; Hsiao Wen, "Shanghai Prostitutes Begin Their Lives Anew," *Women of China* 2 (1957): 24–27.

[94] *Dagongbao*, November 27, 1951, p. 1; *Xinwen ribao*, November 27, 1951, p. 4.

[95] Yang Jiezeng, head of the Shanghai *funü laodong jiaoyangsuo*, 1952–1958, personal interview, December 12, 1986; Cao Manzhi, personal interview.

They did not want to accept reform, and by no means did all of them wish to leave the life and marry respectably (*congliang*). Ones [who did] were extremely exceptional. Those in this category, of the ones I encountered, were often not even one in a hundred. Very few among those who lived well wished to voluntarily give up the trade. In general, after a prostitute had been in the brothel half a year, her psychology changed.[96]

Wu Caifeng and Wang Acai indeed might have made inspiring speeches to their captive sisters, but their exhortations fell on suspicious and terrified ears. When the female staff of the Women's Labor Training Institute saw the tear-streaked, sullen faces of their new charges, they knew that winning the trust of these women would be difficult and that altering their behavior might require coercion.

The reform process did not get off to a smooth start. True, the women were provided with living conditions better than those enjoyed by many Shanghai residents. Each was assigned a bed, a quilt, a wool blanket, sheets, two washbasins (for feet and face), toothpaste and toothbrush, chopsticks, and two food bowls.[97] They were permitted to wear their own clothes and were treated courteously by the staff.[98] They were well-fed, and their rooms were kept warm. But when Cao Manzhi went to address them as part of their orientation, he found himself the target of an innovative spontaneous protest—a cry-in:

> I went to where they lived. There was a rather high stage, and I stood on it and prepared to give them a speech. Just as I started to talk, one of the prostitutes cried out: "Sisters, cry!" (*Jiejie meimei, ku!*) It was very effective: as soon as she called out, more than three hundred people began to cry simultaneously. Every single one cried in a truly broken-hearted way. At first their tears were false, but the more they cried the sadder they became. "Now we are in the hands of the CCP. Before we could get by, but this time we don't know if we'll live or die." The more they thought about it, the sadder they became. Some cried out, "Mama, where are you? Your child can't even write to you!" They said all kinds of things. They cried without stopping for two hours. I sat there. I asked the head of the guards to bring me a stool, and I sat and watched them cry.... When they had almost finished crying, it was time to send in food for them. They all got their bowls filled, and then they dumped their food on the floor. All of them. Not one ate.
>
> I knew their state of mind. Later I talked with several of them, and they said, "When we began to cry, it was to put some pressure on you. But after that it was genuine. We were crying over very sad things. We didn't know where you would send us. Maybe you would execute us. Maybe you would

96 Cao Manzhi, personal interview.
97 *Dagongbao*, November 27, 1951, p. 1.
98 Yang Xiuqin and Xu Huiqing, personal interview, November 11, 1986.

draw our blood. When troops fight in battle don't they lose blood?" etc. Their thinking was unbelievably confused. But not a single one of them thought that the CCP had come to save her.[99]

The Reform Process

The first step in winning the trust of the "sisters" (who after the roundup were never referred to as prostitutes) was to treat their venereal disease and other illnesses. This in itself was a problematic process, since many of the women believed that their blood was being drawn to be sold on the open market. Medical examinations were begun on their third day in the Women's Labor Training Institute, and the group prognosis was grim: half the 501 women suffered from venereal disease, while a full 90 percent had health problems ranging from heart disease and tuberculosis to ringworm.[100] In addition, a majority were addicted to opium or heroin (*baifen*), and forced withdrawal made them listless and frantic by turns.[101]

The municipal government spared no expense on the medical treatment of the "sisters," ultimately spending RMB 180,000 on the cure of venereal disease alone.[102] Doctors were brought in from the Shanghai Venereal Disease Clinic to treat the women at a specially equipped facility inside the Women's Labor Training Institute; those in need of more extended care were sent out to local hospitals and their bills paid by the city.[103] Scarce penicillin was diverted from the PLA and gradually replaced salvarsan, which required a longer course of treatment.[104] Perhaps more than any other feature of the reform program, the medical treatment ultimately convinced the women that the reformers meant them no harm and that if they were worth the expense to cure then perhaps there was a place for them in the new society.[105]

---

[99] Cao Manzhi, personal interview.

[100] He Wannan, "Dangwu digou hua dangnian" [Speaking of the times when we cleaned up the dirt], *Minzhu yu fazhi*, January 1984, p. 21.

[101] *Dagongbao*, November 30, 1951, p. 4; Yang Xiuqin and Xu Huiqing, personal interview, November 11, 1986.

[102] He Wannan "Dangwu digou hua dangnian," p. 21.

[103] Le Jiayu and Xu Chongli, former medical personnel at Shanghaishi xingbing fangzhisuo [Shanghai Venereal Disease Clinic], personal interview, Shanghai, November 17, 1986; Yang Jiezeng, personal interview.

[104] Cao Manzhi in Yang Jiezeng and He Wannan, *Shanghai changji gaizao shihua*, pp. iii-iv; Le Jiayu and Xu Chongli, personal interview, November 17, 1986.

[105] Cao Manzhi, personal interview; Yang Jiezeng, personal interview, December 12, 1986.

The second step was to organize an extensive series of classes for the women, who spent half of every day in study. Since the majority of the group was illiterate and illiteracy had often been a factor in their being "tricked" into consenting to their own sale, some of the classes focused on achieving an elementary-school level of literacy.[106] But the most important task of the classes was to instill a sense of class consciousness, in keeping with the government's view of their dual nature: they had to be made to hate the old society and recognize their oppression in it, and they had to recognize that their own past actions were less than glorious, were now in fact illegal, and must not be repeated.[107] Much of the teaching was geared to the psychological state of the individual women in the classes, as reported by their own team leaders (duizhang):

> Depending on what they were thinking at the time, we would educate them accordingly. There was all kinds of thinking among them. Some of them felt that it was better to be on the outside doing nothing all day, while here they had to love labor, to work and produce, so they were unwilling. We talked about this in the classes, and educated them. We told them that this was bad for their own health and a hindrance to society.[108]

Teaching the women to think of themselves as members of a single oppressed group meant minimizing the factors that divided them. Like most Shanghai residents, prostitutes could identify their place of origin and felt a special kinship with those from the same region who spoke the same dialect they did. In other sectors of the Shanghai work force, native-place kinship was accompanied by hostility to those from other regions.[109] Though prostitution was very much structured by native-place origins,[110] individual prostitutes apparently identified each other by brothel rather than native place, and all spoke Shanghai dialect, so place of origin was not an insuperable obstacle to the creation of a shared identity. The women were also divided by the class of customers they had once serviced; high-class sing-song girls had little in common with working-class streetwalkers. Nevertheless, when women from all along the hierarchy of prostitution were confined together in the Women's Labor Training Institute, the differences in status were apparently less important than the common facts of confinement and reform.[111]

---

[106] Xinwen ribao, August 22, 1952, p. 4; Shanghaishi minzhengju, "Shanghaishi youmin, jinü gaizao gongzuo" [The work of reforming vagrants and prostitutes] (N.p., October 1959), p. 2.

[107] Shanghaishi minzhengju, "Shanghaishi youmin, jinü gaizao gongzuo," p. 2.

[108] Yang Xiuqin and Xu Huiqing, personal interview, November 11, 1986.

[109] Honig, Sisters and Strangers, passim.

[110] Hershatter, "Hierarchy of Shanghai Prostitution."

[111] Yang Xiuqin and Xu Huiqing, personal interview, November 11, 1986. This account is necessarily based on the recollections of reformers rather than subjects. It is certainly

A key factor in reforming the women was to break their emotional ties to the madams. Several weeks after the roundup, the Women's Labor Training Institute organized a large accusation meeting at which women publicly confronted their former bosses (who sometimes had had ownership rights over them).[112] At this meeting, some of the most extreme practices of the madams were dramatically denounced.[113] Yet this did not conclude the process of dissociation from the madams. Seven months after the roundup, when the institute began a formal evaluation of the women's progress, each woman was told to make a self-criticism. One confessed that she had remained in contact with her former madam, even leaving her child with the madam for safekeeping. As a result of this campaign she broke relations with the madam and took her child back.[114]

The third important feature of the reform regimen was involvement in productive labor. The women spent half of each day working in one of the institute workshops, which produced primarily socks and towels. In the minds of the reformers, imparting an actual skill was less important than cultivating the habit of working.[115] The women earned a regular wage for this work; it was the first experience for some of receiving and controlling their own earnings.[116]

Undergirding and reinforcing all of these aspects of reform—medical treatment, education, and labor—was the establishment of regular collective routines and daily habits.[117] The women rose at 6:30 each day and spent most of their time in organized activities. They were divided into teams (*dadui*), subteams (*fendui*), and small groups (*xiaozu*), each of which had a group leader and additional women in charge of study and daily life. The small-group leaders were elected by the women themselves.[118] Though women could not leave the compound at will, they were permitted to meet regularly with their relatives, and eventually a

---

possible that former prostitutes would recall native-place and status alliances differently.

[112] On the different arrangements under which women entered brothels, including pawning and outright sale, see Gail Hershatter, "Prostitution and the Market in Women in Early Twentieth-Century Shanghai," in Patricia Ebrey and Rubie Watson, eds., *Marriage and Inequality in Chinese Society* (Berkeley: University of California Press, 1991), pp. 256–285.

[113] Yang Jiezeng, personal interview, December 12, 1986.

[114] Seventeen of the women had brought children into the Women's Labor Training Institute with them, and subsequent births brought the number of resident children to forty-nine by August 1952. *Xinwen ribao*, August 22, 1952, p. 4.

[115] Shanghaishi minzhengju, "Shanghaishi youmin, jinu gaizao gongzuo," pp. 2–3.

[116] He Wannan, "Dangwu digou hua dangnian," p. 22.

[117] Shanghaishi minzhengju, "Shanghaishi youmin, jinü gaizao gongzuo," p. 3.

[118] Huang Yunqiu and Wang Dingfei, former staff members at Funü laodong jiaoyangsuo, personal interview, Shanghai, November 4, 1986.

system of asking for leave to return home for visits was established. These visits home were used both as rewards and as means of assessing the women's progress toward release:

> Their Sisters' Group (*jiemei xiaozu*) had to evaluate and examine and decide who could go out. Their family also had to work on it. We also asked the masses in the area to work on it, to help us investigate just what they did after they went out on leave. Before they went out on leave they had to say when they would be back. Some went out overnight; some went out in the morning and came back in the evening. The great majority returned on time and voluntarily reported to the staff what had happened that day—they had helped wash clothes at home, cleaned the house, cooked, etc. After we listened we investigated to see whether it was true. So we made contact with their families and asked them what they had done when they went home and also asked the masses, was it true that after they came home they did not go out, was there any activity. In this way we knew whether they were good or not. So this system of asking for leave was very useful.[119]

By means of all of these routines, the behavior of the women, and apparently their thinking as well, were gradually modified.

The success of the reform was put to a dramatic test in September 1952, when a second group of prostitutes, almost twice as big as the first, was rounded up. These were unlicensed prostitutes who had continued to work the streets after prostitution was formally banned, as well as bar hostesses, masseuses, and others who sold sex regularly.[120] They were picked up in one night in a well-coordinated police sweep (*piaoke*):

> They were everywhere on the street in ones and twos.... The trucks were hidden in advance in the lanes. The method was a bit savage. One of them would "hook" her, and ... [then] our plainclothesmen would come out and stuff a handkerchief in her mouth. Otherwise she might call out.... We also tied them up, [but] some jumped off the truck, and one almost died; it took two days [of treatment] to save her.[121]

From the moment of their violent arrest, these women were more difficult for the Women's Labor Training Institute staff to deal with than the first group:

> The second group was different from the first—they made a lot more fuss. Among them were many hoodlums, and some who were very young. They were not like the first group, who it seemed had been sold into the brothels. These were people who engaged in hoodlum activities. Some came from homes that were not badly off, and some were even students. They

[119] Yang Jiezeng, personal interview, December 12, 1986.
[120] Yang Jiezeng and He Wannan, *Shanghai changji gaizao shihua,* pp. 49–50.
[121] Cao Manzhi, personal interview.

willingly engaged in prostitution. So they were antagonistic at being brought in.[122]

The new group tripled the population resident at 418 Tongzhou Road, and many of the new inhabitants were given to loud arguments and fighting. The staff responded by putting women from the first group in charge of the newcomers, and they repeated this procedure when a third group of five hundred women, most of them taxi dancers, was rounded up.[123] (Subsequent inmates were brought in singly, not in large groups.) This work utilized the street wisdom that ex-prostitutes could bring to bear on reforming their sisters; it also gave the earliest inmates a chance to demonstrate the extent of their personal reform.

Release

Beginning in 1953, the Women's Labor Training Institute began to release its reformed inmates. The women had three main destinations. Those with relatives in the countryside were generally released to the custody of their families. The institute contacted the local government in a woman's native place to make sure that the family could take her back, then met with the family members. Sometimes this involved reuniting women with families they had not seen since they had been kidnapped; sometimes it meant sending them back to husbands who knew full well that they had been prostitutes, who had indeed sent them to Shanghai to try to make a living. In every case, the institute staff tried to ensure that the woman would not be discriminated against, be rejected by her family, or return to prostitution.[124] It is not known how successful this effort was in securing the full reacceptance of these women into their rural communities, but apparently few returned to prostitution.[125]

A second group of women, those whose attitude and performance had been best or who had relatives in Shanghai, were assigned factory jobs and sent home to their families. A third group, those with no family to return to, were sent to state farms in Gansu, Ningxia, or Xinjiang, accompanied (apparently permanently) by some of the Women's Labor Training Institute staff. For many of them, a chance at a respectable marriage was part of the agreement:

> Xinjiang had no women, and most people couldn't find wives. Some of these prostitutes had no home to return to, and as prostitutes it was difficult

---

[122] Yang Xiuqin and Xu Huiqing, personal interview, November 11, 1986.

[123] Ibid.

[124] Yang Jiezeng, personal interview, December 12, 1986.

[125] Yang Xiuqin and Xu Huiqing, personal interview, November 11, 1986.

for them to find mates, so we introduced them [to the Xinjiang units]. The ones who went to Gansu went because they were short of labor there, and they could take their families. We explained the conditions there to them, and what they would do there. Those who wanted to go signed up; those who didn't want to go didn't have to. In 1955 more than five hundred went to Xinjiang.[126]

Regardless of where the women were sent, the staff regarded it as part of their work to see that the women were reunited with their mates and that unmarried women were married off. Staff were aided in the latter enterprise by unmarried men who, hearing that the institute contained a number of unmarried women, wrote requesting a spouse:

Some unmarried men knew the situation at the Women's Labor Training Institute and voluntarily wrote letters saying that they were unmarried and had also suffered in the old society, so they sympathized with the bitter experience of these people and wanted to find this kind of a mate. These people were workers; some were merchants. We didn't accept everyone who wrote. First we investigated their work and family situation. After that we found someone about the same age, and if she was willing, we introduced them.[127]

The staff's matchmaking duties did not end when a woman was released, as a former head of the institute recalled:

Later, if they started courting a man in the factory, we sought him out for a talk and let him know about her past, in order to avoid his going back on his word after marriage and causing problems. We also asked that the woman herself explain things to the man. Some people, after they learned about the past of these women, understood that they were victims of the old society and loved them even more.[128]

After 1953, inmates of the Women's Labor Training Institute were increasingly not former prostitutes, but juvenile delinquents who had appeared after 1949. In 1958, its original mandate fulfilled, the institute closed its doors. In all, more than seven thousand women had been the subjects of reform there.[129]

Conclusion: Reformers Compared

In the 1920s, the Shanghai Municipal Council was a reluctant reformer, forced into that stance by the zealous campaigners of the Moral

---

[126] Ibid.
[127] Yang Jiezeng, personal interview, December 12, 1986.
[128] Ibid.
[129] Yang Jiezeng and He Wannan, *Shanghai changji gaizao shihua,* p. 124.

Welfare League. The members of the SMC preferred a regulatory approach that protected the public health by inspecting prostitutes and licensing brothels, thereby requiring them to conform to certain standards of cleanliness and order. The Moral Welfare League activists believed in suppression of prostitution, which they denounced as a form of "commercialized vice" that should not be licensed and thereby condoned by state authority (in the form of the municipal government). Although the SMC was the governing body of the International Settlement, it was subject to decisions taken by open meetings of the ratepayers. In the 1920s, it was required to carry out the licensing and elimination of brothels over the considered objections of many of its members. Though it had a monopoly on governmental power in the Settlement, it was subject to the consent of the governed. Because they were organized, vocal, and persistent, the members of the Moral Welfare League effectively captured a reluctant state authority and bound it to their agenda for moral reform.

No such rift was visible in the ranks of the 1950s reformers. The campaign to eliminate prostitution was carried out by organs of the municipal government, who evidenced a high degree of unity and coordination. Acting on a resolution passed by the municipal Consultative Conference, the Public Security Bureau, the Civil Administration Department, the Health Department, the Democratic Women's Federation, and the residents' committees all carried out their appointed tasks. The police arrested brothel owners and took in prostitutes. The Civil Administration Department ran the Women's Labor Training Institute, which housed, treated, and reeducated the women. The Health Department allocated resources for their medical treatment. The Women's Federation provided staff members for the institute and neighborhood cadres to reinforce the work of supervision of the women and their families. The residents' committees used informal surveillance to guard against any resurgence of prostitution.

Coordinating all these efforts, though largely invisible in the public record of the abolition campaign, was the Communist Party. The CCP approach toward prostitution had been developed in the rural districts of the liberated areas and honed in the cities of the north, which came under Communist control before Shanghai. The head of the Civil Administration Department, Cao Manzhi, was a veteran of abolition campaigns in Shandong and elsewhere. He understood the theoretical underpinnings of the CCP position and had the organizational skills and clout to administer an effective program. Unlike the 1920 effort, the 1951 campaign was conducted by a unified state authority with a well-developed position on prostitution, a government that was impervious to outside pressure (had there been any in favor of another approach) and that apparently enjoyed a great deal of popular support for its efforts.

Although the representatives on the SMC in 1920 came from the most powerful nations on earth, in Shanghai they were far from omnipotent. Their authority was limited. So was their reform effort, which was aimed at eliminating brothels from the International Settlement rather than abolishing all forms of prostitution and reforming individual prostitutes. Even this limited effort, however, failed, in part because they had no authority over the area of Shanghai outside the International Settlement, and many brothels responded to the campaign by moving their operations to the French Concession or the Chinese-controlled area. It failed, as well, because a foreign government in Shanghai could not begin to ameliorate the social system of which prostitution was a part. The SMC could not or did not provide extensive welfare facilities for displaced prostitutes; it made no attempt to punish traffickers or discourage customers; it did nothing to quell the fears or silence the protests of the many commercial establishments that indirectly derived some revenue from prostitution. It took the brothel, and only the brothel, as its unit of regulation. Anything that happened outside the brothel walls—including unlicensed prostitution, the sale of women and children, and the interweaving of prostitution with the rest of the urban economy—was beyond the scope of the state.

In contrast, the CCP-guided government of the 1950s controlled not only all of Shanghai, but the countryside from which most prostitutes came. It could send reformed prostitutes back to their native villages or despatch them to far-flung regions to take up new lives. It was engaged in a massive restructuring of the economy that made it possible to find employment for ex-prostitutes. To settle the women in stable households, it even took on the role of matchmaker. In the lanes of Shanghai it built, with popular support and participation, a network of mutual supervision linked to state authority that made it difficult and dangerous for prostitutes, madams, and traffickers to resume operations. The reach of the state in the 1950s was both wide and deep, making it a far more powerful entity in the lives of Shanghai residents than the imperialists it excoriated had ever been.

Although the 1920s reformers could not agree on whether prostitution should be regulated or suppressed, they shared the Victorian assumption that it was a product of human nature, specifically of male sexual desire. They differed largely on the feasibility and practicality of controlling human nature. The regulators argued that since prostitution was natural, it could not be eliminated, and that the state should confine itself to ensuring that the trade was conducted in a licensed locale by hygienic practitioners. The abolitionists, on the other hand, called on men to transcend their nature with the aid of religion, to subordinate their sexual nature to the higher moral law subscribed to by religious men and all respectable women. In using legal means to enforce a moral code, they argued, the government could also strike a blow for women's rights, by helping to secure the freedom of all women from the untrammeled sexual depredations of men.

For the 1950s reformers, there was nothing natural about prostitution; it was a purely social product. They proceeded from the assumption that prostitution grew out of a distorted social system dominated by imperialists and a reactionary Chinese government linked to rural landlords and urban gangs. Imperialists invaded China and damaged its economy, creating rural distress. The Guomindang and its warlord predecessors worsened the rural crisis and shored up landlord power. Displaced peasants, many of them women sold by their relatives, were forced into prostitution or sought it as a means to support their families. Urban power-brokers controlled gangster networks that made money from procuring and brothel keeping, paying off the urban police in the process. Governments both foreign-controlled and native profited from the taxation of prostitution. In this rendering, the entire system of political and social power became a malignant growth that had to be excised if the Chinese people were to live. Prostitution was a small but integral part of that growth; its elimination was an essential part of the cleansing of the Chinese social system.

Both the 1920s and the 1950s reformers saw prostitutes as dually constructed creatures: they were victims, yet they sometimes profited from the circumstances of their victimization. The earlier group, while acknowledging that women were victims of economic pressures that drove them to prostitution, placed far more emphasis on their sexual victimization, since they were repeatedly subjected to the exercise of a male desire they were presumed not to share. Some of the Moral Welfare writings also hinted that prostitutes were vain and greedy women who diverted money that could be spent on charity into their personal adornment. What is most striking about the 1920s discourse on prostitution, however, is that prostitutes themselves were not at the center of it. Very little time or attention was devoted to their circumstances, much less their desires. Instead the discussion focused on the deleterious consequences of "commercialized vice" to the foreign community. This may have happened in part because most of the prostitutes were Chinese, whereas the clientele of concern to the reformers was white. Racism and cultural chauvinism rendered the women opaque to the reformers, who were more concerned to save white men (and women and children) from prostitution than to save the prostitutes from their surroundings. Though foreigners ran welfare institutions like the Door of Hope—which fit nicely with the characterization of prostitute as victim—they talked very little about prostitutes themselves, compared to the amount of time they expended on discussion of "the social evil."

The 1950s reformers, in contrast, placed the prostitute, as victim, squarely at the center of their reform discourse. One among many unfortunates in the "old society," she was nevertheless given a prominent place in 1950s reform writings as a victim of multiple oppressions: economic deprivation, sexual assault, kidnapping, forced labor, denial of medical care, physical abuse. Sexuality and sexual desire, either on the part of the prostitute or her client, were utterly eclipsed in this discourse. In the descriptions by reformers and prostitutes alike, sex was represented either as rape (by landlords, traffickers, brothel owners) or forced labor (during menstruation, after an abortion, on pain of beatings). But as with the campaign of the 1920s, the characterization of prostitute as victim (certainly not as sexual actor) was tempered by dark hints of character defects. Women might easily grow accustomed to a life of luxury, the warning went, a life in which they enjoyed fine clothes and leisure that were not the fruits of their own labor. The reform process was meant not only to detach the prostitute from her exploiters and to heal her physical and psychological wounds, but to accustom her to labor, thereby readying her for productive employment and mending any character flaws induced by her previous life. These two characterizations coexisted uneasily: if a woman supported a brothel owner through her forced and degraded sexual labor—if she was, in fact, repeatedly victimized by the exploitation of that labor—then how could she also be a social parasite? Nevertheless, the two images of victim and parasite had something important in common: neither granted women any agency in determining the conditions of their own pre-Liberation existence. Instead agency, in the form of the opportunity to construct oneself anew, was bestowed by a prostitute's wholehearted participation in the process of reform.

Both reform discourses, then, rendered the prostitute partially invisible by portraying her as essentially passive. Though this undoubtedly reflects in part the lack of control that prostitutes in twentieth-century Shanghai had over their bodies, their labor, and their sexuality, it also reflects the uneasiness that both groups of reformers felt in dealing with women cut loose from the respectable social controls imposed by the family. The 1920s reformers failed to eradicate prostitution because they could not alter the social system that had detached these women from their families. The 1950s reformers succeeded, and restored Shanghai prostitutes to the ranks of respectable wives and mothers, as part of a much larger effort to reconstitute the family system[130] and "renaturalize" women into it.

[130] Judith Stacey, *Patriarchy and Socialist Revolution* (Berkeley: University of California Press, 1984), passim.

CHAPTER SIX

Progressive Journalism and Shanghai's Petty Urbanites

Zou Taofen and the Shenghuo Enterprise, 1926–1945

WEN-HSIN YEH

In his last words, addressed to the Chinese Communist Party (CCP) in Yan'an in summer 1944 as he lay stricken with cancer, Zou Taofen (1895–1944), the publisher of Shanghai's Shenghuo Bookstore, briefly recounted his lifelong struggle to help gain China's national liberation and political democratization. Reaffirming his commitment to progressive cultural mobilization, he respectfully tendered a deathbed request that he be accepted, posthumously, as a member of the Communist Party.[1] The Central Committee of the Party replied that it was deeply honored and solemnly accepted the request, grieved as it was by the news of Zou's demise.[2]

Zou Taofen's death at 7:20 A.M. on July 24 marked the beginning of the Central Committee's thorough incorporation of his life into the Party's history. The wording of Zou's last request lent itself readily to such political use, although, tellingly enough, controversies later arose over the authorship and, by implication, the authenticity of Zou Taofen's will.[3] Numerous commemorative ceremonies were held in Communist

---

[1] Mu Xin, *Zou Taofen* (Hong Kong: Sanlian, 1959), p. 331. As this chapter goes to press, Zou Taofen's oldest son, Zou Jiahua, is widely rumored to be the top candidate likely to become China's next premier.

[2] See the Central Committee's telegram to Zou's family on September 28, 1944. Ibid., pp. 332–333.

[3] Most accounts suggest that Zou Taofen's last words were written by Xu Xuehan, a Party member and a New Fourth Route Army liaison officer who had been instructed by the Party's command in northern Jiangsu to look after the ailing Zou Taofen in Shanghai. Xu Xuehan himself states that he prepared a draft will upon Zou Taofen's request when the latter's health was rapidly deteriorating under the attack of cancer. Xu insists, however, that Zou Taofen himself wrote the version that was later carried to Subei and Yan'an. See Xu Xuehan, "Linzhong qian de Taofen xiansheng," in Zou Jiali, ed., *Yi Taofen* (Shanghai: Xuelin chubanshe, 1985), pp. 388–389.

base areas to mark his death. In addition, left-wing circles in Chongqing, the wartime capital of the Nationalist government, organized on October 1 a mass rally led by such eminent figures as Song Qingling, Lin Boqu, and Guo Moruo that was attended by thousands of college students and "vocational youth" (*zhiye qingnian*), already employed and out of school. The rally, claiming to be faithful to Zou Taofen's lifelong goals and beliefs, was turned into a mass demonstration against the government's suppression of civil rights. Like the funeral procession for Lu Xun in Shanghai in 1936, the commemorative service for Zou Taofen provided the left wing with a much publicized occasion to display widespread popular discontent against the Nationalist regime.[4]

The memory of Zou Taofen was not allowed to fade. Despite his last wish to be buried in Yan'an, on June 22, 1946, he was given a spectacular funeral in Shanghai's Rainbow Bridge Public Cemetery. Numerous former associates and political allies attended the ceremony. Once again, a crowd was gathered to give voice to political discontent, registering a strong popular protest against the Chiang Kai-shek government's imputed responsibility for the civil war about to break out between the Nationalists and the Communists.[5] Shen Junru, Zou's long-time friend, delivered the eulogy. To carry on Zou's unfinished tasks, the assembled mourners vowed to "fight for the victory of democracy."[6]

In May 1949, the triumphant People's Liberation Army crossed the Yangzi River and entered Shanghai, where progressive journalists led by editors such as Zou Taofen had long agitated for a Communist victory. Two months later the Party commemorated the fifth anniversary of Zou's death. On that occasion Zhou Enlai, the Party's cultural leader, pronounced that Zou's life history was exemplary of "the journey traveled by Chinese intellectuals toward progressivism and revolution."[7]

Zhou's remarks defined the political meaning of the memory of Zou Taofen's life for decades to come. In the 1950s Zou Taofen was hailed as a standard-bearer of progressive culture, a paragon in his dedication to the people, and an exemplary model to Chinese intellectuals undergoing thought-reform.[8] Upon the tenth anniversary of his death in 1954 the Party published Zou's collected essays.[9] Thereafter he was annually hailed in newspapers, journals, and commemorative meetings until the outbreak of the Cultural Revolution in 1965, when savage attacks were leveled

---

[4] Mu Xin, *Zou Taofen*, pp. 337–338.
[5] Ibid., p. 341.
[6] Fudan daxue xinwen xi yanjiu shi, ed., *Zou Taofen nianpu* (Shanghai, 1982), p. 154.
[7] Mu Xin, *Zou Taofen*, p. 341.
[8] Zou Jiali, *Yi Taofen*, pp. 561–564.
[9] Mu Xin, *Zou Taofen*, p. 341.

against both Zou's memory and the persons of his surviving associates at the Sanlian Bookstore, the enterprise he helped found in the 1930s.[10]

A barrage of favorable biographical portraits and memoirs resumed after 1978. With the "moderates" and "pragmatists" in place as the helmsmen of the Party in Beijing, Zou Taofen was once again fondly remembered by numerous former comrades and referred to deferentially for his contribution to the making of the 1949 revolution.[11] During the decade of Deng Xiaoping's "four modernizations" Zou Taofen was presented not only as the "Voice of the People" but also as a pioneer in professional journalism and the scientific management of publishing enterprises.[12] In 1984, upon the fortieth anniversary of his death, Zou Taofen was praised as a great political commentator, journalist, and publisher; a mentor to the patriotic youth of the 1930s and 1940s who helped shape an entire generation of Chinese that grew up during the War of Resistance (1937–1944); and a man whose fervor and dedication informed the countrywide network of the Shenghuo and Sanlian bookstores that he had built into a bastion of progressive propaganda, uniting people of all classes and backgrounds toward a common national goal.[13]

In death, and in the pantheon of early revolutionary martyrs, Zou Taofen was, in the final presentation of the political significance of his personal history, designated as the "Voice of the People" because in life he had allowed himself to become the "Voice of the Party." In life he had lavished praise on the Communist leadership for their courage, moral rectitude, patriotism, and social ideals. He had shared their immediate political goals and had joined them in harshly criticizing Chiang Kai-shek's arbitrary power and oppressive police state. He was the prototypical "progressive intellectual," an inspiration for a whole generation of politically aroused youth. In death the perpetuation of Zou's memory fell under the management of the now bureaucratized cultural agency of the new regime, which continually renewed his reputation by enhancing him with attributes that unfailingly served the evolving policies of the Communist Party-state.

After 1949, complete agreement was assumed to have existed between the "People" and the "Party" in the early days of the revolution, since Party and People were assumed to be identical. The

<hr>

[10] Zou Jiali, Yi Taofen, pp. 568–569.

[11] Ibid., pp. 574–581.

[12] See, for example, Yu Yueting, "Taofen de caifang zhi dao," Xinwen daxue, no. 7 (October 1984), pp. 53–56; Qian Xiaobo and Lei Qunming, eds., Taofen yu chuban (Shanghai: Xuelin chubanshe, 1983).

[13] Xu Xuehan, "Taofen tongzhi dui Zhongguo chuban shiye de weida gongxian," Chuban shiliao, no. 3 (December 1984), p. 2.

reification of Zou Taofen as a paragon was not merely the result of Zou's co-optation by the Chinese Communist Party, however, but also a major indicator of the fundamental changes in the nature of public discourse that accompanied the victory of the Communists in 1949 and the final consolidation of the Party's cultural hegemony. The process of establishing that cultural hegemony began long before the Communists won the civil war and constituted a vital dimension of the larger competition for state power.

Zou Taofen's contribution to this process, simply put, was to create a collective means of giving pluralistic voice to the largest audience China then had: the urban sojourning youth of Shanghai and other cities. In those prerevolutionary days before the Party-state molded the populace into one, the "people" was amorphous and fragmented; it spoke, when it managed to, through many voices. Zou Taofen emerges clearly as one of the few journalists during the years spanning the two revolutions of 1927 and 1949 who, by wide recognition, succeeded in consistently articulating with forcefulness the common wishes expressed in a significant chorus of those voices. His writings enabled Shanghai's urbanites to constitute themselves as a new kind of reading audience. Using the immensely popular "Readers' Mailbox" column in *Shenghuo zhoukan* (Life weekly), Zou Taofen linked the personal plights of thousands of individual readers with the perceived public plight of the country as a whole, thereby helping transform urban middle-brow anxieties about one's self into political concerns about the nation.

The crucial ingredient of Zou's column was its personal focus. Soon, however, as the national crisis intensified in the early 1930s when Japan expanded its dominion over China, this urban readership was channeled into a more impersonal and detached mode of mass expression that ultimately came under the organizational auspices of the Chinese Communist Party. After the War of Resistance broke out in 1937 and Zou Taofen's Shanghai-based publishing enterprise was compelled to emigrate upstream along the Yangzi to China's hinterland, the Communists stepped in to offer their support for the Shenghuo Bookstore. This development was not seen as an organizational take-over, but rather as timely strategic assistance much welcomed by Zou as he intensified his endeavor to achieve national salvation.

But there was a price to pay for this assistance. In the midst of wartime dislocation, mobilization, and intensification of patriotism, a change of discourse took place, and the plurality of the voice was lost. In the early 1930s the Shanghai-based publisher and editor of *Shenghuo zhoukan* was writing from concrete individual experience outward to social forms. A decade later the Communist-supported bookstore was disseminating publications written from an external social norm inward toward the individual. This new cultural hegemony amounted to the production of a state-created voice that claimed to be the vox populi.

When the Shenghuo publishing enterprise returned to Shanghai at the end of the War of Resistance, it reappeared in this much altered form. The story of Zou Taofen's life as the Voice of the People, therefore, cannot but be read as a transformation of major significance. It chronicles a sea change in the relationship between the publisher and his audience: from multiple expressions authentically exchanged with a readership of sharing individuals (many of whom sojourned as "petty urbanites" in Shanghai) to a new collective national audience captured in the organizational net of the Party-state and identified in the Communists' "religion of capital letters" simply as the "People."[14]

The *Shenghuo zhoukan* and Its Audience

In the history of publishing, the May Fourth Movement of 1919 was memorable particularly as a moment when the outburst of patriotic sentiments and cultural reexamination characteristic of the movement found expression in the mushrooming of student journals on school campuses across the country.[15] But the national influence of May Fourth publications tended to be limited to urban intellectual circles. Even though May Fourth intellectuals advocated the use of vernacular Chinese as a means to reach a larger audience, critics such as Qu Qiubai were quick to point out that their writings were in fact inaccessible to the general public because of the liberal use of idioms and concepts borrowed from the West.[16] The organ of the Chinese Communist Party, *Xiangdao* (The guide), and the organ of the Socialist Youth Corps, *Zhongguo qingnian* (Chinese youth), were no exceptions. These journals devoted considerable space to the plight of the Chinese laboring class, but the readership was composed primarily of members of the young educated elite.

---

[14] The "religion of capital letters" (*religion des majuscules*) is, of course, Émile Zola's term.

[15] For a pioneering study of the May Fourth Movement, see Chow T'se-tsung, *The May Fourth Movement: Intellectual Revolution in Modern China* (Cambridge, Mass.: Harvard University Press, 1960). For a general treatment, see Jerome Grieder, *Intellectuals and the State in Modern China* (New York: Free Press, 1981). For the most recent interpretation, see Vera Schwarcz, *The Chinese Enlightenment: Intellectuals and the Legacy of the May Fourth Movement of 1919* (Berkeley: University of California Press, 1986).

[16] Paul G. Pickowicz, *Marxist Literary Thought in China: The Influence of Ch'u Ch'iu-pai* (Berkeley: University of California Press, 1981).

Meanwhile, a large middle- and lower-middle-class audience in cities such as Shanghai and Suzhou devoted itself to the avid consumption of a middle-brow literature written in traditional literary style.[17] The literary section of Shanghai's largest daily, *Shenbao,* printed old-fashioned fiction featuring "talented scholars and beautiful women," wise magistrates, heavenly emissaries, martial heroes, and knights-errant. The paper in the 1920s was also a stronghold of the "Mandarin Ducks and Butterflies" genre of entertainment, composed by contemporaries in classical Chinese and invoking a world of romance and adventure. The popularity of these forms of fiction stimulated the production of numerous pirated editions. Many were made available for a few copper cash at street-corner stands where they were sold or lent to the city's shop clerks, apprentices, office workers, secondary school students, and so forth. Intellectuals bent upon reforming the minds of the people, however, deplored the popularity of these tales, which were often deemed frivolous, superstitious, and tradition-bound fantasies that exercised a pernicious influence on young minds by diverting their attention from reality.

In this context the publication of *Shenghuo zhoukan,* edited by Zou Taofen, acquires special significance. Like middle-brow entertainment fiction, *Shenghuo* reached a large audience among elementary and normal school teachers and what came to be known as "petty urbanites" (*xiao shimin*): literate clerks and apprentices in trade, manufacturing, the professions, and public and private service sectors, who were members of the "old" as well as the "new" middle classes. On the eve of its closure by the Nationalist authorities in late 1933, *Shenghuo zhoukan* had attained a weekly circulation of 150,000 copies, the highest record of distribution ever reached by a periodical in modern Chinese publishing history before 1949.[18] Unlike the "Mandarin Ducks and Butterflies" fiction, however, *Shenghuo* engaged, in a simple language and often brief statements, in serious commentaries on contemporary affairs and introduced its readers to a wide range of social science publications that were considered "progressive" or sympathetic to social reforms. In the wake of the Manchurian Incident of September 18, 1931, and the Battle of Shanghai of January 1932, furthermore, the journal took a strong stance in favor of

---

[17] See Perry Link, *Mandarin Ducks and Butterflies: Popular Fiction in Early Twentieth-Century Chinese Cities* (Berkeley: University of California Press, 1981).

[18] Mu Xin, ed., *Zou Taofen,* pp. 53–54. Each copy was in turn circulated privately, reaching an estimated urban audience at least three to four times the figure of publication. See Leo Lee and Andrew Nathan, "The Beginnings of Mass Culture: Journalism and Fiction in the Late Ch'ing and Beyond," in David Johnson, Andrew Nathan, and Evelyn S. Rawski, eds., *Popular Culture in Late Imperial China* (Berkeley: University of California Press, 1985), pp. 360–417, for an estimate of the size of readership for fiction and journalism.

immediate armed resistance against Japanese military encroachment in China and evolved into a rallying point for popular patriotic mobilization during the "national salvation movement" of the 1930s. *Shenghuo zhoukan* under the editorship of Zou Taofen was thus unique in the sense that it was an extremely popular middle-brow journal of diversion that dealt, at the same time, with serious social and political subjects.

The success of *Shenghuo zhoukan* eventually laid the foundation for Zou Taofen's larger publishing enterprise, the Shenghuo Bookstore. After the authorities closed the journal in 1933, Zou Taofen's later journalistic publishing activities were essentially attempts to duplicate its success and regain its interrupted momentum. *Shenghuo zhoukan* also served as a prototype for other Republican liberal-left publishers demanding political change and social reform. It inspired the creation of several progressive journals, such as *Dushu shenghuo* (Study life) and *Zixiu* (Self-study), that pursued a variation of *Shenghuo's* editorial policies, engaging a comparable audience of urban youth first drawn into the world of printed words and oppositional politics through Zou Taofen's writings.[19]

Unlike either the serious journals directed toward May Fourth intellectuals or the frivolous fiction produced for urban middle-brow escapists, *Shenghuo zhoukan* was intended to enlighten as well as entertain. This

---

[19] In October 1948, as a further affirmation of the progressive character of the *Shenghuo* publishing enterprise that had begun under Zou Taofen's guidance, Shenghuo Bookstore was merged with two other progressive publishing houses—the Dushu (Study) Bookstore founded by the assassinated Li Gongpu and the Xinzhi (New knowledge) Bookstore that grew out of Xue Muqiao's study group on the agrarian economic crisis. The new entity, the Sanlian Bookstore, is a national operation that continues into the present day. Shen Jingzhi, "Cong sifu tici shuoqi," in *Shenghuo, Dushu, Xinzhi Sanlian shudian chengli sanshi zhounian jinian ji* (Hong Kong, 1978), p. 23. Zou was obviously well regarded by the Chinese Communist Party during periods of relaxation. Numerous articles, essay collections, and books have appeared since 1949, affirming Zou's accomplishment as "the voice of the people," "a great patriot," "a brilliant model for intellectual self-reform," "a journalist who dedicated his life to the masses." See the appendix to Zou Jiali, *Yi Taofen*, pp. 547–581, for a comprehensive listing of writings on Zou Taofen that appeared between 1944 and 1985. Progressive publishers of the 1930s and 1940s fell victims during the Cultural Revolution. In Zou's case, note that there is a dearth of favorable portraiture between 1965 and 1977.

The *Shenghuo* phenomenon was significant from yet another perspective. While the early Chinese Communist Party in Shanghai concentrated its efforts on the political mobilization of the industrial workers, recent studies show that the Party's success in that regard was limited, despite the occurrence of numerous strikes, including major outbursts such as the May Thirtieth Movement of 1926. The city's workers were divided by native-place associations, and the recruitment process in particular was dominated by the influence of the city's notorious Green Gang. Factory strikes thus were often manipulated by factional political interests outside the workshops. While the Party might have had some success in reaching members of the working class through evening schools and literacy classes, furthermore, it appeared to have enjoyed little success in engaging the workers through printed materials.

formulation, which gave the journal a special niche in the publishing market, can be traced to the journal's origin in 1925 as the organ of the Shanghai-based Chinese Society for Vocational Education (Zhonghua zhiye jiaoyu she).[20]

The Chinese Society for Vocational Education was founded in 1913 by Jiangnan gentry leaders and Shanghai entrepreneurs such as Mu Ouchu, the cotton magnate, and Huang Yanpei, the head of the Jiangsu Provincial Educational Association, who believed in the efficacy of educational reform and economic modernization for the strengthening of the nation.[21] It was a critical institutional expression of a growing alliance between the "Shanghai capitalists," whose economically dominant interest in Shanghai's modern banking system was to be "nationalized" by Chiang Kai-shek's regime in 1935,[22] and Jiangnan local notables and fellow townsmen, whose dominant influence in Shanghai's cultural and educational enterprises permitted them to play a critical role as a "loyal opposition" to the Nationalists in the 1930s and ultimately as a "third force" (*Di sanzhong ren*) in the Democratic Alliance (Zhongguo minzhu zhengtuan tongmeng, or Minmeng) during the civil war.[23] Representing the liberal conscience of Shanghai's upper-crust bourgeoisie in a decade that witnessed such major incidents of student nationalism and working-class protest as the May Fourth Movement and the May Thirtieth Movement, the goal of the society was to reach down and address the educational needs of the striving and aspiring lower-middle-class "vocational youth" (*zhiye qingnian*)—young men of secondary school age and above who were supporting themselves by working in both the traditional and modern sectors of the economy and thus could not continue their formal studies through college.

Because vocational education stressed pragmatic knowledge and training, in the secondary school circles of the time it stood as a novel alternative to the ideal of "moral education," or textual learning and ethical cultivation of the traditional Confucian sort. At the same time, because it

---

[20] *Zou Taofen nianpu*, p. 24.

[21] On the association, see Wen-hsin Yeh, *The Alienated Academy: Culture and Politics in Republican China, 1919–1937*, (Cambridge, Mass.: Council on East Asian Studies Publications, Harvard University Press, 1990), pp. 119–121.

[22] Parks Coble, *The Shanghai Capitalists and the Nationalist Government, 1927–1937* (Cambridge, Mass.: Council on East Asian Studies Publications, Harvard University Press, 1980), passim.

[23] On the political views and publishing activities of the Third Force during the civil conflicts between the Nationalists and the Communists in the 1940s, see Suzanne Pepper, *Civil War in China: The Political Struggle, 1945–1949* (Berkeley: University of California Press, 1978). On Zou Taofen's participation in Minmeng, see Taofen, "Raoyun le de hua," *Dazhong shenghuo*, no. 25 (November 1, 1941): 603.

also emphasized general knowledge about the individual and society, vocational education differed from the conventional training offered in old-fashioned trade and crafts apprenticeships. It represented a curious hybrid of schooling and craftsmanship that confounded conventional expectations about the separation between the bookish learning of the literati and the practical skills of tradesmen and artisans. At the same time it aptly reflected the combined values that Shanghai's modernizing social and financial elites jointly sought to promote among their prospective employees.

The audience that *Shenghuo zhoukan* targeted thus possessed a distinct profile. This readership was literate, but most individuals were deprived of formal educational opportunities after only a few years in school. Financial difficulty was often cited as the reason for this inability to continue on into college, since Western-style colleges and universities in those days charged tuition and fees, and it cost a considerable sum to maintain a particular style of college life. Indeed, members of the so-called vocational youth envied college students as the lucky few able to afford a stylish and carefree existence. At the same time *zhiye qingnian* saw themselves as members of a status group that, like the college educated, wore gowns rather than short clothing to work and labored with their intellects rather than their muscles. The vocational youth, in short, stood at the bottom rung of the gowned. There was the fear, on the one hand, of falling off the social ladder and becoming degraded to a mere laborer. There was, on the other hand, a keen awareness of their own inferior standing vis-à-vis those above them and a fierce resolve to move ahead.[24]

When Zou Taofen was invited to assume the editorship of *Shenghuo zhoukan* in October 1926,[25] he was being asked to take charge of the journal on behalf of the gentry and entrepreneurial elites of the Chinese Society for Vocational Education, who were dedicated to elevating the economic skills of *zhiye qingnian*.[26] Although an estimated three hundred thousand individuals in the commercial and service sectors of Shanghai could be referred to as vocational youth, the majority of these men were

[24] Wang Zhixin, "Chuan changshan ren de kutong," *Shenghuo* 2.47 (September 25, 1927): 348–350.

[25] Under its first editor, Wang Zhixin, the journal in its first year of existence adopted a didactic tone and commented dutifully on Shanghai's employment scene. Circulation was less than two thousand copies, most of which were distributed free.

[26] Zou Taofen's involvement with the Society for Vocational Education began in 1922, when he was recommended by Huang Yanpei to become the society's editor and English secretary. Zou was responsible for editing the monthly *Jiaoyu yu zhiye* (Education and vocation) and the society's series on vocational education. See *Zou Taofen nianpu*, p. 22.

employed in small enterprises comprising a handful of employees, pursuing profits in hundreds of different trades in all parts of the city. As a "class" the vocational youth represented a highly diverse work force with pronounced differences in training, background, career trajectory, and personal prospects, not to mention native-place loyalties and master-disciple bonds.[27] The single most common trait, apart from age and urban residence, was literacy.[28] The challenge Zou Taofen faced, therefore, was to use reading as a medium to forge among *zhiye qingnian* a distinct sense of social reference that might lead them to look beyond the confines of their immediate work places and neighborhoods.

Zou Taofen was a suitable choice as editor of *Shenghuo zhoukan* not only because he shared the society's faith in modern economic development and education as an instrument of social reform, but also because he himself was no outsider to the gentry and entrepreneurial circles that sponsored the journal.[29] Although a native of Fujian, he had graduated from Shanghai's St. John's University, the exclusive Episcopalian college heavily favored by the sons and daughters of the bourgeoisie. Like the scions of the Jiangnan and Ningbo elites who dominated Shanghai's finance, commerce, and industry, Zou was at ease moving about in the hybrid Sino-Western milieu of Shanghai's business world. Upon graduation he landed a series of jobs as English secretary and newspaper editor through personal introductions in that circle.[30] Such an outlook and style

---

[27] For a comparable social landscape, see William T. Rowe, *Hankow: Commerce and Society in a Chinese City, 1796–1889* (Stanford, Calif.: Stanford University Press, 1984), pt. 2, and *Hankow: Conflict and Community in a Chinese City, 1796–1895* (Stanford, Calif.: Stanford University Press, 1989), pt. 1. On native-place ties in Shanghai's work force, see Emily Honig, *Sisters and Strangers: Women in the Shanghai Cotton Mills, 1919–1949* (Stanford, Calif.: Stanford University Press, 1986), pp. 57–78.

[28] On popular literacy in late imperial and modern China, see Evelyn Rawski, *Education and Popular Literacy in Ch'ing China* (Ann Arbor: University of Michigan Press, 1979), passim; Leo Lee and Andrew Nathan, "The Beginnings of Mass Culture: Journalism and Fiction in the Late Ch'ing and Beyond," in Johnson, Nathan, and Rawski, *Popular Culture,* pp. 360–417.

[29] Zou Taofen, *Jingli* (Shanghai: Shenghuo shudian, 1937), pp. 138–140. Zou Taofen was the weekly's most prolific contributor and sole editor until his departure, forced by government censorship, on a trip to Europe and America in July 1933. Zou Taofen joined Madame Sun Yat-sen's League for the Protection of Civil Rights in January 1933. Yang Quan, the secretary general of the league, was assassinated by the Nationalist secret service in June 1933. Compelled by circumstances, Zou Taofen embarked upon his journey to Europe on July 14, 1933. *Zou Taofen nianpu,* pp. 51–55.

[30] Zou Taofen graduated from the Episcopalian St. John's University in Shanghai in July 1921. His first job was as an English secretary to Mu Ouchu, owner of the Housheng Cotton Mill and founder of the Shanghai Textile Exchange. His St. John's connection, meanwhile, landed him a string of temporary positions as English secretary, teacher, and lecturer at *Shenbao,* in the Y.M.C.A. Middle School, and in the Baptist Shanghai College.

and such connections brought denunciations shortly after the Northern Expedition that *Shenghuo zhoukan* was a mouthpiece of the "Shanghai capitalists," who were to come under such heavy political pressure during the Nanjing decade.[31]

Prominent as the bourgeois connection seemed to be, Zou Taofen's early life, based on his own account, suggested a different biographical motif. Like many other major figures in the CCP pantheon such as Lu Xun and Qu Qiubai, Zou Taofen came from a landed gentry family in decline and acquired a keen appreciation of genteel poverty in his formative years. He was deeply attached to the memory of his mother, who died at the age of twenty-nine when Zou was twelve. Part of that memory centered upon experiences with scarcity when the family lived in Fuzhou on his father's irregular income as an expectant (*houbu*) official. In Zou's later portraiture his father seemed curiously remote from the wants of the family, although he saw to it that the son received a classical education in literary Chinese. His mother (a native of Haining, Zhejiang, from a long line of nationally eminent scholars and officials of the High Qing), whom Zou described later as "one of the most beautiful women that I have ever known," was often left to her own means to provide for the children. She would send her maid to the nearby temple for charity rice, while she paced the floor at home with one of Zou's younger siblings in her arms. "I used to sit in a small chair nearby and follow her movements with my eyes, wondering why her face was so pale and her thoughts so deep, not knowing that what I saw was the portrait of poverty."[32]

Although his St. John's education opened doors for him into the Sino-Western circles of Shanghai's financial and industrial elites, Zou's college experience also reinforced his sense of self-reliance and striving. More than socially acceptable to the Shanghai bourgeoisie because of his cultural accomplishments as a classically trained son of the traditional gentry, Zou Taofen was nonetheless economically inferior by St. John's standards. One of the most prestigious and exclusive missionary institutions in Central China, the St. John's student body comprised many of the indulged children of the wealthy Jiangnan and Ningbo-Canton comprador elite. Zou Taofen, however, had to support himself through

---

Ibid., p. 21. On St. John's University, see Wen-hsin Yeh, *Alienated Academy*, pp. 49–128.

[31] The most explicit attack on *Shenghuo* as a "capitalist mouthpiece" came from He Yuseng, the compiler of a chronological biography of Sun Yat-sen and the editor of the *Revolutionary Army Daily*, a Nanjing-based Nationalist Party publication, shortly after the Nationalists established themselves in Nanjing. He Yuseng's letter to the editor was dated October 17, 1928. "Dafu yifeng yanli zebei de xin," *Shenghuo* 4.1 (November 18, 1928): 6–8.

[32] Zou Taofen, "Wo de muqin," in *Jingli*, pp. 296–299.

college with a variety of library and tutoring chores and contribute to the educational expenses of a younger brother at the same time. An avid reader of English-language publications, he earned pocket money by writing up essays with information taken from American science journals and sports magazines and selling them to Shanghai newspapers and periodicals.[33]

Zou Taofen deliberately mentioned these experiences at St. John's in *Shenghuo zhoukan* not only because they contributed to the basically pro-American and bourgeois liberal stance of the journal before the Manchurian Incident of 1931, but also because Zou often used autobiography to encapsulate his unique standing as a facilitator of communication between the worlds of *Shenghuo*'s high-minded sponsors and the journal's hard-working readers. As one among the Shanghai elite who knew the challenge of financial stress, Zou Taofen consciously resorted to personal anecdotes to inspire vocational youth to press on with their hard climb into the higher ranks of Shanghai's middle-class society.[34] The construction of an autobiographical narrative in this early stage of his publishing career was thus already fused with a broadly defined enterprise of ideological conversion. Zou Taofen was in that sense one of the first popularizers in modern China to subsume the discrete significances of incidents in his own life into a meaningful system of broadly constructed political beliefs.

This blending of biographical narrative into a middle-class ideology was done with a heavily moralistic overtone. The early issues of *Shenghuo zhoukan* elaborated upon the central belief that personal qualities matter and that individual efforts produce results. "Moral cultivation" (*xiuyang*) of ethically correct attitudes at work and in leisure was deemed crucial to personal professional success.[35] By using that venerable moral term, inseparable from the long history of neo-Confucianism, in the 1920s to praise such un-Confucian activities as the pursuit of national political prestige and the advancement of personal economic ambition, Zou illustrated the degree to which tradition could be invoked in defense of modern values.[36]

---

[33] Zou Taofen, *Jingli*, pp. 21–23.

[34] Ibid., pp. 42–43, 54–58, 64–65.

[35] See, for example, Yang Xianjiang, "Qingnian xiuyang lun—faduan," *Shenghuo* 1.1 (October 11, 1925): 4–6; Yang Dinghong, "Qingnian congshi zhiye yihou yingyou de taidu," *Shenghuo* 1.33 (June 6, 1926): 195; Enrun, "Gongzuo yu pinxing zhi guanxi," *Shenghuo* 2.2 (October 31, 1926): 8–9.

[36] Under a conservative regime, the invocation of *xiuyang* could also serve as a form of self-defense. In the 1940s, when the Nationalist government charged that the Shenghuo Bookstore was indoctrinating its employees politically in small in-house group discussion sessions, Zou Taofen replied that the sessions were merely intended for the general *xiuyang*

Few of *Shenghuo*'s messages under Zou Taofen were "original." The journal, however, did light upon a strategy of presentation that, in a highly personalistic and anecdotal tone, wed aspirations for higher personal status to the volatile economic scene of contemporary Shanghai. The concrete form of this strategy was the Readers' Mailbox (*Duzhe xinxiang*): a letters-to-the-editor column that, for the first time in the history of Chinese publishing, provided average literate youths with a forum to give voice to themselves. The Readers' Mailbox offered hundreds of individual voices an opportunity to tell their personal stories in detail. In the column, through the mediating voice of the commenting editor, a general profile of the urban sojourning experience began to emerge, described in its own language and judged by its own chosen criteria. The editor's voice, meanwhile, continually stressed *xiuyang* as the key to success and affirmed the connection between wealthy individuals and respectable nation-states, thereby unleashing and legitimizing the social strivings of petty urbanites who saw their own ambitions projected countrywide on *Shenghuo*'s printed pages. These ambitions, however, were only to be frustrated later during the political instability and economic recession of the 1930s—a disappointment that eventually launched the self-styled "vocational youth" upon a course of transformation into politically charged "progressive youth," energized by the contemporaneous rise of the Democratic Alliance and the expansion of the Shenghuo enterprise when China went to war with Japan.

The Work Ethic

In *Shenghuo*'s depiction of the work place, hardship or *ku* (bitterness) was recognized as a basic condition in the lives of vocational youth. Hardship was understood as long hours of strenuous work and lack of nourishment, relief, and diversion—conditions typical among old-style trades and crafts apprentices in traditional China. In fact, such hardship was regarded as necessary in training a master tradesman. Employers were quoted as instructing new apprentices: "Young people ought to learn diligence and to endure hardship!"[37] In this sense, the apprentice's "hardship" was neither unique to Shanghai nor specific to the 1920s,

---

of members of his publishing enterprise. While the earlier *xiuyang* was deemed as indispensable to individual success in a visibly modernizing nation, the later *xiuyang*, by comparison, was resolutely aimed at raising the political consciousness of the masses for the creation of a new socialist society.

[37] Wu Weizhong, "Liu Bannong suo quxing jinxiang de xuetu ku," *Shenghuo* 2.9 (December 19, 1926): 54.

since it was present nearly everywhere from preindustrial England to late imperial China.

By drawing the vocational youth into the world of printed words and dissolving the boundaries previously separating school students and trade apprentices, however, *Shenghuo zhoukan* was instrumental in generating a new sense of hardship and bitterness: that of an unfortunate young man who, by dint of working instead of attending school, had been "deprived of an education" (*shixue*). The essence of hardship in this sense was less oppression than deprivation. It derived less from the work experience of shop and trade than from a glimpse into the world lying beyond and a comparison with others differently employed. "The life of an apprentice is full of hardship," wrote Liu Bannong in his long poem *The Hardships of Apprenticeship*. "The young man apprentices himself in the hope of mastering the crafts of a trade. But the master teaches neither reading nor arithmetic!"[38]

Instead, the master was likely to invoke "diligence" as an ethical injunction to justify his subjugation of the apprentice:

At dawn the apprentice is ordered to open up the store and to sweep the floor; at dusk he is shown the floor to sleep on and is told to stay alert. He is the cook in the kitchen when free from the store, and he attends chores in the vegetable garden, too. The mistress has a small child. She orders: "You, young man! Hold and take care of the baby for me!" The baby lets out a wail. The mistress erupts in rage. She rises from her chair and pounds on the table. Her abusive words deliver insults to the apprentice's parents! Endlessly from morning till afternoon, the apprentice runs east to fetch liquor and juice, and west to buy vegetables and bean curd; he waits at the table three meals a day; he serves the tea when visitors come; he rolls the tobacco when the master needs a break. By the front door he responds to the summons of the customers. By the back door he washes the pots and urns! Without a moment's rest he is hurried around from sunrise to sunset.[39]

In Liu Bannong's poetic representation, the apprentice lives in constant fear of the master and the mistress. No matter how hard he works and how pleasant he forces himself to be, "still, the master's blows fall on his head like a heavy rain." The apprentice's very existence as a household consumer inflames his employers' stinginess: "His shoes are worn and he mends the holes in the middle of the night with tears in his eyes. The mistress minds the oil that is being burned in the lamp. Repeatedly she says her curses! His meals are leftovers that fail to satisfy

---

[38] Ibid.
[39] Ibid.

his hunger. In the summer he is given no shirts to wear. In the winter he shivers in rags."[40]

Such stinginess was, in all likelihood, widespread at an earlier time. What was new in the 1920s was the poet's denunciation of the master for his "inhuman" denial of the apprentice's basic needs. The young man is pushed to endure the "unnatural," so that even his illness is denied authenticity: "In December the master eats cakes and the apprentice works on the stone and the mortar. In the summer the master eats melons and cools off in the shade while the apprentice tends the fire by the stove and boils the water. The apprentice is ill. The master shouts: 'How dare you lazybones pretend to be ill!' "[41]

But a man's natural capacity for reflection, the poet goes on to show, is irrepressible, even in the midst of a hectic life. When the apprentice rinses rice by the river upon the order of his mistress, "the water in the river is as clear as a mirror.... The apprentice sees his own pale face in the mirror. He thinks to himself: 'I, too, was born to human parents!' "[42] The poet thereby turns to the reflective capacity of all human beings. Shenghuo, likewise, was predicated upon a faith in vocational youth's innate capacity to look toward sources of useful knowledge and general enlightenment.

Vocational youth often wrote letters to the Readers' Mailbox complaining about the oppressiveness of their masters and the tedium of their chores. But sometimes they went beyond discrete complaints and began identifying institutional causes for their malaise. One such reader, for example, criticized "the deficient educational system of this present era of transition" that had failed, on the one hand, to impart useful knowledge to the educated, and, on the other, to rectify societal contempt for manual laborers. "As a result of such social prejudices," Hong Gengyang wrote, "many young people of middling background are kept idle, living off the inheritance of their fathers and elder brothers rather than making a living on their own.... With this many consumers and only a handful of producers... how can the nation not be impoverished?" Hong urged a renewed emphasis on vocational education to give the productive members of society a much-deserved opportunity for education. Vocational youth might thereby aspire to a horizon of unlimited social mobility, much as "Abraham Lincoln had been able to rise from modest employments to the American Presidency."[43]

---

[40] Ibid.

[41] Ibid.

[42] Ibid.

[43] Hong Gengyang, "Kai hu yan zhi," Shenghuo 2.49 (October 9, 1927): 383–384.

Shenghuo's editorials amply criticized the institutional failures that discontented Republican China's urban vocational youth. But even when the journal spoke harshly of old-fashioned employers' backwardness, it went no further than urging them to reform. Instead of calling for a structural overhaul of society, *Shenghuo* placed the burden of personal advancement squarely upon the shoulders of the individual. A young man's career was said to hinge critically upon his attitude toward work or upon his ability to take the initiative. By way of didactically illustrating this road to commercial success, *Shenghuo* routinely featured the biographies of affluent merchants, whose life stories were held up for emulation (see Appendix).

Shenghuo also drew upon the classical philosophers for personal inspiration, quoting the neo-Confucian masters more for their concrete instructions on discrete situations than for their ontological speculations. Sun Xiafeng's instructions on learning were cited, for example, by way of emphasizing that the acceptance of hardship was the key to personal success. Sun admonished scholars who complained that they had failed the examinations because of financial worries and personal difficulties, saying: "These people fail to understand that learning is acquired precisely at these junctures of poverty, illness, setbacks, and disappointments."[44] Wang Yangming, the fifteenth-century moral philosopher of the School of Mind, appeared in the pages of *Shenghuo* as a practical adviser on the psychology of effective personal persuasion. "The best way to admonish a friend is to speak to him sincerely and to offer him ample guidance," the Ming master was quoted as saying. "Exhaust your sincerity and feeling, and exhaust, too, your sense of delicacy and thoughtfulness. [If you do so,] your friend may hear you well and may be willing to follow your advice. Move him by touching his feelings. If you condemn and denounce, and allow your friend no breathing space, you are provoking him to respond violently."[45] And Zeng Guofan, leader of the nineteenth-century school of statecraft thought, was constantly cited to counsel patience, to advise against avoidance of hardship, to urge postponement of gratification, to demand meticulous attention to detail, and to preach "reverence" (*jing*) and "persistence" (*heng*).[46]

---

[44] *Shenghuo* 2.8 (December 12, 1926): 50.

[45] Ibid., 2.10 (December 26, 1926): 60.

[46] Bi Yuncheng, "Qingnian zhi chenggong," *Shenghuo* 2.11 (January 16, 1927): 65–66. At the same time, *Shenghuo* moved beyond the neo-Confucian masters to the Confucian classics to seek moral authority for the work ethic expounded in the journal. The commentaries in the *Book of Changes*, for example, instruct: "Heaven moves on ceaselessly. The gentleman improves upon himself ceaselessly." From this line *Shenghuo* derived teachings on the virtues of diligence, savings, and efficiency. Wang Zhixin, "Chuxu de yichu,"

Even when they were not quoting from the moral philosophers, *Shenghuo*'s authors composed didactic essays imbued with the spirit of the Confucian ethical tradition. Only a small number of individuals are gifted with talents at birth, the readers were told, but all could strive to attain virtue, which should lead to a state of spiritual composure. "Those who are pure in virtue enjoy the pleasure of innocence, and they will not lose this state of mind as a result of changing circumstances."[47]

Shenghuo's messages in the 1920s to "vocational youth," in short, consistently emphasized neo-Confucian *xiuyang* or individual moral self-cultivation. Far from demanding institutional changes to dramatically alter social relationships, the early *Shenghuo* asked vocational youth to take to heart the moral teachings of the neo-Confucian masters, to make the best of their circumstances, to exercise self-control, and to cultivate spiritual composure. Poverty was no hindrance to a young man's eventual advancement, because personal success was not the gift of birth but the result of discipline and resolve. The essential message was simply that steady effort to perfect one's performance might make it possible for any young man to rise to the top of Shanghai's commercial and industrial world. Should that somehow fail to be the case, then proper moral cultivation would bring virtuous contentment in its stead.

Although *Shenghuo*'s didactic essays on the work ethic stressed the importance of individual merit, contemporary sources agreed nearly unanimously that kinship ties and personal connections outweighed all other factors when it came to placement in Shanghai's job market. Tradesmen were often interconnected through native-place associations and master-disciple relationships, and these ties grew even stronger when conjoined with matrimonial affiliations. Normative claims that governed familial relationships were extended to work relationships as well.

Shenghuo's ethical stance, with its universalistic implications, was not intended to displace the reality of particularism altogether. But the journal did emphasize that kinship and personal ties alone were insufficient to guarantee results. It held out the belief that a just system of rewards for the virtuous in fact existed even within the personalistic familial network. As the business environment itself underwent modernization, furthermore, individual competence and accomplishment were seen as gaining in importance. Numerous anecdotes in the pages of *Shenghuo* showed that a well-placed young man owed his success not to connection but to effort or that when two equally well connected candidates

Shenghuo 2.11 (January 16, 1927): 68–69; Lu Guiliang, "Tian ye zuo shenghuo," ibid., p. 68.

    [47] Yangyi, "Dexing—fuwu zhi dier tiaojian," ibid., pp. 66–67.

sought the same post, the one with the superior personal qualities was awarded the prize.[48]

When personal qualities were elevated to such central importance, career success depended not only upon what one did during work hours, but even more upon how one used one's spare time. As far as *xiuyang* was concerned, there was no boundary. If one succumbed to the temptations of gambling and prostitution, among other vices, the inevitable result was indebtedness and eventually embezzlement.[49] Consequently, it was the employer's legitimate business concern—as well as his paternal duty as the teacher-master—to seek to ensure that such-and-such a young employee used his leisure time constructively.[50]

Where did career success supposedly lead? *Shenghuo's* stories of successful merchants usually concluded with the hero becoming the master of his own enterprise. A businessman who had thus attained his financial manhood became, at the same time, the head of a patriarchal household consisting often of wife and children, younger brothers and sisters, nephews and nieces, maids, servants, and perhaps other dependents. He also commanded an entourage of apprentices, accountants, secretaries, chauffeurs, and clerks. A well-established merchant was, above all, centrally situated in an extended network of social relationships that encompassed kin, friends, neighbors, fellow traders, and *Landsleute*. This order of things ideally fused features of the old with the new. But whether an enlightened state of mind informed this male-centered nexus of authority was entirely dependent upon the master: there were no structural provisions for embracing modern values without abandoning traditional virtues.

But the modernizing economy of the city, with its larger commercial organizations and heavier capital outlay, was rapidly taking away from numerous petty employees the prospect of becoming the owners of their own businesses. In the new industries and professions a style of work life was emerging that produced experiences devoid of the certitude and dignity associated with successful tradesmen of the old school. Diligence and dedication were still much in demand. Whether old-fashioned virtue was to bring the promised rewards of success and happiness, however, was increasingly called into question, as the following profile by Zou Taofen of a miserly proofreader shows:

---

[48] Taofen, "Ji," *Shenghuo* 3.25 (May 6, 1928): 269; Bi Yuncheng, "Huiwei," *Shenghuo* 3.34 (July 8, 1928): 381–386.

[49] Bi Yuncheng, "Yi ge fuche," *Shenghuo* 3.12 (January 22, 1928): 129–130.

[50] See Wang Zhiyi, "Zhengdang de yule fangfa," *Shenghuo* 2.1 (October 24, 1926): 1–2, on "musts" and "must-nots" in recreation.

There is a certain proofreader who works for a Shanghai newspaper. Fifty-five years old, he has worked in this position for some twenty or thirty years. His monthly salary was ten-odd kuai at the beginning. He now makes fifty kuai a month.

The proofreader's home town is an industrial center on the Shanghai-Nanjing Railway line. He goes home annually just once toward the end of the year. The rest of the time he spends entirely in Shanghai, where he stays in the office of the newspaper and rarely goes anywhere.

He allows himself three silver dollars a year for pocket money. He deposits his salary with the newspaper's cashier and not with a bank because he fears that the latter may go out of business. He never remits his salary but always asks someone to carry it home, because he refuses to pay for the remittance. He will not take a tram if he carries no luggage on his annual trip home. He walks the entire distance from the newspaper's office on Wangping Street to the train station. He always rides in the fourth-class paupers' train.

His shoes and socks are all made by his wife back in the country. He sends his dirty laundry home for her to wash. A round-trip train ride from Shanghai to his home village takes about three hours. He always puts on his fur gown on the first day of the twelfth month on the lunar calendar. He changes his clothing once a month. He always changes into his summer gown on the first day of the sixth month on the lunar calendar, and remains so dressed for one month. Regardless of the actual conditions of the weather, he never changes his routine.

It costs about a dime for a haircut in the barber shop. This man always gets a monkish shave from the traveling barbers who rest their tools in front of the English cemetery. The shave costs eighteen copper coins. He never goes to the bathhouse. Nor does he ever use the post office. He finds proofreading quite gratifying. He never bothers to learn about the contents.

He finds the seven days that he spends at home rather boring. He hands all his money over to his wife. He has already accumulated several thousands of [ounces of] gold. His sons are all established, and they have children of their own. This proofreader intends to retire at the age of sixty. After retirement he plans to head home to the countryside.[51]

Zou Taofen's portrait of this particular sojourner was detailed, realistic, and firmly embedded in time and space—in sharp contrast to the timeless and ritualized portraits that he drew for Shanghai's icons of success. Yet Zou presented this profile without much comment, except to marvel at the man's frugality in the midst of Shanghai's dazzling opulence.

---

[51] Luoxia, "Fanhua Shanghai zhong de qijian zhe," *Shenghuo* 3.33 (July 1, 1928): 371–373.

For most of *Shenghuo zhoukan*'s readers this sketch of a hard-driven white-collar employee provided a rare glimpse into a strange new world that was burgeoning in Shanghai's modern high-rise office buildings in the foreign concessions. Such a lonely, nameless, and anomic existence of rigid routines and limited prospects was dramatically different from the extravagant life of illustrious members of the city's Chamber of Commerce. Zou's portrait introduced the very real possibility that with the metropolitanization of economic life a father could be severed from his extended household, and a man given to work could be without a home. Such could be the lot awaiting the majority of vocational youth once their apprenticeships were over.

Although *Shenghuo* preferred not to undermine its promotion of economic modernization by stressing the dehumanization of modern times, the concentration of tens of thousands of youthful sojourners of marriageable age in Shanghai's trades, crafts, and industries did nonetheless draw the journal's attention to the question of personal family circumstances. Consequently, *Shenghuo* emphasized the need to constitute a new sort of urban home separate from the extended lineages back in the countryside. Although the idea was by no means irreconcilable with images held by the old patriarchs, it was a different kind of nuclear family that the new members of the Shanghai bourgeoisie were expected to create in order to have, after all, a home of their own.

Family

Shenghuo's progressive image in the late 1920s was framed by Zou Taofen's emphatic projection of the ideal of the *xiao jiating* (small household): the nuclear family consisting of the married couple and their unmarried children. The term acquired meaning in opposition to the *da jiazu* (big family, clan): the traditional extended family that continued to be the norm in vast areas of Republican China. Briefly put, while the *da jiazu* had sanctified the Confucian ethical norms of filial piety and female chastity, functioning for centuries as the foundation of lineage power in rural areas, the *xiao jiating* was Western in inspiration and urban in its constituency.

Along with the ideal of the new nuclear family came a cluster of related changes ranging from open social interaction between men and women, a free choice of marriage partners as opposed to arranged marriages, and separate residence for the young couple from the groom's parental lineages, to complete ownership and disposition over the couple's properties and greater provisions for the eventuality of a divorce. These new practices, combined with the insistence that marriages must

be built upon the emotional bond uniting the conjugal couple instead of
the conventions governing a young woman's entry into the groom's
extended household, constituted a radical challenge to the customary
norms that had governed marriages and families for thousands of years.

Shenghuo's discussion of the *xiao jiating* engaged the interest of many
urban youth, including women students. In his attacks on the traditional
norm Zou Taofen did not reprint such controversial essays and short
stories as "A Critique of Filial Piety" and "Diary of Miss Sophie," which
manifested the defiant rejection by May Fourth intellectuals of these Confucian ethical beliefs.[52] Rather, Zou focused upon the tangible aspects of
everyday arrangements between two modern marriage partners, making
terms such as "the sweetness of love" and "the quest for happiness" a
part of the everyday speech of petty urbanites.[53]

Shenghuo reported approvingly, for instance, that Chiang Kai-shek and
Song Meiling used endearments such as "darling" and "dear" in English
with each other and noted enthusiastically how these linguistic usages
contributed to the tenderness of a family's atmosphere.[54] The journal
pointedly noted by way of contrast that it was common in many parts of
rural China for a girl to be referred to as a piece of "money-losing merchandise" (*peiqian huo*) and for a daughter's marriage to be called the
"sale" (*mai*) of the bride.[55]

Shenghuo's readers responded with cris de coeur that reflected their
own clash with traditional attitudes about love and marriage. "My family
is old-fashioned.... When my elders arranged a marriage contract for me,
they evaluated the groom's family status and assets, but paid no attention
to his personal qualities.... My father intends to marry me off to the
decadent son of a corrupt bureaucrat!... I have been very close to someone lately.... Our love led to physical intimacy... and I am carrying the
consequence of our love!... My father threatens to put me to death."[56] A
characteristic letter to the Readers' Mailbox read in part:

> Dear Editor: Your journal has assumed a major responsibility in transform-
> ing social customs.... Your stance on the *xiao jiating* speaks the mind of us
> unmarried youth.... I am nineteen, with an elementary school education,
> and have been employed in business for three years. My income is just
> enough for my personal expenditure. My parents, however, are putting

[52] Chow Tse-tsung, *The May Fourth Movement,* p. 306; Jonathan D. Spence, *The Gate of Heavenly Peace: The Chinese and Their Revolution, 1895–1980* (New York: Penguin, 1981), pp. 259–261.

[53] Taofen, "Wu ai," *Shenghuo* 3.44 (September 16, 1929): 521–522.

[54] Bianzhe, "Tianme de chenghu," *Shenghuo* 4.31 (June 30, 1929): 347.

[55] Xizhen, "Xiangxia ren bing bu wangu," *Shenghuo* 4.29 (June 16, 1929): 319–320.

[56] Taofen, "Yifeng wanfen poqie qiujiu de xin," *Shenghuo* 4.46 (October 13, 1929): 519.

pressures on me to get married soon.... I have learned from reading your journal that financial independence is critical.... I have also learned about the evils of arranged marriages.... But how am I ever to find opportunities for interaction with women? There are few opportunities for that in Shanghai. Nor can I ever afford the huge expenses of Shanghai's social clubs.... I am unwilling to go along with my parents' arrangements. On the other hand, I am fearful of their displeasure.... What am I supposed to do?[57]

Many such letters conveyed a sense of extreme urgency: a wedding to take place within a week, a deadline imposed by the family, a threat to cut off financial support forthwith, a declaration of intent to pursue legal actions unless immediately satisfied, and so forth. *Shenghuo* regularly reported the suicides committed by young men and women caught in their various personal dilemmas. Youthful rebellion against paternal authority was clearly not without tears and risks. Zou Taofen usually spoke firmly but prudently in the face of such domestic crises. The editor's opinions at such critical junctures were treated by the panicked or confused correspondents as no mere editorial commentary but as a guidance for action. Meanwhile, the publication of their correspondence gave *Shenghuo*'s other readers a chance to reflect upon their own circumstances and to voice their thoughts as well, as they witnessed the unfolding of the drama. Readers writing for help and advice were thus often assured of the moral support of a chorus of voices as they embarked upon their quest for an unconventional solution.

And recommended solutions could certainly turn out to be unconventional. Take, for example, *Shenghuo*'s coverage of the illicit affair between Huang Huiru, a young woman from a highly respectable family, and Lu Genrong, a servant in her brother's household. Miss Huang had been engaged to marry a certain Mr. Bei, scion of a leading Suzhou comprador family that even held a seat on the Shanghai Municipal Council. For some reason the engagement was broken, and Huang Huiru began an illicit affair with her brother's servant. The secret came to light when Miss Huang became pregnant and the brother filed a public suit against the servant in the municipal court. Shanghai's "mosquito press" blazoned the titillating scandal across their front pages.

Shenghuo followed the story closely. But unlike the rest of Shanghai's newspapers, which righteously relished every detail of the poor woman's plight, *Shenghuo* used the scandal as an occasion to examine certain normative assumptions. Through a careful reconstruction of the case, Zou Taofen showed that Miss Huang's brother was a characteristically old-fashioned and self-centered man with rigid notions of status and

---

[57] Mao Jindao, "Fumu cuihun shenji," *Shenghuo* 3.33 (July 1, 1928): 377–378.

propriety. What prompted him to bring suit against Lu Genrong was not so much his stated sense of duty to avenge the insult suffered by his sister as his determination to punish the servant for the latter's insolence toward himself. Worse yet, even as Miss Huang later expressed the wish to marry her lover, the brother ignored her plea and sued for revenge, bringing her public disgrace.[58]

Zou Taofen, meanwhile, was equally critical of the servant, Lu Genrong. He concluded from Mr. Lu's manner of speaking that the man did not have an enlightened understanding of the meaning of love. He had simply taken advantage of his mistress in her moment of distress, assuming, like many others, that her broken marriage contract was enough of a social disgrace to make her "fair game."[59]

Huang Huiru thus emerged in *Shenghuo*'s pages not as the principal perpetrator and hence the guilty party in a scandalous case of illicit sex, but as an unfortunate victim much maligned by males who followed norms that condoned their callousness. "We view Miss Huang as a decent woman," Zou wrote, "whose misfortune was entirely the result of familial and social circumstances."[60] Huang Huiru, to be sure, was not a heroine to be emulated. But her disgrace underscored the inadequacy of existing norms for male behavior. In the judgment of *Shenghuo* she deserved sympathy and support rather than shame and condemnation, and any man who would step forward at this time to rescue her with true love deserved to be admired as a hero.[61] Zou's commentaries were so effective in introducing an unconventional perspective into the case that they drew numerous letters from young women readers supporting Miss Huang and sympathizing with a woman whose name was irreparably damaged by status degradation and illicit love.[62]

It was common in those days for a sojourning young man to learn with surprise that he was engaged to be married. The news would be broken to him in a letter from home. During his next visit back to the province at the time of the annual spring festival he might find himself becoming a groom, his bride a total stranger to him but nonetheless his parents' choice. After the marriage had been consummated the groom

[58] Bianzhe, "Women lianxi Huang Huiru nüshi" *Shenghuo* 4.3 (December 2, 1928): 24–26; 4.4 (December 9, 1928): 36–38.

[59] Ibid.

[60] Taofen, "Yihou she qu Huang nüshi de bianshi 'hero'," *Shenghuo* 4.5 (November 16, 1927): 41.

[61] Ibid.

[62] Hu Yaochang, "Shehui duiyu Huang nüshi he ruci zhi canku," *Shenghuo* 4.11 (January 27, 1929): 111–112.

would have used up his holidays. He would then leave for Shanghai by himself, too insecure financially to take his new wife along, too unhappy with her or too conventional not to concur with the parental expectation that the bride stay behind to wait on her in-laws. Excerpts from the following letter identify a pattern of common problems:

> I come from an old-fashioned family. My marriage was arranged for me....I was 14 when engaged. I tried to get to know her, but without success.... The mere mentioning of the idea to annul the engagement was greeted with such horror by both sets of parents; a divorce would be a sheer scandal.... She was utterly uneducated and stubborn. I was completely put off by her. I left home three days after the wedding.... I have been reading about the new marriages. It is absolutely beyond my power to transform her into a lovable wife.... I found it necessary for my future as well as for hers to obtain a divorce. Are there legal entanglements? May I fall in love with someone else before I divorce her?[63]

While sexual impetuosity and the freedom to love served as powerful solvents in attacks against the *da jiazu,* the *xiao jiating* that was subsequently brought forth was hardly the height of romantic passion. Once married, the ideal couple began the construction of a new domestic order. The heart of this order was the nuclear home: a neat and immaculate place managed by a full-time housewife.[64] The home provided material comfort and emotional solace to its members. In it children were born, nurtured, and educated to health and happiness. In such homes dinner, when the patriarchal head of household returned from work, was the high point of the day. Visitors heard only the gentle voice of the mistress, the laughter of the children, and the singing from time to time with piano or violin accompaniment.[65]

Shenghuo made it clear, however, that not every woman was naturally competent in such a situation. Young wives in old-style extended households, in particular, had typically been socialized to preoccupy themselves with other women—mothers-, grandmothers-, and sisters-in-law, aunts, cousins, nieces, maids, female visitors, and so forth—rather than with their husbands. An assemblage of women was characteristically noisy and gossipy, needlessly mindful of ritual details and hopelessly bogged down by trivialities. Women, especially illiterate ones, furthermore, tended to excite each other's conservative instincts and superstitious beliefs. They could become alternately quarrelsome, hysterical,

---

[63] Zou Taofen, ed., *Duzhe xinxiang waiji* 1:80–83.

[64] See, for instance, Bi Yuncheng, "Yige heyu lixiang de jiating," *Shenghuo* 3.8 (December 25, 1927):81.

[65] Baoyi, "Lixiang de jiating," *Shenghuo* 2.7 (December 5, 1926):42. See also Xinshui, "Jieshao jiating yule fangfa de xinjianyi," *Shenghuo* 2.20 (March 20, 1926):136–138.

vicious, or simply shrill. Such women made sorely deficient mothers, if the primary function of mothering was not simply to raise but also to edify the young. Such women also made undesirable wives, since they deprived their unfortunate spouses of much needed peace and tranquillity at home after a long day of hard work in the office.

As homemakers, moreover, young wives of extended families made poor managers, since their household economy was firmly controlled by the mother-in-law. Few in an extended family had much sense of personal financial accountability, in fact, because assets as well as liabilities were communally owned and managed. Individuals led lives that matched their social standing rather than their financial means, and both men and women were unproductive and inefficient.[66] Hu Shi, for instance, complained that time seemed to have no value for many of his countrymen, who whiled away the whole day either chatting in tea houses or visiting friends. Women of affluent families in particular often knew little better than killing their time with frivolous diversions such as gambling, opium smoking, and theater going.[67]

For there to be young women suitably fit to perform their modern wifely and motherly roles in the xiao jiating, therefore, women must be permitted to acquire an education in new-style schools. "Women are often enslaved by men, exploited, manipulated, and pushed around, without means to independence," lamented Wang Xiaozhong in a letter to the Readers' Mailbox, making an observation that had become commonplace in Republican urban circles.[68] Women's standing had to be improved. The benefits of literacy and solid common sense alone were enough to justify education for women, not to mention the additional training in home economics, child rearing, beautification, and the social skills of a middle-class hostess. Already in Republican cities a new breed of cultured women was being brought forth through these schools. Compared with old-fashioned ladies, these women saw the importance of speaking softly and conducting themselves with style. Those who had attended missionary schools had even acquired a love for Western visual arts and music for the elevation of the spiritual state of everyone in their future families.[69]

[66] Sheng Peiyu, Wu Shen, "Liangwei nüshi duiyu da jiazu de yijian," Shenghuo 2.50 (October 16, 1927): 394.

[67] Hu Shi, "Shijian bu zhiqian," Shenghuo 2.7 (December 5, 1927): 43–44; Sheng Peiyu, "Shu kan hao tan," Shenghuo 3.2 (November 13, 1927): 15; Wang Jianrui, "Shanghai funü li de maotouying," Shenghuo 3.3 (November 20, 1927): 26.

[68] Wang Xiaochong, "Yige nande de nüzi," Shenghuo 2.2 (November 1, 1926): 12.

[69] Too much education in reality could sometimes pose a problem, though, as was evidenced by, for example, "the undeniable fact that the Jinling College for Women has a

Beneath her feminine surface, *Shenghuo*'s ideal middle-class housewife was a hard-headed home economist, a dedicated domestic manager, an effective disciplinarian for her children, and a good neighbor on behalf of the family. The venerable Confucian notion of an "able wife and good mother" (*xian qi liang mu*) still applied. These women, in short, were supposed to attain happiness by asking of themselves the same sort of eclectic work ethic that supposedly led the vocational youth to success. In contrast to their men, however, these women were to use such a combination of modern and traditional disciplines primarily in the domestic setting. A mother was to take up jobs outside the home only when the children were fully grown. Reputable choices for middle-class women were restricted, furthermore, to a narrow range of tendering positions as teachers, tellers, and nurses in schools, banks, and hospitals.

Despite women's indispensability in the *xiao jiating,* the mainstay of this happy new order was still the hard-working man who was, ideally, both the provider and the protector. It was the earning capacity of the male head of the household that made the *xiao jiating* financially possible. "A young man's financial independence is the precondition for his marriage," advised Zhuang Zexuan, a prominent educator and author of guidebooks for youth.[70] Zou Taofen also advised youth to put off getting married until they could safely do so without indebting themselves to their relatives.[71]

It was important for the young husband to support his family himself, rather than depend upon income from his paternal lineage, because financial independence would enable the couple to "extricate" (*tuoli*) themselves from the *da jiazu,* to raise the issue of forming a *xiao jiating,* which was the first step toward breaking away from the web of entangled relationships that characterized the extended family.[72]

If the journal ever attempted a systematic critique of traditional familial relationships, it was in Zou Taofen's extensive rendition of two American novellas that featured a Western woman marrying a Chinese man. The translations, accompanied by extensive editorial commentaries, provided point-by-point comparisons between China and the West of the assumptions governing courtship, marriage, and family life, as seen

large number of old spinsters among its graduates." Cai Xiyue, "Dakai Jinling nüda xiaokan kankan," *Shenghuo* 4.31 (June 30, 1929): 348.

[70] Zhuang Zexuan, "Hunyin de xianjue wenti," *Shenghuo* 2.16 (February 12, 1927): 103–104.

[71] Yin, "Shou jingji yapo er xiangdao jieyu de yiwei qingnian," *Shenghuo* 2.7 (December 5, 1927): 54–55.

[72] The term *tuoli* (extricate, break away from, separate oneself from) occurs repeatedly in the family literature of this period.

through the eyes of Sino-Western couples supposedly at ease in both cultures.[73]

In both stories the couples met and married in the West, triumphing together over the social barriers and cultural prejudices that at first separated them. Once married the Chinese husbands took their English or American bride back home to meet the extended network of relatives. In each case, despite the family's large gentry fortune, the reserve of good will, and the new couple's high standing among their kinfolk, the return to the husband's birth place nearly destroyed the romantic bond between the devoted spouses. The wife found herself strangely idle, prevented from looking after the couple's affairs. Men and women were kept socially separated. Meanwhile, she was drawn into endless rituals that required her attendance on her mother-in-law.

Although Zou Taofen eschewed a categorical denunciation of traditional ethics by way of explanation, it was obvious in his presentation of these mixed marriages that he believed the norms of respectability and propriety in old-fashioned extended families prohibited emotional expressiveness, stifled individual initiatives, and forced the healthy and robust into a ritually correct life of boredom and lethargy. In the end, in fact, the husbands died of inexplicable illnesses, prompting their foreign wives and Eurasian children to embark upon a journey back home to the West.

Because every *xiao jiating* in Shanghai during the 1920s represented a purposeful choice over and against the prevailing norm of the *da jiazu,* one of the most critical roles for the heads of nuclear households was to act as a negotiator on behalf of the integrity of the conjugal unit vis-à-vis their own extended lineages. The burden fell almost exclusively upon the husbands, for women were bound by Confucian norms that effectively silenced them on such issues. Without the husbands' active assertion of such integrity there could be no operative nuclear family. The issue did not arise for Sun Li of the Dalong Iron Works on Shanghai's Gordon Road because Sun's decision to take a wife was prompted simply by the necessity to send a woman home to his village about three hundred *li* from Shanghai to wait upon his elderly parents.[74] Conversely, the attempts of many other men to mediate often put them in an unenviable situation between their parents and wives.[75]

---

[73] The two stories are "Yiwei Meiguo ren jiayu yiwei Zhongguo ren de zishu" and "Yiwei Yingguo nüshi yu Sun xiansheng de hunyin." The former was serialized in vols. 2–3, the latter in vols. 3–4.

[74] Sun Li, "Liangnan," *Shenghuo* 4.5 (December 16, 1928): 50.

[75] Li Guochong, "Ying peng ying," *Shenghuo* 4.6 (December 23, 1928): 59.

Shenghuo's readers expressed their concerns over familial issues by sending in a large number of letters on the subject. Roughly speaking, these fell into two categories. On the one hand was the image of the ideal *xiao jiating:* an urban-based nuclear family that reflected, in many ways, the political economy of the vocational youth, as well as the aspirations of new-style educated women. On the other was the representation of the existing extended families as "rural," "traditional," "oppressive," "unhealthy," "unproductive," and "immoral." In the depiction of the editors as well as the readers, personal and property relationships in the *da jiazu* were seen as not only stifling the genuine expression of human feelings, but also permitting unworthy individuals to abandon their basic social responsibilities with impunity. The creation of the *xiao jiating* thus represented not only the urban vocational youths' endeavor to carve out a domestic space of their own, but also an effort on their part to contain and rectify the pernicious influence of the rural hinterland that threatened to submerge everyone in a morass of evil customs, closed minds, poverty, ignorance, superstition, inefficiency, and irresponsibility.[76]

Bourgeois in social constituency and conservative in moral instincts, the arguments in favor of the *xiao jiating* were nonetheless regarded as "progressive" and even "revolutionary" in later official Chinese Communist historiography because they represented a first step against a system that had privileged not only the male but also the elderly. In its own context in the 1920s this brand of bourgeois individualism, combined with a Confucian ethic of personal accountability and pragmatic moralism, was enormously popular among the upwardly mobile urban vocational youth, because it both addressed a central fear and expressed an important wish.

As urban middle-class employees surveyed the landscape, they saw—as *Shenghuo* had vividly shown in its columns of commentaries and reports—the vast rural hinterlands of China in the grip of famine, flood, banditry, and marauding bands of soldiers and rioting peasants, while becoming at the same time hopelessly lost to opium and gambling.[77] By contrast, they saw the city not only as a place of employment and opportunity, but also as a mindfully constructed space of tree-lined boulevards, public parks and gardens, seafaring vessels, and sky-reaching office

---

[76] Qian Zhuanggong, "Nongcun shenghuo jiyi gailiang zhi dian," *Shenghuo* 2.1 (October 24, 1926): 4–5.

[77] Yang Chizhi and Bianzhe, "Nongmin yundong yu baodong," *Shenghuo* 2.13 (January 30, 1927): 82–83; Taofen, "Tianzai renhuo," *Shenghuo* 6.34 (August 15, 1931): 725; Xueshi, "Hankou shuihuan zhong zhi shehui biaoxian guan," *Shenghuo* 6.34 (August 15, 1931): 733–735.

buildings, the creation of modern technology and artistic imagination. Sojourn in the city was a life of hard work and healthy recreation; of rich cultural experience in the theaters, movie houses, and music halls; of out-door activities and Western-style sports in the park—all in a setting made much safer than the countryside by the availability of modern medicine and the presence of a municipal police force.[78] Was this man-made cityscape not the country's best defense against the hopelessness and loss of will in rural China? To stem the tide of disaster that was ris-ing from the countryside, therefore, an urban-based middle-class new order of hard work, self-sufficiency, domestic felicity, and personal pro-ductivity seemed indeed the best that anyone could strive for, not so much for the self, but—in the political language of the nation-state—"for the creation of a healthy society" and "the happiness of the people."[79]

Love and the Law

Like Lu Xun, Zou was outraged by the oppressive reification of tradi-tional morality, and he was certainly capable of high-sounding denuncia-tions against the ritually correct marriages of the past.[80] In his role as a pragmatic counselor to the young, however, Zou's voice was typically rea-sonable and restrained, and he wrote in a direct and simple style. The grievances of his young correspondents often went on page after page. The editor's response, on the other hand, was reducible to no more than a handful of practical rules of thumb.

Zou Taofen's understanding of love was straightforward enough: true love entails a serious moral commitment; it must never be confused with either sexual licentiousness or emotional blackmail. In practice, this basic insight translated into but a few axioms. Do not seek happiness at the expense of others. Do not send false signals during courtship. Always take full responsibility for what you have done. In case of disputes, always try gentle persuasion before confrontation. Never give in to coercion or manipulation. Men should always recognize their responsibility to their dependents, and not speak lightly of divorce. Women, however, should recognize their own basic rights to a decent existence, whether they choose to divorce or not. Zou argued strongly

---

[78] Wang Zhiyi, "Zhengdang de yule fangfa," *Shenghuo* 2.1 (October 24, 1926): 1–2; and "Gaizao dushi de yanjiu," *Shenghuo* 2.2 (October 31, 1926): 9–10.

[79] Sheng Peiyu, Wu Shen, "Liangwei nüshi duiyu da jiazu de yijian," *Shenghuo* 2.50 (October 16, 1927): 394.

[80] On Lu Xun, see Leo Ou-fan Lee, *Voices from the Iron House: A Study of Lu Xun* (Bloomington and Indianapolis: Indiana University Press, 1987).

against women committing suicide out of despair: "Always remember that you are, first of all, human, whether you are a wife or not."[81]

There was an obvious effort to seek simple solutions to complex problems, and Zou's advice to the young was nearly always measured and realistic. "You should again plead with your mother and hope that she may change her mind," he often advised. "Perhaps your uncle may put in a few good words on your behalf to your father. You must be patient and not despair." "Do you have a close friend or relative to whom you may turn for a few days till your father's rage subsides?" "You must remember that it's easier to insist on a cancellation of the marriage contract before the wedding has taken place than ask for a divorce afterwards. Insist!" Patience and persistence combined were clearly seen as the most effective means of persuasion in the long run.

After the founding of the Nationalist government in 1927 new laws were put into effect that substantially altered—at least on paper—the conditions governing marriage and divorce. Anyone over twenty was entitled to sign his or her own marriage contract, for example, without parental consent. Only natural parents, and not grandparents, uncles, aunts, brothers, in-laws, and so forth, had the authority to arrange for the marriages of minors. In theory, divorce had become a legal option much more accessible than before to women.[82]

Zou cited the new laws whenever applicable, consulting attorneys on his readers' behalf and providing information on court procedures and expenses. "The law says that when a marriage contract is signed without the consent of the principals who are minors, he or she may disavow the contract when reaching adulthood at the age of twenty. Who does your grandmother think she is, to defy the law of the land?" "The Ministry of Education has banned secondary school students from getting married while still in school. Your in-laws are defying the ministry's order when they demand that your sixteen-year-old daughter be married at this time. If the groom's family seems so thick-headed, it certainly portends serious problems after marriage. It's better to cancel the marriage and save your daughter from future anguish."[83] The law, however, was far from adequate in offering protection to the privately abused, and divorce was in reality difficult to obtain. Zou would sigh with resignation: "Perhaps your sister may seek the help of the local women's association, though I

---

[81] Mengsheng, "Jiujiu wo jiejie de xingming," *Shenghuo* 3.40 (August 19, 1928): 476–477.

[82] Kathryn Bernhardt, "Women and the Law: Divorce in the Republican Period," paper prepared for the Conference on Civil Law in Chinese Society, University of California at Los Angeles, August 1991, pp. 1–2.

[83] *Waiji* 1:218–219.

doubt that they are effectual. I am truly sorry to say that there seems to be no better way other than urging her not to give up hope."

Where the law failed to reach, the publisher and his readers offered moral support.

> I am sorry to hear that your fiancé turned out to have another lover. For-
> tunately you are not yet married, and you have a lover of your own. The
> law says that an engaged person may not have an affair with a third person.
> Such a happening constitutes sufficient ground for the dissolution of the
> marriage contract. Since you are over twenty years old and have received a
> secondary education, you may consider fleeing from home and supporting
> yourself with a job as a last resort to escape from the wedding. Your father
> need not worry about being legally liable to your fiancé's family, since you
> are no longer a minor. You must, of course, plan carefully for your travel in
> order to assure safety.[84]

In due course the cluster of individual cases presented in the pages of the journal became established precedents that created a framework of references among themselves. "What you may try under the cir-cumstances is to flee from home, as Miss Shen had done in a similar situation," wrote Zou. With an expanding repertoire for personal action, an audience that was called into existence by its shared interest in *Shenghuo* thus began to constitute itself as a social group with its own collective memory, unique language, distinct values, and shared culture.

The State

When *Shenghuo* invoked the law in defense of the young, it implicitly accepted the new party-state of the Nationalists as an active participant in the articulation of cultural norms. It pinned its hopes on the capacity of the modernizing state, through its enlightened cadres, to loosen the grip of the "evil gentry and local bullies" on provincial affairs, thereby undermining the basis of power of many conservative lineages. Meanwhile, despite the journal's pronounced individualistic ethic, there was a paradoxical acceptance of the power and function of the state. Inherent in its personalistic style of edification and steadfast endeavor toward the creation of a new cultural consensus were tendencies that lent themselves to an authoritarian construction of the sociopolitical order—untenable, though, as such a construction must be if stripped of a clear sense of communal support and moral legitimacy.

Although *Shenghuo* reported little on the activities of the Nationalists before the 1927 Revolution, the journal expressed considerable

---

[84] Ibid., pp. 57–58.

enthusiasm once the Nanjing government was founded. About December 29, 1927, the day that the Manchurian military governor pledged his allegiance to Nanjing, it commented excitedly: "One flag over China!"[85] And at the time of Sun Yat-sen's state funeral ceremony, which was made into a film for many Shanghai residents to view in the movie theaters, Zou Taofen reported on the audience's thunderous applause when Sun's portrait came on the screen and their quiet tears and solemn silence as Sun's coffin was seen carried down the temple steps by uniformed guards.[86]

The Nationalists' professed ideology, as stated in Sun Yat-sen's *Three Principles of the People,* addressed many issues of concern to vocational youth. Sun's Third Principle, that of "People's Livelihood," in particular, sought to combine state ownership of basic industries and the infrastructure with fully private enterprise in other economic sectors, while simultaneously paying equal attention to the twin tasks of rural revival and urban construction. It promised a future of vibrant economic growth without sharp social stratification, using the power of the state as tax collector to equalize the distribution of wealth and subsidize general welfare and education.

But it soon became clear that the Nationalist government of Chiang Kai-shek was in fact pursuing military and political policies that belied the legacy of the party's own Founding Father. Instead of a period of political stability and economic construction, the founding of the new government in 1927 marked only the beginning, instead of the end, of the Nationalists' use of military means in its quest for national political power. After a succession of local wars with regional warlords in North China, Chiang Kai-shek turned to conduct a series of military campaigns in Jiangxi in an effort to annihilate his one-time revolutionary comrades and now Communist rivals, who had managed to set themselves up in rural soviets. As these civil conflicts raged on, foreign powers, and especially the Japanese, intensified their exploitation of China's political instability, inciting local insurgents and provoking diplomatic incidents against the central authority in Nanjing.

The government thus turned increasingly to the Shanghai bourgeoisie for means to help pay for its staggering military expenses. To make matters worse in the eyes of the middle classes, Nanjing refused to permit them a voice in the political process commensurate with the share of

---

[85] Li Gongpu, "Quan Zhongguo zhiyou yizhong guoqi le," *Shenghuo* 4.17 (March 24, 1929): 174.

[86] Taofen, "Kanle Sun zongli guozang dianli yingpian," *Shenghuo* 4.34 (July 21, 1929): 375.

financial obligation it imposed upon them. In response to criticisms the government further tightened its control over the formation of political groups outside the party's control and censored dissenting views even more.

Meanwhile, drought and flood devastated extensive areas of China's interior in the early 1930s, and the government's popularity plummeted. Masses of famine-stricken refugees poured into large cities in search of relief, shocking middle-class residents with their destitute despair. Urban bankruptcies and unemployment rose alarmingly toward mid-decade, partly in response to the global economic depression that had finally reached Shanghai in full force. Not only were the Nationalists callous about such massive suffering; the regime took advantage of the economic disarray to seize managerial control of China's leading banks and responded to criticisms of its covetousness and malfeasance by having such dissidents assassinated.[87]

Shenghuo's coverage of current events in the early 1930s reflected its perception of doom and disaster under the Nationalists.[88] As the journal turned increasingly critical of the Nationalists, its initial reaction was to stress all the more the importance of self–help for the betterment of the lot of the petty urbanites. If the party-state was failing in its promise to fulfill its responsibilities to the nation, then members of the urban middle class—with their skills, virtues, knowledge, and discipline—would take it upon themselves to change the country's prospects. To prepare themselves for such tasks as well as to bring forth a viable urban political force, *Shenghuo,* along with its original sponsor, the Chinese Society for Vocational Education, strongly supported a variety of cultural and educational activities loosely referred to as "vocational," "social," or "popular." These activities ranged from alternative educational plans such as vocational training, mass literacy programs, correspondence schools, evening classes, lending libraries, and reading clubs to other forms of acculturation in music, drama, arts, and sports.[89]

---

[87] The most infamous case of this was the assassination of Shi Liangcai, the publisher of *Shenbao.*

[88] On the government's bureaucratism, see Qiuxing, "Women jinri suo zui xuyao de shi shenme?" *Shenghuo* 4.15 (March 10, 1929): 148; Taofen, "Bukan shexiang de guanhua," *Shenghuo* 5.1 (December 1, 1929): 1; on selfishness and irresponsibility, see "Mou yuanlao de liumang wenti," *Shenghuo* 5.8 (January 19, 1930): 113; on famine in Shanxi, "Ji Zha Liangzhao jun tao Shan zaishi," *Shenghuo* 6.12 (March 14, 1931): 253–254; on popular protest, "Minyi suozai," *Shenghuo* 6.25 (June 13, 1931): 509; on the state of gloom, "Guoqing yu guoai," *Shenghuo* 6.42 (October 10, 1931): 893; on Nationalist appeasement of the Japanese, "Guonan yu xuechao," *Shenghuo* 6.52 (December 19, 1931): 1153.

[89] See, for example, Taofen, "Qingkan jiaoyu jijin de gongxiao," *Shenghuo* 6.14 (March 28, 1931): 285; Zhu Jin, "Women de dushu hezuo," *Shenghuo* 6.14 (March 28, 1931): 299–300.

Zou Taofen's relationship with the Nationalists soured all the more precipitately, therefore, when the Nanjing government—as part of its "partification" (*danghua*) policies in education—imposed regulations that forced prospective students to prefer state-accredited institutions of learning, directly threatening the operation of night schools, literacy classes, correspondence courses, and autodidactic study sponsored by the urban gentry and entrepreneurial reformers of the Chinese Society for Vocational Education.[90]

Just as these projects were being curtailed, so also was the editing of *Shenghuo* suddenly encumbered by new censorship rules requiring government review of all manuscripts prior to publication. Zou Taofen responded angrily to Nanjing's attempt, through the Bureau of Social Affairs of Shanghai, to impose control on the press. He spoke out repeatedly on freedom of speech and stressed the importance of unrestricted access to information and an independent public opinion to a truly popularly based political system. Before long *Shenghuo* was attacking highly placed Nationalist officials for corruption, accusing them of perpetrating vices such as opium smoking and suggesting that the self-styled followers of Sun Yat-sen had betrayed the master's teaching and degenerated into selfish despots.[91]

A complete break with the government came with the Manchurian Incident of September 18, 1931. Under Zou Taofen's editorship, *Shenghuo zhoukan* embraced the cause of armed resistance against Japanese military encroachment without qualification. Zou denounced Chinese military commanders in the field for extreme cowardice and attacked Chiang Kai-shek's government for nonresistance.[92] He lamented that Nationalist leaders showed greater interest in domestic struggles for power than in defending the interests and dignity of the nation. In a clear move toward an attempt to call forth the urban populace, he urged Shanghai's college students to organize themselves for citywide protests and demonstrations.[93] In addition, he called for the organization of a

---

[90] When the new Ministry of Education introduced rules requiring all college applicants to present a diploma from accredited secondary schools before they were allowed to sit for college entrance examinations, for example, Zou Taofen charged that the sons and daughters of the poor would be seriously disadvantaged. The weekly printed numerous exchanges between Zou and Zhu Jingnong, the minister of education, on matters regarding school accreditation. On the significance of Nationalist regulations on higher education, see Wen-hsin Yeh, *Alienated Academy,* chap. 5.

[91] Zou Taofen, "Yapian gongmai minyi ceyan," *Shenghuo* 7.42 (October 22, 1932): 825.

[92] Taofen, "Wu ke yanshi de jiduan wuchi," *Shenghuo* 6.41 (October 3, 1931): 873.

[93] Taofen, "Dui quanguo xuesheng gongxian de yidian yijian," *Shenghuo* 6.40 (September 26, 1931): 854.

volunteer military corps and began using his journal to launch fund-raising campaigns for armed resistance against the Japanese in Man-churia.

The choices before the Chinese people, Zou commented grimly, were either death or dishonor, either resistance or the degradation of slavery.[94] The journal printed eyewitness accounts of Japanese massacres of women and children, accompanied by photographs of captured Chinese soldiers being herded away, their hands tied behind their backs, by Japanese sol-diers with drawn bayonets.[95] A vital nerve had apparently been touched: letters from the readers poured in, filled with despair and outrage—anger against both the Japanese and their own government. The fund drive drew impressive responses, with children, women, and petty wage earners sometimes giving their entire savings.[96] The circulation of the journal soared, pushing newsstand sales to a record circulation of nearly 150,000 copies. Encouraged by such momentum, Zou Taofen and his friends began planning for a newspaper, the *Shenghuo Daily,* that prom-ised to be even more responsive than the weekly to popular moods and interests.[97]

In due course the editorial voice grew shrill and defiant, and criti-cisms of the Nationalists' appeasement policies toward the Japanese crowded out discussions of most other subjects in the pages of *Shenghuo.* As the Nanjing government repeatedly ordered its troops to withdraw under Japanese military pressure, Zou Taofen openly declared that government incompetence and irresponsibility were ''sowing the seeds of revolution.''[98] Growing ever more hostile to the Nationalist regime, *Shenghuo* began speaking of domestic classes of ''oppressors'' who were ''beyond the touch of conscience and above the rule of the law,'' versus the vast majority of an unarmed and suffering people.[99] ''We are but common civilians with neither politically organized forces nor the preparations to seize political power,'' Zou warned. With the National-ists showing not a trace of Sun Yat-sen's ideals and with the nation in

---

[94] Taofen, "Yizhi de yanli jiandu," *Shenghuo* 6.40 (September 26, 1931): 854.

[95] Jizhe, "Shangxin canmu," *Shenghuo* 6.42 (October 10, 1931): 913–914; Taofen, "Guoqing yu guoai," *Shenghuo* 6.42 (October 10, 1931): 893; "Shenghuo guonan canxiang huabao," *Shenghuo* 6.44 (October 24, 1931): 991–994.

[96] See, for instance, "Benshe wei choukuan yuanzhu heisheng weiguo jianer jinji qishi," *Shenghuo* 6.48 (November 21, 1931): 1071–1072; "Juankuan zhuxiang zhe laihan zhi yiban," *Shenghuo* 6.48 (November 21, 1931): 1080.

[97] Taofen, "Chuangban *Shenghuo Ribao* zhi jianyi," *Shenghuo* 7.9 (March 5, 1932): 114–116.

[98] Taofen, "Zhengfu guangbo geming zhongzi," *Shenghuo* 6.49 (November 28, 1931): 1081.

[99] Ibid.

crisis, however, "for their self-defense as well as for the defense of the nation, the people (*minzhong*) may have to rise up and take a last stand!"[100]

This radical turn in political inclination signified not so much an abandonment of Zou's earlier socio-moral philosophy, however, as it did a shaken faith in creating a better society through individual efforts. His earlier beliefs had been predicated upon the assumption that socioeconomic construction could be brought about by private endeavors without resort to political means. His encounter with the Nationalist regime, however, had impressed upon him the futility of attempts to preserve the autonomy of private initiatives from political interference. Zou continued to advocate the necessity of striving to improve one's own lot in the world, but there was an element of resignation in his voice, born out of a bleak assessment of Chinese political realities. There was a belated recognition that no homes or careers were secure from the arbitrary power of an intrusive state. Nor were individual means ever adequate to stem the disastrous effects of irresponsible state policies on civilian lives. Revolutionary means for the creation of a new political system and a new society were necessary, consequently, before anyone would be allowed to enjoy peacefully the fruit of his honest hard labor.[101]

A major rhetorical shift occurred when *Shenghuo* became preoccupied by patriotism and turned into a journal of political commentary. The bourgeois construction of individual happiness began to give way to a new vocabulary of societal welfare and collective well-being. In 1932, when Zou Taofen kindled in the pages of the journal a debate on sexuality, the discussions were conducted primarily in abstractions, in striking contrast to the journal's earlier personalistic style. Gone were the images of middle-class couples in their private homes and gardens with children and maids. What emerged after several months of debate was a distinct emphasis on the creation of social institutions such as collective child-care arrangements and maternal welfare systems designed to attain rational, decent conditions for the benefit of all.

The rhetorical shift of *Shenghuo* coincided with other alterations in the journal's editorial stance. As the shadow of war lengthened, the chatty and relaxed tone of the earlier issues and the humane concern for the plight of striving youth and struggling women gave way to high-sounding, strident statements about the honor and shame of the nation. The hopeful mood about a better personal economic future, the romantic

---

[100] Ibid.

[101] Zou Taofen's response to Liang Shaowen, in "Hangao lüci," *Shenghuo* 5.32 (July 20, 1930): 541.

idealization of an urban home of one's own, and the pride attached to
the attainment of autonomy and manhood gave way to frustration and
despair. The Nationalist government was seen as responsible for its
people's plight. As the petty urbanites were urged to set aside self-
centered concerns and set a new course for the country to follow, intimate and involved narratives on things at hand were displaced by stirring
treatises that called for the creation of a unified People—all expressed in
the absolute and abstract language of progressive political mobilization.

From the "Voice of the People" to the "Voice of the Party"

Zou Taofen's political sympathy for the Chinese Communist Party
developed gradually in the late 1930s. His transformation within a
decade from a hopeful follower of the Nationalists to a firm supporter of
the Chinese Communist Party was intimately connected with his
responses to Japanese military aggression in China. In 1936 Zou was a
major leader of the National Salvation Association (Jiuguo hui) in Shanghai, which agitated for armed resistance against the Japanese. In fact, he
was among the "Seven Gentlemen" arrested early on the morning of
November 23 by the Nationalist authorities for their vocal criticisms of
Chiang Kai-shek's policy of *annei rangwai* (first put down the internal
[Communists], then expel the external [Japanese]).[102] Even after Nationalist soldiers fired back against the Japanese in July 1937 and the two parties entered the Second United Front, Zou and his colleagues continued
to irritate the authorities with their demand for the democratization of
the political process. Much of this activity centered upon the Shenghuo
Bookstore.

The Shenghuo Bookstore, which grew out of the publishing enterprise
of *Shenghuo zhoukan,* was, before the war, a Shanghai-based operation
with two small branch offices in Canton and Wuhan.[103] As a business
enterprise it trailed far behind the leading publishers of the city—the
Commercial Press, the Zhonghua Bookstore, and the Nationalist-
supported Zhengzhong Bookstore—in terms of assets, publications, and
circulation. As a clarion of political consciousness, however, Shenghuo
Bookstore was, together with Dushu Shenghuo and Xinzhi bookstores,
one of the leaders of progressive publishing after the mid-decade in

---

[102] Parks M. Coble, *Facing Japan: Japanese Politics and Japanese Imperialism, 1931–1937*
(Cambridge: Council on East Asian Studies Publications, Harvard University Press, 1991),
pp. 289–297.

[103] Shao Gongwen, "Jinian Shenghuo shudian wushi nian," *Chuban shiliao,* no. 2 (December 1983): 131.

Shanghai, with a publication list that stressed contemporary sociopolitical and economic subjects. Despite repeated denials at the time in the presence of the government's censors, all three enterprises had been penetrated by members of the Chinese Communist Party by 1935. Nevertheless, before the outbreak of the war in 1937 the Communist influence was diffused and clandestine.

The crucial development that permitted bonds to form between the Communists and the National Salvation Movement of Shanghai was the series of patriotic campaigns of the mid-1930s, when many sectors of society rallied around the common cause of Chinese patriotism.[104] Since progressive publishers were at the forefront of this patriotic mobilization, their ranks were among the first penetrated by a growing Communist influence. The alliance took shape, however, at a time when the Communist Party was in considerable organizational disarray in the wake of the Long March.[105] The reorganization of the Party in Shanghai in

---

[104] Xu Xuehan, "Huiyi quanguo gejie jiuguo lianhehui pianduan qingkuang," in Zhonggong Shanghai shiwei dangshi ziliao zhengji weiyuan hui, ed., *Yierjiu yihou Shanghai jiuguohui shiliao xuanji* (Shanghai, 1987), pp. 405–406; Wu Dakun, "Dang yu jiuguohui," in ibid., pp. 407–408. The National Salvation Association (NSA) in Shanghai was able to mobilize a large number of the city's vocational youth, along with writers, students, workers, elementary school teachers, and middle-class women, to form organizations of their own. These organizations in turn became constituent elements of the NSA, which was loosely formed and coordinated, giving ample opportunities to individual members of the Communist Party to exercise their influence as dedicated organizers. These individuals, who generally kept their Party membership a secret, succeeded in forging important personal links with the leadership of the NSA and its constituent bodies. See Wan Han, "Yierjiu yundong hou Shanghai dixia dang gongzuo luxian de zhuanbian," in ibid., p. 315; Lu Zhiren, "Guanyu Shanghai zhiye jie jiuguo hui de yixie qingkuang," in ibid., pp. 417–418; Yong Wentao, "Huiyi Dang dui Zhijiu de lingdao he Shanghai renmin de kangri jiuwang yundong," in ibid., pp. 411–412.

[105] Communication with the Central Committee of the Party was not resumed until some time after the Red Army reached its new base in northern Shaanxi. In the wake of such major setbacks and in the middle of important changes in political strategy, numerous rounds of reorganization took place in the Party's Jiangsu and Shanghai committees. Preexisting committees on literature, arts, drama, the film industry, and so forth, previously headed by Zhou Yang, were restructured. Overlapping committees with newly designated and often competing functions were set up, while the chain of command became tangled and confused with the arrival of new appointees from northern Shaanxi. See Li Fanfu, "Guanyu yijiusanwu zhi yijiusanqi nian Shanghai dixiadang douzheng de yixie qingkuang," in ibid., pp. 379–380; Qian Junrui, "Jiuguohui nei de dang zuzhi qingkuan," in ibid., p.387; Wu Dakun, "Dang yu jiuguohui," in ibid., p. 408. At first, contact with northern Shaanxi was assured by the presence of these individuals, many of whom were northerners, representing the Central Committee. After 1936 a southerner took charge in the form of Pan Hannian, the highest-ranking Party representative in the Shanghai area throughout the war. Pan began his career as a member of the Literary Creation Society and as an assistant editor of a series of minor publications in the 1920s in Shanghai. After a stint with the Red Army in the Jiangxi Soviet, Pan traveled from Zunyi in Guizhou to Moscow. In 1936 he was sent

1936–1937 was precisely an attempt to revitalize the party by riding this swelling tide of patriotism.[106]

Zou Taofen had no formal contact with the Party until sometime in 1938, well after the outbreak of the Sino-Japanese war in Shanghai in August 1937. Like other progressive publishers at the time, Shenghuo Bookstore found itself confined to the foreign concessions after the Nationalist troops pulled out of Shanghai in November 1937. The enterprise was thus cut off from the urban middle-class audiences that had formed the backbone of its readership.[107]

As Japanese control over the Chinese sectors of Shanghai tightened, Zou decided to try temporarily to relocate his publishing enterprise upstream along the Yangzi in Wuhan. There Zou met Zhou Enlai, the head of the Eighth Route Army's liaison office in central China.[108] The meeting was arranged by Hu Yuzhi (1896–1985), a former editor of the influential monthly *Dongfang zazhi* (Eastern Miscellany), an NSA activist during 1935–1936, and a close associate of Zou Taofen in the Shenghuo Bookstore enterprise. Not until well after 1949 was it revealed that Hu had also been a secret member of the Chinese Communist Party since the early 1930s.[109]

Zou Taofen and his colleagues quickly adjusted themselves to a new set of publishing circumstances in wartime Wuhan. On the one hand, the war gave them a renewed sense of mission and responsibility. To mobilize resistance, Shenghuo published pamphlets and drawings that told stories of Chinese victories over the Japanese in very simple language.[110] On the other hand, the war forced publishers to combine resources. Shenghuo merged its biweekly *Kangzhan* (War of resistance), for example, with the weekly *Quanmin* (The people) to form a new

---

back to Shanghai as the Comintern's representative and the CCP Central Committee's top coordinator of underground activities in the lower Yangzi valley. See Wang Yaoshan, "Yijiusanqi nian qian Shanghai de kangri jiuwang yundong he dixia dang zuzhi de zhengli gongzuo," in ibid., p. 382; Hu Yuzhi, "Pan Hannian tongzhi yu jiuguohui," in ibid., p. 386.

[106] Until the Second United Front policies gave the urban cells of the Party a new lease on life, the Shanghai underground in the mid-1930s remained small and secretive. Within the National Salvation Association the Party cultivated new members slowly and cautiously.

[107] Xue Muqiao, "Huiyi Xinzhi shudian he *Zhongguo nongcun*," *Shenghuo, Dushu, Xinzhi Sanlian shudian chengli sanshi zhounian jinian ji*, p. 40.

[108] Shao Gongwen, "Jinbu wenhua chuban shiye liang xianqu—Hu Yuzhi yu Zou Taofen," *Chuban shiliao*, no. 6 (December 1986): 33.

[109] "Hu Yuzhi tongzhi shengping," *Chuban shiliao*, no. 6 (December 1986): 2. Hu Yuzhi rose to become the chief of the daily *Guangming ribao* and a vice-chairman of the Standing Committee of the People's Congress after 1949.

[110] Shao Gongwen, "Jinian Shenghuo shudian wushi nian," *Chuban shiliao*, no. 2 (December 1983): 131.

weekly entitled *Quanmin kangzhan* (People's war of resistance) that was
coedited by two of Zou Taofen's NSA comrades, Shen Junru and Liu Ti.
Both the content and the format of the new journal were simplified to
reach a larger audience, no longer mainly confined to the literate urbanites of the coastal cities, but now necessarily expanded to include the
semiliterate masses of the interior.

Although it was the outbreak of the war that drastically altered the
circumstances of publishing, *Shenghuo's* new editorial voice was audible
already in mid-decade, as the call for arms gained in momentum. In
1936, as he gave himself to the publication of the newspaper *Shenghuo
Daily,* Zou Taofen wrote openly to his readers on his editorial policies,
telling them that he had in mind a paper that was to be "the daily,
indispensable spiritual food for all 500 million Chinese ... a collective
enterprise of all producing members of this society, with news and commentaries contributed directly by workers, peasants, office employees,
and students from all parts of the country."[111]

In retrospect, one of the most telling cultural consequences of the
outbreak of the war in 1937 was the forced rustication of the urban-
based liberal publishers of the lower Yangzi cities along with their
readers, who were compelled to leave the littoral and penetrate the
towns and villages of China's vast hinterland.[112] When the nation itself
was under military attack, all justifications were withdrawn, it would
seem, for the urban vocational youth to continue carving out the modernizing cities as their own separate space, shielded from the backwardness
of the rural homeland. What the nation needed urgently was the simple,
powerful messages of unity and mobilization that were to become the
"daily, indispensable spiritual food for all five hundred million Chinese"
consisting of an overwhelming majority of peasants and workers, rather
than the petty urbanites alone.

Shenghuo Daily proved to be short-lived. The journal that became
most distinctly associated with the Shenghuo Bookstore in the late 1930s
was the weekly *Dazhong shenghuo* (Mass life), inaugurated in Shanghai in
November 1935, closed down by the government after sixteen issues,
revived in Hong Kong on May 17, 1941, for another thirty weeks, only to
end abruptly on December 6 at the outbreak of the Pacific War. Its main
themes were "unity," "resistance," and "democracy," and it was widely

---

[111] *Zou Taofen nianpu,* p. 90.

[112] See Ch'ien Chung-shu, *Fortress Besieged,* tr. Jeanne Kelly and Nathan K. Mao (Bloomington: Indiana University Press, 1979), passim, on the theme of rustication in the Sino-
Japanese War.

regarded as the prototypical organ of the National Salvation Movement.[113]

To the extent that the Readers' Mailbox continued to be featured in *Dazhong shenghuo*, it merely served to underscore the new journal's differences from the earlier *Shenghuo*. To a former *Shenghuo* reader who wrote to urge that Zou Taofen dispense the sort of personal advice he used to give, Zou replied that the goal of the new journal was, indeed, to become much more "progressive" than ever before. "The giant wheels of the epoch (*shidai*) roll on," Zou wrote; "the epoch that brings forth *Dazhong shenghuo* is utterly different from the epoch of *Shenghuo*."[114] *Dazhong shenghuo*'s "epoch" was no longer a time for individualism. Rather, a young person should endeavor to be "a brave and progressive fighter for the masses in conjunction with the collectivity," because "it is only from the liberation of the collectivity that individuals find their personal liberty."[115] To one skeptical reader who voiced doubts about *Dazhong shenghuo*'s categorical denunciation of the existing order, Zou Taofen, in less than subtle ways, politely suggested that the correspondent was perhaps not a wholehearted friend of the people.[116] As the bulk of the journal now consisted of contributions by an illustrious roster of Communist intellectuals—Hu Sheng, Hu Qiaomu, Qian Junrui, Xia Yan, Mao Dun, Zhang Youyu—who were assembled to enlighten their audience on the truth of politically correct thinking, the Readers' Mailbox was duly transformed into an evaluative exercise. Readers wrote in either with a comment or a report, and these were judged by the editor on the basis of the correctness of their thought, with praise and blame distributed accordingly.

Despite the economic dislocation of the war, Shenghuo began in 1938 to set up a national network of branch stores that would encompass the major centers in Nationalist-controlled northwestern, western, and southwestern China as well as the mountain towns and population centers in base areas and border zones that lay in central and southern

---

[113] Zou Taofen, *Huannan yusheng ji* (Beijing: Sanlian shudian, 1958), p. 66.

[114] For "epoch" (*shidai*), see Lung-kee Sun, "Chinese Intellectuals' Notion of 'Epoch' (*Shidai*) in the Post–May Fourth Era," *Chinese Studies in History* 20.22 (Winter 1986/87): 32; and Leo Ou-fan Lee, "In Search of Modernity: Some Reflections on a New Mode of Consciousness in Twentieth-Century Chinese History and Literature," in Paul A. Cohen and Merle Goldman, eds., *Ideas Across Cultures: Essays on Chinese Thought in Honor of Benjamin I. Schwartz* (Cambridge: Council on East Asian Studies Publications, Harvard University Press, 1990), pp. 120–121.

[115] Xu Fengshi, "Qiwang," *Dazhong shenghuo* 1.2 (November 23, 1935): 62–64.

[116] Liang Ziqi, "Yanlun de lichang he taidu," *Dazhong shenghuo* (new), no. 6 (June 21, 1941): 140–143.

China behind enemy lines. At the height of this ambitious effort of expansion no fewer than fifty-five branch stores were opened in Xi'an, Chongqing, Changsha, Guilin, Lanzhou, Guiyang, Nanchang, Kunming, Fuzhou, Changde, Jinhua, Hengyang, Liuzhou, Nanjing, Yichang, Enshi, Wanxian, Meixian, Yulin, and so forth.[117]

Although it was vigorously denied at the time, much of Shenghuo's expansion in 1938 was made with the assistance of the Communist Eighth Route Army. The location of many of the branch stores was dictated by the presence of an Eighth Route Army liaison office in that particular town. In city after city, underground Party organizations helped prepare the ground for the bookstore by guiding Shenghuo's managers through the social, political, and cultural intricacies peculiar to each locale. Party members provided critical introductions into local society, smoothing the way for such necessary operations as renting a suitable work space, generating a much-needed pool of local applicants to fill the bookstore's clerical positions, promoting its publications among local secondary and elementary school teachers and students, and mobilizing the local readership to assist in a variety of chores from painting and furnishing the store to purchasing supplies, collecting mail, advertising, and evading the local government censors.[118]

Shenghuo's employees jumped from fewer than thirty in 1937 to nearly five hundred in 1939.[119] The overall organization of the bookstore underwent a fundamental transformation at the same time. Zou Taofen was only one among a number of political allies sharing the top management of the bookstore.[120] A standing committee of the board of directors was created in the Chongqing head office of the firm, while decisions on publications were entrusted to an editorial committee cochaired by Hu Yuzhi (whose Communist Party membership was still undisclosed), Shen Zhiyuan, and Jin Zhonghua (who received the appointment after 1949 of deputy mayor of Shanghai).[121] The organization within the Chongqing head office, meanwhile, became complex. Directly under the standing committee of the board was the head store of Chongqing, which housed the general management office of all Shenghuo branch stores. The

---

[117] Shao Gongwen, "Jinian Shenghuo shudian wushi nian," p. 131.

[118] Ibid., p. 132.

[119] Zou Taofen, *Huannan yusheng ji,* p. 77.

[120] Zhongguo Guomindang zhongyang weiyuan hui dangshi weiyuanhui, ed., *Zhonghua minguo zhongyao shiliao chubian* (Taipei: Zhongyang wenwu gongyingshe, 1981), vol. 1, p. 543.

[121] Shao Gongwen, "Jinian Shenghuo shudian wushi nian," p. 132. In 1938 Ai Hansong served as the secretary to the committee, which was composed of Zou Taofen, Liu Ti, Shi Mei, Liu Simu, Shen Zijiu, Zhang Zhongshi, Ge Baoquan, Mao Dun, and Dai Baitao.

branch stores in turn managed the smaller branches and sales outlets in their respective sales territories.[122]

The main Shenghuo bookstore in Chongqing handled retail, whole-sale, and mail orders, as well as promotion, and operated independent of the head office. With an estimated annual sales volume of more than 400,000 yuan, Chongqing was the most profitable of Shenghuo's opera-tions.[123] No other wartime publishing enterprise had such a widespread national network of distribution outlets. But Shenghuo Bookstore was unique in two other regards as well. First, it made its several hundred employees shareholders of the bookstore and organized them into study societies and discussion groups that focused attention on left-wing social science theories and current events.[124] Second, the bookstore, in Chongqing in particular, functioned as a kind of cultural service center, creating a network of writers, professors, journalists and other cultural figures bound together through interlocking committee memberships.

Zou Taofen encouraged Shenghuo employees to read as a means of professional self-improvement. Among the reading materials recom-mended to all members of the store was the weekly *Shenghuo shudian dianxun* (Store newsletter).[125] The objectives of the *Newsletter*, according to Zou, were to keep the employees informed of the store's business plans, to supply market information about the publishing industry, to report on cultural events, and to introduce individual employees to their colleagues.[126] In addition, members of the editorial board contributed articles to the *Newsletter*, which thus printed Zou and Hu's thoughts on the store's management philosophy as well as reflections upon its cultural mission. The weekly was intended to be "a publication for the education of all employees in life, thought, and professional expertise, a forum to unify the spirits of our colleagues and to generate a common effort toward the goals of mass culture and national liberation."[127]

---

[122] *Zhonghua minguo zhongyao shiliao chubian,* vol. 1, pp. 543–544. Individuals in the headquarters were given special responsibility to establish direct contact with politically sensitive areas such as Xinjiang.

[123] Ibid., pp. 544–545. The bulk of Shenghuo's published works was printed, prior to the fall of Canton that cut off transportation from coastal to inland China, in Shanghai. In the latter half of the war Shenghuo turned to several printing houses in Chongqing, includ-ing a certain Guiyang Commercial Printing House which, the authorities charged, was also the printer of Mao Zedong's works.

[124] Ibid., p. 544.

[125] The first issue of the *Store Newsletter* appeared on January 22, 1938, in Hankow. The last issue appeared on January 31, 1941, in Chongqing. One hundred eight issues were printed, the later ones appearing bimonthly because of financial difficulty. Qian Xiaobo and Lei Qunming, *Taofen yu chuban,* p. 191.

[126] Qian Xiaobo and Lei Qunming, *Taofen yu chuban,* p. 191.

[127] Ibid., p. 192.

The Nationalist authorities charged that this use of the publication amounted to a form of in-house political training. Because prominent left-wing figures also employed the *Newsletter* as a forum to discuss progressive publishing strategies during wartime, the periodical further conveyed the impression of being a bulletin for left-wing, and even CCP, strategic planning. Issue number 40 of the *Newsletter*, for example, which appeared in December 1938, printed Mao Zedong's communication to Li Gongpu and Du Jue, both progressive publishers, discussing how their activities might not suffer disruption in the event that the Japanese occupied the major cities in Fujian, Guangdong, Hunan, Hubei, and Shanxi, where their publishing had previously been based. Mao urged the publishers to build outlets in guerrilla territories, to work closely with the resident Red Army units, and to be self-sufficient in capital and equipment.[128] Mao's remarks appeared to outline the basic strategy eventually followed by progressive publishers in border areas controlled by the Eighth Route and the New Fourth armies.

The Chongqing main store, meanwhile, was active in organizing fellow publishers and cultural figures in the Nationalists' wartime capital into associations. It routinely hosted social gatherings, evening programs, and lectures featuring well-known progressives and Communist leaders. Among the prominent speakers presented to the public on these occasions were Ye Jianying, Dong Biwu, Bo Gu, and Kai Feng. Zhou Enlai made two presentations, in February and June of 1939. These were hosted by Zou Taofen (who was a regular presence at such gatherings) and attended primarily by an in-house audience eager to discuss the war and the future of China.[129]

The main store also created a service department devoted to its readers' cultural needs. The services it offered ranged from recommendations of reading materials to general information about cultural events. Shenghuo invited readers to browse freely so that the store was virtually turned into a public reading room.[130] Many branch stores became centers for the distribution of progressive materials, meeting places for progressive youths, and ultimately intelligence-gathering posts and communication links for the Eighth Route Army.[131] Although "vocational youth" had by no means lost their significance as a clientele, Shenghuo's readership in the 1940s was defined primarily in terms of their progressive political

---

[128] Ibid., p. 194.

[129] Shao Gongwen, "Jinian Shenghuo shudian wushi nian," p. 142.

[130] *Zhonghua minguo zhongyao shiliao chubian,* vol. 1, p. 547.

[131] Zou Taofen, *Huannan yusheng ji,* pp. 69, 77; Liu Ti, "Ta he renmin dazhong zai yiqi," in *Yong zai zhuinian zhong de Taofen xiansheng* (Shanghai: Shenghuo shudian, 1947), p. 74.

leaning rather than urban middle-class employment.

The Nationalist Party Central Committee's Bureau of Statistics and Investigation (BSI, Zhongtong) concluded as early as June 1940 that Shenghuo Bookstore and the newspaper *Xinhua ribao* (New China daily) were the Communists' two most important propaganda organs outside Yan'an. The BSI report stated that the bookstore "used cultural services and activities as a cover to penetrate deeply into many circles of society. It lured the public into these open activities and then proceeded to influence them according to a hidden agenda."[132]

The Guomindang's propanganda and security departments resorted to a combination of means to battle the growing influence of progressive journalists secretly allied with the Communist Party in areas under the government's control. In 1938 the Chongqing government revived a censorship regulation that permitted Nationalist censors to edit original manuscripts before publication and to bring journals and newspapers to a virtual standstill by the simple tactic of delay. Even more directly, the authorities forcibly closed a number of Shenghuo branches and coerced Shenghuo's main store into merging with the government-owned Zheng-zhong Bookstore.

On April 21, 1939, Shenghuo's branch store in Xi'an was raided by the Nationalist police. The raid was carried out with considerable brutal-ity. More than eighteen hundred copies of books and journals were car-ried away, along with the bookstore's papers and accounts. The police even stripped the bookstore of its furniture, some pieces of which later on reportedly reappeared in the Nationalist-run Chinese Cultural Service Center in Xi'an. The manager, Zhou Minghuan, was repeatedly interro-gated about Shenghuo's communication with the Communists in Yan'an. Afterwards he was thrown into prison, and eventually died in a concen-tration camp.[133]

During the next eight months a similar fate befell Shenghuo branches in Tianshui, Nanzheng, Wanxian, Yuanling, Ji'an, Linchuan, Nancheng, Ganzhou, Jinhua, Lishui, Lihuang, Fuzhou, Nanping, Qujiang, Meixian, Lanzhou, Hengyang, Guiyang, Guilin, Chengdu, and Kunming. More than forty managers were imprisoned as a result of these raids. Other branches were forced to close down, meanwhile, in the face of the Japanese advance. By early 1940, only six of Shenghuo's branch stores remained, in Chongqing, Guiyang, Kunming, Chengdu, Guilin, and

---

[132] "Zhongyang diaocha tongji ju bianzhi, Shenghuo shudian, Xinhua ribao Diaocha bao-gao," in *Zhonghua minguo zhongyao shiliao chubian*, vol. 1, p. 543.

[133] Zou Taofen, *Huannan yusheng ji*, p. 72; Shao Gongwen, "Jinian Shenghuo shudian wushi nian," p. 133.

Qujiang. When the Nationalist Army launched a surprise attack on the Communist New Fourth Army in southern Anhui in January 1941, Nationalist police and secret service squads simultaneously assailed Communist allies elsewhere. All the remaining branches of Shenghuo, except the main store in Chongqing, were pillaged and closed down.[134] In each of these raids the authorities charged that the bookstore was a major communications post for the Communists. According to the police, not only were Shenghuo's publications slanderous of the Nationalist authorities; local branches of the bookstore were centers for recruiting and indoctrinating subversive elements.[135]

Zou Taofen, who had been a member of the government's National Political Assembly since 1938, was outraged by these raids and accusations. To protest, he quit his seat as a member of the "National Salvation Association faction" in the assembly; and then, having exposed himself to government retaliation, secretly made his way out of Chongqing with the help of underground networks run by the Chinese Communist Party.[136] Thereafter Zou was to take refuge in the Communist areas of Guangdong and Jiangsu, never again to resume management of the Shenghuo enterprise.[137]

Meanwhile, if the Nationalists had hoped by closing down the Shenghuo Bookstore network to deal a fatal blow to the dissemination of progressive ideas, they were soon disappointed. The Chongqing branch of Shenghuo had developed close working relationships with several publishing organizations—Xinzhi Bookstore, Shanghai Magazine Company, Xinsheng Bookstore, Huazhong Bookstore, Sichuan Bookstore, and so forth—by sharing subscription lists, printing each other's advertisements, shuffling operating funds from one operation to another; these nominally distinct enterprises were in fact run by a handful of individuals serving on overlapping editorial boards. In addition, frequent contact was maintained with a variety of left-wing organs, from the liaison offices of the Eighth Route Army in Nationalist areas, the work teams that were sent out to villages in North China behind Japanese lines, the amateur drama troupes that propagated patriotism with one-act plays performed at street corners and village fairs, the Chongqing office of the Democratic Revolutionary Society, and the job agencies for war refugees, to the information

---

[134] Shao Gongwen, "Jinian Shenghuo shudian wushi nian," p. 134. In one of the most brutal operations, Fang Jun, the manager of the southern Anhui branch, was killed by the Nationalist police.

[135] Zou Taofen, *Huannan yusheng ji*, p. 74.

[136] His old friend Huang Yanpei also served in the Assembly as the leader of the "Society for Vocational Education faction."

[137] Zou Taofen, *Huannan yusheng ji*, p. 74.

centers and newspaper reading rooms that coordinated Chinese-language news coverage on the war front.[138] Outside Chongqing, similar relationships existed between former Shenghuo branches and other Communist Party operations as well.[139] Some of these outlets used several names in dealings with the outside world in attempts to confuse both the censors and the secret service.[140]

Consequently, the Nationalist crackdown on Shenghuo Bookstore in 1941 merely scratched the surface of the front itself. After the closure of many of its stores, the resources and expertise that Shenghuo represented—its editors, manuscripts, inventory, and, most important, the *zhixing,* or plates of published materials, along with intangible assets such as long-established relationships with progressive authors, subscription lists, mail order accounts, and business relationships with paper suppliers, printers, advertisers, library subscribers, vendors, and street distributors—continued to be used by other Communist-supported publishing organs under a changed name.

By mid-1942, Zou Taofen had been escorted by the Communists from Guangdong to the New Fourth Route Army area in northern Jiangsu, where he joined a group of fellow progressives, intellectual and literary figures who had followed a similar path to allegiance to the Communist Party. Zou participated enthusiastically in the cultural programs of the Party: he was an earnest pupil of Party ideology rather than a master in his own right. Meanwhile, the Communist Party in Yan'an formally sent Zhang Youyu to take charge of the Shenghuo Bookstore in Chongqing.

In 1943, the Party sent another representative, Huang Luofeng, to Chongqing. Huang's charge was to unite the entire progressive publishing business in Chongqing under the single command of the Party. Huang began his work with Shenghuo, combining, without much difficulty, the resources and operations of Shenghuo with those of two other progressive publishers, Dushu and Xinzhi. The combined operation of these three bookstores was formally known, after November 20, 1945, as the Chongqing branch of the Sanlian Bookstore.[141]

---

[138] *Zhonghua minguo zhongyao shiliao chubian,* vol. 1, p. 548. Nationalist agents believed that the leadership of these respective organizations met frequently, and suggested that Shenghuo management had access to Communist safe houses on No. 4, Kuanzi Lane, and Nos. 13–14 on the Daxiang at the Golden Purple Gate in Chongqing.

[139] The fifty-some Shenghuo branches that constituted the national network in fact included a number of bookstores with a different name. In Binxiang, for example, Shenghuo's outlet was named the Yongzhi Bookstore; in Luxian, alternately the Tuojiang Bookstore and the Luxian Bookstore; and in Changsha, the Minzhong Bookstore.

[140] *Zhonghua minguo zhongyao shiliao chubian,* vol. 1, p. 544.

[141] Shao Gongwen, "Jinian Shenghuo shudian wushi nian," pp. 135, 138.

In December 1943, Huang Luofeng further succeeded in bringing together nineteen progressive publishing houses under the General Association of the New Publishing Industry (Xin chubanye lianhe zongchu). Huang became the chairman of the new association's executive board, which later sponsored the opening of the Associated Bookstore (Lianying shudian) in Chongqing.[142] Through Huang's assiduous efforts the association eventually encompassed thirty-some publishing houses, most of which labored under the yoke of the Nationalist censorship laws. Vigorously led by the Communist Party, these progressive Sichuanese publishers began to act unanimously, signing joint statements and presenting a range of trade-related demands to the Nationalist government vis-à-vis the supply of paper, printing costs, postal restrictions, and the like.[143]

Shenghuo's Shanghai branch underwent a similar process of transformation and became, during the latter half of the war with Japan, a major supplier of publications and intelligence to the headquarters of the New Fourth Army in northern Jiangsu. It collaborated closely with Dushu and Xinzhi in northern Jiangsu to form a new bookstore, the Huabei Bookstore.[144]

Zou Taofen remained in northern Jiangsu, still under the protection of the Communist Party, while the "socialization" of publishing radically transformed Shenghuo into an appendage of the CCP propaganda apparatus. By now cancer had taken Zou Taofen by the throat, and he was escorted to Shanghai for medical treatment. In the terminal stage of his illness Zou lost his voice. He was hospitalized under an assumed identity as Ji Jinqin, a shopkeeper, and after ultimate silence fell his body was sent to the mortuary under that name.[145] Within the month the

---

[142] Zhang Jinglu, a veteran publisher from Shanghai, was appointed general manager of the association. Wan Guojun and Xue Dichang were appointed assistant managers. The new bookstore drew its editors almost entirely from the original three progressive bookstores: Shenghuo, Dushu, and Xinzhi. He Lisun was its general manager and Zhong Qiuyuan its assistant manager.

[143] Shao Gongwen, pp. 135–136. During the civil war period (1946–1949) the Chongqing branch of the Sanlian Bookstore came under the leadership of the Chinese Communist Party's Chongqing Municipal Committee. At that time the bookstore was the major publisher of progressive journals and books in southwestern and western China. It often ran full-page advertisements in the *Xinhua ribao,* and it worked hard to promote Chairman Mao's published writings. It further took on the responsibility of information gathering, collecting all "counterrevolutionary" publications for the reference of the Party's Central Committee in Yan'an. Ibid., pp. 138, 140.

[144] Ibid., p. 137.

[145] *Zou Taofen nianpu,* p. 150.

initial Party celebrations of his accomplishments as the "Voice of the People" had commenced.

Without him but under Party control, the Shenghuo enterprise continued. The Huabei Bookstore, which upon Zou's death was renamed the Taofen Bookstore by the Central Committee of the Party, was given the important assignment in the civil war of 1947–1949 of bringing all progressive publishing houses in Shanghai under one organization.[146] This consolidation led to the creation of the Shanghai Association of the New Publishing Industry and the Shanghai Association of Employees of the New Publishing Industry.[147] In the fall of 1948, managers of Shenghuo, Dushu, and Xinzhi bookstores met in Hong Kong. Upon the instruction of the Communist Party, they announced their merger and the creation of an all-China Sanlian Bookstore.[148] By then, Zou Taofen's former Shenghuo enterprise had been thoroughly transmuted from the "Voice of the People" of prewar Shanghai to the voice of the Chinese Communist Party and its new national audience of targeted readers. There was no longer a separate space for individuals with a voice of their own to present their personal expression. Instead, all voices were mobilized to speak in unison, led by the Party to take on collective issues concerning the nation and the people.

This is not to say that progressive publishers of the 1930s could have chosen otherwise once they lost their Shanghai base and had to endure harsh wartime censorship and police persecution during the 1940s. By then if the "Voice of the People" were to remain audible at all it had to be amplified by the organizational apparatus of the Communist Party. Under these circumstances, the absolute "Voice of the People" was found only in disciplined unison, which was orchestrated by the Chinese Communist Party. But this stirring unanimity entailed great strength as well as a vital cost. By discovering the power of the masses in this new "Voice of the People," Zou Taofen and other progressive intellectuals unwittingly lost the many individual voices of the people they once had heard and had helped articulate in all their diversity and differentiation.

---

[146] Ibid., p. 144.
[147] Ibid., p. 140.
[148] Ibid., p. 143.

APPENDIX: *Shenghuo*'s **Success Stories**

Biography One

Zhu Yinjiang was a native of Jiading. As a young man, he served as a poor shop apprentice. Early one morning, as Zhu was passing by the Jiuji Wood Store, he was suddenly drenched by a downpour of water from the second floor. The mistress of the store was emptying her wash basin.

Zhu Yinjiang did not change his color. The mistress, however, was apologetic. She asked her husband to summon Zhu Yinjiang. When he came, the master and mistress were both favorably impressed by the young man's composure. The master offered to take Zhu into his store. Zhu replied that his own master had been kind to him, and he did not wish to betray his trust. The owner of the wood store consulted Zhu's master and obtained permission for Zhu to change employer.

Zhu Yinjiang was thus hired by the wood store as a street runner. Grateful to his master and mistress for their attention, Zhu worked with extreme dedication. He quickly earned their respect and trust and was soon promoted to cashier. The master gave Zhu Yinjiang his oldest daughter as a wife. This first wife soon died. The master then gave Zhu his second daughter in wedlock. The second wife died, too. The master again conferred one of his daughters upon Zhu. When the master himself died, Zhu was granted management of the store, which prospered greatly. Meanwhile, Zhu took his master's natural heir under his wing and helped teach him how to become a merchant-gentleman in his own right.[149]

Biography Two

Xue Liquan was orphaned at a tender age. Lacking uncles and brothers, he was without support in this world. Via the introduction of fellow townsmen, he became an apprentice in a paint and dye store. Xue was diligent, dedicated, and modest. He was soon promoted to clerk.

Xue was frugal with his handsome salary. By saving one thousand yuan in five years, Xue Liquan managed to open up his own dye and paint store with a number of his colleagues as partners. At this time the cost of dye was low. Xue bought four to five thousand yuan worth of

---

[149] Cheng Zhichao, "Linli manshen er buxiao zhi Zhongguo shiye jia," *Shenghuo* 2.7 (December 5, 1926): 43.

goods. Then the European War broke out, and import of German dye was disrupted. Xue's stock rose in value many times over, and he made several tens of thousands of yuan.[150]

Biography Three

Yuan Xuetang, a native of Yangzhou, was also orphaned at a tender age. At eighteen, relatives got him a job as a trainee in a Shanghai arsenal. Although his position was low, he worked conscientiously; and although he had never been to school, he spent his spare time teaching himself how to read newspapers and write letters. After becoming literate, Yuan was assigned to the chemistry department, where he learned how to conduct experiments and was promoted to a research position. On his own he invented a new medicinal drug. Using the several tens of yuan that he had saved as working capital, he manufactured the new drug and consigned it for sale to a grocery in the nearby market town of Gaochangmiao. His customers grew in numbers.

A few years later Yuan consigned his medicine to a pharmaceutical outlet in Shanghai. The owner of the store, however, usurped the use of Yuan's packaging and brand name, the Chicken. Thereupon Yuan Xuetang opened up his own pharmacy, the Jihuatang, on Yunnan Road in the International Settlement. His medicines were efficacious. He himself was diligent and sincere. His customers were always treated courteously and amicably. Yuan's medicines sold widely in Shanghai, and he was eventually able to market his medicines as far north as Manchuria and as far south as Guangdong.[151]

All three of these men were prominent Shanghai merchants. Zhu Yinjiang, for instance, was a board member of the Chamber of Commerce of Shanghai County and, in that capacity, a delegate to the Shanghai Federation of Merchant Associations that negotiated the peaceful surrender of Shanghai to the Nationalist Northern Expedition Army in April 1927.[152]

---

[150] Wei Buchan, "Zuoguo xiaoxiao yanliao dian xuetu de Zhongguo fuwong," *Shenghuo* 2.11 (January 16, 1927): 67.

[151] Shen Weixia, "You Yitu er chenggong zhi fendou qushi," *Shenghuo* 2:21 (March 27, 1927): 145–146.

[152] See the roster of Shanghai Federation of Merchant Associations in Shanghai shi dang'an guan, ed., *Yijiu erqi nian de Shanghai shangye lianhe hui* (Shanghai: Renmin chubanshe, 1983), p. 10.

Although these men were flesh-and-blood Shanghai entrepreneurs, their biographical sketches, written in a stylized semivernacular Chinese, imparted a timeless quality characteristic of traditional moral portraiture. Events occurred merely to test one's character, which ultimately accounted for business success or failure according to an ethical profile constructed with centuries-old rhetorical devices.

Biography One, for instance, started with a conventional portrait of a respectable merchant-gentleman of the traditional sort: public-minded and generous, devoted to such time-honored philanthropies as relief for the poor and endowments for elementary schools.[153] His success story, which culminated in the conclusion of three marriages and the inheritance of his master's store, approached the wildest possible fantasy imaginable by struggling vocational youth. Such gentlemanly stature and extraordinary fortune were well deserved, however, because Zhu earned them at two critical encounters in his early life. The first, the humiliating drenching with the bedpan, allowed Zhu to display remarkable self-control along with considerable deference to status. The second was Zhu's initial refusal to change masters, which resonated with so many episodes in popular historical lore.[154] Deferent composure and unstinting loyalty have long been regarded as marking unusual personalities of great promise.[155]

The opening paragraphs of Biography Two, meanwhile, were paraphrases of the opening statements in a celebrated essay by Li Mi, an official of the Three Kingdoms and Wei-Jin period whose private life was officially glorified as exemplary of genteel poverty and filial piety.[156] Indeed, the image of an orphaned child shivering in rags in the winter is so common (in stories such as that of the "twenty-four filial paragons," for instance) that there is little originality in such a sentence as "He had no winter clothing to keep him warm."

Similar phrases were used in Biography Three to suggest the deprivation of the innovator's childhood. The image there of a studious young man seizing every spare moment to educate himself has received at least

---

[153] For profiles of traditional gentry-merchants, see Rowe, *Hankow: Conflict and Community*, pp. 91–186, passim.

[154] See, for instance, episodes in the *Romance of the Three Kingdoms*, especially chapters 25–28.

[155] These traits were immortalized in such legendary biographies as that of Zhang Liang in the *Record of the Grand Historian*. See "Liuhou shijia," *Shiji* (Beijing: Zhonghua shuju, n.d.), *juan* 55, pp. 2034–2035.

[156] For the full text, see Li Lingbo, "Chenqing biao," *Zhaoming wenxuan*, pp. 520–521; also Zhuge Liang, "Chushi biao," *Zhaoming wenxuan*, pp. 513–514.

one full-blown treatment in the opening chapter of the eighteenth-century classical novel *Rulin waishi* (The scholars), not to mention numerous other sources.

CHAPTER SEVEN

Migrant Culture in Shanghai
In Search of a Subei Identity

EMILY HONIG

Pre-Liberation Shanghai was a city of immigrants where social groups were often defined by native-place identity.[1] From the mid-nineteenth century, when the city's development as a large commercial and industrial metropolis began, laborers, merchants, and entrepreneurs came mostly from three areas: Guangdong, Jiangnan (the Ningbo-Shaoxing region of Zhejiang and the Wuxi-Changzhou area of Jiangsu), and Subei (roughly, the area of Jiangsu north of the Yangzi River). Which of these areas one hailed from was critical in shaping work opportunities, residential patterns, cultural activities, and social status. Hierarchy was structured largely according to local origins: the elite was composed primarily of people from Guangdong and Jiangnan, the unskilled service sector staffed mostly by migrants from Subei. Identity as a Ningbo native connoted wealth and urbanity as certainly as a Subei identity was associated with poverty and ignorance (even though not all migrants from Ningbo were wealthy nor all from Subei poor).

The belief in the existence of a despised group called *Subei ren* (or, in more popular and slightly more derogatory parlance, *Jiangbei ren*) has been central throughout Shanghai's development as a modern industrial center. From the early twentieth century, calling someone a *Jiangbei ren* or, even worse, a "Jiangbei swine," has been one of the most common curses in Shanghai dialect. *Jiangbei ren* was one of the most frequent identities ascribed to individuals in daily newspapers, and almost all Shanghai residents could identify the so-called Subei villages, the shack settlements or slums where many Subei natives lived. If a single group of

---

[1] From 1885 to 1935, Shanghai natives accounted for an average of only 19 percent of the population of the International Concession and 26 percent of the Chinese-owned parts of the city. Zou Yiren, *Jiu Shanghai renkou bianqian de yanjiu* [Research on changes in the population of old Shanghai] (Shanghai: Shanghai renmin chubanshe, 1980), 112–13.

people in Shanghai was consistently despised and discriminated against, it was migrants from Subei, who at the time of Liberation in 1949 represented approximately one-fifth of the city's population.[2]

Yet the notion of a Subei identity, pervasive as it appeared to be, was in some ways an anomaly in Shanghai. While native place defined quasi-ethnic groups in Shanghai, most such groups were associated with a clearly defined place: Ningbo-ese were from Ningbo, Cantonese from Canton. Subei, however, is neither a city nor a province, but rather a region with no obvious boundaries or consistent definition. Most literally, it includes all of Jiangsu north of the Yangzi River, from Haimen and Nantong in the south to Xuzhou in the northwestern corner. Yet, depending on whether one's definition is based on geographic, economic, or linguistic criteria, Subei could be defined as the area of Jiangsu north of the Yangzi and south of the Huai; it could exclude areas on the northern bank of the Yangzi (such as Nantong and Haimen); it could also include areas on the southern bank of the Yangzi, such as Zhenjiang. Exactly who was included as a Subei native was therefore debatable.

Even the areas that are uncontestably part of Subei—Yangzhou in the south to Yancheng, Funing, and Huai'an in the north—represent a region marked by extreme diversity. The area in the north, as the name of its major city, Yancheng (Salt City), suggests, consists of land reclaimed from the sea, suitable for little but producing salt and raising pigs. The land farther inland is not so salty and hence can support cotton crops. Still farther west, stretching south toward Yangzhou and Taizhou, the land is broken by a series of lakes and marshes and is thus wet enough to grow rice. As the transshipment point on the Grand Canal, Yangzhou had been one of China's major trading cities through the mid-Qing dynasty. If these areas had anything in common, it was only that they were poor when compared to the famed prosperity of Jiangnan and that their population spoke variations of Yangzhou dialect—which belongs to a dialect group entirely different from that of the Wu dialect spoken in Jiangnan. Yet the notion of a Subei identity implied a commonality of experience including far more than shared poverty and speech.

This chapter attempts to look more closely at the meaning of Subei identity in Shanghai: what it meant both to those who used the term and to the Subei natives it allegedly described. It is not a history of migrants

---

[2] Very little information about the number of Subei people in Shanghai is available, largely because most published census data breaks down the Shanghai population by province—not district—of origin. According to the only available statistic, there were 1,500,000 people from Subei in Shanghai in 1949. The entire population of Shanghai at that time was 5,062,878. Xie Junmei, "Shanghai lishi shang renkou de bianqian" [Historical changes in the population of Shanghai], *Shehui kexue* 3 (1980): 112.

from northern Jiangsu, but rather an exploration of how they defined themselves in Shanghai: under what circumstances, if any, natives of such places as Nantong, Yangzhou, and Yancheng believed they shared a common geographic origin, heritage, culture, and experience in Shanghai that could be described by the label *Subei ren*. Did Subei people think of themselves as *Subei ren*, or was it simply a social category used by others to describe them?

These questions are important, for the belief in *Subei ren* was a central ingredient in the development of a Shanghai identity, equated primarily with the culture of Jiangnan immigrants. Shanghai identity can be understood only in contradistinction to "the other" against which it defined itself, and Subei people represented that "other." Moreover, the conflict between Subei and Jiangnan natives was by far the most salient native-place cleavage in Shanghai, one that affected almost every aspect of Shanghai life. The economic, social, cultural, and sometimes even political history of Shanghai is in no small part the working out of this conflict. Understanding social organization as well as the relationship between class and native place identity in the immigrant city of Shanghai thus requires analysis of the antagonism between these two largest immigrant groups. The antagonism begins with names and identities: was there really a group called *Subei ren*? Jiangnan and Subei natives, we shall see, had very different answers to this question.

"Them"

Most non-Subei people in Shanghai believed that despite economic, linguistic, and cultural differences among districts north of the Yangzi, Subei people shared a common identity and represented a homogeneous group. From at least the mid-nineteenth century, it was assumed that migrants from any part of northern Jiangsu could be described by the categorical term *Subei ren* (or *Jiangbei ren*). From the 1870s through the 1940s, newspapers only rarely identified someone as being a native of Yancheng, Yangzhou, or Huai'an. (In contrast, individuals from Wuxi were invariably identified as *Wuxi ren*, those from Ningbo as *Ningbo ren*. They were never grouped together under the rubric *Jiangnan ren*, a category that existed only at the national level.) People from north of the river were identified as generic *Jiangbei ren* or occasionally as someone "speaking with a Jiangbei accent." (Speech was the only marker of a Subei identity.) Likewise, accounts of "Jiangbei shack dwellers" and, at times of floods, of "Jiangbei refugees" commonly appeared in the popular press. Some accounts, referring to the "Jiangbei *bang*" implied that Subei migrants represented not only a coherent, homogeneous group, but a united one as well.[3] *Subei ren,* in other words, was one of the major social categories used to identify individuals in Shanghai.

The notion of *Subei ren* as a social category must be understood in the context of the vastly different economies of southern and northern Jiangsu. Although Subei (particularly Yangzhou) had once been renowned for its prosperity, by the early twentieth century it was as famed for its poverty as was Jiangnan for its wealth. Its decline began in the late Qing, hastened by the replacement of the Grand Canal by sea transport and the shift in the course of the Yellow River in the mid-nineteenth century. From then on, cycles of floods, famine, and poverty characterized large portions of Subei.[4] The impoverishment and decline of Subei was made all the more conspicuous by the simultaneous rapid economic development of Jiangnan, which by the mid-nineteenth century had replaced the north as a magnet for merchant capital and was quickly becoming China's most urbanized, industrialized, and consequently wealthy region.[5]

The relative wealth and poverty of the two parts of Jiangsu was reflected in patterns of migration. Subei, it seemed, was a notorious producer of refugees. From the time of its decline in the nineteenth century, we find records of "Jiangbei refugees" heading south to Jiangnan, where they farmed land the natives considered undesirable, did coolie labor in the cities, or tried to survive by begging or taking advantage of the relief agencies that provided food and shelter. Whether they migrated to rural areas or cities, Subei refugees were the scourge of Jiangnan: they were considered a source of social disorder, and local officials engaged in continual efforts to send them back to their Subei homes.[6] The notion of *Subei ren,* then, is based on the presence throughout Jiangnan (including Shanghai) of large numbers of poverty-stricken refugees who spoke an unfamiliar dialect and were therefore perceived as somewhat foreign.

The notion of *Subei ren* as a social category must also be understood in the context of their status in the Shanghai labor market. In general, Subei people did the least lucrative and least desirable jobs in Shanghai. They dominated the ranks of unskilled laborers, representing the majority of rickshaw pullers, dock workers, construction workers, night soil and garbage collectors, barbers, and bathhouse attendants. In factories that

---

[3] Examples of the use of the term *Jiangbei ren* can be found in almost any issue of Shanghai's daily newspaper *Shenbao.* For some specific cases, see March 7, 1872; March 7, 9, 13, 1915; April 24, 1915; September 28, 1915.

[4] Emily Honig, "The Politics of Prejudice: Subei People in Republican-Era Shanghai," *Modern China,* July 1989, 253–57.

[5] Ibid.

[6] Ibid.

employed people from both Jiangnan and Subei, Subei natives were concentrated in the dirty, physically demanding, and low-paying jobs in the
workshops. Their concentration in these jobs was not simply a result of
their being poverty-stricken refugees from floods and famine, willing to
do almost any work. It was also because, in a job market where personal
connections were critical, they lacked the home-town ties to members of
the elite that their Jiangnan counterparts could draw on. Moreover,
Jiangnan employers, who regarded Subei natives as equivalent to a
different—and inferior—ethnic group, preferred to hire workers with
whom they shared a "common language," both literally and metaphor-
ically.[7]

The status of Subei natives, in both Jiangnan and Shanghai, as
refugees who were equated with "coolie" labor gave rise to the belief that
they constituted a distinct and coherent ethnic group. The conviction
that a coherent group called *Subei ren* existed was expressed in descriptions of a "Subei character." Observers of the Jiangsu rural economy,
who often wrote in popular magazines such as *Dongfang zazhi* (The
Eastern miscellany), went to great lengths to describe the differences
between the character of Subei and of Jiangnan natives. "In general,
Jiangnan people are civilized whereas Jiangbei people are coarse," wrote
Wang Peitang.[8] "People dislike [Subei people] because they are dirty and
rude," stated another description.[9] A third, slightly more specific,
observed that "in terms of personality, Jiangnan people are soft and
flexible, while Jiangbei people are firm and tough.... In terms of customs, religion, and superstition, Jiangnan people tend to be more civilized and open-minded."[10] That these beliefs shaped public perceptions
of Subei people in Shanghai is suggested by the explanations offered by
factory managers for their preference to not hire workers of Subei origins:
they were perceived as "dirty," "coarse," and "harder to handle."[11]

In addition to these personality traits, Subei people also allegedly
shared a common experience in Shanghai. Almost every Republican-
period discussion of Subei and/or Subei people repeats the partly inaccurate observation made in a 1930 issue of *Dongfang zazhi*:

> Men and women who have grown up in Jiangnan, every year see people
> from Jiangbei come to the cities and towns of Jiangnan to become peddlers,

---

[7] For a more extensive analysis of the reasons Subei people were tracked into certain
jobs, see Honig, "Politics of Prejudice," pp. 253–65.

[8] Wang Peitang, *Jiangsusheng xiangtu zhi* (Changsha, 1938), p. 369.

[9] Luo Manyan, "Jiangnan yu Jiangbei" [Jiangnan and Jiangbei], *Renyan zhoukan* 1:9
(June 23, 1934): 389.

[10] Zhao Ruheng, chap. 8, p. 189.

[11] Interview with He Zhiguang, 1980.

factory workers, rickshaw drivers, and do all the lowest class jobs. They
live, eat, and raise their children on small, dilapidated boats. . . . Actually, the
majority of workers in Shanghai's cotton industry, manufacturing industry,
heavy industry, cart pullers, rickshaw drivers, dock workers, and coolies are
Jiangbei people. The poor people in Nanshi, Zhabei and Pudong, Xujiahui
and Tushanwan all demonstrate the hard lives of Jiangbei people.[12]

The few articles chronicling the plight of Subei people in the 1920s and
1930s confirmed this belief in their common experience as poverty-
stricken shack dwellers and coolie laborers in Shanghai. One such article, for instance, described the areas where Subei people lived as "truly
tantamount to hell."

They live in straw huts that are very cheap to build, [and] there are often
fires in their settlements. They eat food that is hardly better than
garbage. . . . They are not very sanitary. They change their clothes only once
every week or two. . . . Most men are rickshaw pullers, construction, dock, or
transport workers. Most women are maids, servants, or work in silk
filatures. One can say that they do the lowest strata of jobs. Jiangbei men
are often in fights; the women are often raped. They have little legal protection because they are so ignorant.[13]

Sometimes the attributes of Subei people were expressed more crudely,
as in a fictitious dialogue between a Ningbo and a Subei native, published
in the Shanghai daily paper in 1932. "You Jiangbei people are all a
bunch of low-class nothings!" exclaimed the man from Ningbo. "Just
look: the people who empty toilets and pull rickshaws in Shanghai are
all you Jiangbei people. And most kidnappers and criminals are you
Jiangbei people, too."[14]

---

[12] Feng Hefa, *Zhongguo nongcun jingji ziliao* [Materials about the Chinese rural economy]
(Shanghai: Kaiming shuju, 1935), vol. 1, pp. 361–62. Also quoted in Wang Peitang, *Jiang-*
susheng xiangtu zhi, p. 365 (originally Wu Shoupeng in *Dongfang zazhi* 27:7 [April 10,
1930]: 69). Also quoted in Luo Meihuan, "Jiangsu Jiangbei gexian de meiluo—qi yuanyin ji
qi jiuji banfa" [The decline of each county in the Jiangbei part of Jiangsu—the causes and
methods of salvation], *Jiangsu yuebao* 1:2 (December 20, 1933): 70. Also quoted in Jiang
Junzhang, "Jiangsusheng shidi gaiyao" [An outline of the history and geography of Jiangsu
Province], part 4, *Jiangsu yanjiu* 2:3 (March 25, 1936): 7–8.
Despite the author's claim, few Subei natives were in fact employed in industries other
than cotton spinning and silk reeling. For a more extensive discussion of the role of Subei
people in the Shanghai labor market, see Emily Honig, "Native Place Hierarchy and Labor
Market Segmentation: The Case of Subei People in Shanghai," in Lillian Li and Thomas
Rawski, eds., *China's Economy in Historical Perspective* (Berkeley: University of California
Press, forthcoming).
[13] Jin Yuan, "Jiangbei ren zai Shanghai" [Jiangbei people in Shanghai], *Nüsheng* 4
(1934). Another article making similar generalizations about Subei people in Shanghai is
Cao Hui, "Jiangbei funü shenghuo gaikuang" [The general condition of women in Jiangbei],
Nüsheng 2 (1934): 10–11.
[14] "Ningbo ren yu Jiangbei ren" [Ningbo people and Jiangbei people], *Shenbao,* April 14,

Political events sometimes highlighted and intensified the belief in Subei people as a coherent social category. For example, when a large number of women silk filature workers began to organize a union in 1924, Subei women were singled out as the culprits. One factory owner dealt with the labor unrest by firing all the women from Subei, whether they were involved or not; workers from Jiangnan who may have been involved in organizing were not fired. According to at least one account, the labor activities of women silk workers at this time generated popular antagonism toward Subei people.[15]

The most dramatic and significant instance of a political event consolidating the belief in Subei people as a coherent group was the Japanese attack on Shanghai in 1932. Public reaction both reflected the conviction that *Subei ren* represented a homogeneous group and hardened a prejudice against them. Subei people came to be despised during this period as they were scapegoated for the criminal activity that plagued many Shanghai districts during the Japanese attack. Almost every day , articles in the local papers bore titles such as "Jiangbei hoodlums rob and loot people in Zhabei."[16] As many Chinese evacuated Zhabei, according to one report, "a large number of Komponese [*Kompo* is the pronunciation of *Jiangbei* in Wu-based Shanghai dialect] were seen busy along the Chapei areas digging into doors of the evacuated civilian houses to commit theft."[17] In other words, the perception of Subei people as criminals and hoodlums was intensified.

More serious than the association of Subei people with crime was the belief that they collaborated with the Japanese. As one writer observed, "After the war [the January 28 incident] a new term appeared: Jiangbei traitor."[18] The alleged collaboration of Subei people with the Japanese was manifested in several ways. First, the puppet government (the "Great Japan New Political Affairs Bureau") established by the Japanese in the Zhabei district of Shanghai in April 1932 was described as the machination of Subei people. Common knowledge, though not completely accurate, held that the leaders of the puppet government were all *Subei ren*. The associate director, Wang Du, was from Funing; the chief of police, Chang Yuqing, was chairman of the North Jiangsu Residents Guild of Shanghai and owner of a bathhouse on Nanjing Road; the chief

---

1932.

[15] *Shibao*, February 28, 29, 1924; March 3, 1924. Also see "Kankan Jiangbei ren" [Looking at Jiangbei people], *Jingbao*, March 1, 1924. I am grateful to Gail Hershatter for calling my attention to this article.

[16] *Shenbao*, March 8, 1932; *Shibao*, March 10, 1932.

[17] Shanghai Municipal Police Files, D-3325, March 3, 1932.

[18] *Shenbao*, April 4, 1932.

detective, Yao Zhitu, was also a Subei native. Although Gu Zhuxuan, the most well known Green Gang leader of Subei origins (and also very active in the Subei native-place association in Shanghai), did not hold a public office, he was nevertheless powerful in the administration of the puppet government.[19]

Despite the high-ranking positions held by Subei people in the puppet government, not all its members were from Subei. The traffic superintendent, Chen Ajing, was a native of Ningbo; Li Fei, the chief police inspector, came from Tianjin.[20] Moreover, the head of the administration, Hu Lifu, was from Anhui. Yet even articles that focused on him propagated the conviction that these so-called traitors were all *Jiangbei ren*.[21]

Perhaps more influential than the association of Subei people with leadership of the puppet government was the belief that large numbers of Subei migrants in Shanghai were actively assisting the Japanese. Newspaper articles with titles such as "Uneducated Jiangbei people in Zhabei are willingly being used by the Japanese," noted that Subei people wore armbands symbolizing the Japanese flag. "They look so stupid and disgusting," the writer of one article exclaimed, "but under the wing of the Japanese they have become really arrogant."[22] Other articles accused "ignorant and illiterate" Subei people of being "bought" by the Japanese to work as spies.[23] In addition, Chinese pictorial broadsheets sold on the streets of the International Settlement included illustrations with subtitles such as "Execution of Kompo men who were employed as Snipers by the Japanese," "The arrest of Chinese (Kompo men) who were paid $30 per day for carrying land mines for the Japanese," and "Twenty or thirty sampans plied near the O.S.K. Japanese Wharf by Kompo men engaged in smuggling motors for military purposes."[24]

A final aspect of the perception of Subei people as collaborators with the Japanese was the belief that the population of Subei itself was transporting food and supplies for the Japanese. As in the accusations of collaboration in Shanghai described above, writers stressed the relative ignorance of Subei natives. A report from Nantong in the Shanghai daily

[19] *China Weekly Review*, April 9, 1932; *Shenbao*, April 7, 1932; Shanghai Municipal Police Files, D-3445, April 18, 1932.

[20] Shanghai Municipal Police Files, D-3345, April 18, 1932.

[21] *Shenbao*, April 16, 1932. This misrepresentation may be due to the inconsistent definition of Subei. To many Shanghai residents anyone from north of the river who spoke something resembling Subei dialect was a *Subei ren*. Hu Lifu might therefore qualify. That he operated a bathhouse in Shanghai, an enterprise associated with *Subei ren*, may also help account for the conviction that this most notorious traitor was from Subei.

[22] *Shenbao*, March 11, 1932.

[23] *Shenbao*, May 11, 1932.

[24] Shanghai Municipal Police Files, D-3660, March 10, 1932.

Shibao, for example, observed that "at each of the docks along the river in Jiangbei there are ignorant, stupid people . . . using large junks to cross the river secretly and assist the enemy."[25]

In other words, in 1932 there developed an overwhelming association of Subei people with collaboration. Not surprisingly, the prejudice against Subei people became particularly virulent and blatant during this period. According to some reports, people who wanted to hire maids or rickshaw drivers refused to hire people from Subei; some refugee centers even refused to admit people of Subei origins.[26] The head of one Subei native-place association complained that "anyone who does not speak Shanghai dialect is accused of being a 'Jiangbei traitor.'"[27] Even two years later, according to one social commentator, "Whenever the name *Jiangbei* is mentioned in Shanghai, no matter who one is talking to, their expression immediately changes to contempt and disgust."[28]

It is difficult to know whether the majority of collaborators were actually from Subei or whether Subei people were simply being used as scapegoats. Certainly, Subei people were not the only, or even the most notorious, collaborators in Shanghai. Wang Jingwei, for instance, hailed from Canton—yet no reference was made to "Cantonese traitors." Nevertheless, it would not be surprising if some Subei people in Shanghai worked for the Japanese. Zhabei, the district occupied by the Japanese, was a working class district where large numbers of Subei natives lived in shack settlements. Most were poor and perhaps not averse to taking jobs that would give them money, regardless of its origins. Ultimately it does not matter whether Subei people really were collaborators or not; more significant is the popular perception that they were and the discrimination against them that ensued—a discrimination that both reflected and intensified the belief that they constituted a coherent social category.[29]

---

[25] *Shibao,* March 6, 1932.

[26] *Shenbao,* April 4, 1932. Also see Cao Hui.

[27] The complaint was made by the head of the Huai-yang-tong lühu tongxianghui. See *Shenbao,* March 19, 1932.

[28] *Shenbao,* April 13, 1934.

[29] Given the legacy of 1932, one would expect that the subsequent Japanese attack on and occupation of Shanghai would have deepened the perception of "Jiangbei collaborators." However, there is surprisingly little evidence that this was the case. A number of Subei natives were in fact associated with the puppet regime of that time. Chang Yuqing, a famed 1932 "collaborator," became even more renowned in the late 1930s for his association with the Japanese. In addition, Wu Shibao, a Gaoyou native, whose allegedly hideous and deformed features generated the nickname "Rotten Wintermelon" (*lan donggua*), was a major figure in the Japanese-run police force (see Xue Gengxin, "Wo jiechuguode Shanghai banghui renwu" [Shanghai gangsters with whom I came in contact], in Zhongguo renmin zhengzhi xueshang huihi Shanghaishi weiyuanhui wenshi ziliao gongzuo weiyuanhui, ed., *Jiu*

"Us"

What we have observed thus far are the beliefs of the Jiangnan-based Shanghai elite, specifically their conviction that Subei people had all the attributes of a distinct ethnic group—common geographic origin, character, and shared experience in Shanghai. But what about Subei people themselves? Did they partake of the belief that they constituted a coherent, homogeneous group with a shared identity? Did they, in other words, perceive themselves as a distinct ethnic group?

Since the idea of Subei as a place and Subei people as a category emerged only in conjunction with the development of Jiangnan and Shanghai, it is not surprising that a sense of Subei ethnic identity, if it were to exist at all, would be forged only through the experience of migration and living in the "south." The majority of Subei people had most likely not even heard the term *Subei* before coming to Shanghai. Furthermore, when they first arrived, they appear to have identified not as *Subei ren,* but rather as natives of the particular district from which they came, much as Italian migrants to the United States saw themselves as Genoese, Venetians, Neapolitans, Sicilians, and Calabrians rather than as Italians.[30] "Ethnicities rarely coincided with the initial self-identification of the industrial recruits," observes Eric Wolf about migrants to the United States, "who first thought of themselves as Hanoverians or Bavarians rather than as Germans, as members of their village or parish (*okolica*) rather than as Poles, as Tonga or Yao rather than as 'Nyasalanders.'"[31] So Subei people too, initially thought of themselves not as "Subei-nese," but as Yangzhou-, Yancheng-, or Nantong-ese. Did their sense of identity change over time?

Shanghai de banghui [Shanghai: Shanghai renmin chubanshe, 1986], p. 107; Zhuan Xiangyuan, *Qingbang daheng: Huang Jinrong, Du Yuesheng, Zhang Xiaolin waizhuan* [Green Gang bosses: biographies of Huang Jianrong, Du Yuesheng, and Zhang Xiaolin] [Hong Kong: Zhongyuan chubanshe, 1987], pp. 201–202). Nevertheless, Subei people as a group never seem to have been singled out or scapegoated; almost no articles in the press identified Subei people as collaborators.

Despite the brevity of the Japanese attack of 1932 compared to the war from 1937–1945, its legacy in terms of the construction and stigmatization of the category "Subei people" was far more profound. That Subei people were not perceived as more inclined to be collaborators during the latter period failed to negate the perceptions formed earlier. Even in the 1980s, when I raised the subject of Subei people with retired factory workers, many complained that Subei people had collaborated with the Japanese.

[30] Jonathan D. Sarna, "From Immigrants to Ethnics: Toward a New Theory of 'Ethnicization,'" *Ethnicity* 5 (1978): 371.

[31] Eric Wolf, *Europe and the People without History* (Berkeley and Los Angeles: University of California Press, 1982), p. 381.

At first glance, it appears that Subei migrants to Shanghai gradually accepted the belief that they formed a coherent group, that by the late 1910s local identities had gradually given way to a growing sense of Subei identity. This is the picture that emerges if we use the organizations they formed, specifically native-place associations, as an index of their self-identity. Previous scholars have assumed that no native-place associations from Subei existed in Shanghai. Preliminary research, however, shows that although the Subei native-place associations were never as large or powerful as those from Jiangnan areas (such as the Ningbo Guild), most Subei districts did have associations in Shanghai.[32]

More significant here is the number of associations that represented Subei as a whole. A Jiangbei Natives' Preservation Association (Jiangbei tongxiang weichi hui) existed in the early 1920s; in 1936 an Office for the Confederation of Shanghai Sojourners from Each District in Subei (Jiangbei gexian lühu tongxianghui lianhe banshichu) was formed.[33] During the late 1940s, the number of Subei-wide organizations in Shanghai multiplied. These included a Service Society for Subei Sojourners in Shanghai (Subei lühu tongxiang fuwushe) and a Relief Committee for Shanghai Sojourners from Each Subei County (Subei geshu lühu tongxiang jiuji weiyuanhui), as well as a Subei Refugee Center (Subei nanmin shourongsuo), a Subei Nursing Home (Subei yanglao yuan), and a Subei Compulsory Primary School (Subei yiwu xiao xuexiao).[34] Aside from the sheer fact of their existence, little is known about any of these organizations or about their members or activities. Their existence, though, suggests that a Subei identity was replacing or supplementing the more local

---

[31] The only study that deals extensively with guilds and native-place associations in Shanghai is Tadashi Negishi, *Shanhai no girudo* [The guilds of Shanghai] (Tokyo, 1951). His study makes no reference to Subei associations in Shanghai.

[32] The data about these organizations are fragmentary at best: archival records are only available for the late 1940s; for the preceding decades we must rely on scattered references to the associations that appear in local newspapers and other published sources.

[33] For the Jiangbei tongxiang weichi hui, see *Shibao,* April 11, 1919; May 13, 20, 1919; *Shenbao,* July 7, 1925. For the Jiangbei gexian lühu tongxianghui lianhe banshichu, see *Shenbao,* February 13, 1936. Another Subei-wide organization existed in 1932, the Office for the Confederation of Native Place Associations of Huai'an, Yangzhou, and Nantong (Huai-yang-tong lühu tongxianghui lianhe banshichu). See *Shenbao,* March 19, 1932. Nothing is known about the membership, activities, or longevity of any of these organizations.

[34] Subei nanmin shourongsuo, Shanghai Municipal Archives (6-9-223). The Subei yanglao yuan is referred to in *Shanghai shirenzhi* [Atlas of the Shanghai elite], p. 80. The Subei yewu xiaoxuexiao is referred to in Subei nanmin jiuji huiyi Shanghai banshichu, ed., "Shanghai Subei nanmin jiuji baogao" [Report on the salvation of Subei refugees in Shanghai] (February 1947), Shanghai Municipal Archives, in records of Subei nanmin jiuji yeyi Shanghai banshichu (6-9-225).

Yangzhou or Yancheng identities. The charter of the Service Society for Subei Sojourners in Shanghai, for example, declared the society's goal of helping Subei natives win the respect they deserved for their contribution to Shanghai's development.[35]

Closer scrutiny of the native-place associations, however, calls into question the Subei identity that their existence might seem to represent. First, these organizations were not always established by Subei people themselves. For example, the Organization to Save Subei Refugees (Subei nanmin jiuji xiehui), formed in 1946, was initiated and directed by Du Yuesheng, a Pudong native, and several individuals from Zhejiang and Anhui, as well as influential people from Subei such as the Green Gang leader Gu Zhuxuan.[36] Likewise, the Subei Flood Relief Organization, formed in August 1947, when a severe flood destroyed large parts of Xuzhou and Haizhou, was organized by "Shanghai citizens."[37] Some organizations bearing the name "Subei" therefore represented the benevolence of non-Subei people concerned with the plight of this destitute community. While the rosters of some organizations indicate that the founders and members were all of Subei origins, the above examples caution us from assuming that organizations with the name Subei inherently represent the efforts of Subei natives.

Second, most of the Subei-wide organizations appear to have been short-lived. That after 1925, for instance, no references to the Jiangbei Natives' Preservation Association exist, suggests it may have disbanded. Likewise, the Association for Sojourners from Each District in Subei, formed in 1936 in response to a major strike of rickshaw pullers (most of whom hailed from Subei), seems to have dissolved once the strike ended.

Not only were the organizations short-lived, but the basis of the bond represented by their formation seems to have been precarious. The truth of this assertion is suggested by the comments of the chairman of the first meeting, in 1936, of the Office for the Confederation of Shanghai Sojourners from Each District in Subei. "The groups from each district have no spirit of unity," he complained. "Every day the number of migrants from Subei districts increases, but it is impossible to unify them."[38] Likewise, Zhu Hua, from Dongtai, founder of the Service Society for Jiangbei Sojourners in Shanghai, bemoaned that although "the majority of people [in Shanghai] are countrymen from Jiangbei, they have very

---

[35] "Jiangbei lühu tongxiang fuwushe luqi" [Record of the founding of the service society for Jiangbei sojourners in Shanghai] (Shanghai Municipal Archives, 6-9-228), 1946.

[36] Records of Subei nanmin jiuji xiehui, Shanghai Municipal Archives.

[37] *Da gongbao,* August 15, 1947.

[38] *Shenbao,* February 13, 1936.

little contact among themselves, and this is a pity."[39] Little wonder, then, that many of these organizations and confederations were formed in response to specific issues such as famine relief or a strike and then disbanded once the issue was resolved.

A final qualification of the Subei-wide identity represented by these organizations is that they were often overshadowed by the existence—if not proliferation—of associations representing natives of specific Subei districts in Shanghai. From at least the 1910s, for example, Yangzhou migrants had their own association, the Yangzhou Guild, and later an Association of Sojourners in Shanghai from the Eight Counties of Yangzhou.[40] By the early 1930s, separate associations for sojourners from Dongtai, Xinghua, Huaiyin, and Haimen also existed.[41] And by the late 1940s, these were joined by associations for Funing, Yancheng, Huai'an, Nantong, Baoying, Qidong, Taixing, Taixian, Gaoyou, and Rugao.[42] Almost every Subei district could boast its own native-place association in Shanghai.

Not only were the majority of associations locally based, but the issues that concerned them tended to be locally defined as well. Only rarely did associations become involved in an issue of concern to migrants from another Subei district. This fact is perhaps most dramatically exemplified by an incident that absorbed and enraged Shanghai's Yangzhou community in 1934—the publication by Yi Junzuo of *Xianhua Yangzhou* (Musings of Yangzhou), a book that primarily describes the history, people, and places of interest to tourists in Yangzhou. In part, Yi's book reads like an advertisement for Yangzhou and its famed culture, praising Yangzhou people for being particularly refined and distinct from their cruder Subei brethren. "Jiangbei people have a coarse personality," he observed, "but Yangzhou people are refined. Although Yangzhou is in Jiangbei, from early on it became 'Jiangnan-ized.' "[43] These compliments notwithstanding, Yangzhou natives felt the book insulted their reputation. More specifically, they objected to the author's statements (1) that prostitutes were the pride of Yangzhou; (2) that Yangzhou was cluttered by

[39] "Jiangbei lühu tongxiang fuwushe luqi," Shanghai Municipal Archives, 6-9-228, 1946.

[40] The Yangzhou Guild (Yangzhou bashu gongsuo) is referred to in *Shenbao*, January 4, 1917. Records for the Yangzhou baoshu lühu tongxianghui for 1946–47 are held at the Shanghai Municipal Archives. The association is also referred to in *Shenbao*, September 2, 1931.

[41] The Huaiyin association is referred to in *Shenbao*, November 26, 1936; the Haimen association in *Shenbao*, December 7, 1936; the Xinghua association in *Shenbao*, December 10, 1931; the Dongtai association in *Shenbao*, September 8, 1931.

[42] Records of all these associations are all held at the Shanghai Municipal Archives.

[43] Yi Junzuo, *Xianhua Yangzhou* (Shanghai: Zhonghua shuju, 1934), p. 28.

chamber pots and the sight of natives relieving themselves in public; and (3) that Yangzhou people were notorious collaborators—first with the Manchus, more recently with the Japanese.[44]

No sooner did the book appear than the Association of Sojourners from the Eight Counties of Yangzhou in Shanghai called an emergency meeting to plan a protest. The heads of the association held a press conference and denounced the book as "an insult to all the people of Yangzhou." They demanded that Yi resign from his position as director of the Editing and Censorship Office of the Jiangsu Provincial Bureau of Education and later filed suit against him. Meanwhile, they asked that stores at least refuse to sell the book, preferably burn it.

The results of their efforts are not clear. More significant here, however, is that this was a strictly Yangzhou-defined issue in Shanghai. It was the Yangzhou community that was offended and the Yangzhou community that responded. The attempts to rectify the book's insults were organized entirely by the Yangzhou native-place association in Shanghai. No other Subei native-place association came to its assistance or defense. (Nor did the Yangzhou association involve itself in issues concerning natives of other Subei districts. For example, when Gu Zhenghong, from Yancheng, was killed in 1925, the Yangzhou associations did not join the Association of Jianghuai Sojourners in sponsoring a memorial.) It is clear, then, that the district-based native-place associations for the most part represented local identities.

No discussion of the Subei native-place associations would be complete without reference to the Association of Jianghuai Sojourners in Shanghai (Jianghuai lühu tongxianghui). Of all the associations—Subei-wide or district-based—this was the single most enduring and powerful association of Subei natives in Shanghai. Established at the time of the May Fourth Movement in 1919, it continued to exist through the late 1940s, by which time it had branch offices in most of the districts where Subei people lived in Shanghai and operated a school as well.[45] This association, at first glance, seems to represent an identity that extended beyond specific localities. And it did: according to its 1947 charter, it encompassed the districts of Huai'an, Huai'yin, Lianshui, Siyang, Yancheng, and Funing, the majority of its members coming from those areas.[46] It did not, however, serve natives of *all* of Subei: those from the southern part of Subei, such as Yangzhou, Taixing, or Nantong, were not affiliated with the Jianghuai association. In other words, while the

---

[44] *Shenbao,* July 12, 1934; July 17, 1934.

[45] The Jianghuai Primary School is referred to in *Da gongbao,* July 4, 1947.

[46] Jianghuai lühu tongxianghui, Shanghai Municipal Archives, 6-5-954, 1946–47.

Jianghuai association may have represented a belief in the commonality of experience of migrants from "Jianghuai," it reinforced the profound sense of difference between natives of northern and southern Subei.

This split is corroborated by other associations that represented several Subei districts, for almost all were federations of northern or southern districts. For example, in the 1940s, an Association for Sojourners in Shanghai from Nantong, Rugao, Chongming, Haimen, and Qidong (Tong-Ru-Chong-Hai-Qi lühu tongxianghui) served natives of the southernmost part of Subei, while an Association for Sojourners in Shanghai from Yancheng and Funing (Yan-Fu lühu tongxianghui) represented those from the north.[47]

We have seen, then, that the existence of several Subei-wide organizations cannot be immediately equated with the emergence of a Subei identity among migrants from northern Jiangsu. Instead, if organizations are at all indicative of identity, they suggest the persistence of localism and perhaps a growing sense of commonality among natives of specific parts of Subei, such as Jianghuai. It does not appear, in other words, that the conviction held by the Shanghai elite that Subei people represented a coherent group with a common heritage and experience was shared by Subei people themselves. This perception becomes overwhelmingly evident if we shift our focus from organizations to the beliefs and experiences of Subei migrants to Shanghai.

We cannot know how all, or even most, Subei people identified themselves, nor can we know how the self-identity of individuals changed over time or how the self-identity of migrants from a Subei district in the 1870s differed from their counterparts' in the 1940s. Nevertheless, the fragmentary evidence provided by interviews with individuals who migrated from Subei to Shanghai in the 1930s and 1940s as well as data about their cultural practices, work, and residential patterns, sketches their persisting localism and the northern/southern Subei rift suggested above.

The more local identities of migrants from Subei are expressed, first, in attitudes toward one another, as migrants from different Subei districts often went to great lengths to distinguish themselves. For example, a cook at the Yangzhou Restaurant in Shanghai insisted, "Our customs were completely different from those of Yancheng natives. Our language was different and our food was different, too. Yancheng people ate

---

[47] For the Tong-Ru-Chong-Hai-Qi lühu tongxianghui, see Subei nanmin jiujihuiyi Shanghai banshichu, ed., "Shanghai Subei nanmin jiuji baogao," February 1947, Shanghai Municipal Archives (6-9-225). The Yan-Fu tongxianghui is first mentioned in *Shenbao*, May 10, 1937. Its records for 1946–47 are held at the Shanghai Municipal Archives (6-9-956).

yams while we ate rice. We don't consider Yancheng people as belonging to our same native place."[48] That natives of one Subei district did not
consider those from another to be *tongxiang ren* is confirmed by the
admission of Xia Keyun, himself from Huai'an, that "if someone came to
Shanghai from Huai'an we would help him, but if he came from Yangzhou we'd ignore him."[49] They did not, in other words, share a common
Subei identity.

The sense of separateness expressed by people of different Subei origins sometimes extended to attitudes of hostility or condescension, particularly among natives of the more prosperous southern parts of Subei.
People from Yangzhou, for instance, frequently expressed precisely the
same attitudes of scorn and disgust toward Yancheng people that Jiangnan natives more commonly expressed toward Subei people as a group.
Their sense of superiority was occasionally so extreme that they insisted
Yangzhou was not part of Subei at all. For example, in explaining why
the bathhouse bosses hired only people from Yangzhou, one man, himself
a pedicurist from Yangzhou, said:

> It was because we people from Yangzhou know how to speak well; we speak
> in a rather cultivated way. It was important for the service people to speak
> well or the customers would not come. Our speech is very careful and soft,
> while theirs [people from Yancheng] is very crude—*wawawawawa*. We were
> much more refined, while Subei people were very coarse; we were very
> sophisticated, while they were very poor.
>
>   Even though we were from Yangzhou, people still used to call us "Jiang-
> bei folk." It was derogatory and it upset us. We knew we were from Yang-
> zhou and were not really Jiangbei folk, but they did not know the
> difference.[50]

A similar desire to exclude one's native place from the definition of Subei
and thereby deny one's Subei identity was expressed by the late-
nineteenth-century reformer Zhang Jian. Himself a native of Nantong, he
declared that Subei consisted only of areas immediately south of the
Huai, such as Yancheng, Funing, and Huai'an. By implication, neither
Yangzhou nor the more southern districts of Haimen or Nantong were
part of Subei.[51] Natives of the two areas, as far as he was concerned, did
not share a common Subei identity.

The local identities of Subei migrants were not simply attitudinal; they
were also expressed in the migrants' separate cultural activities. This

[48] Interview with Zhou Dianyuan, Yangzhou fandian, August 24, 1988.
[49] Interview with Xia Keyun, Shanghai Coal Handling Co., August, 4, 1988.
[50] Interview with Xu Liansheng, Shanghai Yudechi Bathhouse, November 12, 1986.
[51] Liu Housheng, *Zhang Jian zhuanji* [Biography of Zhang Jian] (Shanghai: Kexue chubanshe, 1953), p. 250.

division is particularly evident in local opera, one of the favorite forms of entertainment for Subei natives. While most Subei districts could boast their own distinctive opera, Yangzhou and Huai opera were the two most frequently performed in Shanghai. (The latter, also known as Jianghuai opera, originated in the rural areas of Huai'an, Yancheng, and Funing.[52]) Natives of these two parts of Subei favored performances of opera from their respective regions. The Yangzhou barber Zhou Dianyuan recalled that before 1949, "we went to hear Yangzhou opera at the Taiyuan *fang*. The audience was all Yangzhou people, especially barbers. But we never went to Huai opera!"[53] Conversely, Subei dock workers, few of whom were from Yangzhou, preferred Huai opera performed at tea houses in their neighborhoods, such as the Kaitian teahouse in Pudong or the so-called Forty Room (*sishi jian*) in Nanshi.[54] Huai opera drew its audience not only from the ranks of dock workers, but from almost all migrants from the northern Subei areas of Yancheng, Funing, and Huai'an. "Before [1949], we used to all like to go to Huai opera," recalled rickshaw puller Zhang Ronghua. "We liked Xiao Wenyan. There was also Yangzhou opera, but we liked to see Jianghuai opera."[55]

Residential patterns are yet another indicator of the predominantly local identities of Subei people in Shanghai. Although most Shanghai people associated all Subei people with shack settlements, Subei people themselves recognized much more subtle patterns within the "Subei villages," as natives of different districts congregated in particular alleys. "Before 1949," recalled Xia Keyun, "we'd say, 'That's the Hubei alley. That's the Yangzhou alley. And that's the Huai'an alley.' "[56] Dock worker Cheng Jinfan believed that the Pudong area of Yangjiadu was inhabited mostly by Taizhou people; Zhang Ronghua, a former rickshaw puller, recalled that almost everyone who lived in the shack settlement bordering North Zhongshan Road in Zhabei was, like him, from Yancheng; and the Zhabei district of Shenjiatuo was, according to a shoemaker from Yangzhou, the purview of fellow Yangzhou natives.[57]

---

[52] Zhongguo xijujia xiehui and Shanghaishi wenhuaju, eds., *Zhongguo difang xiqu jicheng; Shanghaishi juan* [Compendium on Chinese local opera: Shanghai] (Beijing: Zhongguo xiju chubanshe, 1959), pp. 1–17.

[53] Interview with Zhou Dianyuan, Yangzhou Restaurant, August 24, 1988.

[54] Interview with Xia Keyun, Cheng Jinfan, and Pan Jingan, Shanghai Harbor Coal Handling Co., August 4, 1988.

[55] Interview with workers at Zhabei district sanitation bureau, November 3, 1986.

[56] Interview with Xia Keyun.

[57] Interview with Cheng Jinfan, Shanghai Coal Handling Co., August 4, 1988 (?). Interview with workers at Zhabei district sanitation bureau, November 3, 1986. Interview with retired people at Zhongxing Street Residence Committee, 1986.

Household registration records that would make possible a more systematic study of the relationship between local origins and residential patterns in Shanghai are not available. Membership lists of native-place associations, however, which often include addresses of their members, provide some corroboration to the impressions of Subei natives described above. Although the majority of lower-class Subei natives did not join the associations, the residence patterns of those who did join can still suggest the ways in which people from particular localities clustered together in Shanghai. For instance, a sizable community of Jiangdu natives resided in lanes number 68 and 82 on Jiaozhou Road; lanes 42, 51, and 162 of Yuyao Road as well as lanes 793–95 on Pingliang Road were dominated by people from Yancheng and Funing; a large number of Huai'an natives lived in lane 68, Changshou Road.[58]

It would be misleading to suggest that these patterns were absolute and that all Subei migrants lived in lanes or shack settlements surrounded by people from their precise locality. These patterns most likely varied by class, with the wealthier members of the "Subei community" scattered throughout Shanghai, for they could afford more desirable housing. Indeed, the native-place association records indicate that directors of the various associations, all men of considerable wealth, lived in the International Settlement and French Concession, alongside natives of Jiangnan districts. (They were still seen as Subei natives, in spite of their financial means.) The overwhelming majority of poor, working-class Subei migrants, though, were dependent on personal and native-place connections (*tongxiang guanxi*) to find a place to live and therefore tended to cluster together. It is impossible to determine what percentage lived with natives of the same locality compared to those who "mingled" with natives of different Subei districts. Compared to the perception of Jiangnan natives that all Subei people lived together in shack settlements, however, there was a significant amount of segregation according to specific local origins. This residential segregation both reflected and reinforced the more local identities of Subei people in Shanghai.

Residential patterns suggest that certain aspects of their experience in Shanghai perpetuated the distinctions and divisions among Subei migrants, militating against the formation of a broader Subei identity. Such distinctions and divisions are even more evident if we examine patterns of employment, which suggest that no common "Subei" work experience existed. Instead, employment patterns often reinforced and

---

[58] See Huai-yang lühu tongxiang fulihui, 1948, Shanghai Municipal Archives, 6-9-246; and Jianghuai tongxianghui, Shanghai Municipal Archives, 6-5-954; Huai'an lühu tongxianghui, Shanghai Municipal Archives, 6-5-993.

reproduced the more local identities of Subei migrants.

Although, as observed above, non-Subei people associated all Subei people with coolie labor, Subei people themselves were aware of a much more complex division of labor in which migrants from each Subei district concentrated in particular jobs. The most important division was between people from Yangzhou and those from the more northern areas of Yancheng, Funing, and Huai'an. In general, Yangzhou natives had jobs requiring slightly more skill and offering better working conditions than those dominated by people from farther north, reflecting perhaps the prosperity of Yangzhou compared with Yancheng, Funing, and Huai'an. Although some Yangzhou natives could be found among almost all the jobs dominated by Subei people—rickshaw pulling, dock loading, night soil and garbage collecting—they were particularly known for their domination of the so-called three knives—barbers, bathhouse pedicurists, and cooks.[59] Yangzhou was famous as an exporter of barbers, particularly to Shanghai, and the head of the barbers' guild in 1920, Chen Sihai, was a Yangzhou native.[60] People from Yancheng and Funing, in contrast, could claim dominance of the rickshaw-pulling profession. A survey of the native place of rickshaw pullers in 1934–35 showed some 53 percent coming from Yancheng and Funing, whereas only 17 percent hailed from the area near Yangzhou.[61]

The hierarchy of jobs dominated by Yangzhou and Yancheng-Funing people was confirmed by the pride and resentment expressed by people from each of those areas. People from Yancheng knew they could not aspire to enter the occupations controlled by the Yangzhou *bang*. "The jobs done by people from Yangzhou were much better than ours," a man from Jianhu (near Yancheng) observed bitterly. "Their work was easier and lighter. Being a barber was much better than pulling rickshaws! The worst work was hauling night soil carts, collecting garbage, and sweeping the streets. Not many Yangzhou people did those kinds of jobs. They were mostly in barber shops and bathhouses."[62]

More important than the precision or consistency of these divisions is the consciousness of Subei natives that they existed, for almost all Subei

---

[59] Wu Liangrong, "Shanghaishi Subeiji jumin shehui biandong fenxi" [An analysis of social mobility among Subei natives in Shanghai], in Shanghai shehuixue xuehui, ed., *Shehuixue wenji* [Collected essays on sociology] (Shanghai: 1984), p. 177.

[60] Li Cishan, "Shanghai laodong qingkuang" [The condition of labor in Shanghai], *Xin qingnian* 7:6 (1920): 48–49.

[61] Shanghaishi chuzu qiche gongsi, *Shanghai jiedao he gonglu yingye keyun shiliao jiangji* [Compendium of historical materials on the Shanghai street and road business and public transport] (Shanghai, 1982), pp. 127–29.

[62] Interview with Zhou Guozhen, Zhabei District Sanitation Bureau, 1986.

people I interviewed could identify the native-place origins of workers in various occupations. Former dock worker Xia Keyun, for instance, explained that "Yangzhou people did service jobs; Yancheng people pulled rickshaws, and Nantong natives pulled *tache* and *laohu che* (dragon carts). People from Taizhou liked to sell things, so they sold peanuts and snacks to us dock workers from Huai'an."[63] Another Subei native originally from Yangzhou described a division of labor as follows: wok repairers were from Gaoyou county; cobblers and sanitation workers from Jiangdu county; barbers, pedicurists, and cooks from Yangzhou city.[64] These descriptions may or may not accurately reflect social reality. As no surveys of workers in these occupations exist, we can only draw on people's memories and beliefs. Yet these beliefs are as significant as reality, for they suggest the ways in which people experienced work as perpetuating the distinctions and boundaries among natives of different Subei districts.

These distinctions, as with residential patterns, were not absolute, and certainly many Subei people worked in occupations employing natives of several Subei districts. Cotton mills and silk filatures, for example, employed women from almost every part of Subei. While such mixing did not always contribute to the creation of a broader Subei identity, it did occasionally bring together natives of several districts. A report of a strike at a silk filature in the early 1920s both highlights the local identities and illustrates an instance when they were at least temporarily overcome. "In the past, people referred to Yancheng and Taixing as 'small feet' and 'big feet' [referring to the presence or absence of foot binding]," remarked the author. "But in this case the two groups (*bang*) were able to cooperate. Women workers belonging to the Yancheng *bang* went to the women's office of the Taixing native-place group (*tongxiang Taixing bang nügong chu*) to ask for strike support."[65] Apparently, under more ordinary circumstances, women from the two districts did not get along, much less see themselves as sharing a common "Subei" identity. The division between the Yancheng and Taixing women (emphasized by the special office for women of the Taixing *bang*) was broken down in this case only by the exigencies of a strike.

Dock workers, too, came from a variety of Subei districts: Taixing and Nantong, as well as Yancheng, Funing, and Huai'an. Although

[63] Interview with Xia Keyun and Jiang Sanxiao, Shanghai Harbor Coal Handling Co., August 27, 1988.
[64] Interview with retired people at Zhongxing Street Residence Committee, Zhabei, 1986.
[65] *Minguo ribao*, August 11, 16, 1922. I am grateful to Elizabeth Perry for calling my attention to these reports.

workers from each district tended to concentrate in particular jobs, some interaction took place, as attested to by their work chants. On the one hand, workers from each Subei district brought with them chants of their own native place. The chants of Nantong, Yangzhou, and Huai'an were completely different from one another. On the other hand, though, workers on the Shanghai docks adopted chants from districts other than their own, depending on which was most rhythmically appropriate to the job they were performing. Those who hauled sacks of cargo on their backs (*gang*), for example, sang chants from Nantong, which had a strong beat, while workers who teamed up to carry cargo on shoulder poles preferred the rhythm of Yangzhou chants—even though few were themselves from Yangzhou.[66] This "blending" of customs had its limits, however. Subei natives, for instance, despite their contact with workers from Hubei, were unwilling to adopt Hubei chants. "The Hubei chants," exclaimed Xia Keyun (after imitating one), "sound like the songs of minority people to me!"[67]

Thus, although working together led Subei natives to adopt the chants of workers from Subei districts other than their own, a knowledge of which chant came from which district persisted, and a broader Subei identity was not forged among dock workers.

The above discussion has stressed the ways in which the more local identities of Subei people were perpetuated in Shanghai. It is important to point out, however, that what appears to be a continued insistence on distinctions among Subei migrants of different local origins was sometimes an expression of class difference. In other words, the line separating class and native-place identities was often blurred; and as we saw in the attitude of the Jiangnan elite toward Subei people as a group, native place sometimes functioned as a metaphor for class. The class dimension of the local identities maintained by many Subei people in Shanghai is evident in a theme underlying many of the attitudes and practices described above: the disdain of those from southern Subei for those from farther north. Most often, it was people from the southern areas of Nantong, Haimen, and Yangzhou who wanted to disassociate themselves from natives of the more northern districts of Yancheng, Funing, and Huai'an.

---

[66] Interview with Xia Keyun and Jiang Sanxiao, Shanghai Harbor Coal Handling Co., August 27, 1988.

[67] Interview with Xia Keyun, August 4, 1988, Shanghai Harbor Coal Handling Company. The attitude of Subei migrants toward their fellow workers from Hubei was disdain at best, and fights often broke out between the two groups. Such a brawl in 1926 between Subei and Hubei workers over unloading at the Pudong docks resulted in the drowning of two Hubei natives. *Minguo ribao,* July 8, 1926 (courtesy of Elizabeth Perry).

Because southern Subei tended to be more prosperous than the northern districts, southern Subei was often the first destination for migrants
from farther north. Refugees from Yancheng and Huai'an eking out a living by collecting garbage were a familiar sight to those who grew up in
Yangzhou in the 1930s. We have also seen that migrants from southern
Subei generally obtained better jobs in Shanghai than their compatriots
from the north. Profiles of members of native-place associations from
the two areas further attest to the economic differences between these
migrant communities in Shanghai. We can look, first, at the educational
experience of members of the northern Huai'an and southern Nantong
native-place associations (table 1). The most notable differences are that
more members of the Nantong association had advanced degrees (a total
of 13 percent compared to 2.4 percent of the Huai'an association
members); a far greater percentage of the Nantong association had middle school education (79.8 percent for Nantong, compared to 9.3 percent
for Huai'an); and the number of illiterate or semiliterate members of the
Huai'an association far surpassed those from Nantong (24.9 percent for
Huai'an, 1.0 percent for Nantong).[68]

Differences in the social and economic status of the migrant communities from northern and southern Subei districts are also evident in
occupational patterns. Data are available for occupations of members of
native-place associations from the northern area of Huai'an and southern
areas of Yangzhou and Haimen in the late 1940s (table 2). Here, too,
we see that members of the Yangzhou and Haimen associations were
employed in more lucrative and prestigious jobs than were those in the
Huai'an association. Whereas businessmen and professionals represented
95 percent of the Yangzhou and 63 percent of the Haimen associations'
members, they comprised only 6 percent of the members of the Huai'an
association. And whereas 52 percent of members of the Huai'an association were workers, only 1 percent of the Yangzhou and 5 percent of the
Haimen association were employed as workers.[69]

The membership of these native-place associations does not necessarily represent a cross-section of migrants from the districts they
represent. The vast majority of migrants never joined the associations,
and little is known about what qualified certain individuals for membership. Nevertheless, as a rough index of the economic and social status of

---

[68] These statistics are based on the 1947 membership lists of the Nantong lühu tongxianghui and the Huai'an lühu tongxianghui, both held at the Shanghai Municipal Archives.

[69] These data are compiled from the membership lists of the Haimen lühu tongxianghui,
the Yangzhou 7 xian lühu tongxianghui, and the Huai'an lühu tongxianghui. This material
is held at the Shanghai Municipal Archives.

Table 1

Educational Experience of Members of Native-Place Associations

Education	Huai'an (N/%)	Nantong (N/%)
University	3 (0.9)	10 (3.3)
Law school	1 (0.3)	7 (2.3)
Specialized school	2 (0.6)	18 (5.9)
Teachers college	2 (0.6)	5 (1.6)
Upper middle school (*gaozhong*)	2 (0.6)	65 (21.4)
Middle school (*zhongxue*)	12 (3.7)	68 (22.4)
Lower middle school (*chuzhong*)	16 (5.0)	109 (36.0)
Upper primary school (*gaoxiao*)	8 (2.5)	0
Primary school (*xiaoxue*)	17 (5.3)	0
Private academy (*sixu*)	91 (28.4)	18 (5.9)
Literate	21 (6.6)	0
Roughly literate	27 (8.4)	0
Illiterate	53 (16.5)	3 (1.0)
No education listed	65	0
TOTAL	320	303

the various Subei communities, these data illuminate the prosperity of the communities of migrants from southern Subei relative to those from the north. Thus, when natives of the southern districts distinguished themselves from natives of the north (such as the pedicurist who insisted people like him from Yangzhou were not *Subei ren*), they were not expressing native place identities alone, but were insisting upon class differences as well, even among the "Subei folk" perceived as uniformly poor by the Jiangnan-based elite.

It would be misleading to conclude that Subei people never thought of themselves as constituting a coherent social category before 1949, although the paucity of instances in which they left an explicit record of Subei consciousness makes it difficult accurately to determine the frequency or longevity of this consciousness. One of the few such instances was during the Japanese attack in 1932, described above. In response to accusations that they were collaborators, people from Subei districts spoke out in their own defense. "For someone who is from Jiangbei," complained one man in a letter to the editor of a local magazine, "walking on the street and hearing people make fun of us feels worse than being a Chinese in a foreign country." He criticized the public for blaming all Subei people for the activities of what he believed constituted only a small minority of Subei collaborators.[70] Other Subei natives, rather than

[70] Bing Qian, "Jiangbei ren sanzi" [The three words "Jiangbei ren"], *Shenghuo zhoukan* 7:20 (May 21, 1932): 311.

Table 2
Occupations of Members of Native-Place Associations

Occupation	Huai'an (N/%)	Yangzhou (N/%)	Haimen (N/%)
Government	2 (0.6)	4 (1.0)	18 (8.4)
Lawyer	1 (0.3)	20 (5.0)	5 (2.3)
Teacher	2 (0.6)	2 (0.5)	26 (12.0)
Accountant	0		
Doctor	1 (0.3)	1 (0.3)	21 (9.8)
Business	18 (5.1)	355 (89.2)	80 (37.2)
Journalist	0	13 (3.3)	
Engineer	0		2 (0.9)
Factory supervisor	9 (2.6)		
Company employee	3 (0.9)		
Store clerk	6 (1.7)		
Factory worker	93 (26.6)	3 (0.8)	8 (3.7)
Dock worker	18 (5.1)		
Rickshaw puller	8 (2.3)		
Sanitation	4 (1.1)		
Service	6 (1.7)		
Warehouse worker	31 (8.9)		
Moneylending	20 (5.7)		
Artisan	1 (0.3)		1 (0.4)
Peddler	5 (1.4)		
Unlisted/unclear	123		53
TOTAL	351	398	214

denying the accusations, rallied their compatriots to behave more patriot-ically. The Office of the Association of Sojourners in Shanghai from Huai'an, Yangzhou, and Nantong issued a statement that, while deploring the accusation that Subei people were traitors, admitted that "some of our people have totally lost their hearts and minds and are helping the enemy." It threatened those Subei people found guilty of collaboration with severe punishment.[71] According to one report, a group of Subei intellectuals printed and posted leaflets calling on their fellow *Subei ren* to stop working for the Japanese. "Dear pitiful Jiangbei compatriots," began the leaflet. "We have long been aware of the nature of your daily life, but there is nothing we can do [now].... You must please tolerate it for the time being and we will find a way to help you in the future. You

[71] *Shenbao,* March 19, 1932.

cannot only think of your own narrow interests. Please do not help the Japanese kill people and start fires.... Wake up! Wake up!" The poster was signed by "a tearful *Jiangbei ren*."[72]

These statements may be interpreted as signifying a consciousness among Subei natives that they belonged to a coherent group or at least a recognition and acceptance of the label *Subei ren* imposed on them by the Jiangnan elite. They do not, however, show that all, or even most, Subei natives subscribed to this belief. Instead, the pleas are issued by members of the Subei elite, and as such they express a kind of class anxiety: concern, among the literati, that the activities of their less-wealthy, less-educated compatriots will tarnish their own reputation. How the majority of poorer Subei natives responded to the accusations of collaboration and to the pleas of their compatriots remains unclear.

That "Subei solidarity"—even if only among the elite—emerged in the context of the Japanese attack is not surprising, for as studies of ethnic identity elsewhere have shown, "ethnic unity, ascribed by outsiders, was accepted as part of the defense against prejudice and hostility." Adversity, argues Jonathan Sarna in an essay describing the transition "from immigrants to ethnics," is what caused immigrants to the United States to transcend their village identities and accept a national identity ascribed them by "outsiders."[73] And if there was ever a time when Subei people in Shangahi experienced adversity, the early 1930s was it. As noted above, this may well not have been the first instance of migrants from northern Jiangsu displaying an acceptance of the "Subei identity" formulated by the Jiangnan elite of Shanghai. Yet if such an identity emerged earlier, it was most likely in the context of similarly adverse circumstances. Furthermore, it was most likely a similarly temporary and perhaps class-based sense of identity that may well have dissipated once the intense hostility toward Subei people subsided.

Conclusion

What we have seen is that Subei people represented something akin to an ethnic group in the eyes of Jiangnan natives. They were perceived as coming from a homogeneous region defined largely by its poverty and dialect and, once in Shanghai, as having a shared experience as coolie laborers, shack dwellers, and collaborators. Among people who had actually migrated from districts north of the Yangzi, however, a Subei-wide identity was fleeting, at best, and more often muted or nonexistent.

---

[72] *Shenbao*, March 10, 1932.

[73] Sarna, "From Immigrants to Ethnics," pp. 372–74.

This attitude confirms the findings of anthropological studies of ethnicity, which have frequently observed the difference between the definition of a group imposed by "outsiders" and the "insiders'" definition of themselves. For example, in a classic study of ethnicity in Bornu, anthropologist Ronald Cohen contrasts the Kanuri people's belief that groups of non-Muslim people in the southeast represent a coherent group called Kirdi, whereas the Kirdi see themselves as belonging to a number of distinctive ethnic groups. "The problem becomes more complex," observes Cohen, "when it is realized that in Kanuri-dominated towns such people often accept the dominant group's term and claim they are Kirdi. Only much closer questioning elicits their home-based subjective identifications."[74]

That the persistence of more local identities is commonly found in studies of ethnicity and immigrant cultures, however, does not account for the insistent belief in the category *Subei ren* by the Jiangnan elite and its function in the historical development of Shanghai. The ascription of a Subei identity established, in part, "the other" against which Jiangnan natives could define themselves and claim, eventually, a Shanghai identity. Shanghai dialect derived from the Wu dialect of Jiangnan and differed from (and excluded) the Yangzhou-based dialects of Subei; Shanghai local opera (*huju*) was based on Jiangnan traditions, as opposed to the Yangzhou and Huai operas of the north; Shanghai cuisine, too, derived from Jiangnan tastes. To be a *Shanghai ren* was to be urbane and sophisticated like the Jiangnan elite, in contradistinction to the crude, backward natives of Subei. Subei became the yardstick against which modernity in Shanghai was defined.

The Subei identity, however, was more than a mirror for Jiangnan people's self-definition in Shanghai. It was also a metaphor for class, as the discourse about Subei people was often one about wealth versus poverty. To be poor in Shanghai, to live in the slumlike straw-hut settlements, to perform undesirable jobs such as pulling rickshaws or collecting night soil, was to be a *Subei ren*. Finally, as evidenced in the case of the Japanese attack of 1932, the belief in the social category *Subei ren* provided Shanghainese with a scapegoat, a means of assuaging their own potential guilt: there were no collaborators, only "Subei collaborators."

That Subei natives themselves rarely shed their more local identities to evidence a Subei consciousness was almost irrelevant to the belief in the social category *Subei ren*. In the immigrant city of Shanghai,

---

[74] Ronald Cohen, "Ethnicity: Problems and Focus in Anthropology," *Annual Review of Anthropology* 7 (1978): 382.

Jiangnan natives constituted the elite and as such had the power to establish the terms of discourse, both about social categories constructed according to native-place identities as well as who qualified as a truly native Shanghainese.

CHAPTER EIGHT

"The Pact with the Devil"

The Relationship between the Green Gang and the Shanghai French Concession Authorities, 1925–1935

BRIAN G. MARTIN

This chapter analyzes the relationship that developed in the late 1920s and early 1930s between the Green Gang bosses, in particular Du Yuesheng, and the Shanghai French Concession authorities. In doing so, it seeks to address one of the major questions in the social and political history of Shanghai in the early twentieth century: that is, what was the nature of the relationship between gangster organizations and the foreign administrations, and what did this mean for the character of foreign rule in Shanghai? In a partial answer to this question, the chapter argues that in the French Concession, at least, there did exist a significant community of interests between the French authorities and Du Yuesheng's gangster organization that reflected institutional and administrative imperatives and not merely transient arrangements between corrupt individuals. However, this relationship was not unchanging over time. The balance of forces within it reflected the degree to which the gangsters could translate their "comprador" functions (assisting in the control of the Chinese population and the maintenance of social order) into the exercise of actual power within the Concession and the degree to which the French authorities could resist or control this phenomenon. At the same time, it also reflected the influence on these internal developments of such external factors as changes in the Chinese and French political environments. It was precisely because of its fluid nature that this cooperative relationship played such an important role in the emergence of a system of organized crime in Shanghai.

Gangsterism and Shanghai

By the early twentieth century, Shanghai had become notorious as a center of large-scale criminal activity. Although there are no reliable figures for the total number of gangsters in Shanghai, the most commonly cited estimate for the 1920s and 1930s was about a hundred thousand, which represented just over 3 percent of the city's population at that time.[1] Most of these were members of the Green Gang, which was the predominant secret society–cum-gangster organization in Shanghai. According to a names list of prominent Green Gang members published in the early 1930s, more than 10 percent were resident in Shanghai; this was the greatest concentration of Green Gang leaders in any city in China.[2]

This development reflected the irresistible economic and institutional opportunities afforded the gangsters by the foreign settlements. As the leading commercial and industrial center in China, Shanghai attracted peasants and merchants from all over the country to work in its factories and commercial firms. As a result, the city's population burgeoned dramatically in the first thirty years of the twentieth century. The population for the whole of Shanghai virtually trebled in the brief twenty-year period 1910–1930, increasing from just over one million to just over three million. The population increases in the foreign settlements were even more dramatic. In the International Settlement, the population doubled between 1895 and 1910 and doubled again between 1910 and 1930, while that of the French Concession almost tripled between 1895 and 1915 and more than tripled again between 1915 and 1930.[3] The greater part of this increase was provided by immigrants from other parts of China, principally the Jiangnan and Jiangbei regions. In the International Settlement, for example, immigrants from other regions of China

---

[1] Ma Yinchu, "Guanyu jinyan wenti zhi jige yaodian" [Several important points concerning the question of opium suppression], in Ma Yinchu yanjiang ji [Collection of the lectures of Ma Yinchu] (Shanghai: Commercial Press, 1928), vol. 4, p. 280; Carl Glick and Sheng-Hwa Hong, Swords of Silence: Chinese Secret Societies Past and Present (New York: Whittlesey House, 1947), p. 252; E. O. Hauser, Shanghai: City for Sale (New York: Harcourt, Brace, 1940), p. 252.

[2] Chen Guoping, Qingmen kaoyuan [The origins of the Green Gang] (Shanghai: Lianyi chubanshe, 1946), pp. 281–313.

[3] Luo Zhiru, Tongji biao zhong zhi Shanghai [Shanghai in statistics] (Nanjing: Academia Sinica, 1932), p. 21, table 29. The figures given by Luo are as follows. For the whole of Shanghai: 1910: 1,185,859; 1930: 3,112,250. For the International Settlement: 1895: 245,679; 1910: 501,541; 1930: 1007,868. For the French Concession: 1895: 52,188; 1915: 149,000; 1930: 434,807.

made up more than 89 percent of the total population in 1895, more than 82 percent in 1910, and more than 90 percent in 1930.[4]

Thus, in the early years of the twentieth century, Shanghai was a city of immigrants, and one where the social cohesion of the Chinese population was tenuous at best. In this situation the role of native-place networks gained in significance, and these provided the basis for whatever social organization existed among the Chinese population. This fact was of enormous importance in the development of organized crime in the city. Most of the gangsters were themselves immigrants; many of them were local thugs, landless peasants, disbanded soldiers, salt smugglers, and rural police constables attracted by the enhanced opportunities for criminal activities provided by Shanghai.[5] The native-place system, therefore, became the basic building block of gangster organizations. Many gangster bosses restricted their area of operations to their fellow provincials, as did Gu Zhuxuan (1885–1956) in the International Settlement and Jin Jiulin in the French Concession, both of whose power bases were provided by their fellow immigrants from Subei.[6] The gangsters used native-place networks to organize protection rackets, to interpose themselves as middlemen between their native-place group and other such groups, to mediate relations between their fellow-provincials and petty officialdom in the various municipalities of Shanghai, and to gain control of the labor market and transform it into a lucrative racket.[7]

The large influx of Chinese immigrants into Shanghai in the 1910s and 1920s and the attendant increase in gangster activities posed serious problems of social order and control for the city's police authorities. These authorities, however, were ill equipped to deal with such problems. Shanghai was not one city but three cities—the Chinese city, the International Settlement, and the French Concession—each with its own administrative, legal, and (most important) police systems. There was little or no institutional cooperation among the three separate police authorities, and what cooperation did occur was ad hoc. The lack of

---

[4] Ibid., p. 27, table 43.

[5] According to the names list provided by Chen Guoping, the overwhelming majority (62 percent) of the Green Gang leaders he lists as resident in Shanghai actually came from other parts of China, notably Subei, Shandong, and the Ningbo region. Chen Guoping, *Qingmen kaoyuan,* pp. 281–313.

[6] Wang Yangqing and Xu Yinghu, "Shanghai Qinghongbang gaishu" [A general account of the Green and Red gangs in Shanghai] in *Shehui kexue,* no. 5 (May 1982), p. 64.

[7] Zhu Bangxing et al., *Shanghai chanye yu Shanghai zhigong* [Enterprises and workers in Shanghai] (Shanghai: Shanghai renmin chubanshe, 1984; reprint of 1939 ed.), passim; Shanghai kexueyuan jingji yanjiusuo [Economic Research Institute of the Shanghai Academy of Social Sciences], ed., *Liu Hongsheng qiye shiliao* [Historical materials on the enterprises of Liu Hongsheng], (Shanghai: Shanghai renmin chubanshe, 1981), vol. 1, pp. 314–315.

formal cooperation between the two foreign jurisdictions was all the more remarkable given their shared interests in maintaining their respective colonial authorities. The degree of isolation between the foreign administrations was reflected in the admission by the acting French consul-general, Jacques Meyrier, to the French Municipal Council in the wake of the May Thirtieth Incident in 1925 that no direct telephone link existed between the police authorities of the French Concession and the International Settlement.[8] The problem was exacerbated by the fact that the three municipalities were not merely civic administrations but also separate national jurisdictions, and therefore routine police functions (such as criminal investigations and the maintenance of local order) could and did take on the character of exercises in international relations. The frustrations to which such a situation gave rise were well summed up by the commissioner of the Municipal Police of the International Settlement in the following extracts quoted by Feetham in his report on the question of extraterritoriality to the Municipal Council in 1931:

> While the police forces do cooperate with each other to the best of their ability in the circumstances, full cooperation is impossible because of fundamental differences in ideas of police administration. Prevalence of crime in one area is not likely to give cause for anxiety to the police in another area; in fact, there is no exchange of information between the three authorities in connection with the general state of crime. There is no central police control.

> Further while the principles on which the police administrations of the three independent areas of a large city work, differ as fundamentally as they do in Shanghai, and while political expediency gives rise to continual friction, there can be no real cooperation between the different police authorities in suppressing crime.[9]

Such a situation of divided and conflicting police jurisdiction allowed the gangsters to flourish and to extend their own organizational systems. They could set themselves up in one jurisdiction and conduct armed robberies, kidnapings, and narcotics trafficking in the other two jurisdictions, and they could safeguard their base by bribing the local beat policemen and even relatively senior police officials.[10] During periodic police

Social Sciences] (Shanghai: Shanghai renmin chubanshe, 1981), vol. 1, pp. 314–315.

[8] Conseil d'Administration Municipale de la Concession Française à Changhai, *Compte-Rendu de la Gestion pour l'Exercice 1925, Séance du Conseil du 9 Septembre 1925*, p. 140.

[9] *Report of the Hon. Richard Feetham, C.M.G., to the Shanghai Municipal Council* (Shanghai: North China Daily News and Herald, 1931), vol. 2, pp. 159 and 83, respectively.

[10] In 1922, for example, the French consul-general, Auguste Wilden, dismissed the entire personnel of one police post (composed of a sergeant and four constables) for taking bribes from local gangsters. M.A. Wilden, Consul-General de France à Changhai, à Son

crackdowns they could avoid any substantial loss to their position by moving between jurisdictions. It was for eventualities such as these that the various gangster groups entered into agreements and formed loose alliances among themselves. Indeed, it can be argued that the Shanghai gangsters successfully transferred to this Sino-foreign urban environment the rural bandits' classic strategy of establishing their "lairs" in the no-man's-land between two or more county or prefectural administrations: by 1920 Shanghai had become a veritable urban Liangshanpo. To enhance their security even further, the gangsters frequently bribed the consuls of countries enjoying extraterritoriality in order to gain such extraterritorial privileges for themselves and so escape criminal prosecution in the International Settlement and French Concession Mixed Courts. In the early 1920s the Portuguese, Spanish, and Chilean consuls-general enjoyed a lucrative business selling the rights of citizenship of their respective countries to a large number of local Shanghai gangsters. Included in this number were Du Yuesheng, who enjoyed Portuguese citizenship, and the Guangdong narcotics "king," Ye Qinghe, who claimed to be a Chilean protégé.[11]

The situation was further complicated by the fact that gangsters also formed the basis of the Chinese detective squads in both the International Settlement and the French Concession. The Chief of the Chinese Detective Squad of the Shanghai Municipal Police (SMP) in the 1910s and 1920s was one Shen Xingshan. Shen was also the principal leader of the gangster organization known as the Big Eight Mob, which controlled the narcotics traffic in the International Settlement in the late 1910s and early 1920s, and many of his lieutenants were also members of the Municipal Police's Chinese detective squad.[12] Indeed, the Big Eight

Excellence Monsieur Poincaré, President du Conseil, Ministre des Affaires Étrangères à Paris, Consulat-General de France à Changhai, Shanghai, le 18 Février 1924, Direction des Affaires Politiques et Commerciales, *Asie: Océanie* (hereafter, Direction), no. 34, E515.4.

[11] *North-China Herald,* August 25, 1923; August 30, 1924; October 25, 1924; February 7, 1925; March 7, 1925; May 2, 1925. The League of Nations, Advisory Committee on Traffic in Opium and Other Dangerous Drugs, Minutes of the Seventh Session, Geneva, August 24–31, 1925, C.602.M.192/1925, p. 109; J.T. Pratt, "Memorandum Respecting the Opium Problem in the Far East," Foreign Office, August 10, 1929, FO 4749/4749/87.

[12] Although the Big Eight Mob's operations were taken over by the French Concession Green Gang in the mid-1920s and its organization was absorbed into the latter's, nevertheless its influence persisted among the Chinese detectives of the Shanghai Municipal Police. The chief of these detectives in the 1930s, one Lu Liankui, was not only a Green Gang member but also a follower of Ji Yunqing, one of the eight leaders of the Big Eight Mob. Zhang Jungu, *Du Yuesheng zhuan* [Biography of Du Yuesheng] (Taibei: Zhuanji wenxue congkan, 1980), vol. 1, pp. 124, 136; Jiang Hao, "Qingbang de yuanliu ji qi yanbian" [The origins and evolution of the Green Gang], in *Jiu Shanghai de banghui* [The gangs of old Shanghai], ed. Zhengzhi xieshang huiyi Shanghai shi weiyuanhui wenshi ziliao gongzuo weiyuan-

Mob had such a grip on the SMP Chinese detective squad that one former China coast journalist observed rather sardonically that "almost every Chinese detective on the [SMP] force had a criminal record."[13] Shen's opposite number in the French Concession was Huang Jinrong. That this situation continued throughout the lives of the foreign settlements would seem to indicate deliberate policy rather than mere chance occurrence. The probable rationale for this policy was that the co-optation of selected gangster groups was the most cost-effective way of maintaining order among and control over the settlements' Chinese populations. The police forces of both settlements were, after all, essentially colonial forces whose main task was to ensure the security of the colonial administrations and the lives and property of the imperial powers' citizens, not the enforcement of *law* among the subject (Chinese) population. Given that the gangster/detectives' function was to mediate the coercive power exercised by the colonial authority over the indigenous Chinese population, their role was in effect that of "compradors of violence." This general rationale was doubtless reinforced in the Shanghai situation by the enormous problems of social control posed by the continuous large increases in the Chinese population throughout this period and by the specific problems for police control posed by the separate national jurisdictions. Whatever the reasons for this policy, its effect was to strengthen and, to a degree, institutionalize gangster organizations in the foreign settlements. The access to foreign authority that the gangster/detectives gained by virtue of their role in the system of control strengthened their power and enhanced their status among other gangster groups. Indeed, their role gave them a certain legitimacy within the settlements' colonial power structure, and some of them, such as Huang Jinrong, were even decorated by the colonial authorities for services rendered.[14]

hui [Work Committee of Historical and Literary Materials of the Shanghai Municipal Committee of the Chinese People's Political Consultative Conference] (Shanghai: Shanghai renmin chubanshe, 1986), pp. 61, 66. For further information on the Big Eight Mob, see Brian G. Martin, "Warlords and Gangsters: The Opium Traffic in Shanghai and the Creation of the Three Prosperities Company to 1926," in John Fitzgerald, ed., *The Nationalists and Chinese Society, 1923–1937: A Symposium* (Melbourne: University of Melbourne, History Department, 1989), pp. 44–71.

[13] John Pal, *Shanghai Saga* (London: Jarrolds, 1963), p. 19.

[14] Shi Jun, "Shanghai sandaheng de goujie he douzheng" [Cooperation and conflict among Shanghai's three big bosses], in *Jiu Shanghai de banghui,* p. 32.

The Balance of Forces in the French Concession

The strategic nature of the relationship between certain gangster groups and the foreign authorities in Shanghai was most clearly demonstrated in the French Concession in the 1920s and early 1930s. Unlike the International Settlement, where executive authority was exercised by a Municipal Council overseen by the Consular Body, executive power in the French Concession was concentrated in the hands of the French consul-general, who exercised it through the issuance of consular ordinances, with the Municipal Council serving in a purely advisory capacity. One of the key powers enjoyed by the consul-general was his control over the Concession's police force (La Garde Municipale), which, in the words of one consul-general, was answerable "directly and solely to the Consul-General."[15] The personnel of this force (both French and Vietnamese) was almost exclusively former soldiers, and its chief throughout the period 1919 to 1932, E. Fiori, was an artillery captain in the Army Reserve who had seen extensive service with the French army in Morocco.[16] The paramilitary nature of the Concession police was also reflected in its responsibilities, which, in addition to the regular policing of the Concession, included providing for the external security of the Concession. As Consul-General Wilden noted in early 1924, the police provided, "in case of troubles, the principal element of the body responsible for the defence of the Concession."[17] Thus, both in its composition and in its diverse responsibilities, the French Concession police constituted a typical example of a colonial police force.

Despite the large powers enjoyed by the consul-general, successive consuls-general were preoccupied by the relative weakness of the Concession's system of security compared with that enjoyed by the International Settlement. Although this concern became critical only during the events of late 1926 and early 1927, it had been a factor in the calculations of the French Concession authorities since World War I. Indeed, Fiori had been appointed in 1919 with the specific brief to transform the police into an effective instrument for the defense of the Concession and so lessen its dependence in security matters on the International Settlement.[18] This sense of vulnerability reflected the fact that throughout the early 1920s budgetary constraints made it difficult to maintain the strength of the police force at levels adequate even for regular policing functions, a problem that was compounded by the huge increases in the

---

[15] Wilden à Poincaré, February 18, 1924.

[16] Ibid.; *North-China Herald,* February 18, 1928.

[17] Wilden à Poincaré, February 18, 1924.

[18] Ibid.

Concession's Chinese population during this same period. Another factor that contributed to this concern with security matters was the doubtful legal standing of the 1868 Règlements, which provided the constitutional basis of the Concession. It was argued that, since these had been supported by force majeure, they could be invalidated by force. As one contemporary authority noted: "The Règlements have their origin in the same vague treaty provisions as the [International Settlement] Land Regulations. The Règlements have been supported by force and could be invalidated in the same manner by a strong Chinese government."[19]

The recognition of the Concession's vulnerability on security matters was aggravated by the metropolitan French government's belief that the Concession represented the most important center of French influence in the Far East. Such an attitude led the local French administration to emphasize French authority at every opportunity and to meet all challenges, real or imagined, to that authority no matter from what quarter they might emanate. In this context local French officials came to believe that the International Settlement itself, by the very fact of its proximity to the Concession, constituted a challenge to continuing French authority within the Concession.[20] This anxiety was clearly expressed in the minute the Ministry of Foreign Affairs submitted to the Council of Ministers at the height of the Shanghai crisis in January 1927. It said in part:

> The French Concession in Shanghai is, by far, the most important centre of French influence in the Chinese seas. [It has] contributed in the greatest measure to the maintenance of our prestige in China. A failure on our part would have disastrous consequences for all our economic and moral interests in the Far East.[21]

This preoccupation with security concerns predisposed French officials to seek allies where they could to support the efforts to maintain French authority and prestige within the Concession. One such ally was Huang Jinrong (1868–1953), a member of the Chinese detective squad and a gang boss. Although Huang had joined the French Concession police in 1892, it was not until World War I that he emerged as the leading Chinese figure in the police force and the predominant gangster boss in the Concession. Because of the large number of French police

---

[19] William Crane Johnstone, *The Shanghai Problem* (Stanford, Calif.: Stanford University Press, 1937), p. 103.

[20] This was a major reason in the desire by both Meyrier and Naggiar to reform the French Municipal Council in 1925–1926. See the following section.

[21] Ministère des Affaires Étrangères, "Note en vue du Conseil des Ministres: Défense de la Concession Française de Shanghai," le 10 Janvier 1927, Direction, E515.4.

officers who returned to France for war service at this time, the French consul-general carried out a reorganization of the police force that devolved greater responsibilities on the Chinese members of the force. As a result, Huang was promoted to chief superintendent, and many of his close associates, such as Cheng Ziqing and Jin Jiulin, were also appointed to senior positions.[22] Huang's usefulness to the French authorities derived from the close relations he had developed with local gangster groups associated with the Green and Red Gang systems, such as the Big Eight Mob and the Thirty-Six Mob, although Huang himself did not finally become a formal member of the Green Gang until 1923. He was also active in a group called the One Hundred and Eight Warriors, which brought together the leading Chinese detectives working for the foreign authorities and therefore provided him with a regular channel to his colleagues in the International Settlement.[23] Through these connections, Huang was able to assist the chief of the Sûreté (the detective squad) to effect such periodic police "clean-ups" as that in 1922 when thirteen separate gangster mobs (with a total of 124 members) were arrested in the course of the year.[24] In much the same way, Huang was able to mobilize the necessary muscle to help the French authorities break the Chinese shopkeepers' strike in the wake of the May Fourth Incident of 1919.[25] It was for such services that Huang earned the popular nickname "the Great Wall of peace and order in the French Concession."[26]

At the same time, Huang used his position as the Sûreté's leading Chinese detective to further his own economic interests and increase his influence with the leading gangster organizations in Shanghai. From his headquarters in the Ju Bao Teahouse, Huang regulated the activities of armed robbers, kidnappers, and narcotics smugglers and managed his many diverse economic interests. He owned a string of theaters and bathhouses, and he either protected or controlled all of the opium *hongs,* gambling joints, and brothels in the French Concession.[27] As part of

---

[22] Shi Jun, "Shanghai sandaheng."

[23] Xiang Bo, "Huang Jinrong shilüe" [A biographical sketch of Huang Jinrong], in *Jiu Shanghai de banghui,* pp. 131–132. Cheng Xiwen, "Wo dang Huang Jinrong guangjia de jianwen" [What I saw and heard as Huang Jinrong's butler], in ibid., pp. 148–149.

[24] Wilden to Poincaré, July 9, 1923, Direction, no. 16, E515.4.

[25] *Shenbao,* June 8, 1919, cited in Shanghai shehui kexueyuan lishi yanjiusuo, ed., *Wusi yundong zai Shanghai shiliao xuanji* [Selected historical materials on the May Fourth Movement in Shanghai], 2d ed. (Shanghai, 1980), p. 768.

[26] Xiang Bo, "Huang Jinrong shilüe," p. 132; Shanghai shehui kexueyuan zhengshi falu yanjiusuo shehui wenti zu [Social issues section of the Political and Legal Institute of the Shanghai Academy of Social Sciences], ed., *Da liumang Du Yuesheng* [Big gangster Du Yuesheng], (Beijing: Qunzhong chubanshe, 1965), p. 6.

[27] Xiang Bo, "Huang Jinrong shilüe," p. 132; *Da liumang Du Yuesheng,* p. 6; Xu Chucheng, *Du Yuesheng zheng zhuan* [A true biography of Du Yuesheng] (Hangzhou:

these operations, he regularly paid out bribes to his French colleagues
and superiors in the police force. It might be remarked in this context
that two successive heads of the Sûreté, Messrs. Traissac and Sidaine,
Huang's nominal superiors, lost their positions in 1924 and 1925,
respectively, for turning a blind eye to the involvement of Chinese detectives in the gambling and narcotics operations in the Concession.[28]
Despite Huang's corruption of superiors, his position, nevertheless,
derived from his influence with French officialdom. It was his position
within the Concession police force, particularly in the 1910s and early
1920s, that gave him standing with other gangster groups in Shanghai
and enabled him to build up his own gangster following. This standing
allowed him to develop a close working relationship with those gang
bosses who belonged to the Green Gang system without his formally
being a member of that system until very much later in his career. Thus
it was that Huang Jinrong's position as a gang boss was defined and con-
strained by his membership of the police force.

By the mid 1920s Huang's most senior lieutenant was Du Yuesheng
(1888–1951), whose career formed the basis of the most famous of
Shanghai's "rags to riches" stories of the 1930s. Born into obscure
poverty in Gaoqiao village, Pudong, Du began his career as an assistant to
a fruit vendor in Nandao, and, in his early twenties, went on to become a
petty gangster and gambler who frequented the brothels, gambling joints,
and opium dives clustered around the Chinese dock area of Shiliupu.
During this period in the early 1910s he joined the Green Gang and
became a follower of Chen Shichang, a small-time gangster boss active in
the opium traffic in Shiliupu. After working for a time as an opium
trafficker and informer for the Chinese detective squad of the French
Concession police, Du was introduced to Huang Jinrong and proceeded
to make himself indispensable to the Huang household. Over a period of
years Huang progressively devolved responsibility for the management of
the various rackets in which he had an interest on Du Yuesheng, and
consequently by the the mid 1920s Du controlled all Huang's opium
interests.

Huang Jinrong and his associates, however, were not the only group
that the French officials used to mediate their relations with the Chinese
population of the Concession. Another powerful group closely associated

Zhejiang renmin chubanshe, 1982), pp. 14–15.
  [28] M.A. Wilden, Consul-Général de France à Shanghai, à Son Excellence Monsieur le
President du Conseil, Ministre des Affaires Étrangères à Paris, Consulat-Général de France à
Changhai, Shanghai, le 21 Juillet 1924, Direction, no. 34, E515.4; Meyrier à Son Excellence Monsieur le Ministre des Affaires Étrangères, Telegramme no. 2, Shanghai, le 11 Janvier 1926.

with the Concession authorities was the so-called gentry-councillor clique, which was composed of influential Chinese businessmen who were also Roman Catholics and/or returned students from France.[29] The two leading members of this group in the 1920s and 1930s were Zhu Zhiyao (1863–1955) and Lu Baihong (1873–1937). Both Zhu and Lu belonged to leading Chinese Roman Catholic families from Jiangnan who could trace their Catholicism back to the seventeenth century and were active in Catholic evangelical and philanthropic work in Shanghai. Both, for example, were involved with the creation of the Shanghai branch of the Union for Chinese Catholic Action (Unio Actionis Catholicae Sinarum) shortly after that organization was established in 1912, while Lu also ran the Hospice de St. Joseph in Nandao. In 1926 Lu went to Rome and had an audience with Pope Pius XI, who conferred on him papal decorations in recognition of his work with Catholic Action. Zhu and Lu were also leading merchants with strong links with the Zhejiang financial clique (notably with Zhu Baosan and Yu Xiaqing) and extensive interests in shipping, public utilities, and real estate in the Shanghai area.[30]

Other members of this clique included Wu Zonglian (a former Chinese Minister to Italy), Lu Songhou (former Chairman of the Nandao municipality), Zhu Yan (co-director of the Institut Technique Franco-Chinois), and Wei Tingrong (a director of the Credit Franco-Chinois and the Da Da Bank and the son-in-law of Zhu Baosan).[31] That members of this group had forged close links with the French Catholic establishment and the Vatican commended them to the local French authorities, particularly as France still maintained at that time an interest in the promotion of Catholicism as part of the cultural aspect of its China policy. Moreover, a number of them, such as Wei Tingrong and Zhu Yan, were involved in promoting French financial and educational interests in Shanghai and therefore contributed indirectly to the strengthening of French authority within the Concession. In fact, when the French, as

---

[29] Yang Shi, "Shanghai tan liumang daheng yishi san ce" [Three anecdotes about the Shanghai gangster bosses], *Dang'an yu lishi*, no. 2 (1986), pp. 88–89.

[30] Zhu Wenwei, "Zhu Zhiyao," in *Minguo renwu zhuan* [Biographies of leading figures of the Republic] (Beijing, 1984), vol. 4, pp. 236–242; Howard L. Boorman, ed., *Biographical Dictionary of Republican China* (New York: Columbia University Press, 1968), vol. 2, pp. 4–451; *China Weekly Review*, September 13, 1930; John Fitzsimmons and Paul Maguire, eds., *Restoring All Things: A Guide to Catholic Action* (London: Sheed and Ward, 1939), pp. 78–80; Kenneth Scott Latourette, *A History of Christian Missions in China* (New York: Macmillan, 1929), p. 741.

[31] *China Weekly Review*, January 3, 1931; *Gendai Chūka minkoku Manshukoku jimmeikan* [Biographical dictionary of contemporary China and Manzhouguo] (Tokyo: Gaimusho Johobu, 1932), pp. 75, 113, 147.

part of the Sino-French Agreement of 1914, agreed to appoint two non-participating Chinese councillors to the Municipal Council to advise the consul-general on matters relating to the Chinese population, they appointed them from the ranks of these Catholic gentry.[32]

There is no doubt that a relationship of some kind existed between this "gentry-councillor clique" and prominent Shanghai gangsters. Both Zhu and Lu dealt with at least one leading member of the Big Eight Mob in the course of their business activities in the early 1920s, and there were suggestions that some sort of recognition concerning spheres of interest in the French Concession existed between them and Huang Jinrong's group.[33] However, as the gangsters sought to enlarge the areas of their interests and the degree of their influence with the French administration, this tacit compact broke down, and both groups engaged in both covert and overt conflict for power and influence in the late 1920s.

The Changing Balance: The Competition for Influence, 1925–1927

In the mid-1920s (specifically in the period 1923–1925), major changes in the power relations between the various gangster groups in Shanghai resulted in the emergence of Huang Jinrong's gangster organization to a position of predominance among them. These developments were related to changes in the organization of the narcotics trafficking in Shanghai. In this period Huang's group took over the Big Eight Mob's opium trafficking operations in the International Settlement and absorbed that gangster group into its own organization. At the same time, Huang's group successfully capitalized on the confused military and political situation in the Jiangnan area following the local Anfu militarists' defeat in the Zhejiang-Jiangsu War of September–October 1924—and the consequent breakdown of the Anfu militarists' control over the opium traffic in Shanghai—to consolidate their own control over that traffic. This was achieved with the creation of the Three Prosperities Company in early 1925.[34]

---

[32] Dong Shu, "Shanghai fazujie de duoshi shiqi" [An eventful period in the Shanghai French Concession], in *Shanghai shi tongzhiguan qikan* 1:4 (1934):1022; Zhu Menghua, "Shanghai fazujie de gongdongju ji Xunbufang" [The Municipal Council and police headquarters of the French Concession], in *Shanghai difang shi ziliao* [Materials on Shanghai local history], vol. 2 (1983), p. 81.

[33] Huang Yongyan, "Du Yuesheng dajin dada lunchuan gongsi jingguo" [The takeover of the Dada Steamship Company by Du Yuesheng], in *Jiu Shanghai de banghui*, p. 289; Yang Shi, "Shanghai tan liumang."

[34] For further details of these developments, see Martin, "Warlords and Gangsters."

These external changes involving the extension of the power and organization of the group as a whole were accompanied by changes within the group that saw the emergence of a new leadership combination. Huang's position as the all-powerful gang boss had been seriously weakened by the humiliation of his arrest by He Fenglin over the Lu Lanchun affair in 1923. Huang's arrest had been ordered by Lu Xiaojia, the son of Lu Yongxiang (the Anfu warlord who controlled Shanghai and Zhejiang), after Huang had assaulted him for creating a disturbance during a performance by the local Chinese opera star, and Huang's current paramour, Lu Lanchun. The affair created serious tensions between the gangster bosses and the local Anfu militarists, and Huang was released from prison only by the intercession of his two subordinates Zhang Xiaolin (1877–1940) and Du Yuesheng. Zhang, based on his close personal relations with the leading Zhejiang militarists, acted as the gangster bosses' liaison with the local Anfu warlords; and it was he who was largely responsible for negotiating Huang's release. Du, however, was the main architect of the group's strategy for gaining control of the Shanghai opium traffic, and he used his control over this revenue-generating racket to further his own leadership ambitions. By 1925, therefore, Huang's dominant leadership role had been replaced by a joint leadership of Huang, Du, and Zhang, in which real power was exercised by the latter two, particularly Du Yuesheng.[35]

As part of the process of consolidating their control over the Shanghai opium traffic, these Green Gang bosses sought to secure their base of operations within the French Concession. There are indications that the gangsters first approached influential French members of the Municipal Council, in particular the leading French lawyer and legal counsel for the Concession, Du Pac de Marsoulies, in order to reach some kind of tacit understanding with the French.[36] The Concession authorities were

---

[35] Ibid. On the Lu Lanchun affair see Huang Guodong, "Du men huajin" [Reminiscences about Du's household], in *Jiu Shanghai de banghui*, pp. 255–256; Jiang Shaozhen, "Du Yuesheng," *Minguo renwu zhuan* 1 (1978): 314.

[36] The acting consul-general, Meyrier, in his report to the French minister noted the allegations that one reason why Du Pac stood in the Municipal Council elections of January 1925 was his desire to set up an opium trafficking organization. Du Pac was associated with the Shanghai opium traffickers. He was the defense lawyer in the Ezra opium case that involved the leading Guangdong opium merchant, Ye Qinghe, and withdrew from the case in rather intriguing circumstances. See the reports in the *North-China Herald,* January–June 1925. See also M. J. Meyrier, Consul, gérant le Consulat-Général de France à Shanghai, à Son Excellence Monsieur de Martel, Ministre Plenipotentiaire de la République Française à Pékin, Annex in M. D. de Martel, Ministre Plenipotentiaire de la République Française en Chine, à Son Excellence Monsieur Edouard Herriot, Président du Conseil, Ministre des Affaires Étrangères à Paris, Légation de la République Française en Chine, Pékin, le 10 Février 1925, Direction, no. 41, E515.4.

interested. Throughout the early 1920s they had argued that the policy
of opium prohibition was a failure, and the chief of police, Fiori, openly
urged the legalization of the trade in 1924 and 1925. In this he was not
alone; many other foreign officials held similar views, including Sir
Francis Aglen, the inspector-general of customs.[37] A principal reason for
these calls for legalization, apart from the impossibility of adequately
policing the policy of prohibition, was that a legalized trade could be
licensed and thus generate revenue for both the Chinese government and
the Shanghai foreign settlements. Opium farms at that time were a standard means of raising official revenues in European colonies in the Far
East, and the French officials in Shanghai had the example of the lucrative farm in (French) Indo-China that raised 15 million piastres in revenue in 1923 alone, or 21 percent of the French administration's budget
for that year.[38] Moreover, the security problems that confronted the Concession authorities in late 1924 and early 1925 in the wake of the
Zhejiang-Jiangsu War graphically illustrated the need for an expanded
police force. Revenue was, therefore, the major consideration in the
French authorities' response to the gangsters' overtures in early 1925,
and subsequent events confirmed the importance of revenue as a motiva-
tion.

The main obstacle to a policy of open licensing of the opium trade
was international and Chinese public opinion mobilized by the powerful
(and basically Protestant) missionary lobby in organizations such as the
International Anti-Opium Association and the Chinese National Anti-
Opium Association. The effective work performed by these bodies
prevented either the Chinese government or the Shanghai consular body
from requesting the foreign powers to reappraise the 1912 Hague Convention and allow the public licensing of the opium trade. The local
French administration, however, decided to defy this pressure and
entered into secret negotiations with the Three Prosperities Company, in
the person of Du Yuesheng.[39] These negotiations, held over the three-

---

[37] Wilden à Poincaré, July 9, 1923; Wilden à Poincaré, February 18, 1924; Conseil
d'Administration Municipale, *Compte-Rendu de la Gestion pour l'Exercice 1924, Rapports pour
l'Année 1924: Rapport de la Garde Municipale,* p. 296; idem., 1925, p. 258.

[38] *North-China Herald,* December 6, 1924.

[39] The following is based on the minutes of meetings and the text of the contract
between Du Yuesheng, acting on behalf of the Three Prosperities Company, and certain
French officials and businessmen provided in Douglas Jenkins, Consul-General, to the
Secretary of State, Washington, American Consulate General, Shanghai, China, March 16,
1931, State Department Decimal File, 893.114 Narcotics/208. Other sources used for this
section are *Da liumang Du Yuesheng,* pp. 14–15; Xue Gengshen, "Jindai Shanghai de
liumang" [The gangsters of modern Shanghai], *Wenshi ziliao xuanji,* no. 3 (1980), p. 163;
Ferdinand Mayer, United States Minister, to the Honorable, the Secretary of State, Washington, Peking, April 23, 1925, State Department Decimal File 893.114/528; *Minguo ribao*

month period April–June 1925, involved senior members of the municipal administration and leading French businessmen, including the chief of police, Captain Fiori; the chief administrative officer of the Concession, M. Verdier; M. Speelman (a local banker); M. Blum (the managing director of Ullmann et Cie); M. Galvin (a local pharmacist); and Doctor Hibert (a medical practitioner). The sources suggest that the acting consul-general at the time, Jacques Meyrier, was represented in the negotiations by Galvin and Blum and that he used the services of Li Yingsheng, the manager of a jewelry store on the rue du Consulat owned by Du Yuesheng, as an intermediary between himself and the Three Prosperities Company. On June 1, 1925, an agreement was finally reached; it established an officially protected opium distribution and retail network in the Concession in return for large regular payments to the French police and a body described in the contract as "the European committee." The arrangements were tightly controlled by the French police. According to the terms of the contract, all arrangements were to be made with Captain Fiori, with whom the Three Prosperities Company was to maintain a close and regular liaison, and its personnel were to be registered with the French police. As some informed observers later remarked, an opium tax farm had been established in effect, if not in name, in the French Concession.[40] These semiofficial arrangements were of quite a different order from the corruption of individual police and municipal officials that had obtained in an earlier period. They put the relationship between the gangsters and the French authorities on a new, more regular and systematic basis, and in so doing created new opportunities for the gangsters.

These new opportunities, however, were not immediately realized, mainly because of the emphasis the French administration continued to place on its relations with the gentry-councillor clique. In late 1924 the consul-general, Auguste Wilden, turned to this group for assistance in dealing with the security crisis facing the Concession as a result of the

[Republican daily news], July 25, 1925.

[40] The contract stipulated that the French police would arrest and prosecute only those opium dealers who were not members of the Three Prosperities Company and whose opium consignments did not bear the combine's chop. Jenkins to Secretary of State, March 16, 1931. In a dispatch of mid-1930, the British consul-general in Shanghai referred to the Green Gang bosses as "the 'opium farmers' of the French Concession." Consul-General Brenan to Sir M. Lampson, Shanghai, May 29, 1930, FO 3570/184/87. Other sources that imply a semiofficial arrangement regarding opium between the gangsters and the French authorities are Shanghai Municipal Police, Special Branch Section 2, investigation file D9319, "Memorandum on Mr Tu Yueh-Sheng alias Tu Yuin, July 8, 1939"; China Weekly Review, February 7, 1931, and January 23, 1932.

confused military and political situation in Shanghai in the wake of the Zhejiang-Jiangsu War. That the French chose not to seek help from the gangsters possibly reflected not only the limited role the French still assigned Huang Jinrong's gangster organization but also that the French Concession gangsters themselves were deeply implicated in the military conspiracies of the defeated Anfu forces. All three Green Gang bosses were involved in the abortive scheme of Xu Shuzheng ("Little Xu") in mid-October 1924 to reorganize the defeated Zhejiang forces and continue the struggle along the borders of the foreign settlements, with the option of rushing the settlements in the event of their defeat.[41] The gentry-councillor clique responded to Wilden's request by organizing a militia corps between November 1924 and April 1925 that was officially known as the French Concession Chinese Volunteers (Compagnie des Volontaires Chinois de la Concession Française).[42] This corps consisted of between 150 and 200 men and was controlled by Zhu Zhiyao and Lu Baihong, who were its president and vice-president. Its commander was Wei Tingrong. Although the gentry-councillor clique met most of the company's costs out of a special fund, the French authorities supplied most of its armaments (200 rifles) and contributed $5,000 for outfitting the volunteers. The volunteer corps also boasted six machine guns and an armored car. This corps was similar to the merchant militias organized in Chinese Shanghai, and it greatly enhanced the power and influence of the gentry-councillor clique in the Concession. The French were well pleased with the performance of the volunteers and considered them a major support to the police in the maintenance of public order, especially during the first anniversary of the May Thirtieth Incident on May 30, 1926. As a result, Wei Tingrong was awarded the Concession's highest decoration, the Gold Medal of the French Municipality (Medaille d'Or de la Municipalité Française) in recognition of the services he performed for the French Concession as commander of the Chinese Volunteers.[43]

The position of the gentry-councillor clique was further enhanced by the role that French officials allotted it in their reform of the

---

[41] *North-China Herald,* October 18, 1924, and October 25, 1925; Zhang Jungu, *Du Yuesheng zhuan,* vol. 1, p. 212.

[42] *North-China Herald,* November 22, 1924; *Shanghai Municipal Council Police Daily Report,* July 21, 1925; Fan Shaozeng, "Guanyu Du Yuesheng" [Concerning Du Yuesheng], in *Jiu Shanghai de banghui,* p. 208; M. E. Naggiar, Consul-Général de France à Changhai, à Son Excellence Monsieur le Ministre des Affaires Étrangères a Paris, Consulat-General de France à Changhai, Shanghai, le 10 Septembre 1927, Direction, no. 204, E515.4.

[43] Conseil d'Administration Municipale, *Compte-Rendu de la Gestion pour l'Exercice 1926, Séance du Conseil du 5 Juillet 1926,* p. 142.

Concession's administration. Both Meyrier and his successor as consul-general, P. E. Naggiar, were concerned at the growing influence of non-French foreigners on the Municipal Council, believing that such influence posed a threat to French authority in the Concession. The problem was demographic: by the mid-1920s the French had become a minority in their own Concession. In 1926, according to figures cited by Naggiar, out of a total population in the Concession of 308,000, some 300,000 were Chinese; 7,000 were non-French foreigners, and only 1,000 were French.[44] As part of their strategy for dealing with this problem the French authorities decided to appoint Chinese representatives to the Municipal Council with, for the first time, full rights of participation in the Council's affairs. Such appointments had a double advantage from the administration's standpoint: they met to some degree Chinese nationalist demands for greater representation in the Council and at the same time shored up the French position within the Council. As a result, one of Naggiar's first acts on taking up the position of French consul-general in April 1926 was to appoint two leading members of the gentry-councillor clique, Lu Baihong and Lu Songhou, as full members of the French Municipal Council.[45] In a speech at a reception for Sun Chuanfang in early May, Lu Baihong expressed his satisfaction with Naggiar's actions, which not only provided the Chinese bourgeoisie with full representation in the Municipal Council for the first time, but also served to further strengthen his clique's position within the Concession. In his speech Lu revealed a shrewd understanding of the concerns motivating Naggiar's actions:

> Despite some general difficulties, there is nothing of a vexatious manner to be found in the French Concession.... Thanks to [Naggiar] we [the Chinese councillors] can now take part in the deliberations of the Council and in its decisions. This benevolent attitude will certainly ensure a greater prosperity for the French Concession, and will consolidate the excellent understanding between the Chinese and French residents.[46]

---

[44] M. E. Naggiar, Consul-Général de France à Changhai, à Son Excellence Monsieur de Martel, Ministre Plenipotentiaire de la République Française en Chine à Pékin, Changhai, le 15 Août 1926, Direction, no. 157, E515.4; M. J. Meyrier, Consul, gérant le Consulat-Général de France à Changhai, Changhai, le 21 Septembre 1925, Direction, no. 32, E515.4.

[45] Dong Shu, "Fazujie shizheng yange" [Evolution of the municipal administration in the French Concession], Shanghai shi tongzhiguan qikan 2:3 (December 1934): 759; Naggiar to Martel, August 15, 1926.

[46] M. E. Naggiar, Consul-General de France à Changhai, à Son Excellence Monsieur le Ministre des Affaires Étrangères à Paris, Consulat-Général de Changhai, Shanghai, le 17 Mai 1926, Direction, no. 33, E515.4.

Although Meyrier and Naggiar had earlier considered matching the elected members of the Council with others appointed by the consul-general to ensure (with the casting vote of the French president) a built-in majority, by the end of 1926 Naggiar had decided to completely abolish the elected Municipal Council. On January 14, 1927, it was replaced with an appointed Provisional Commission (Commission Provisoire d'Administration Municipale) on the basis of Article 8 of the 1868 Règlements. Technically, the elected Municipal Council was only suspended temporarily because of "events affecting the order and security of the Concession"; in fact, it was never restored. Of the seventeen members appointed to the Provisional Commission by the consul-general, five were Chinese, and all of them were leading members of the gentry-councillor clique. In a very real sense, the major beneficiaries of Naggiar's administrative coup (apart from the French administration itself) was the clique of Chinese Roman Catholic gentry associated with Zhu Zhiyao and Lu Baihong.[47]

The complex of financial, security, and constitutional problems the French administration faced in the years 1925 and 1926 had enabled both the gangster triumvirate and the gentry-councillor clique to enhance their respective positions within the Concession. The Green Gang bosses not only widened their range of contacts with French officials but also succeeded, to a degree, in formalizing those contacts as a result of the agreement both parties had signed on the opium traffic. They were now better placed than before to develop their political influence in the Concession over the longer term. That this did not happen immediately reflected both that the new leadership needed time to digest the changes in its organization and range of activities and that the gentry-councillor clique dominated the political relationship between the Chinese residents and the French Concession authorities in these years. This clique successfully parleyed its preparedness to accommodate French concerns on security and political matters into substantial influence with successive consuls-general, in particular Naggiar. As a result there appears to have been a degree of covert conflict between the two groups throughout this period, with the Catholic gentry clique attempting to contain the

---

[47] The five Chinese members were Lu Baihong, Lu Songhou, Zhu Yan, Wu Zonglian, and Wei Tingrong. *North-China Herald,* January 15, 1927; Dong Shu, "Shanghai fazujie de duoshi shiqi," pp. 1000–1001; *The China Year Book 1928,* p. 928; M. E. Naggiar, Consul-Général à Changhai, à Son Excellence Monsieur le Ministre des Affaires Étrangères à Paris, Consulat-Général de France à Changhai, Shanghai, le 17 Janvier 1927, Direction, no. 11, E515.4; Conseil d'Administration Municipale, *Compte-Rendu de la Gestion pour l'Exercice 1927, Séance de la Commission Provisoire d'Administration Municipale du 24 Janvier 1927,* p. 8.

increasing ambitions of the gangster bosses. It is possible that Zhu and Lu's group was behind the attempt in early May 1925 to disrupt negotiations on the prospective opium farm. This took the form of an open letter to the acting consul-general calling on him to suppress the opium retail shops scheduled to open "in a day or two" so as to ensure that "the reputation and integrity of the French in Shanghai should be upheld."[48] The sources also suggest that the Catholic gentry, and in particular Wei Tingrong, engineered the resignation of Huang Jinrong from the detective squad in 1925 and that this was one reason for the enmity that came to characterize the relationship between Wei and Du Yuesheng in the late 1920s.[49] Du and Wei were, in a sense, mirror images of one another. Both represented the new leadership in their respective organizations; both were young and extremely ambitious; and both sought to enhance at every turn the power and influence of their group.

The Creation of a New Balance: The Consolidation of Green Gang Influence in the French Concession, 1927–1930

Within weeks of the consolidation of its leading position within the Concession, the position of the gentry-councillor clique was undermined by the grave security crisis that confronted the French authorities in early 1927. This crisis was triggered by the entry of the Guomindang's National Revolutionary Army (NRA) into the Jiangnan region and the Communist-inspired workers' uprisings in Chinese Shanghai in February and March 1927. The French authorities in both Paris and Shanghai were extremely concerned by these developments, and in particular by reports of the seizures of the British concessions in Hankou and Jiujiang in early January 1927. During the first two months of 1927 the French Foreign Ministry was concerned that the weaker defense forces available to the Shanghai French Concession relative to those in the International Settlement would encourage the Chinese to consider the Concession a "soft option" and attack it in preference to the more strongly defended International Settlement.[50]

This crisis, which appeared to have the potential to threaten the very existence of the Concession, forced the French authorities to look hard at

---

[48] *North-China Herald,* May 9, 1925.

[49] Yang Shi, "Shanghai tan liumang"; Xue Gengshen, "Jindai Shanghai de liumang," pp. 162–163; Fan Shaozeng, "Guanyu Du Yuesheng."

[50] Le Ministre des Affaires Étrangères à Monsieur le Ministre des Colonies, Minute, 26 Février 1927, Direction, no. 232, E515.4; Le Ministre des Affaires Étrangères à Monsieur le Ministre des Colonies, le 10 Janvier 1927, Direction, E515.4.

their defense resources. In the course of this review, they dismissed the Chinese members of the police force and the volunteers as incapable of providing an effective defense "in the event of anti-foreign disorders."[51] Events had overtaken the gentry-councillor clique. They had never felt the need to develop contacts with the underground Guomindang (GMD) organization in Shanghai and dealt only with the local warlord authorities. They therefore lacked the necessary connections with the new forces on the Chinese political stage and were thus of little use to the French during the critical early months of 1927. In contrast, the gangster bosses did enjoy a working relationship with the various revolutionary parties active in Shanghai, and they also had links with Jiang Jieshi (Chiang Kai-shek). Their long-standing relationship with the GMD, dating from the 1911 Revolution, when Chen Qimei was the military governor in Shanghai, was maintained throughout the 1920s. In 1924, for example, Du Yuesheng extended his protection to Chen Lifu when the latter set up an underground GMD organization in Shanghai.[52] The French authorities, therefore, turned to the gangster bosses, and in particular to Du Yuesheng. These French overtures neatly balanced those from the Right GMD, who were also seeking the gangster bosses' assistance against the Communists in Shanghai. Du agreed to assist the French in maintaining order in the Concession in return for French-supplied weapons. On February 26 Naggiar dispatched a request for 300 rifles and 10,000 cartridges; by early March the figure had increased to 600 rifles plus 150 revolvers and 1,000 steel helmets.[53] These were the

---

[51] Le Ministre des Affaires Étrangères, "Note en Vue du Conseil des Ministres: Défense de la Concession Française de Shanghai," le 10 Janvier 1927, Direction, E515.4; M. E. Naggiar, Consul-Général à Changhai, à Son Excellence Monsieur le Ministre des Affaires Étrangères à Paris, Consulat-Général de France à Changhai, Shanghai, le 11 Février 1927, Direction, no. 45, E515.4.

[52] For a detailed discussion of the relations between the French Concession Green Gang bosses and the GMD at the time of "Party purification," see Brian G. Martin, "The Green Gang and 'Party Purification' in Shanghai: Green Gang–Kuomintang Relations, 1926–1927" (paper presented to the Symposium on the Nanking Decade, 1928–1937: Man, Government and Society, University of Hong Kong, August 15–17, 1983); Shanghai Municipal Police Special Branch, Section 2, Investigation File D9319, "Memorandum on Mr Tu Yueh-sung alias Tu Yuin, July 8, 1939."

[53] "Memorandum of Mr Woodhead's Interview in Peking with M. Wilden, French Minister, on October 21, 1932," enclosure in Mr Ingram to Sir John Simon, Peking, December 26, 1932, FO 1380/7/87; Le Ministre des Affaires Étrangères à Monsieur Le Ministre de Guerre, Minute, le 2 Mars 1927, Direction, no. 386, E515.4; De Martel, le Ministre de France à Pékin, à le Ministre des Affaires Étrangères, Telegramme, Pékin, le 5 Mars 1927, Direction, no. 118, E515.4; E. Naggiar, Consul-Général de France à Changhai, à Son Excellence le Ministre des Affaires Étrangères, Telegramme, Shanghai, le 6 Mars 1927, Direction, no. 57, E515.4; Le Ministre des Affaires Étrangères à Monsieur le Ministre de la Guerre, Minute, le 9 Mars 1927, Direction, no. 444, E515.4.

weapons Du's gangsters used to effect the anti-Communist coup in mid-April. Du quickly implemented his side of the bargain when he personally intervened to prevent Chinese merchants and their employees in the French Concession from joining the Communist-sponsored general strike of February 20–24 and thus ensured that the strike did not take root in the Concession.[54] The French, for their part, facilitated Du's preparations for the anti-Communist purge. In addition to providing arms and an armed guard for the headquarters of the China Mutual Progress Association (an organization established by the gangster bosses to implement the purge), Captain Fiori arranged a meeting between Du Yuesheng and Stirling Fessenden, the chairman of the Shanghai Municipal Council, at which the latter granted Du's armed gangsters the right of passage through the International Settlement to attack the Communist positions in Zhabei.[55] It is probable that the French used the gangster bosses as their intermediaries in establishing contacts with the GMD's NRA; these contacts were an important element in their strategy to maintain the security of the Concession during the months of February, March, and April 1927.[56]

By these means the Green Gang bosses, and especially Du Yuesheng, emerged as one of the major beneficiaries of the anti-Communist coup of April 12, 1927. At a time of acute crisis they had effectively served the political interests of both Jiang Jieshi's group within the GMD and the French authorities. In the process, they successfully parlayed their standing with one group into increased influence with the other and thus encouraged perceptions among both groups of their indispensability. This perception in turn created new opportunities for the gangster bosses, such as mediating, on a functional basis, the tensions and frictions in the relations between the new Nationalist government authorities in Shanghai and the colonial authorities of the French Concession. This was one characteristic of the role Du Yuesheng performed in the late 1920s and early 1930s. Within the French Concession the crucial assistance the gangster bosses had provided the authorities during the crisis of February–April began the process by which they progressively displaced the gentry-councillor clique as the major center of Chinese power in the Concession.

---

[54] Martin, "The Green Gang and 'Party Purification.'"

[55] Ibid.; John B. Powell, My Twenty-Five Years in China (New York: Macmillan, 1945), pp. 158–159.

[56] M. E. Naggiar, Consul-Général de France à Changhai, à Son Excellence Monsieur le Ministre des Affaires Étrangères à Paris, Consulat-Général de France à Changhai, Shanghai, le 29 Mai 1927, Direction, no. 130, E515.4.

An important aspect of the accord reached in February 1927 between Du Yuesheng and Captain Fiori, acting on behalf of the gangster bosses and the French consul-general, respectively, was the latter's agreement to protect the extension of the gangsters' economic power (in the form of opium and gambling rackets) in the Concession. This agreement marked the beginnings of a clear community of interests between the French authorities and the gangsters, in which the former tolerated the latter's rackets in return for their assistance in maintaining the security and internal order of the Concession. The French themselves ruefully referred to this arrangement as "the pact with the devil" (le pacte avec le diable).[57]

An important aspect of this pact was the reaffirmation of the 1925 agreement on opium trafficking and the extension of the narcotics distribution network within the Concession. Opium was sold so openly in the Concession that an investigation conducted in early 1931 revealed that the local Chinese regularly referred to the system as an "official monopoly."[58] An indication of the degree of involvement of French officialdom in the opium traffic is revealed by the strenuous efforts French officials made in the late 1920s to try to persuade the representatives of the other foreign powers to overturn the 1912 International Opium Convention and again legalize (and tax) the opium trade. During the discussions by the Shanghai consular body in early March 1928 of the GMD's proposed Anti-Opium Law, which would have established a form of official monopoly, the French acting consul-general, Meyrier, strongly argued the case for the creation of a monopoly system in the Shanghai foreign settlements. In the course of his argument, Meyrier revealed that he personally knew that the Three Prosperities Company was prepared to contribute directly to the treasuries of both administrations the sums it then expended on "bribes" in the event that the monopoly system was instituted.[59] In July of the same year, Naggiar, who was then head of the Asiatic Department of the Ministry of Foreign Affairs, put the same argument to members of the British Embassy in Paris.[60] Unfortunately for the French, the British and American governments refused to consider a

[57] Personal communication from Professor Jean Chesneaux; "Memorandum of Mr Woodhead's Interview in Peking with M. Wilden"; Brenan to Lampson, Shanghai, May 29, 1930, FO 3570/184/87.

[58] H. G. W. Woodhead, *The Truth About Opium in China* (Shanghai: Shanghai Evening Post and Mercury, 1931), p. 58.

[59] Sir M. Lampson to Sir Austen Chamberlain, Peking, May 29, 1928, FO 42990/127/87.

[60] Mr N. M. Henderson to Sir Austen Chamberlain, Paris, July 7, 1928, FO 3621/244/87.

revision of the Hague Convention, and so the policy of official connivance in the drug traffic continued in the French Concession. This
connivance even extended to the French armed forces in the Far East
with reports that French gunboats on the upper Yangzi were used to con-
voy French flagged vessels known to be engaged in running guns to
Sichuan and opium to Shanghai.[61]

In addition to his opium rackets, Du Yuesheng also developed major
gambling interests in the Concession in the late 1920s, which greatly
increased his financial power. He conducted negotiations with Fiori and
Verdier (the Concession's chief administrative officer) in the course of
1927, and early in 1928 five large gambling joints catering to wealthy
Chinese were opened in various locations throughout the Concession.
Du Yuesheng directly controlled all of them; they were managed by key
lieutenants of his Small Eight Mob and protected by a special strong-arm
squad of five hundred gangsters under the control of one of his principal
lieutenants, Gao Xinbao. The largest and most notorious of these gambling houses was the Fusheng (also known as "Number 181" from its
address on the Avenue Foch). This was a large, three-storied, foreign-
style house in which one could engage in all types of Western and
Chinese forms of gambling and for whose use Du paid 4,000 silver taels
each month. In addition to such prestigious locations, Du also controlled
innumerable gambling dives catering to working-class gamblers in the
area around Baoxing li. The revenue generated by these gambling joints
together with that of the opium retail shops provided Du with the capital
to establish the Zhonghui Bank in 1929, which in turn was the means by
which he successfully penetrated the financial and commercial world of
Shanghai in the 1930s.[62]

In addition to his financial interests, Du Yuesheng used the pact with
the French authorities to further his political ambitions within the Concession. The instrument of this policy was the French Concession
Chinese Ratepayers' Association (CRA). This organization was established in mid-January 1927 with the avowed purpose of representing
the interests of the Chinese ratepayers in the Concession. From the
outset, however, it was controlled by Du Yuesheng and his colleagues.

---

[61] George M. Graves, "The Opium Problem in Central China," Report to Walter A.
Adams, American Consul-General, American Consulate-General, Hankow, China, September 29, 1932, U.S. Department of State, Decimal File 893.114 Narcotics/419.

[62] Da liumang Du Yuesheng, p. 34; Shanghai Municipal Police, Special Branch Report,
"Memorandum on Mr Tu Yueh-Sheng"; Xue Gengshen, "Jindai Shanghai de liumang"; China Weekly Review, July 25, 1931; Zhang Jungu, Du Yuesheng zhuan, vol. 2, pp. 86–89; Shi
Yi, Du Yuesheng waizhuan [An unofficial biography of Du Yuesheng] (Hong Kong: Daye,
1962), pp. 68–69. On the Zhonghui Bank, see Da liumang Du Yuesheng, p. 40.

The three Green Gang bosses were joint chairmen of a twenty-one-man Preparatory Committee that formally established the association during the first six months of 1927 and whose headquarters was either in or near Du's home on the rue Wagner. The Preparatory Committee numbered at least two more gangsters in its membership: Shang Mujiang (a close associate of Zhang Xiaolin) and Cheng Zhusun.[63] The Green Gang bosses also firmly controlled the association's supervisory committees and joint chairmanships "elected" by the association's members in 1929 and 1931.[64]

The gang bosses launched their drive for political power in the Concession in the immediate aftermath of the anti-Communist purge. In late April 1927 the CRA began to pressure the French authorities to meet its demands for the election of all Chinese members of the Provisional Commission (instead of their appointment by the French consul-general), to increase the numbers of Chinese members from five to eight, and to appoint six Chinese advisers to the consulate-general.[65] These aims had the dual purpose of promoting the CRA itself (and hence the gang bosses) as the legitimate spokesman for the Chinese residents of the Concession and to undercut the position of the gentry-councillor clique, whose members made up all the Chinese representation on the Provisional Commission. The French authorities' decision in July 1927 to follow the International Settlement and raise the Concession's rates by 2 percent provided the gang bosses with the ideal issue to push their political demands. In early July the CRA presented the Provisional Commission with its demands, including the ambit claim that all matters concerning the Concession's administration should be submitted to the CRA for its approval. If accepted, this demand would have enabled the CRA to appropriate the functions of the Provisional Commission. It was in fact an obvious attempt by the gangster bosses to pressure the French by capitalizing on current Chinese Nationalist hostility to extraterritoriality

[63] *Shanghai shi nianjian 1936* [Shanghai municipal yearbook for 1936], pp. V45–V46. Shang Mujiang was a Green Gang boss from Hangzhou who had moved to Shanghai and was very close to Zhang Xiaolin. See *Gendai Chūka minkoku Manshukoku jimmeikan,* p. 171. Although there are no similar biographical details for Cheng Zhusun, circumstantial evidence would suggest that he too was a Green Gang member.

[64] *Shanghai shi nianjian 1936* gives the following details: The supervisory committee elected in the 1929 elections of the Chinese Ratepayers' Association consisted of Huang Jinrong, Du Yuesheng, and Jin Tingsun (one of Du's senior lieutenants); the three-man joint chairmanship was held by Zhang Xiaolin, Shang Mujiang, and Cheng Zhusun. In the 1931 elections, the supervisory committee was composed of Huang Jinrong, Zhang Xiaolin, and Jin Tingsun; the joint chairmanship was held by Du Yuesheng, Shang Mujiang, and Cheng Zhusun.

[65] Dong Shu, "Shanghai fazujie de duoshi shiqi," p. 1022.

and the GMD's intervention in the contemporaneous rates dispute in the International Settlement. The other demands dealt with the real issues at stake: the abolition of the rates increase and the election of the Provisional Commission's Chinese members by the CRA. In mid-July the CRA appointed Du, Zhang, and Shang Mujiang to negotiate with the French authorities on its behalf. As a result of these negotiations, a compromise was reached. Although the Green Gang bosses failed to obtain the election of the Chinese members of the Provisional Commission, they did win the right to have the CRA elect nine Chinese advisers to the Provisional Commission. All nine advisers were drawn from the CRA's Executive Committee and included Du Yuesheng, Zhang Xiaolin, Cheng Zhusun, and Shang Mujiang. The French obtained the gangsters' acceptance of the increased rate, which was to be reviewed in six months.[66]

Despite this compromise, the CRA continued to press throughout the latter half of 1927 for the election of the Chinese members of the Provisional Commission. In an open letter to the Concession's Chinese ratepayers in late November 1927, the CRA argued that the effectiveness of the existing Chinese councillors was severely restricted because they were appointed by the French consul-general and not elected by the Chinese ratepayers. In the context of the hostility between the Green Gang bosses and the gentry-councillor clique, this statement was not merely, or even primarily, a plea for greater democracy in the Provisional Commission but an attack on the clique's self-assumed right to represent Chinese interests in the Concession. At the same time, the CRA attempted to strengthen its legitimacy by appropriating current GMD terminology on political democracy. In the letter it described its aims as "to promote the capacity for self-government" and to develop "the spirit of self-government."[67]

In January 1928 Du Yuesheng and Zhang Xiaolin used the resumption of negotiations on the increased rate to bargain for Zhang's admission to the Provisional Commission. In return the French continued to collect the increased rate; as a sop to the ratepayers, they agreed to increase the police force by two hundred men. Zhang's appointment to the Provisional Commission was one of the last acts of Naggiar as consul-general, and he acknowledged that it was a quid pro quo for the services

[66] *North-China Herald,* July 9, 1927, and July 30, 1927; *Shanghai shi nianjian 1936,* p. V46; *Da liumang Du Yuesheng,* p. 29; Dong Shu, "Shanghai fazujie de duoshi shiqi," p. 1021.

[67] *Shenbao,* November 17, 1927, cited in Dong Shu, "Shanghai fazujie de duoshi shiqi," p. 1021.

rendered by the gangster bosses during the security crisis a year before.[68] Zhang's membership on the Provisional Commission was a major victory for the Green Gang bosses, and it was consolidated eighteen months later by Du Yuesheng's own appointment as a councillor in July 1929. In his inaugural speech on taking his seat in the Provisional Commission on July 17, 1929, Du stated that the basic work of the Commission was that of Sino-French administration.[69] This was a calculated remark implying that in future the main business of government in the Concession could be pursued only through collaboration between the representatives of the Chinese population and the French authorities. At the same time, by stating that this should occur within the Provisional Commission, he was asserting an equivalence between that body and the French administration that it had never enjoyed and never been intended to enjoy. Du asserted this equivalence because the Provisional Commission had (as of mid-1929) become the power base of the gangster bosses in the Concession.

If the membership changes to the Provisional Commission in 1928 and 1929 represented an increase in power for the Green Gang bosses, by the same token they represented a serious diminution in the power of the gentry-councillor clique. Both Zhang and Du gained their seats on the Commission at the expense of Lu Songhou and Wu Zonglian, two aged members of the clique. Although the clique still retained three of the five Chinese seats, real influence had shifted from them to Du and Zhang. This shift was clearly revealed by the Wei Tingrong affair in mid-1929. Within a week of his taking his seat on the Commission, Du had his old rival Wei Tingrong kidnaped and spirited away to Pudong. Such a brazen attack on a leading member of the gentry-councillor clique caused consternation within French officialdom. According to a Shanghai Municipal Police report, the French authorities threatened to close down

[68] *North-China Herald,* January 21, 1928, and February 4, 1928; Dong Shu, "Shanghai fazujie de duoshi shiqi"; Edwin S. Cunningham, American Consul-General to the Honorable the Secretary of State, Washington, American Consulate-General, Shanghai, China, February 11, 1928, Political Conditions in the Shanghai Consular District During the Month of January 1928; M. E. Naggiar, Consul-Général de France à Changhai, à Son Excellence Monsieur le Ministre des Affaires Étrangères à Paris, Consulat-Général de France à Changhai, Shanghai, le 9 Janvier 1928, Direction, no. 7, E515.4; Conseil d'Administration Municipale, *Compte-Rendu de la Gestion pour l'Exercice 1928, Séance de la Commission Provisoire d'Administration Municipale du 16 Janvier 1928,* p. 9.

[69] Conseil d'Administration Municipale, *Compte-Rendu de la Gestion pour l'Exercice 1929, Séance de la Commission Provisoire d'Administration Municipale du 17 Juillet 1929,* p. 138; M. E. Koechlin, Consul, Charge du Consulat-Général de France à Changhai, à Son Excellence Monsieur le Ministre des Affaires Étrangères à Paris, Consulat-Général de France à Changhai, Shanghai, le 9 Août 1929, Direction, no. 96, E515.4.

the opium traffic unless Wei was released. The incident also created a rift between Du and Zhang Xiaolin. The relationship between the two bosses had never been easy, and Zhang possibly considered that Du had overreached himself and had endangered the basis of the gangsters' power in the Concession (their control of the opium traffic) for the dubious satisfaction of settling accounts with a bitter rival. Whatever the reason, Zhang abruptly resigned his position as cochairman of the CRA on August 1, 1929, and left Shanghai for Dairen. The affair was finally brought to an end when, after a tense three months, Wei was finally released in mid-September 1929 in a raid conducted by all three police forces in Shanghai.[70] Whatever the immediate costs to Du's position, he had in kidnaping Wei delivered a symbolic message to the gentry-councillor clique on where power now lay in the new balance of forces within the French Concession.

The coping stone to the edifice of gangster political power in the Concession was provided by Consul Koechlin's agreement in late 1930 that the CRA should elect the Chinese members of the Commission. This agreement was the result of protracted negotiations conducted throughout 1930 that again involved the gangsters' use of the rate issue to gain leverage with the French authorities. Among other factors that influenced Koechlin's decision was undoubtedly the crucial role played by Du Yuesheng in bringing to an end the long-drawn-out strike of the French Tramways Union from June to August 1930. On October 31, therefore, Koechlin sent a letter to the CRA in which he conceded the principle of election of the Chinese councillors and requested that the CRA endorse the five Chinese members already serving on the Commission. The CRA complied, and on November 18, 1930, it convened an extraordinary Congress that formally endorsed the five sitting Chinese members and elected nine special advisers to the various committees of the Provisional Commission.[71] These developments represented a complete victory for the Green Gang bosses, and in particular Du Yuesheng. He now controlled the Provisional Commission, and the leaders of the gentry-councillor clique were dependent on his favor for the retention of their positions on the Commission. A new balance of forces had emerged in the power structure of the French Concession.

---

[70] "Confidential Report on Traffic in Opium in Shanghai," Enclosure in Sir M. Lampson to Mr. A. Henderson, Peking, October 22, 1929, FO 6548/69/87; Consul-General Brenan to Sir M. Lampson, Shanghai, May 29, 1930, FO 3570/184/87; *Shanghai shi nianjian 1936*; Fan Shaozeng, "Guanyu Du Yuesheng."

[71] *China Weekly Review*, July 5, 1930; Dong Shu, "Shanghai fazujie de duoshi shiqi," pp. 1023–1024; *Shanghai shi nianjian 1936*; Zhu Menghua, "Shanghai dazujie de gongdongju ji Xunbufang."

The Balance Overturned: The Ascendancy of the Green Gang Bosses and the Crisis of Authority in the French Concession, 1930–1932

In addition to his political gains in the Provisional Commission, Du Yuesheng's position in the Concession was also enhanced by his successful mediation of industrial and social disputes. Such mediation was an important aspect of the pact between Du and the French authorities and represented, from the latter's point of view, a significant contribution to the maintenance of the internal security of the Concession. The most important industrial disputes in this period occurred in the principal public utilities concern in the Concession, the French Tramways and Electric Light Company (La Compagnie Française de Tramways et d'Éclairage Électrique de Changhaï), and in particular the strikes in December 1928 and June–August 1930.[72] In undertaking the mediation of these strikes, Du was not solely concerned with increasing his standing with, hence his "indispensability" to, the French authorities. Such a policy would merely have reflected a dependent relationship between himself and the French. By the latter half of 1930, Du was intent on building up an independent power base within the Concession, and part of his strategy for achieving this end was to gain control over organized labor in the settlement. Therefore one major purpose of his mediation of the 1928 and 1930 strikes was to gain control of the French Tramways Union (FTU). This was accomplished in the period 1930–1931. Once he had control of the FTU, which organized the workers in one of the most strategically placed industries in the Concession, Du had the advantage of the French authorities.

Du's strategy was facilitated by the fact that industrial disputes, such as those in the French Tramways Company, were not matters of concern solely to the Concession authorities. Agencies of the municipal government of greater Shanghai, such as the Bureau of Social Affairs, together with the Shanghai GMD Party Branch claimed an interest in the Chinese populations of the foreign settlements, and both organizations were actively involved with the 1928 and 1930 disputes in the French Tramways Company.[73] This was a local manifestation of the new Nationalist government's general policy to reclaim those areas of the nation's sovereignty that had been lost to China. In the four-year period 1927–1930 the Nanjing government had regained tariff autonomy, successfully negotiated the withdrawal of Japanese troops from Shandong

---

[72] Brian G. Martin, "Tu Yueh-sheng and Labour Control in Shanghai: The Case of the French Tramways Union, 1928–1932," *Papers on Far Eastern History*, no. 32 (September 1985), pp. 99–137.

[73] Ibid.

after the Jinan Incident, fought (and lost) a brief war with the Soviet Union over the latter's control of the Chinese Eastern Railway, and obtained the rendition of the British naval base at Weihaiwei. After putting the foreign powers on notice that it sought the abolition of extraterritoriality, it launched a diplomatic offensive toward this end in late 1930 and early 1931.[74] As part of this policy the Chinese authorities in Shanghai took every opportunity to assert their claims to authority over the foreign settlements, and this attitude ensured that even relatively minor incidents became the subjects of diplomatic exchanges.

This was the context within which Du conducted his mediation of social and industrial disputes in the Concession. The French used him to "manage" their relations with the local Chinese authorities in the resolution of disputes involving the Chinese population of the Concession, while the Chinese authorities found Du to be a useful instrument in furthering their own interests in the Concession. Du, for his part, used his relations with the one to gain increased leverage with the other and so increase his own power and influence. Good examples of this triangular relationship and of the way in which local fracases could become international incidents were provided by the Wu Tonggen Affair of September 1928 and the Xin Dingxiang Affair of October–December 1930.[75] In both cases a Chinese worker was murdered by French marines (a tram driver in the case of Wu and a sampan ferryman in the case of Xin); the Shanghai Party Office and the Shanghai trade unions mobilized public protests in which demands were made to abolish extraterritoriality, and the affairs became the subject of diplomatic exchanges between the Chinese and French authorities. On each occasion both parties accepted Du's mediation of the incident, and in each case he negotiated a compromise settlement that took the immediate heat out of the affair, met the political needs of the local French and Chinese authorities, and provided some material relief to the victims' bereaved families. In addition, Du strengthened his own relations with both Chinese and French officialdom as a result of his successful negotiations.

By early 1931 Du's control of the Provisional Commission and the local trade unions together with his close and complex relationship with the Chinese authorities had caused many informed foreign observers to

---

[74] Akira Iriye, *After Imperialism: The Search for a New Order in the Far East, 1921–1931* (New York: Atheneum, 1969), pp. 227–299; Harold M. Vinacke, *A History of the Far East in Modern Times* (New York: Appleton-Century-Crofts, 1950), pp. 456–461.

[75] For the Wu Tonggen Affair, see Martin, "Tu Yueh-sheng and Labour Control," pp. 108–109. For the Xin Dingxiang Affair, see Ma Chaojun, *Zhongguo laodong yundong shi* [A history of the Chinese labor movement] (Taibei: Zhongguo laogong yundong shi biansuo weiyuanhui, 1958), vol. 3, pp. 1019–1021.

conclude that the gangsters and not the French administration ran the Concession. The British and International Settlement authorities were particularly concerned by this development and the adverse implications it held for the foreign position generally in Shanghai. In late 1929, for example, the Shanghai Municipal Police provided the British consul-general with a confidential report on the situation in the French Concession which stated that Captain Fiori was chief of police in name only and that real power was exercised by Du Yuesheng and his gangster colleagues.[76] Eighteen months later, in March 1931, the British consul-general in a report to his Minister in Beiping observed that not only did the Green Gang bosses have complete control of the Concession's affairs but that they were in a position to destroy the French administration if they considered it in their interests to do so. His report said in part:

> The truth of the matter is ... that the local French authorities are so entirely in the hands of the people who control the traffic in opium and gambling that they are unable to break loose, even if they so desired. It pays the ring at present to support the French administration, but I have little doubt that they could bring it tumbling to the ground and that they *would* do so if any serious attempt was made to cut off their sources of income.[77]

By mid-1931 it was commonly believed that public order had so broken down that a crisis of authority existed in the French Concession. As a result, it was seriously suggested that the commanders of the United States and British defense forces in Shanghai be formally requested to station some of their troops in the residential section of the Concession in order to protect the lives and property of their nationals resident there.[78]

These developments were a cause of some concern to the French government in Paris not only because of the threat they posed to French authority in Shanghai, but also because of the great damage they inflicted on French prestige in the Far East generally. For these reasons, in mid-1930 it dispatched Auguste Wilden, a former consul-general in Shanghai, as the new French minister to China with the specific brief to investigate the situation in the Shanghai Concession. Wilden's investigations were hampered by the obstructive tactics adopted by the French officials in Shanghai, notably Koechlin, whom Wilden described as "obviously hostile," and Fiori, who was "evasive and furtive." Finally, Wilden reluctantly concluded that it was impossible to reform the situation through

---

[76] "Confidential Report on Traffic in Opium at Shanghai."

[77] Consul-General Brenan to Sir M. Lampson, Shanghai, March 31, 1931, Enclosure in Sir M. Lampson to Mr A Henderson, Peking, April 13, 1931, FO 3225/22/37.

[78] *China Weekly Review,* July 18, 1931.

the existing local French officials, who were too deeply involved with the gangsters.[79]

While Wilden searched for an appropriate strategy to deal with the problems in the Concession, the situation deteriorated further with the publicity given to the gambling rackets in early 1931. Between 1929 and 1931 the International Settlement authorities had progressively closed down all the gambling joints and dog racing tracks (Luna Park and the Stadium) in the settlement, which meant that by 1931 the Green Gang bosses had a virtual monopoly of gambling rackets in Shanghai. One reason for the International Settlement's policy was its desire to prevent the question of gambling (which was formally proscribed under Chinese law) from becoming an issue in the negotiations between the Chinese government and the foreign powers concerning extraterritoriality. As a result, many foreign officials feared that the continued open operations of the Green Gang's gambling joints in the French Concession could seriously undermine the response of the foreign powers to the Chinese government's diplomatic offensive in early 1931 for the rendition of the foreign concessions. For this reason the British consul-general put pressure on Koechlin in February 1931 to clean up the gambling rackets. The French authorities, however, procrastinated, responding with a few carefully managed raids that left the Green Gang gambling joints largely undisturbed.[80]

Nevertheless, the pressure was increasing on Green Gang interests in the Concession, and Du Yuesheng developed a dual strategy to meet it. On the one hand, he sought to strengthen his relations with the Nanjing government and, on the other, he used his power within the Concession to keep the local French officials from capitulating to this pressure. A breakthrough was achieved in the relations between the French Concession Green Gang bosses and the Nationalist government at a meeting between Du Yuesheng and Jiang Jieshi in Nanjing in early May 1931. Since 1928 a major area of friction in these relations had been the periodic proposals for an official opium monopoly put forward by the Nationalist government (particularly by T. V. Soong, the finance minister) and the gangsters' fears that such a monopoly would undermine their own arrangements in the Jiangnan area. At the Nanjing conference, however, Jiang Jieshi agreed that the officials designated to run the proposed opium monopoly would be appointed by the Nationalist government only after selection by the Green Gang bosses. Furthermore,

[79] "Memorandum of Mr Woodhead's Interview in Peking with M. Wilden."

[80] Brenan to Lampson, March 31, 1931; *China Weekly Review*, May 23, 1931; May 30, 1931; June 6, 1931; June 13, 1931.

control of the opium distribution networks in the Jiangnan area was to remain with Du Yuesheng and his colleagues. In return, Du pledged Green Gang support for Jiang Jieshi's anti-Communist campaign and to use his gangster resources to assist in the destruction of the Communist underground in Shanghai.[81] One immediate result of this agreement was that the gangsters, with the future of their financial interests now guaranteed, ended their lukewarm attitude to the Nationalist government's campaign against extraterritoriality and swung the CRA in support of the government's negotiations for the rendition of the French Mixed Court, which were then just getting under way.[82] At the same time, Du Yuesheng used his control of industrial labor to encourage the local French officials in their opposition to Wilden. Although the strike in July 1931 by the garbage coolies of the French municipality had its own separate causes, strong circumstantial evidence suggests that Du used the strike to demonstrate his power in the Concession and intimidate the French authorities.[83] The strike effectively paralyzed the French Concession, and it was in this context that a number of observers spoke of a crisis of authority in the Concession. From the point of view of the gangsters, the strike did have a salutary effect on the local French officials. When Captain Fiori, in response to pressure from the consular body, launched his drive against gambling in September 1931, it was conducted in such a way as to minimize its impact on Green Gang interests.[84]

---

[81] See *Dagongbao* (Shanghai), May 1, 1931, for the report of the Green Gang bosses' summons to Nanjing. Harold R. Isaacs, "Five Years of Kuomintang Reaction," *China Forum,* May 1932, p. 18.

[82] Edwin S. Cunningham, American Consul-General, to the Honorable Secretary of State, Washington D.C., "Political Report for May 1931," American Consulate-General, Shanghai, China, June 5, 1931, Department of State, Decimal File 893.00PR Shanghai/36.

[83] Martin, "Tu Yueh-sheng and Labour Control," pp. 129–130, 133; *North-China Herald,* July 7, 1931; *China Weekly Review,* July 18, 1931; Edwin S. Cunningham, American Consul-General, to the Honorable the Secretary of State, Washington, D.C., "Monthly Political Report for May 1931," American Consulate-General, Shanghai, China, June 5, 1931, Department of State, Decimal File 893.00PR Shanghai/38; Conseil d'Administration Municipale, *Compte-Rendu de la Gestion pour l'Exercice 1931, Rapport des Services de Police, Titre IV Section Politique,* p. 300. Among the reasons that can be adduced to suggest manipulation of the strike by Du Yuesheng are the following: the curious fact that the French authorities refused to take emergency measures despite protests by foreign residents of the Concession, the rapidity with which the strike spread from the garbage coolies to involve all employees of the Municipal Council and the suggestions of coercion involved, the very generous strike settlement that was estimated to cost the ratepayers an extra 400,000 taels a year, and finally the official French description of the strike as having "an especially anti-French character."

[84] *China Weekly Review,* September 5, 1931; September 19, 1931; September 26, 1931.

The outbreak of conflict between Chinese and Japanese forces in the Shanghai area on January 28, 1932, brought the crisis in the French Concession to a head. Both sides tried to manipulate the security crisis to their own advantage: Du Yuesheng and the gangsters in a bid to preserve their power and influence, Wilden and those French officials associated with him to ease out Koechlin and Fiori and to remove Du Yuesheng's influence from the Concession. Immediately hostilities commenced between Chinese and Japanese forces, Vice-Admiral Herr, commander of the French Far East Fleet and overall commander of French forces in Shanghai, took over all authority from the civil officials of the Concession and proscribed the opium and gambling rackets. At the same time, Koechlin called out Du's gangsters ostensibly in support of the French forces in the defense of the Concession, and the streets were filled with more than a thousand of Du's "special agents" sporting tricolor armbands and carrying weapons supplied by the French police. Their purpose was to create such confusion as to effectively disrupt the French forces' security operations and so compel the martial law authorities to rescind their proscriptions on the opium and gambling rackets. Herr had apparently been forewarned of Du's tactics, however, and he moved decisively against the gangsters; within a few days he had cleared them from the streets.[85]

At the same time, Wilden, in accordance with an earlier decision, announced the appointment of Meyrier and Fabre, consul-general and chief of police in the Tianjin French Concession, as the new consul-general and police chief in Shanghai.[86] Koechlin, now under considerable pressure, was compelled to seek Du's resignation as a member of the Provisional Commission. Du tendered his resignation in a letter dated February 15, 1932, in which he cited, among other things, his financial and commercial commitments and his involvement with the Shanghai Martial Law Committee, which precluded his further membership on the Provisional Commission. Koechlin, however, did not announce Du's resignation until February 29, 1932.[87] In the intervening fortnight Du undoubtedly engaged in last-minute efforts to avoid its acceptance. However, Koechlin no longer exercised any effective authority: his actions

---

[85] La lumière, June 18, 1932, cited in China Weekly Review, September 10, 1932; Shenbao, February 19, 1932, cited in Da liumang Du Yuesheng, p. 32; The Peking and Tientsin Times, June 28, 1932; China Weekly Review, March 19, 1932.

[86] "Memorandum of Mr Woodhead's Interview in Peking with M. Wilden."

[87] "Shanghai fazujie dangju youguan yierba shibian wenjian xuankan" [Selections from French Concession documents relating to the Shanghai Incident of January 28, 1932], Dang'an yu lishi [Archives and history], no. 2 (1985), p. 26; Conseil d'Administration Municipale, Compte-Rendu de la Gestion pour l'Exercice 1932, Séance de la Commission Provisoire d'Administration Municipale du 29 Février 1932, p. 34; Da liumang Du Yuesheng, p. 32.

were now controlled by Minister Wilden and Vice-Admiral Herr, and in any event he had to salvage what he could of his professional career. A strange sequence of events now unfolded. Within a fortnight of the public acceptance of Du's resignation from the Provisional Commission, three leading members of the Concession died within a week of one another from what Meyrier described as "a sudden illness" (une maladie foudrayante): Du Pac de Marsoulies of "double pneumonia"; the former consul-general Koechlin of "smallpox" en route to France; and Colonel A. Marcaire, commander of French land forces in Shanghai, of "pneumonia."[88] Rumors circulated almost immediately that all three had been murdered by Du in revenge for the actions taken against his interests in the Concession, but no convincing evidence has been found to substantiate such rumors. Nevertheless, the circumstances of the deaths—including the fact that they involved key French officials involved in the pact with the gangsters and all occurred within a week of one another (March 11–19, 1932)—and the lack of any adequate explanation as to the manner in which the alleged fatal diseases were contracted are certainly suspicious. Some possible hint of the real nature of the deaths was provided by Meyrier in his homily to Koechlin and Marcaire when he described the men as having "died for France in the service of our concession" (morts pour France au service de notre concession).[89]

Whatever the true nature of these deaths, they ushered in a five-month period (March—July 1932) of bitter conflict as Du Yuesheng deployed all his resources in an effort to preserve his position in the face of the determined efforts by Meyrier and Fabre to prize him out of the Concession. During this period protracted negotiations were held between Du and Meyrier for the removal of the Three Prosperities Company from the Concession. These negotiations were conducted in an extremely tense atmosphere, in which Meyrier and Fabre were first offered bribes and then had their lives threatened. When these tactics failed to move the local French officials, Du used his connections with leading Chinese to have them intercede on his behalf with senior French officials and politicians. As a result, Zheng Yuxiu (Soumay Tcheng) and Madame H. H. Kung went to Paris in mid-April 1932 to lobby French

---

[88] Conseil d'Administration Municipale, *Compte-Rendu de la Gestion pour l'Exercice 1932, Séance de la Commission Provisoire d'Administration Municipale du 14 Mars 1932*, p. 44; *Séance de la Commission Provisoire d'Administration Municipale du 24 Mars 1932*, pp. 53–54; *North-China Herald,* March 15, 1932; March 22, 1932; *China Weekly Review,* March 26, 1932.

[89] Conseil d'Administration Municipale, *Séance de la Commission Provisoire d'Administration Municipale du 24 Mars 1932,* p. 54.

government officials and French politicians on Du's behalf, while Madame Wellington Koo lobbied Wilden in Beiping.[90] Both attempts, however, were unsuccessful. With the failure of these missions Du fell back on his last remaining (but most powerful) weapon—his control of organized labor in the Concession. He orchestrated a strike in the French Tramways Company and timed its outbreak for the week preceding Bastille Day (July 14, 1932) to maximize its impact on the French authorities.[91] This stratagem worked, and with the outbreak of the strike on July 7, French troops and police were mobilized to patrol the main thoroughfares of the Concession.[92] Four days into the strike, Meyrier made contact with Wu Tiecheng, the mayor of greater Shanghai, in order both to end the strike and seek an arrangement for the removal of Du's opium business from the Concession. After further negotiations they finally reached an agreement by which Du could run his narcotics operations from Nandao under the auspices of Wu's newly created opium monopoly in greater Shanghai; the French would assist in transporting his opium stocks out of the Concession. By the end of the year, Du had dissolved the Three Prosperities Company; he ran his narcotics operations from a "Special Service Department" within the Shanghai Peace Preservation Corps, which was commanded by his crony Yang Hu.[93] Thus, by November 1932 Meyrier could assure the British consul-general that the opium combine had been removed from French territory and that Du Yuesheng was no longer allowed to interfere in the Concession's affairs.[94]

A Balance Restored: The Reassertion of French Authority in the Concession, 1932–1935

Meyrier's primary task during his three years as consul-general was the reassertion in the Concession of French consular authority, which

---

[90] "Memorandum of Mr Woodhead's Interview in Peking with M. Wilden," *China Forum*, April 16, 1932; *Da liumang Du Yuesheng*, p. 36.

[91] Martin, "Tu Yueh-sheng and Labour Control," pp. 134–135; Zhu Bangxing, *Shanghai chanye yu Shanghai zhigong* pp. 360–361.

[92] Da Yun, "Fadian bagong yu women de lingdao" [The French Tramways strike and our leadership] (August 6, 1932), in *Zhonggong 'gongren yundong' yuanshi ziliao huibian* [Collection of original documents on the Chinese Communist "Labor Movement"], vol. 4 (Taibei: Sifang xingzheng bu tiaocha ju, 1982), p. 126.

[93] Consul-General Sir J. Brenan to Mr Ingram, Shanghai, November 7, 1932, FO 1380/7/87; Shanghai Municipal Police, Special Branch Report, "Memorandum on Mr Tu Yueh-sheng," July 8, 1939.

[94] Brenan to Ingram, November 7, 1932.

had been seriously eroded during the tenure of his predecessor, Koechlin (December 1928–March 1932). In his inaugural speech to the Provisional Commission on March 14, 1932, Meyrier outlined his three priorities: preserving order and security in the Concession, improving its administration, and enhancing its prosperity. He emphasized particularly the last two points: "I eagerly desire that calm and peace will return at last to Shanghai, and that we will be able to devote our energies no longer to defence but to the prosperity and good administration of our Concession."[95] Police corruption, the legacy of Fiori, was the first item on the agenda of his program of administrative reform. With the assistance of Fabre he dismissed large numbers of corrupt officers from the force and implemented a wholesale reform of the police structure. Great care was taken in the selection of officers, and the lines of responsibility within the police hierarchy were strengthened, so that by 1935 the Concession had a more disciplined and tightly controlled police system than at any time since World War I.[96]

In the sphere of municipal administration, Meyrier reasserted the primacy of the office of the consul-general over the Provisional Commission. He rarely attended its meetings and communicated with it through his consul, Coiffard, who acted as president of the Provisional Commission. In this way he restored the traditional relationship between the consul-general and the Municipal Council/Provisional Commission, a relationship that had been undermined in the period 1929–1932 when Du Yuesheng had transformed the Provisional Commission into his personal power base with Koechlin attending all its meetings in his capacity as president. In this context Meyrier restored key members of the gentry-councillor clique to their former role as the main intermediaries between the French administration and the Chinese population. Meyrier had a long relationship with this group and had worked very closely with them in the mid-1920s, first as consul to Wilden and then as acting consul-general. This relationship was particularly true of Wei Tingrong, for whom Meyrier had apparently a very high regard and whom he used as a personal adviser on matters affecting the Chinese residents of the Concession. Wei's consistent opposition to Du Yuesheng further increased his standing with Meyrier.[97]

[95] Conseil d'Administration Municipale, *Séance de la Commission Provisoire d'Administration Municipale du 14 Mars 1932*, p. 44.

[96] Conseil d'Administration Municipale, *Compte-Rendu de la Gestion pour l'Exercice 1935, Séance de la Commission Provisoire d'Administration Municipale du 7 Janvier 1935*, p. 4; *North-China Herald*, January 16, 1935.

[97] Conseil d'Administration Municipale, *Compte-Rendu de la Gestion pour l'Exercice 1935, Séance de la Commission Provisoire d'Administration Municipale du 7 Janvier 1935*, pp. 4–5; Huang Guodong, "Du men huajiu," *Jiu Shanghai de banghui*, p. 256. Throughout Meyrier's

In addition to implementing these administrative reforms, Meyrier prosecuted vigorous antiopium and antigambling policies. In late September 1932 the French police played a prominent role in the seizure of a large consignment of opium valued at between Ch$250,000 and Ch$500,000.[98] Moreover, there was a marked increase in the number of drug traffickers and proprietors of opium dens arrested in 1932 over the preceding year. Almost ten times as many traffickers were arrested in 1932 as in 1931 (475 as opposed to merely 48), and almost five times as many opium den proprietors (2,053 versus 465).[99] The crackdown continued throughout 1933 and 1934, when a total of 11,130 drug-related arrests were made. The high arrest rate for drug-related offenses decreased noticeably, however, after Meyrier returned to France. In 1935 the number of arrests totaled 3,234, in 1936, a mere 788.[100] Meyrier also created a Gaming Squad (Brigade des Jeux) for the express purpose of eradicating all forms of Chinese gambling from the Concession. This squad made just over 1,700 arrests each year between 1934 and 1936.[101]

Despite these innovations, however, Meyrier's reforms were strictly limited in their effects. He himself, after all, had played a role when he was acting consul-general in the original agreement with the Green Gang bosses on the opium traffic in 1925. Moreover, he retained the services of certain key administrative personnel, such as Verdier (director-general of municipal services [directeur-général des services municipaux]), who had figured largely in the system as it had operated between 1928 and 1932.[102] In addition, the influence of the Green Gang bosses was still apparent in the Concession. Most members of the French Police's

term of office, Wei was a member of the Provisional Commission's powerful Public Works Committee (his colleague Lu Baihong was a member of the equally important Finance Committee). When Meyrier retired as consul-general in January 1935, Wei resigned his membership on the Provisional Commission. This resignation strengthens the assumption that Wei's influence on the Provisional Commission in the period 1932–1935 reflected his personal relationship with Meyrier. Conseil d'Administration Municipale, *Séance de la Commission Provisoire d'Administration Municipale du 7 Janvier 1935*, p. 5.

98 *The Central China Post*, September 26, 1932; September 27, 1932; *North-China Herald*, September 28, 1932.

99 Conseil d'Administration Municipale, *Compte-Rendu de la Gestion pour l'Exercice 1935, Rapports pour l'Année 1935: Rapport des Services de Police*, p. 341.

100 Ibid., p. 197; Conseil d'Administration Municipale, *Compte-Rendu de la Gestion pour l'Exercice 1936, Rapports pour l'Année 1936: Services de Police*, p. 215.

101 Conseil d'Administration Municipale, *Rapports pour l'Année 1935: Rapport des Services de Police*, pp. 197–198; *Rapports pour l'Année 1936: Services de Police*, p. 215.

102 Conseil d'Administration Municipale, *Séance de la Commission Provisoire d'Administration Municipale du 7 Janvier 1935*, p. 3.

Chinese detective force remained followers of Du Yuesheng's Green Gang group. Zhang Xiaolin, furthermore, not only retained his membership of the Provisional Commission but was honored by the French administration on the occasion of his sixtieth birthday in June 1936.[103] The CRA continued to "elect" the Chinese members of the Provisional Commission, three of whom came from its own ranks, as well as the special advisers to the commission's various committees, who included such prominent Green Gang members as Shang Mujiang and Jin Tingsun. In fact, Du Yuesheng's control of the CRA was strengthened after the association's 1933 election, which abolished the system of cochairmen and replaced it with one chairman (Du) and two vice-chairmen. The new CRA Executive Committee elected in 1933 also contained at least four members of Du's recently established Perseverance Society.[104] The French authorities, moreover, continued to rely on Du Yuesheng's good offices to assist them in the maintenance of social order, as indicated by Du's successful mediation of the serious dispute over the registration of rickshas in the French Concession in August 1935.

In short, Meyrier's policies did not eradicate the power of the Green Gang bosses from the French Concession. They probably were not intended to. Rather, the purpose was to contain that power and to ensure that Du Yuesheng, in particular, did not exert undue influence on the affairs of the Concession. In other words, Meyrier sought to achieve a realignment of forces among the Concession authorities, the gentry-councillor clique, and the Green Gang bosses from which a more stable balance of power would emerge and one in which the French authorities exercised decisive control and the Green Gang bosses played a subordinate although still important role. Meyrier was assisted in this goal by the fact that after 1932 Du Yuesheng had reached an accommodation with the GMD authorities in both Nanjing and Shanghai, greatly extending his political horizons and expanding his scope of influence. Consequently, the French Concession lost its importance as the major focus of his activities. Nevertheless the fact of Du's emergence as a major political figure in Shanghai by the mid-1930s meant that the French

---

[103] Conseil d'Administration Municipale, *Compte-Rendu de la Gestion pour l'Exercice 1933, Séance de la Commission Provisoire d'Administration Municipale du 9 Janvier 1933*, p. 3; *Compte-Rendu de la Gestion pour l'Exercice 1934, Séance de la Commission Provisoire d'Administration Municipale du 15 Janvier 1934*, p. 3; *Compte-Rendu de la Gestion pour l'Exercice 1935, Séance de la Commission Provisoire d'Administration Municipale du 7 Janvier 1935*, p. 5; *Compte-Rendu de la Gestion pour l'Exercice 1936, Séance de la Commission Provisoire d'Administration Municipale du 20 Janvier 1936*, p. 3; *Séance de la Commission Provisoire d'Administration Municipale du 22 Juin 1936*, p. 56;

[104] *Shanghai shi nianjian 1936*, p. V47; *Jiu Shanghai de banghui*, pp. 369, 372, 373, 379.

authorities could not prevent, even had they wished to, a recrudescence of his influence within the Concession. Du Yuesheng and the French reached a new accommodation that reflected the new political situation, a development assisted by the departure of Meyrier in January 1935 and the appointment in 1936 of Naggiar as the first French Ambassador to China.

CHAPTER NINE

Strikes among Shanghai Silk Weavers, 1927–1937

The Awakening of a Labor Aristocracy

ELIZABETH J. PERRY

Studies of the Chinese labor movement generally end their story in the spring of 1927, when Jiang Jieshi's (Chiang Kai-shek's) bloody Shanghai massacre drove a shattered Communist Party out of the cities and into the countryside. From that point on, we are led to believe, the urban proletariat was politically insignificant. The Chinese revolution became a peasant war, fought and won in the rural hinterland.

The focus of Communist activities did indeed shift away from the urban workers after April 1927. But the history of the Chinese labor movement is not identical with Party history. Just as Chinese workers had been active well before the founding of the Communist Party, so they continued their struggles well after the mass executions and forced exodus of Communist labor organizers in 1927. Indeed, certain sectors of the work force grew much more feisty during the Nanjing decade (1927–1937) than they had ever been under Communist inspiration. One such group was the Shanghai silk weavers.

The silk weavers of Shanghai were known in the 1920s as China's "labor aristocrats" (*guizu gongren*). Occupying skilled jobs that paid well, these fortunate laborers were notably absent from the massive workers' strikes that swept through most of the city's factories in that period. While workers in other Shanghai industries responded actively to the spirit of the May Fourth (1919) and May Thirtieth (1925) movements, silk weavers remained quietly at their jobs. By the turn of the decade, however, the situation had changed. As producers of a luxury commodity tailored toward an international market, silk weavers were especially vulnerable to fluctuations in the world economy. That economy brought them prosperity in the 1920s, but a few years later—in the wake of the Great Depression, the Japanese invasion of Manchuria, the disastrous Yellow River flood, and the Sino-Japanese conflict in Shanghai—the picture was notably less bright. Scores of small silk-weaving enterprises suspended operations, putting thousands of Shanghai's skilled weavers out of work.

Strike Waves

The difficulties of the silk-weaving industry were reflected in the strikes of its workers. As figure 1 indicates, the years 1930, 1934, and 1937 all saw massive strike waves among Shanghai silk weavers. The pattern is very different from that which obtained in the city as a whole. For most of the city's workers, 1925–1927 was the period of greatest labor unrest. The years 1930 and 1934, in most Shanghai factories, actually saw a decrease in the level of strike activity; and although 1937 was a year of increased strikes, the magnitude of that increase was far greater among silk weavers than was found in the city as a whole.[1]

The silk weavers' increased protest activity was obviously related to the fact that by the early 1930s their industry had fallen on hard times. As the figures in table 1 indicate, exports of finished silk products fell steadily during the Nanjing decade. But the relationship between economic hardship and labor unrest was not as straightforward as may at first appear, for the depression years saw not only a general *decline* in the silk-weaving industry, but also a fundamental *restructuring* of the industry. While the smaller silk-weaving factories found themselves forced to lay off substantial numbers of workers or suspend operations altogether, a few of the larger concerns continued to expand, thereby coming to dominate the industry. Strike activity, as we will see, was heavily concentrated in these more prosperous enterprises.

The most successful survivor of the depression years was the Meiya Company, founded in 1920 with comprador capital as a small factory of only twelve looms and thirty to forty weavers. Business improved rapidly the following year when the comprador's son-in-law, Cai Shengbai, was hired as general manager. Recently returned to Shanghai from an educational stint at Lehigh University, Cai quickly put his American know-how to use by importing the latest model U.S.-made looms and recruiting educated workers to operate them. Cai's two personnel managers, natives of eastern Zhejiang province, made frequent trips home to Shengxian and Dongyang counties to enlist bright young men and

---

[1] Shanghai Bureau of Social Affairs, ed., *Strikes and Lockouts in Shanghai Since 1918* (Shanghai, 1933); "Jin si nian lai Shanghai di bagong tingye" [Strikes and lockouts in Shanghai during the past four years], *Guoji laogong tongxun* 5:5 (May 1938).

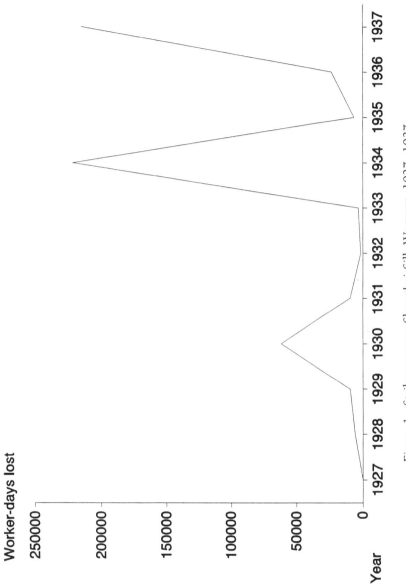

Figure 1. Strikes among Shanghai Silk Weavers, 1927–1937

Table 1
Value of Chinese Silk Piece Goods Exported

Year	Value (Chinese $)
1927	28,223,472
1928	25,987,270
1929	20,484,285
1930	17,827,441
1931	17,695,349
1932	14,754,601
1933	15,648,269
1934	11,289,794
1935	6,987,582
1936	6,217,958

SOURCE: D. K. Lieu, *The Silk Industry of China* (Shanghai, 1940), pp. 256–257.

women as apprentice weavers. Only those who passed a difficult technical test were admitted as apprentices. Thanks to the skill of its
enthusiastic young workers, Meiya had by 1927 developed into the largest silk-weaving concern in all of China, with 408 looms and more than
thirteen hundred employees, more than half of whom were serving a
four- to five-year term as apprentices. To encourage high output among
the young weavers, the company sponsored production contests, paid
generous wages, and provided a variety of services: dormitories,
cafeterias, clinic, library, night school, recreation club, sports teams, and
the like. Aided by such forward-looking management, Meiya in the space
of a decade grew into a ten-factory conglomerate with more than a
thousand looms—nearly one-quarter of all the silk-weaving looms in
Shanghai. Most silk-weaving establishments in the city had fewer than
ten looms in operation.[2]

With both its source of materials and its market outlets more
diversified than other silk-weaving operations, Meiya was better

[2] *Shanghai zhi jizhi gongye* [Mechanized industry in Shanghai] (Shanghai, 1933), p. 175;
Zhu Bangxing, Hu Lingge, and Xu Sheng, eds., *Shanghai chanye yu Shanghai zhigong*
[Shanghai's industries and workers] (Shanghai, 1939), p. 133; Luo Gengmo, "Meiya
gongqiao shimo" [The Meiya workers' tide from beginning to end], in *Zhongguo jingji
lunwen ji* (Shanghai, 1936), p. 227; D. K. Lieu, *The Silk Industry of China* (Shanghai 1940),
p. 191; Zhang Shouyu, *Jindai Jiangnan sizhi gongye shi* [A history of the modern Jiangnan
silk-weaving industry] (Beijing, 1988); *Meiya qikan* [Meiya journal] (Shanghai Municipal Archives nos. 199-48-258 and 199-48-259), 1933/11/16.

positioned to withstand the upheavals of the Depression. As many of its less fortunate competitors fell by the wayside, the Meiya Company continued to enjoy hefty profit margins. By 1934, Meiya's one thousand looms accounted for half of all the silk-weaving looms in operation in Shanghai.[3]

Success itself bred problems for Meiya's managers, however. The highly skilled and productive young employees, aware of the company's prosperity, began to press for additional perquisites. In early 1927 a portion of the Meiya work force—inspired by the urgings of He Datong, a Marxist student who hailed from eastern Zhejiang—engaged in a brief work stoppage to demand a wage increase, greater job security, and recognition of a labor union. Although General Manager Cai initially balked at these requests, he reversed his position when He Datong paid a visit to Meiya headquarters with revolver in hand. The company agreed to a 40 percent wage hike, strike pay, no dismissals without just cause, and subsidy for a labor union. On March 21, 1927, the Meiya union was inaugurated. Shortly after Jiang Jieshi's April coup, however, He Datong was put under surveillance by the Guomindang authorities. When police raided a clandestine meeting of Communist labor organizers, He Datong fled to the street below—only to slip on a watermelon rind. Immediately apprehended, he was executed shortly thereafter at the age of twenty-four.[4]

With the demise of He Datong and the attendant dissolution of the Meiya labor union, the company, in an attempt to improve discipline among its newly hired employees, reneged on its earlier collective agreement. In 1930 a worker was fired on grounds of incompetence, and the remaining employees were required to sign an employment contract that substantially reduced their earlier rights. In protest, weavers at eight Meiya factories (1,229 men and women) struck for two weeks. The outcome was a partial victory for each side: in theory, the 1927 collective agreement would be honored, but at the same time workers would have to submit to an employment contract. Dissatisfied with the result, the weavers struck again two months later, in the summer of 1930. This time the protest lasted thirty-five days and ended with a settlement, negotiated by the Shanghai Bureau of Social Affairs, more favorable to the workers: the 1927 agreement was completely upheld, workers' bonuses were to be distributed, and recently hired temporary workers were to be given permanent-worker status.[5]

---

[3] *Meiya qikan* 1934/8/16: 2.

[4] *Shanghai sichou gongyunshi* [The labor movement of Shanghai silk weavers] (Shanghai, 1985), pp. 13–17.

[5] *Strikes and Lockouts*, 85–86; Number Two Archives (Nanjing), no. 722: 4–226.

The unrest of 1930 spelled not the end, but the beginning, of serious labor-management troubles for Meiya. A few years later, the sharp decline in the price of silk fabric (which dropped by some 50 percent from 1933 to 1934) precipitated another, more dramatic conflict. With a large supply of unemployed silk weavers milling about the city, Meiya's profit-hungry managers decided this was a convenient time to cut labor costs. In 1933, Meiya reduced workers' wages by 10 percent. The following year, the company announced a second round of wage cuts (averaging 15 percent). This time, however, the employees were not so compliant. In the spring of 1934, workers at all ten of Meiya's factories—4,500 men, women, and children—went on strike. Pointing out that the company had enjoyed record sales in 1933, the strikers demanded restoration of their pre-1933 wages. For more than fifty frenzied and often violent days, they pressed their case—with management, city and Party officials, police, and public. In the process the strikers forged links with outside allies, most notably the Communist Youth League. These connections would cost them dearly, for the strike ended with the abrupt dismissal of some 143 workers accused of radical sympathies. But government suspicions notwithstanding, the strike was not simply the brainchild of outside Communist agitators. Its impressive organization and articulate demands were features commonly found in the protest of factory artisans: the classic artisan strike is one in which skilled workers resist capitalist initiatives by recourse to preexisting organizations and moralistic claims. Thus, Meiya weavers practiced a style of politics befitting their reputation as "labor aristocrats."

The unsuccessful strike of 1934 marked the end of this particular type of silk-weaver protest, however. In subsequent years, as weavers became more "proletarianized," outside parties played a greater role in their political activities. With the recovery of Shanghai's textile industry in 1936–1937, dozens of small silk-weaving enterprises reopened. Officially sponsored unions found ready recruits among the recently rehired employees. The 1937 strike wave, which touched more than two hundred of the city's silk-weaving factories, was testimony to the broad reach of the newly established unions. Thanks to government (and gangster) connections, the union-sponsored strikes proved somewhat more successful in attaining their demands, but not without a substantial decline in worker independence.

Had the story of the Shanghai silk weavers ended with the close of the Nanjing decade, it would be a sad tale indeed. By the time of the Japanese invasion in the summer of 1937, the weavers seemed to have lost many of the distinguishing features of a labor aristocracy: pride, control, autonomy. More exploitative forms of management and increased political interference had left these once fortunate workers in a much less enviable position. But of course the Shanghai labor movement did *not* disappear in the wake of the Japanese occupation. During the Sino-Japanese War (1937–1945) and subsequent Civil War (1945–1949) periods, worker activism—inspired increasingly by Communist revolutionaries returned from their sojourn in the countryside—grew in both frequency and political impact. At the forefront of this resurgence in labor unrest stood the silk weavers; proletarianized and politicized by their experiences under the Nanjing regime, these workers were to play a key role in the development of the radical labor movement that eventually helped unravel Guomindang control and usher in a new socialist regime.

"Modern" and "Traditional" Weavers

Who were these silk weavers and how did they manage to become such a significant political force? The numerical strength of Shanghai silk weavers fluctuated dramatically in these years: at the height of the Depression, employed silk weavers numbered fewer than ten thousand, but with the recovery of the industry in 1936–37 more than forty thousand silk weavers were working in the city.[6] Within this sizable and shifting work force, we can distinguish two rather different types of weavers. The most secure and most prestigiously employed group hailed from the eastern Zhejiang counties of Shengxian and Dongyang. These workers were educated young men and women who began their weaving careers with employment in the new, modernized factories of Meiya and other large companies. The move to Shanghai was for them a form of upward mobility. From the more than twenty-five hundred job application forms that remain in the Meiya archives, we can see that the great majority of new recruits came from peasant families. Yet these young weavers, most of whom were were still in their twenties when they entered the factory, were unusual peasant sons and daughters inasmuch as nearly all had received at least an elementary education.[7]

A different sort of worker came from the traditional rural handicraft areas of Hangzhou, Huzhou, and Suzhou. Raised in families that had practiced small-scale silk weaving for generations, these workers tended to be older and less well educated, driven out of their homes in the countryside by the decline of the rural handicraft industry. For them, the

---

[6] "Sizhiye" [The silk-weaving industry] (unpublished manuscript in the archives of the Shanghai Number Four Silk-Weaving Factory, 1982).

[7] Shanghai Municipal Archives, no. 199-48: 1–6.

move to Shanghai represented an unwelcome process of "proletarianization" in which they lost much of the freedom and control characteristic
of traditional artisan production. Such weavers usually worked in small
factories for lower wages and less job security than that enjoyed by their
counterparts in the more "modern" sector of the industry.[8]

The contrast between the two types of weavers is suggested by a look
at their literacy rates. A 1938 investigation among Shanghai silk weavers
found that male weavers from eastern Zhejiang had an amazingly high
literacy rate of 95 percent, with 30 percent having a middle school education, 40 percent a primary school education, and an additional 25 percent at least some minimal degree of literacy. Among women weavers
from eastern Zhejiang, the literacy rate was found to be 35 percent. In
large part, this high literacy level was the result of Meiya's early hiring
practices. By contrast, silk weavers from Hangzhou, Suzhou, and
Huzhou—who comprised the overwhelming majority of workers at
smaller factories—had far lower rates: 20–30 percent literacy among
males and even lower levels for females.[9]

About half of those employed in the Shanghai silk-weaving industry
were women. In the smaller factories, women tended to be confined to
the Preparation Department (zhunbei bu), whereas men worked in the
Weaving Department (jizhi bu), performing the skilled work of operating
the looms. This division of labor by gender perpetuated traditional practice in the Zhejiang countryside; silk weaving had usually been a male
occupation in which weavers were responsible for the operation, maintenance, and repair of their looms. Women, it was widely believed, should
not be engaged in the unseemly behavior of climbing about fixing complicated machinery. At the Meiya Company, Cai Shengbai's new
management procedures led to a break with this traditional division of
labor. Finding that women weavers were often as productive as (or even
more productive than) men, Meiya hired large numbers of female
weavers at wages only 80–90 percent of the pay for males. The intention was to reduce costs as well as to create a more docile labor force,
since popular wisdom held that women workers were less demanding
than men. Weavers at Meiya—whether male or female—were relieved
of the burden of machine repair by specialized mechanics trained at the
Hangzhou Technical Institute.[10]

---

[8] Zhu Bangxing, Shanghai chanye, p. 146.

[9] Ibid., p. 143.

[10] Xu Xijuan, personal interview conducted at the Shanghai Number Nine Silk-Weaving
Factory, 1987/6/2; "Sizhiye"; A Ying, "Chouchang de nügong" [Women workers in the
silk-weaving factories], Shenghuo zhishi, no. 39 (1946), p. 4.

Differences in native place, educational level, and employment conditions were also reflected in the popular culture of these two groups of Shanghai silk weavers. The young, securely employed literates from eastern Zhejiang prided themselves on being sophisticated urbanites, fully attuned to the ways of the big city. When they had saved up some money, they spent it on the accoutrements of a "modern" life-style: Western clothing, leather shoes, trolley rides, movie tickets, foreign food. These young weavers were seldom religious, and their friendship and mutual aid clubs were not of the traditional secret-society or sworn-brotherhood sort. Marriages among them were rarely arranged by family heads back in the countryside; instead they were often love matches with a simple wedding ceremony—or no ceremony at all for those who preferred the cohabitation popular among the Shanghai students whose habits they so admired.

They had not abandoned all their native eastern Zhejiang customs in the move to the big city, however. Many of the silk weavers were talented singers of Shaoxing opera, a skill they parlayed as guest performers in local teahouses. At the Meiya Company, weavers formed a Shaoxing opera troupe that served as the organizational nucleus of the 1927 strike.[11] It was said that their stage experience and penchant for the dramatic made the young weavers effective public speakers; certainly the Meiya strike of 1934 offered ample evidence of their ability to inspire a crowd. Identification with native place was thus still salient among these "modern" labor aristocrats. The early Communist network at Meiya was in fact organized largely along native-place lines.[12]

The largely illiterate workers from Hangzhou, Huzhou, and Suzhou adhered to a rather different set of norms. Peasant-artisans by upbringing and instinct, these traditional weavers brought along much more of their rural heritage to soften the trauma of adjustment to life in Shanghai. Wearing the familiar clothing of the countryside (blue cotton jacket and trousers), they lived together in crowded, squalid conditions. For the most part, they were deeply religious: many were Buddhists, a few were Christian converts, and virtually all believed in the unalterable power of fate. Marriages and funerals were an opportunity to rehearse traditional rituals, complete with raucous drinking and feasting, which reinforced native solidarities. Kinship ties remained strong among these weavers,

---

[11] Li Shufa, interview transcript in the archives of the Shanghai Number Four Silk-Weaving Factory, 1969/12/24; Shen Rongqing, dossier in the archives of the Shanghai Number Four Silk-Weaving Factory, n.d.

[12] Zhou Zhixin, interview transcript in the archives of the Shanghai Number Four Silk-Weaving Factory, 1982/6/5.

who often entered the silk factory in entire families. When these immigrants sought a Shanghai role model for emulation, it was not the student
but the gangster to whom they turned. Sworn brotherhoods, sisterhoods,
and secret societies helped provide some social identity for these
uprooted rustics.[13] As one woman weaver recalled,

> Ten of us in the Preparation Department of the Dacheng silk-weaving fac-
> tory formed a sisterhood. Elder sisters one and two were from Hangzhou,
> as were sisters five and six. On our day off we met at a pavilion in a park
> and the one of us who could write scribbled all our names on a red piece of
> paper. She also wrote our group motto: "Share good fortune and troubles
> alike." The paper was kept by the eldest sister. After the ceremony we all
> went to an amusement center to enjoy ourselves.[14]

Such groups could constitute an important informal support structure
within the factory. The informant above remembered that she once
avoided paying a hefty fine imposed by her supervisor only because her
nine sisters threatened to engage in a slowdown unless she was par-
doned.[15]

   This basic division between "modern" and "traditional" silk weavers
in Shanghai was reflected in their political activities. To oversimplify
somewhat, the literate, urbane workers from eastern Zhejiang (active in
the strikes of 1930 and 1934) tended to undertake well organized protests for clearly articulated demands—demands that might even lay claim
to new rights and resources. Workers from rural weaving backgrounds
(active in the 1936–1937 strikes) tended, by contrast, to engage in
briefer protests that seldom went beyond an effort to reclaim lost ground.
Yet despite this (often blurred) distinction, the gulf separating Shanghai's
silk weavers was not so vast as to preclude cooperation. Unlike the
situation in many of Shanghai's industries, among silk weavers fights
between rival native-place associations were rare—at least until union
organizers purposely stimulated such tensions. Sharing a sense of pride
in their work as artisans, silk weavers were capable of uniting in pursuit
of common goals. While Meiya's educated employees stood in 1934 at
the forefront of agitation among Shanghai silk weavers, workers in
smaller enterprises were quick to lend support. Just as Meiya's General
Manager functioned as an industry leader (having formed the Shanghai
Silk Weaving Employers' Association in February 1934), so his workers
played a vanguard role for other silk weavers in the city.

---

[13] *Shanghai chanye,* pp. 141–143.
[14] Wan Wenhua, interview transcript in the archives of the Shanghai Number Four Silk-
Weaving Factory, 1982/7/21.
[15] Ibid.

The Meiya Strike of 1934

The wage cut that precipitated the famous 1934 Meiya strike was prompted by anxiety over recent market trends. In 1928–1931, buyers in India and Southeast Asia had accounted for more than half the company's total sales. Over the next few years, however, Japanese competitors made significant gains in both markets; by 1934, Meiya's exports had dropped to 28 percent of total sales. While 1933 had certainly been a boom year for the company (with total sales reaching a record high of more than six million yuan), Cai Shengbai feared that the shift to reliance on the domestic market spelled hard times ahead.[16] He therefore hoped to reduce operating expenses in anticipation of a business decline. According to company figures, wages at Meiya comprised an unusually high proportion of operating expenses, equivalent to 18 percent of sales. Thus it was from the payroll that Cai hoped to make the reductions to ward off a feared drop in profits.[17]

Management announced the decision to cut wages on March 2, the day after workers had returned from their New Year's holiday. The following morning, weavers at the company's Number Six factory—the branch that housed Meiya's experimental laboratory and which therefore employed many of its most skilled craftsmen—refused to show up for work.[18]

Protest was no stranger to the artisans at Number Six. Several months earlier, ten of the most skilled craftsmen at the factory (operators of the complicated "five-tiered looms") had started a slowdown to demand higher wages. They were soon supported by others at Number Six: a small progressive reading group that had predated the strike expanded into a larger friendly society (*youyi hui*) of forty to fifty people, which also joined the work stoppage. After a month's agitation, the weavers succeeded in winning the wage hike for which they had struggled. Energized by this victory, the workers at Number Six inaugurated an all-company friendly society, with branches at each of the ten Meiya factories.[19]

Behind the scenes, a clandestine network of politicized workers buttressed the openly established friendly society. At Meiya Number Four, for example, some ten to fifteen weavers had joined the underground Communist Party during the initial years of Guomindang rule.[20] At

---

16 Zhang Shouyu, *Jindai Jiangnan sizhi gongye shi;* Yi Wei, "Meiya chouchang bagong de yanzhongxing" [The severity of the Meiya silk factory strike], *Nüsheng* 2:2 (1934): 2.

17 *Meiya qikan* 1934/8/16.

18 *Shanghai chanye,* p. 151.

19 Ibid., 162.

20 Zhou Zhixin, 1981/12/21.

Number Six, ten weavers had entered the Communist Youth League. Several of these league members elected to remain at their factory over the New Year holiday in 1934, preparing for an anticipated additional round of wage cuts by Meiya management.[21]

Thus there was already an organizational network in place when on March 3 the strikers at Number Six dispatched deputies to the other branch factories in search of support.[22] They went first to nearby Number Nine, which had an all-female work force of relatively unskilled laborers. The superintendent of Number Nine, who happened to be at Meiya headquarters when the strike first began, boasted confidently to the general manager that the docile workers at his factory fully accepted the wage cut and would definitely not join the protest. Much to his chagrin, however, the women weavers at Number Nine were the first to follow the lead of their neighboring strikers. Within a few days the rest of Meiya's workers, except for the apprentices (numbering five hundred youths), had also joined the protest.[23]

Workers at each of the ten branch factories rapidly organized into small groups of about five to ten people. Each small group chose its own group leader, who thereby became a member of that branch factory's strike committee. The ten branch committees, in turn, selected three delegates to form the central strike committee, headquartered at Number Six and chaired by a Communist Youth League member from that factory. Under this central governing committee were established five functional units: general affairs, organization, propaganda, liaison, and security. The general affairs unit handled documents and accounts; the organization division was in charge of registration, investigation, and marshaling of strikers; the propaganda office, directed by another Communist Youth League member from Number Six, solicited monetary contributions and published a weekly newsletter about the strike; the liaison department was responsible for initiating negotiations and keeping in contact with outside parties; the security personnel were charged with

---

[21] Zhang Qi, personal interview at the Shanghai Labor Union, 1987/6/16.

[22] Here I take issue with the otherwise generally valuable account of the Meiya strike by Edward Hammond, who asserts that "organization of the strike proceeded relatively slowly for several reasons, the most important being the lack of any pre-existing organization." Edward Roy Hammond, "Organized Labor in Shanghai, 1927–1937" (Ph.D. dissertation, University of California, Berkeley, 1978), p. 222. The major sources for this chapter—*Shanghai chanye yu Shanghai zhigong,* the Shanghai Municipal Police File, worker interviews, and government and factory archives—offer a much fuller, and quite different, picture of worker organization. None of these informative sources was available to Hammond. Still, Hammond is correct in pointing out that unions played next to no role in the 1934 strike.

[23] *Shanghai chanye,* p. 152.

maintaining order, protecting delegates at meetings, gathering intelligence, guarding factory machinery, provisioning food, and the like.[24]

These rapid organizational developments reflected preexisting informal networks among the workers. At Number Six, for example, the picket group in charge of security comprised a twelve-man sworn brotherhood association that had predated the strike by five years.[25] Native-place bonds were also used in organizing workers. Zhang Qi, a skilled weaver at Number Six who hailed from the Zhejiang county of Pujiang, quickly succeeded in mobilizing the many women weavers at Number Seven who shared his native-place affiliation.[26] Probably because of such long-standing bonds, strikers were notably responsive to the directions of the strike leadership. As one participant recalled,

> During the strike the workers were very disciplined. Every day we went to the factory to receive instructions. When we got to the factory, first we bowed three times in front of a portrait of Sun Yat-sen. Then we followed the instructions of the strike leaders. Some of us were assigned to guard duty, while others were sent out to collect contributions.[27]

Fortified by their remarkable organizational apparatus, the Meiya strikers proceeded to articulate their grievances. On March 9, they issued a statement of their position, notable for its defensive, moralistic tone: "So long as we can survive (*shengcun*), so long as management sustains our survival, we will gladly suffer tribulation and oppression.... All we demand is survival.... Now wages have been cut again and survival cannot be sustained, so why must we continue to suffer day after day? Under such pressures, we have no choice but to resort to our ultimate weapon: strike!"[28]

Judged by comparison with workers in other industries, the silk weavers' plight was in fact not nearly so dismal as the Meiya manifesto suggested. In 1934, silk weavers remained one of the most highly paid groups of workers in Shanghai, below only shipbuilders, printers and mechanics. Their hourly wage rate (Ch$0.087) was a full three times the amount that workers in the unskilled silk-reeling industry received, for example. Moreover, even among silk weavers the Meiya workers were especially fortunate, with wages averaging double those paid to weavers

---

[24] Ibid., p. 152; Shanghai Municipal Police (International Settlement) Files (microfilms from the U.S. National Archives), D-5802.

[25] Yu Lin, interview transcript in the archives of the Shanghai Number Four Silk-Weaving Factory, 1982/5/8.

[26] Zhang Qi, 1987/6/16.

[27] Ge Sulan, interview transcript in the archives of the Shanghai Number Four Silk-Weaving Factory, 1982/7/17.

[28] Luo Gengmo, "Meiya gongqiao shimo," pp. 229–231.

in smaller, more traditional enterprises in the city.[29] Cai Shengbai's wage cuts were designed to bring the Meiya pay scale in line with prevailing wages in the industry, thereby increasing the competitiveness of his products.[30] It was not *absolute* deprivation, but rather the sharp *relative* decline in income, that drove the weavers to protest. As table 2 indicates, in 1934 wages in the Shanghai silk-weaving industry reached their lowest point in five years, a precipitous drop from the high pay that had obtained before the first round of Meiya cuts in 1933.

Meiya's silk weavers hoped to halt their recent reversals by appealing to the sympathy of their employer. They argued that the key issue was the "moral economy" question of whether wages were sufficient to maintain a decent livelihood for a worker's family, rather than the "rational" question of whether wages occupied too high a percentage of company expenses.[31] Having learned from past experience that the Bureau of Social Affairs—the city's official agency for labor dispute mediation—was often ineffective, the strikers decided initially to negotiate directly with Meiya management. Accordingly, the central strike committee notified General Manager Cai Shengbai of its intention to open discussions on the afternoon of March 11 at the Number One factory on rue Bremier de Montmorand in the French Concession.

On the agreed upon day, some forty workers' representatives—accompanied by more than two hundred of their security personnel—arrived on schedule at the appointed location. The general manager did not show up, however; instead he sent word that the negotiation site should be changed to the company's head office, in the International Settlement. Suspicious of the sudden alteration in arrangements, the workers' representatives refused to budge from factory Number One. A party of French police soon arrived on the scene to try to disperse the crowd, which had now grown to some three thousand people. To separate the negotiators from their thousands of supporters amassing outside Number One, an electric fence at the front gate of the factory was activated on orders from General Manager Cai. A battle then ensued between the police, equipped with tanks and machine guns, and the workers, armed just with stones. One woman worker was killed and many others seriously injured in the two-hour fray. The fighting abated only when the workers retreated to a public recreation ground at the city's West Gate. After an emotional mass meeting in which indignant spokesmen rebuked Meiya management for having betrayed their trust,

[29] Number Two Archives, no. 722, pp. 4–224.
[30] Luo Gengmo, "Meiya gongqiao shimo," pp. 228–229.
[31] Ibid., pp. 230–231.

Table 2

Wages in the Shanghai Silk Industry, 1930–1934

(average hourly rates)

	1930	1931	1932	1933
Silk weaving	.096	.091	.112	.104
Silk reeling	.044	.041	.034	.038

SOURCE: *Wage Rates in Shanghai* (Shanghai, 1935), p. 54.

the strikers decided to change strategy and petition the Bureau of Social Affairs for redress.[32]

Following a series of brainstorming sessions to agree on specific demands, in a couple of days the strikers were ready to submit a formal petition to the Bureau of Social Affairs. On March 13 more than a thousand workers marched on Civic Center to present their appeal, requesting that (1) the Meiya management be held responsible for the medical expenses incurred by the injured and for compensation to the family of the deceased worker and also be instructed to issue pay for the strike period and restore the previous wage scale and (2) the French authorities be ordered to bring the police officers responsible for the assault to justice, to compensate the strikers, and to insert an apology in the press providing assurance that such incidents would not be repeated. The Bureau of Social Affairs promised only to give the requests due consideration.[33]

While awaiting some official government action, the strikers turned to the public for support. The heavy-handed tactics of the French police had provided a powerful weapon in the fight for public sympathy. Shortly after the March 11 incident, a strike support committee was established among workers in the eastern district. Weavers in other parts of the city—the French Concession and Nandao in particular—were also quick to lend assistance in the form of both money and moral support. Even Shanghai's rickshaw pullers displayed sympathy for the strike by allowing Meiya propaganda teams to ride free of charge.

To spread their message as widely as possible, members of the Meiya central strike committee—making good use of their literary skills—issued an open letter to the citizens of Shanghai. This manifesto, which was quickly reprinted in the major newspapers, blamed Meiya's general

---

[32] *Shanghai chanye,* p. 153–4; Shanghai Police Files, D-5802.

[33] Shanghai Police Files, D-5802.

manager Cai Shengbai for having ordered the police assault that left one worker dead and dozens more severely wounded and indicted him for failing to share the company's growing prosperity with its workers:[34]

> The Meiya Silk-Weaving Company is the giant of Shanghai's silk-weaving industry. Its business is flourishing, with enormous profits each year. Last year total sales were more than six million yuan, higher than in any previous year. But General Manager Cai Shengbai doesn't understand the meaning of cooperation between labor and management; he only knows how to increase company profits. He uses every possible scheme to exploit the workers. Recently he plotted to make further cuts in wages which are already at the bare minimum, leaving workers unable to maintain a livelihood and giving rise to this strike. Surprisingly, Cai Shengbai not only refused to seek an amicable solution; he has also used force to suppress the workers. On March 11 the workers had chosen representatives to meet with Cai Shengbai at the main factory on Montmorand Road for direct negotiations about conditions for resuming work. At that time Mr. Cai not only purposely avoided the meeting, but also closed the iron gates and activated the electric fence to imprison the workers' representatives who had entered the factory. Moreover, he connived with the French police to dispatch armed troops to surround the workers who were standing outside the factory patiently awaiting news. Suddenly, the police attacked with pistols and iron bars. The unarmed workers suffered many casualties. Woman worker Xu Guifen was killed by a bullet in the head. More than forty workers were seriously wounded, and countless others received lighter injuries. Weak, defenseless women workers comprised most of the wounded. This violent use of foreign police power to murder our compatriots is comparable to the May Thirtieth tragedy. The workers are determined to carry on the struggle. We will not rest until we have expelled the violent, senseless capitalist running dog Cai Shengbai, have eliminated the irrational wage standard, and have avenged the death and injuries among the workers. People of all stations in life, having a sense of justice, must feel anger about this massacre. We hope you will advocate public morality in the form of punishment for the culprits. Moreover, we hope you will offer spiritual and material help to the starving workers.[35]

With this open letter, the strikers drew a sharp and visible line between themselves and management. No longer were China's "labor aristocrats" willing to undertake private negotiations in hopes of appealing to the moral sensibilities of their employer. Now the battle was a public one, which ordinary citizens as well as government agencies were invited to join. It was at this stage that outside Communist organizers,

---

[34] Ibid.; Luo Gengmo, "Meiya gongqiao shimo," p. 229; *Shanghai dijiu sizhichang* [The Shanghai Number Nine Silk-Weaving Factory] (Shanghai, 1983).

[35] Number Two Archives, no. 722, pp. 4–224.

attracted by the apparent class consciousness of this once quiescent group of workers, became more actively involved in the silk weavers' strike.

Tea shops near the Meiya factories, where workers gathered to chat about the progress of their struggle, were a natural focus of Communist mobilization efforts. Under the pretext of looking for friends or relatives, young Communist activists sought out sympathetic types among the tea-house patrons. In this way, they managed to make a few contacts among strikers at factories Number One and Five.[36] Over the next several weeks, resolutions exhorting the workers to more radical activities were issued by a number of Communist agencies: the Shanghai Western District Committee of the Communist Party, the Jiangsu Provincial Committee of the Communist Youth League, and even the Central Committee of the Communist Party (signed by Mao Zedong in Jiangxi).[37] A series of articles in Communist Youth League publications emphasized the need for the Jiangsu Communist Youth League to assume control of the Meiya struggle.[38] Yet, despite this considerable attention, there is evidence that Communist agents were not entirely successful in their efforts to play a commanding role. An internal Party report, seized by the British police in early April, admitted that "although the attitude of the Meiya strikers is good, our own activities still remain outside the struggles." The report bemoaned a "lack of consolidated organization" and chided the workers' strike committee for being "unaware" of the division of responsibility between itself and the Communist Youth League.[39] Such "confusion" was obviously the product of a strike committee that operated independent of outside direction.

Communist agents may not have been fully effective in gaining control of strike leadership, but their efforts had important ramifications all the same. Fear of Communist direction hardened the position of Meiya's management and inclined the state authorities against the strikers. On March 15, the company issued an ultimatum: any worker who had not resumed work by March 17 would be considered to have resigned of his or her own volition, and new hands would be hired as replacements. On March 16, representatives of the strikers were called to the Bureau of Social Affairs to meet with government and Party officials. The

---

[36] Shanghai Police Files, D-5802; *Shanghai chanye,* p. 165.

[37] Shanghai Police Files, D-5802; *Hongse Zhonghua* [Red China] (Jiangxi), nos. 162, 169, 171, 178, 180 (March–April 1934); *Douzheng* [Struggle] (Shanghai), 1934/4/19.

[38] *Tuan de jianshe* [League construction] (Shanghai), no. 13, 1934/3/12; no. 15, 1934/4/13; no. 16, 1934/4/27; *Qunzhong de tuan* [League of the masses] (Shanghai), no. 3, 1934/4/6.

[39] Shanghai Police Files, D-5802.

authorities strongly advised the strikers to resume work immediately, pending mediation by government and Party agencies.[40]

On the morning of March 17, the deadline set by management for a return to work, it was clear that government persuasion had failed to soften the militancy of the strikers. Accordingly, the authorities decided to adopt sterner measures. Plainclothesmen were sent to the various Meiya branch factories to seek out and apprehend suspected ringleaders. At Number Six, an attempted arrest was averted only because an alert member of the strikers' security force managed to sink her teeth into the hand of the policeman before he could complete his assignment! At Number Five, however, workers' pickets proved less effective. A woman weaver by the name of Liu Jinshui was apprehended on suspicion of being a Communist and was carted off to the local police station.[41]

With a martyr to their cause now behind bars, the strikers found it even easier to elicit public sympathy. On the afternoon of March 17, strikers carrying bamboo baskets and white cloth banners inscribed with the characters "Meiya Silk-Weaving Factory Propaganda Group" visited various small silk-weaving concerns in the Jessfield Park and Zhabei districts to request As the propagandists shared recent news of the protest movement, sympathetic listeners filled the bamboo baskets with cash contributions.[42]

The following day, the strikers were ready for a more direct show of strength. At 8:00 A.M. on March 18, more than four thousand workers and supporters gathered at the West Gate police station to demand the release of Liu Jinshui. The officer in charge replied that he had no authority over the case, explaining that Liu had been arrested under direct orders from the Guomindang Central Executive Committee in Nanjing. Dissatisfied with this answer, the crowd refused to disperse. Instead, the protesters settled in for an all-night vigil, spreading themselves across the front gate of the station and into the surrounding streets so that all traffic in the vicinity was brought to a standstill. During the evening, several hundred workers from small silk-weaving factories in the French Concession and Nandao districts joined the sit-in. Merchants in the West Gate area sent food for the strikers, whose ranks were soon swelled by university students sympathetic to the cause. The following morning, dozens of silk weavers from factories in more distant parts of the city also arrived to lend support.[43] At 10:00 A.M., the chief of

---

[40] Ibid.; *Meiya qikan* 1934/8/16, pp. 3–7.

[41] Luo Gengmo, "Meiya gongqiao shimo," p. 234; Shanghai Police Files, D-5802; *Shanghai chanye*, p. 155.

[42] Shanghai Police Files, D-5802.

[43] Ibid.; *Shanghai chanye*, pp. 155–156; Luo Gengmo, "Meiya gongqiao shimo," p. 234.

Shanghai's Public Security Bureau—responding to the intense public pressure—issued orders to release the prisoner.

Overjoyed by this outcome, the victorious protesters led their freed martyr away in a boisterous and triumphant firecracker parade. Flushed with success, the strikers quickly drew up a new and more ambitious set of demands to present to Shanghai authorities. In addition to the restoration of pre-1933 wages, the workers called for full pay during the strike period, a guarantee against dismissals without just cause, elimination of fines as a form of punishment, and equal pay for men and women.[44] This last demand reflected the key role that women weavers were playing in the protest. Meiya's effort to create a more docile labor force by hiring women had evidently backfired. Women casualties in the March 11 incident, women pickets in the strike security force, a woman prisoner—all pointed to the pronounced activism of women workers.[45]

The release of Liu Jinshui gave the weavers an important psychological boost, but unfortunately for them it did not augur a more accommodating attitude on the part of the authorities. To the contrary, public security agents actually stepped up surveillance and arrests among Meiya activists. On March 27, a confidential report by a Guomindang agent sent from Nanjing to investigate the strike concluded that Communist elements had infiltrated the movement. The agent advocated harsh reprisals.[46] Over the next few weeks, more than a dozen strikers were apprehended (and several of them sentenced to detention) for distributing strike literature and soliciting financial contributions.[47]

Once again, however, police intervention worked to expand the strikers' support group. To protest the police intimidation, Meiya's five hundred young apprentices (employed for the most part at Factory Number Eight) stopped work on April 5. The move came as a surprise to management, since the traditional arrangement for apprentices relieved the company of any responsibility for the wages of these youngsters. At the start of their three- to five-year training period, apprentices were required to deposit a security payment of Ch$30 to $50, nonrefundable in the event of leaving the company before completion of the training period.[48] Although apprentices were surely the poorest of Meiya's workers, the fact that they received no wages would seem to have rendered

---

[44] Shanghai Police Files, D-5802; *Shanghai chanye,* p. 153.

[45] Bai Shi, "Zai Meiya bagong zhong duiyu nügong de renshi" [Getting to know women workers in the course of the Meiya strike], *Nüsheng* 4:10 (1934).

[46] Number Two History Archives, no. 722:4–224.

[47] Shanghai Police Files, D-5802.

[48] Lieu, *Silk Industry of China,* p. 222; *Shanghai chanye,* p. 140; Ma Chaojun, ed., *Zhongguo laogong yundong shi* [A history of the Chinese labor movement] (Taibei, 1954), p. 1190.

them unlikely participants in a protest against wage reductions. However, on the day after this group of workers joined the struggle, the strikers issued an updated set of demands that evidenced the concerns of their new recruits. The new list called for the company to abolish the practice of requiring security money from apprentices, to protect apprentices from assault by foremen, and to provide every apprentice with a loom at the end of his or her training period.[49]

With all the employees now on strike, Meiya served as a kind of magnet for other disgruntled workers in the area. Strikers in Shanghai's rubber factory sent delegates to Meiya's central strike committee for advice on how to organize effectively. Workers in Shanghai's pharmaceutical, tobacco, and umbrella industries launched strikes under Meiya inspiration. Even in the interior, in the traditional silk centers of Huzhou and Hangzhou, weavers followed the lead of their city cousins in striking for higher wages and improved working conditions.[50]

The Meiya strike was welcomed not only by other strike-prone workers, but by some employers as well. Other silk-weaving concerns in Shanghai naturally profited from Meiya's work stoppage. Not surprisingly, these rival factories contributed heavily to the strike fund that sustained Meiya's militants during their lengthy protest.[51]

Seeing its market captured by competitors and without even any apprentices to carry on production, Meiya management tried to retaliate. Its first step was to reduce the quality of food still being served in workers' cafeterias. Meat was withdrawn from the already meager menu, and only the cheapest of vegetables were provided. The decline in service was quickly met by heated protest. At Number Nine, two hundred women workers engaged in a brief hunger strike.[52] Weavers at Number Four (led by the secretary of the underground Communist Party branch at the factory) barricaded the superintendent in his room. Police who tried to climb the factory fence in a rescue mission retreated hastily when workers unleashed buckets of night soil from the roof. After two days and nights under siege, the factory superintendent signed a guarantee of improved meals and paid one hundred dollars in food subsidies.[53]

With tensions between workers and management running high, the Bureau of Social Affairs decided to attempt a more active role in settling the dispute. Green Gang leader Du Yuesheng was asked to intervene in

---

[49] Shanghai Police Files, D-5802.
[50] *Shanghai chanye*, pp. 156–157.
[51] Ibid., p. 157.
[52] Shanghai Police Files, D-5802.
[53] *Shanghai chanye*, pp. 157–158; *Meiya disi zhichouchang* [The Meiya Number Four Silk-Weaving Factory] (Shanghai, 1982), p. 33.

the case, but his efforts to talk the strikers into giving up their struggle proved fruitless. With few of his own followers among the Meiya work force, Du was powerless to effect a solution. Pressed by an April 8 cable from Jiang Jieshi ordering an immediate end to the strike, the bureau put together a formal mediation committee consisting of one representative from the Bureau of Social Affairs (as chair), one representative from the Shanghai Guomindang, one representative from the Public Security Bureau, and two representatives each from Meiya management and Meiya workers. With this committee duly constituted, the bureau scheduled an official mediation meeting for the morning of April 10.[54]

Before 10:00 A.M. on April 10, the time when mediation was supposed to commence, hundreds of strikers converged on the Bureau of Social Affairs at Civic Center. Marching two abreast and carrying portraits and statues of Sun Yat-sen, they distributed handbills proclaiming "Labor is sacred" (*laogong shensheng*). Once assembled outside the offices of the Bureau of Social Affairs, the weavers sang their strike theme song—"How sad, how sad, how terribly sad; Meiya workers' wages have been cut so bad"—and chanted in unison, "We want to work! We want to eat!" Much to their consternation, however, it soon became clear that no mediation could take place: Meiya's management had again failed to show. In place of negotiators, Meiya sent word that it had decided to shut down its factories. Since operations were being suspended, mediation was pointless. To demonstrate that the decision was more than idle talk, the company summarily closed the doors of all its workers' cafeterias, leaving the strikers without a regular source of food.[55]

Meanwhile the strikers, insisting that the Bureau of Social Affairs order a reopening of their cafeterias and enforce some acceptable settlement of the dispute, laid siege to Civic Center. At about 6:00 P.M., when the staff of the Bureaus of Social Affairs, Education, and Public Health were preparing to go home for the night, the demonstrators sealed all doors and placed a tight cordon around the building. No one was to be permitted to leave until Meiya's representatives arrived to negotiate. As a cold rain began to fall, thousands of workers settled in to enforce their blockade. One intrepid young protester even delivered her baby in the dank, open air at Civic Center that night![56]

That the Meiya strike should have assumed overtly political proportions is not surprising. As Edward Shorter and Charles Tilly have argued,

---

[54] Luo Gengmo, "Meiya gongqiao shimo," p. 235; *Meiya disi zhichouchang,* pp. 33–34.

[55] Ma Chaojun, *Zhongguo laogong yundong shi,* p. 1191; *Shanghai dijiu sizhichang,* p. 23; *Meiya disi zhichouchang,* p. 34.

[56] Shanghai Police Files, D-1791.

strikes are by their very nature political (as much as economic) modes of activity:

> Workers, when they strike, are merely extending into the streets their normal processes of political participation...and the people whom these displays are intended to impress are not individual employers against whom—for reasons of political convenience—the strike is ostensibly directed, but the political authorities of the land, in the form of either the government itself or powerful members of the polity.[57]

With the Meiya strikers now occupying the heart of Shanghai's municipal government, a large force of police and public security agents was called in. By the next morning, some seven to eight hundred police and six fire engines had reached the scene. In the midst of this confusion, Shanghai's mayor, Wu Tiecheng, arrived at Civic Center and while making his way to his office was surrounded by strikers demanding his help in bringing about a settlement. Alarmed by this direct confrontation, the police decided to charge the workers. Brandishing batons and turning fire hoses on the crowd, they succeeded in dispersing the protesters—but not without inflicting a good many injuries in the process.[58]

This April 11 incident marked a turning point in the Meiya strike.[59] Although the police assault generated public support for the strikers (workers at more than a hundred small silk-weaving factories in the southern and eastern districts of Shanghai staged a brief sympathy strike soon after the April 11 affair), the state authorities had lost any empathy for the workers' cause. Having experienced firsthand the disruptive effects of the strike, Shanghai officials were now more inclined than ever to identify with the position of Meiya's management. Cooperation between capitalists and the state was also promoted by new tactics on the part of Meiya's general manager; during the course of the strike, Cai Shengbai compiled a clipping file of newspaper reports on successful

---

[57] Edward Shorter and Charles Tilly, *Strikes in France, 1830–1968* (London and New York, 1974), p. 343.

[58] Shanghai Police Files, D-5802; *Shanghai chanye*, p. 159.

[59] Recent assessments of the Meiya strike by scholars in the People's Republic of China point to the April 11 protest as evidence of the disastrous effects of the "ultra-leftist" labor policies of the day. By this interpretation, the Meiya strike committee is blamed for having adopted a Wang Ming line of "blind adventurism" in a situation where a moderate strategy of behind-the-scenes negotiation would have been more effective. The ultimate defeat of the Meiya strike, in this view, is attributable to misguided Party policy. Shen Yixing, *Gongyunshi mingbian lu* [Ruminations on the labor movement] (Shanghai: Shanghai Academy of Social Sciences Press, 1987), pp. 140–142. While it is certainly conceivable that the April 11 demonstration escalated tensions to the point where compromise became impossible, it is less clear that the responsibility for this decision should rest with the "ultra-leftist" line in Communist Party labor strategy.

suppression efforts against textile strikes around the world.[60] Perhaps taking a cue from these materials, Cai decided to adopt a more aggressive role in putting an end to the strike. Sharing native-place origins with the director of the Bureau of Social Affairs, Meiya's General Manager reinforced these ties by offering handsome compensation to the director and three of his underlings for their assistance in bringing the strike to a speedy conclusion.[61] The government's hardened attitude was seen in a series of public security moves intended to weaken the strike: a temporary martial law was declared, all public meetings were prohibited, and police were sent to every Meiya factory to round up activists. At Number Four, eleven strike leaders—including the Communist Party branch secretary—were arrested and sent to the Wusong-Shanghai garrison headquarters for detention.[62]

On April 13, the Executive Committee of the Guomindang in Nanjing—which had also been contacted by Cai Shengbai—cabled the Shanghai party branch with orders to take all necessary measures to break the Meiya strike immediately. Party Central expressed alarm over the involvement of "bad elements" (*buliang fenzi*)—a euphemism for Communist agents. By the next morning, the number of arrests at Meiya factories had risen to forty.[63]

Encouraged by these stiff government measures, Meiya management adopted a similarly hard line. Factory dormitories were locked up, forcing the workers to take refuge with friends or roam the streets in search of shelter. (Many workers resorted to sleeping in the public May Thirtieth martyrs' cemetery on the outskirts of town.) Homeless and leaderless, the silk weavers began to lose their fighting spirit.

The central strike committee, weakened by the loss of so many of its key members, found it difficult to retain control over the workers. Meiya's apprentices, enticed by the company's promise to provide them with their own looms if they returned to their jobs, were the first to resume work. Weavers at Number Two and Number Five then asked the strike committee to call off the walkout, threatening to resume work on their own if necessary. In a desperate attempt to salvage the situation, the strike committee announced a mass demonstration to petition city authorities on April 21. More than a thousand bedraggled workers showed up at the local Guomindang headquarters on the appointed day

[60] Shanghai Municipal Archives, no. 199-48-207.

[61] *Meiya disi zhichouchang*, p. 28; Jiang Hongjiao, "Ziwo pipan" [Self-criticism], in the archives of the Shanghai Number Four Silk-Weaving Factory.

[62] Shanghai Police Files, D-5802.

[63] Ibid.

to demand the release of the arrested workers and the immediate reopening of workers' dormitories and cafeterias. The limited nature of the demands (which made no mention of wages) showed the sorry state to which the movement had sunk. Guomindang authorities, confident that they now held the upper hand, were firm in their answer: Meiya would be told to reopen the dormitories, but the workers must resume work at once. Tired and defeated, the silk-weavers were back on the job the next morning, bringing to an end their fifty-one-day walkout.

When they returned to work, the strikers found that things had changed in their absence. They were informed that the factories were being reorganized and that all workers must therefore reregister with the company. The process of reregistration, it soon became clear, entailed an investigation of one's involvement in the strike; as a consequence, 143 activists were dismissed.[64]

On April 27, Nanjing—responding to a direct appeal from Cai Shengbai—instructed the Shanghai authorities to deal harshly with "reactionary troublemakers" in the Meiya strike.[65] Three days later, the forty previously arrested workers were sentenced to varying degrees of punishment: most received prison terms of twenty to forty days; the Party secretary at Number Four, betrayed by two of his fellow cell members, was sentenced to five years behind bars.[66] With this legal verdict, the Meiya protest was brought to an official conclusion. What lessons were to be drawn from this long, and ultimately unsuccessful, exercise in workers' politics? For the Meiya strikers, the lesson was a bitter realization of the limitations of their own power. Theirs had been a classic "aristocratic" protest: organization was based upon small, preexisting networks of workshop friendship; demands were moderate, articulate, and phrased in a moral language with public appeal; outside assistance was welcomed, but leadership remained in the hands of the weavers themselves. Yet, clearly, this style of protest was ineffective against an employer whose search for profits numbed the sense of respect and moral obligation he had once felt for his skilled work force.

If workers harbored any hope that the previously cordial relationship with management might be restored, they were quickly disillusioned. Cai Shengbai, proclaiming that "this dispute has left a scar not on a single person or a single enterprise, but on our entire national industry," proceeded to take retaliatory measures. In the months following the strike,

[64] *Shanghai chanye,* pp. 160–161.
[65] Number Two History Archives, no. 722: 4–224.
[66] Shanghai Police Files, D-5802; Zhou Zhixin, 1981/12/21.

Meiya enforced a 30 percent wage cut, closed all workers' dormitories, and raised prices in factory cafeterias.[67]

Even more disheartening to the defeated weavers was the implementation of a loom rental system, whereby the company leased out its looms to members of the staff to manage on its behalf. With a guaranteed annual rental income, Meiya gained a predictable source of revenue and was relieved of the burden of dealing directly with the workers. Although the company remained responsible for raw materials and sales outlets, matters of hiring, training, and wages were entirely the personal responsibility of the staff members who leased the looms. Under this system, operating expenses were reduced (by about 15 percent) and Cai Shengbai solidified ties with his top staff at the same time that he put a comfortable distance between himself and the ordinary weavers. Among the workers, the loom rental system exacerbated divisions along native-place lines, inasmuch as staff foremen tended to exhibit favoritism toward workers with whom they shared such connections.[68]

In the aftermath of the strike, Meiya's once proud labor aristocrats lost many of the privileges that had previously distinguished them from less fortunate textile workers in the city. At the same time, other large silk-weaving factories in Shanghai, pressed by the general depression in the industry, reduced their scale of operations and adopted a loom rental system similar to Meiya's.[69] This change in the organization of the industry narrowed the gap between "modern" weavers—employed at larger factories with higher wages and better working conditions—and the "traditional" weavers who worked at smaller factories under less desirable terms.

As the structure of the industry changed, its work force attracted more interest from outside parties. The strike of 1934 had drawn attention to the heretofore unnoticed political potential of Shanghai's silk weavers. Earlier labor organizers, of either Communist or Guomindang affiliation, had tended to dismiss the possibility of a major protest among this relatively skilled and well paid group of workers. The Meiya strike, however, generated a new enthusiasm for mobilizing silk weavers.

This newfound interest on the part of outside organizers became evident during the course of the fifty-one-day strike itself. As we have seen, Communist agents attempted—albeit with limited success—to gain a

---

[67] *Qunzhong de tuan,* no. 8, 1934/8/24; *Meiya qikan* 1934/8/16, p. 2.

[68] *Meiya disi zhichouchang,* p. 19; *Shanghai dijiu sizhichang,* p. 31; Fu Yuanhua, interview transcript in the archives of the Shanghai Number Four Silk-Weaving Factory, 1982/12; Shanghai Municipal Archives, no. 199-48-207.

[69] *Shanghai zhi jizhi gongye,* p. 175.

deciding role in the protest. Such efforts were instrumental in igniting the interest of other outside parties as well. The Guomindang, for its part, sent agents (under the guise of newspaper reporters) to try to dilute the wording of strike petitions.[70] Official unions also showed some interest in the conflict, although at the time just one of Meiya's factories (Number Two) was endowed with such an organization. The union at Number Two became active only after the April 11 confrontation at Civic Center, when it worked to persuade weavers in that factory to withdraw support from the central strike committee.[71]

As the dust from the Meiya strike gradually settled, some two to three years after the conclusion of the conflict, a new pattern of silk weavers' politics became visible—a pattern in which officially sponsored unions played a leading role. The weavers gained powerful allies among the authorities, but at considerable cost to their independence and integrity.

The All-City Strikes of 1936–1937

The immediate aftermath of the Meiya strike saw a period of quiescence among Shanghai's silk weavers. Sobered by the defeat of their "modern" spokesmen and still suffering from severe economic depression, the city's weavers were loathe to undertake further struggles. Those strikes that did occur were small in scale and limited in goals. In 1935, the average silk weavers' strike numbered only fifty-five participants, compared to an average of nearly a thousand participants per strike the year before. Occurring in a time of acute depression, the strikes of 1935 were universally unsuccessful in forestalling wage reductions or worker dismissals.[72]

By late 1936, however, recovery in the silk-weaving industry brought an increase in both the frequency and success of protest. Improvement in the industry was due in large measure to illegally imported artificial silk from Japan. Cheap and plentiful, the contraband silk made it possible for small silk-weaving establishments to commence operations with very little capital. By the end of the year, some 480 silk-weaving factories were open in Shanghai, most of them tiny workshops with only a few looms.[73] A total of twenty-nine silk weavers' strikes occurred in 1936, by far the largest number of any year to date. The walkouts were

---

[70] *Shanghai chanye,* pp. 163–164.

[71] Ibid., p. 164.

[72] "Jin si nian lai."

[73] *Shanghai sichou gongye jieduanshi* [A periodized history of the Shanghai silk-weaving industry] (Shanghai, n.d.), p. 3.

brief in duration (averaging eight days) and modest in their goals, but increasingly effective in bringing results. Taking place for the most part among workers in smaller factories that had only recently resumed operations, these protests were a good deal less bold than the Meiya strike two years earlier. Absent now were the demands for gender equality and better treatment for apprentices that had distinguished the 1934 movement. Also missing in 1936 were many women participants. In most cases, these were all-male strikes for limited wage demands.[74] The conservatism and gender segregation that characterized these protests reflected the social composition and structure of work in smaller silk-weaving enterprises. (The one notable exception to this pattern was another Meiya strike. For two weeks in the late summer of 1936, 150 women and 100 men at factory Number Two struck to demand a reduction in the control of labor contractors, abolition of the graded wage scale, and enforcement of better treatment by job foremen.)[75]

The resurgence of widespread unrest among the silk-weaving community attracted the attention of Shanghai authorities, especially in the local Guomindang and Bureau of Social Affairs. Top-ranking officials in both agencies, embroiled in a bitter factional battle for power, saw the feisty silk weavers as a potential social base for their own ambitious designs. Accordingly, representatives of rival factions raced to found state-sponsored unions that would bring the silk weavers under their control.

On December 20, 1936, the first new silk-weavers' union was inaugurated at a meeting attended by six hundred people, including representatives of the Guomindang, the Bureau of Social Affairs, and the Guomindang-sponsored General Labor Union. Known as the District Four Silk-Weavers' Union, the new organization soon claimed three thousand members in 120 factories in the International Settlement east of Hongkou Creek. The chief force behind the union was an employee of the mediation section of the Bureau of Social Affairs. Making use of his native-place connections with weavers at several of the smaller silk factories in eastern Shanghai, he convinced his friends to unionize. The new union had an elaborate organizational structure (not unlike that of the Meiya strike committee), with sections in charge of general affairs, propaganda, mediation, security, organization, and liaison. Under the district union were some thirteen branch unions, controlling the more than one hundred factory committees. Each factory was organized into

---

[74] Shanghai Police Files, D-7506.
[75] "Jin si nian lai"; Shanghai Police Files, D-7506.

small groups, numbering some six hundred in all, of about five members each.[76]

Despite this impressive structure, the new union did not function altogether smoothly. According to police reports, at least two of the branch unions were actively plotting to usurp the leadership of the district union. The Ward Road branch (which included some 800 weavers at forty factories) was closely associated with the District Four Tobacco Workers' Union—a Green Gang–controlled branch of the General Labor Union that hoped to wrest control over silk weavers from rivals in the Bureau of Social Affairs. A second branch union (which included some 350 weavers employed, for the most part, at the Mei-feng factory) opposed the dictatorial manner of its parent union and identified closely with Mei-feng management.[77]

District unions were formed in other parts of Shanghai as well—with politics no less complicated than those of the fourth district. In January 1937 a District Three Silk-Weavers' Union was established in the western part of the city. The instigator, Wang Hao, was a member of the Peasant-Worker Section of the Shanghai Guomindang who had been sent to settle a five-factory strike in late 1936. A follower of Green Gang labor leaders Lu Jingshi and Zhu Xuefan (who were, in turn, top lieutenants of Green Gang chieftain Du Yuesheng), Wang was also a member of the Guomindang's paramilitary corps, the Blue Shirts. Since more than a few silk weavers in western Shanghai had received training from the Blue Shirts, Wang Hao was able to draw on the connection to develop a following among the workers. With official approval from the Shanghai Guomindang, he settled the five-factory strike in a manner satisfactory to the protesters. Using the five factories as a base, Wang then proceeded to establish the District Three Union at a gala ceremony attended by Zhu Xuefan.[78]

Wang Hao's mission to organize the silk weavers was part of a concerted program by his backstage bosses, Lu Jingshi and Zhu Xuefan, to develop a base among labor in preparation for the upcoming National Assembly elections.[79] At the time, Lu Jingshi in particular was involved

---

[76] *Shanghai chanye,* pp. 171–172; Shanghai Police Files, D-7744.

[77] Shanghai Police Files, D-7744.

[78] "Yijiusanqi nian sichou dabagong" [The great silk-weavers' strike of 1937] (1982), in the archives of the Shanghai Number Four Silk-Weaving Factory, pp. 1–2; Zhang Yuezhen, interview transcript in the archives of the Shanghai Number Four Silk-Weaving Factory, 1981/9/23; Zhou Yunqing, "Wo shi zenma canjia geming de" [How I joined the revolution], archives of the Shanghai Number Four Silk-Weaving Factory, 1982/10/4.

[79] Zhang Pingshan, interview transcript in the archives of the Shanghai Number Four Silk-Weaving Factory, 1981/9/29; Zhang Yuezhen, 1981/9/23.

in an intense factional struggle with the director of the Bureau of Social
Affairs (Pan Gongzhan), the head of the Shanghai Guomindang (Wu Kai-
xian), and the acting mayor of Shanghai (Yu Hongjun).[80] Each man had
hopes of cultivating elements within the Shanghai labor movement to
augment his position. The workers welcomed unionization as a means of
improving their situation. As one silk weaver recalled,

> We workers didn't realize at the time that unions were part of a Guomin-
> dang plot to drum up mass votes for its National Assembly. All we knew
> was that organization would give us strength. This fellow Wang, I under-
> stand, was a member of the Blue Shirts. But he had a "leftist" demeanor
> and was really trusted by the workers, who saw that he ate plain noodles,
> rode a bicycle, and lived in modest circumstances.[81]

In February, an officially sanctioned District One Silk-Weavers' Union
was inaugurated in the Nandao area, where six of the Meiya factories
were situated. It took considerable effort to convince the formerly
independent workers at Meiya to join the unionization movement, however. Slowest to register in the new union were the craftsmen at factory
Number Six, where the 1934 strike had originated.[82]

With unions now in place across the city, Wang Hao moved to
assume overall command by setting up a unified "Shanghai Silk-Weavers'
Committee for Improved Treatment." Encouraged by this new committee, the cry for higher wages spread like wildfire throughout the silk-
weaving community. On March 17, under the leadership of Wang Hao's
committee, a mass meeting of more than two thousand weavers was convened at an open field near St. John's University to draw up a unified set
of demands. Requests for higher wages, shorter hours, and a general
improvement in treatment were agreed upon and duly submitted to an
official mediation committee comprised of representatives from the
Bureau of Social Affairs, the local Guomindang, workers, and employers.
Arguing that their industry was recuperating from its earlier depression
and could therefore afford to pay more to its workers, the weavers
demanded an across-the-board raise of 30 percent. After lengthy discussions, the employers consented to a 15 percent increase for workers
earning less than fifty cents a day, but refused to consider raises for those
receiving more than this minimum amount. Since such poorly paid
workers constituted but a small percentage of the silk-weaving

---

[80] *Shanghai dijiu sizhichang,* p. 39; He Zhensheng, "Kang-Ri zhanzheng shiqi Shanghai
fangzhi gongye yu zhigong de yixie qingkuang" [Conditions of the Shanghai silk-weaving industry and its workers during the Sino-Japanese War], *Shanghai gongyun shiliao,* no. 4
(1984), pp. 14–15.

[81] Zhang Yuezhen, 1981/9/23.

[82] *Shanghai chanye,* p. 173.

community, the workers rejected the proposal and began to plan a city-wide strike in support of their demands.[83]

Tensions mounted when various factories around the city received police protection, ostensibly to prevent union intimidation of workers who preferred to remain at their jobs. On March 29, 150 strikers at the Jinxin factory stormed the plant and attacked police who tried to bar them from entering the factory to meet with management.[84] That same day, a crowd of 500 union members marched to the Yuanling silk-weaving factory to try to persuade workers there to unionize. Three of the agitators got into a scuffle with British police stationed at the factory. One of the three hurled a rock at the police sergeant and then tried to outsprint him, but as the English press explained, "Sergeant Lovell had represented the police in the athletic games in 1935 and had no difficulty catching up." Their heads swathed in bandages, the three activists were brought to trial a few days later.[85] Police efforts to slow the pace of unionization only intensified the resolve of union leaders. At midnight on March 30, a united strike of 220 mills and 11,944 workers—by far the largest of the year's labor disputes—was set in motion by Wang Hao's Committee for Improved Treatment. As table 3 indicates, the strike reached all areas of the city.

The rapid spread of the strike was encouraged by Wang Hao's policy of "factory-storming" (chongchang), in which Blue Shirt–trained workers' pickets rushed in and destroyed machinery in factories where workers were loathe to strike.[86] Recent memoirs reveal that at the time underground Communist organizers opposed a general strike in the silk-weaving industry and advocated a more restrained strategy of separate struggles in factories with relatively "enlightened" management.[87] However, although the Communists enjoyed some strength in the District Four Union, overall leadership of the silk weavers was firmly in the hands of Wang Hao.

Wang's tactics aroused criticism not only from underground Communists, but also from his opponents within the Bureau of Social Affairs. Alarmed by this massive work stoppage in one of the city's key industries and hoping to undercut the power base of Wang and his backstage bosses, the Bureau of Social Affairs issued an emergency order declaring an end to the strike. In exchange for returning to their jobs, the strikers

[83] *China Press* (Shanghai), 3/31/1937; *Shanghai Evening Post and Mercury*, 3/31/1937; *Shanghai chanye*, pp. 174–175; *Shanghai dijiu sizhichang*, p. 39).

[84] *China Press*, 3/29/1937.

[85] Ibid., 3/31/1937.

[86] "Yijiusanqi nian sichou dabagong," pp. 5–6.

[87] *Meiya disi zhichouchang*, p. 46.

Table 3

Spatial Distribution of Silk-Weavers' Strike, March 1937

District	Number of Strikers	Number of Factories
International Settlement		
East district	4,000	169
West district	576	7
Other	838	6
French Concession	1,560	20
Nandao	3,000	10
Zhabei	2,000	8
TOTAL	11,974	220

SOURCE: *Shanghai Evening Post and Mercury,* 3/31/1937.

were promised an across-the-board wage increase of 10 percent, bonus payments, elimination of the loom rental system, and a new one-month paid maternity leave program. The offer was generous enough to erode worker enthusiasm for a continued strike; by early April most weavers had resumed work.[88]

The bureau's order proved effective in convincing the workers to end their walkout, but it had far less impact upon the managers, most of whom refused to honor the call for a 10 percent wage hike. During the course of the strike, Meiya's Cai Shengbai—who still chaired the Silk-Weaving Employers' Association—had organized an ad hoc "Committee to Counter the Strike Wave." This committee, funded by an assessment of two yuan per loom, used its resources to fight the compromise solution proposed by the Bureau of Social Affairs.[89] In mid-April Cai took his case to Guomindang headquarters in Nanjing, alleging that unionization efforts by local Shanghai officials were responsible for the rash of labor unrest in the city.[90]

Early the next month, when Jiang Jieshi happened to be hospitalized in Shanghai, the Generalissimo took a personal interest in the struggles still rampant among the city's silk weavers. Perturbed by the daily newspaper accounts of strikes and slowdowns, Jiang called upon municipal authorities to bring a speedy halt to the disturbances. In response, on the evening of May 14 a large contingent of International Settlement police raided the District Four Silk-Weavers' Union, on the pretext that

---

[88] *Shanghai Evening Post and Mercury,* 4/5/1937; *Shanghai sichou gongye,* pp. 20–21.

[89] *Shanghai chanye,* p. 176.

[90] *Shanghai Times,* 4/14/1937; Number Two History Archives, no. 722: 4–19.

the union had intimidated a worker at the Jinxin factory. Documents were seized, seals of office confiscated, and more than twenty workers detained at police headquarters for questioning.[91]

A few days later, representatives of the District Four Union (including the union secretary, an employee of the Shanghai Guomindang) proceeded to the Bureau of Social Affairs at Civic Center to request that the police return the stolen materials and release the union members being held in custody. It was union leaders' hope that a prompt bureau response might forestall yet more strikes on the part of angry weavers in the eastern district.[92]

Authorities in the Bureau of Social Affairs were torn between loyalty to the union they had helped create and pressure from the central government in Nanjing. The intransigence of factory managers had undermined the bureau's strategy of using a unionized Shanghai labor movement for its own political purposes. Nanjing, for its part, shared with the International Settlement fear of a scenario in which the now heavily unionized silk, cotton, and tobacco workers would join hands to take charge of the city's economy. As a local paper explained, "It is not the individual cases which bother the authorities seriously—it is the steady move toward union combination which undoubtedly will play a decisive part in labour relations of the future."[93] Never far from the imaginations of officials in Nanjing was the specter of Communist agents seizing control of a highly organized labor movement. As a pro-Guomindang paper described fears at the height of the all-city weavers' strike:

> The bogey of Moscow is, perhaps, all too often trotted out by labour-scared employers, but definite evidence is in the hands of official circles to show that there is a direct link between current labour agitation and both financial and ideological inspiration from the Kremlin.... It is not only a question of wages which is being raised, but in whose hands is to rest the dominant political power.[94]

In fact, "Kremlin inspiration" played very little part in the silk weavers' spring offensive. The most active group of Communists (denounced as "Trotskyist" by their mainstream opponents in the Party underground) were at the Jinxin factory. There workers refused to accept the Bureau of Social Affairs compromise and continued a lengthy strike to demand a 30 percent wage increase.[95] Undoubtedly this radical

---

[91] *Shanghai chanye,* p. 177; Shanghai Police Files, D-7744; Number Two History Archives, no. 2: 2–1054.

[92] Shanghai Police Files, D-7744; *Shanghai chanye,* 177–178.

[93] *Shanghai Times,* 5/19/1937.

[94] Ibid., 4/3/1937.

[95] *Shanghai chanye,* p. 181.

connection helped to precipitate the May 14 police raid on the District Four Union, for strikers at the Jinxin factory had been using union premises as a center for free food distribution. The union's president, moreover, was a former Jinxin worker with Communist leanings.[96] But on the whole, Communist involvement was not a major factor in the silk weavers' unrest.

Even without much Communist participation, however, the contest was most decidedly a political one in which factions within the Shanghai regime struggled for the upper hand. While state agencies jockeyed for power over the workers, previously submerged rivalries among the silk weavers themselves rose to the surface. On May 24, a gang fight involving more than five hundred unionized workers erupted at Meiya's Factory Number Ten. Workers from the same native-place association as their factory superintendent advocated work resumption, whereas other employees insisted upon a continued strike for better working conditions. From 11:00 P.M. until six the next morning, the weavers fought a bloody battle in front of the mill.[97]

With control of the situation slipping quickly from their grasp, authorities at the Bureau of Social Affairs concluded that the silk weavers' unions must be destroyed. On June 3, the bureau ordered the closing of unions in districts one, three, and four. New unions, less likely to stir up trouble among the workers, were to be established.[98] On June 12, Wang Hao was arrested at the offices of his now defunct District Three Union. When he was released a month later, weavers in the western part of the city welcomed him back with banners and firecrackers.[99]

In the one month remaining before the Japanese invasion, ambitious Guomindang functionaries rushed forth to found new silk-weaving unions. Native-place attachments were used in the struggle to draw workers into the embrace of one or another rival union organizer. Repeated battles between these competing leaders and their fellow provincials indicated the fractionalized state into which the silk weavers had fallen by the summer of 1937.[100] When the Japanese seized control of Shanghai's silk industry in August 1937, they found a once proud "labor aristocracy" in disarray.

---

[96] Shanghai Police Files, D-7744; *Shanghai sichou gongyun shi*, p. 50.
[97] *China Press*, 5/26/ 1937; *Shanghai chanye*, p. 179.
[98] *Shanghai Times*, 6/3/1937.
[99] Shanghai Municipal Archives, no. 199-48-207.
[100] *Shanghai chanye*, pp. 180–181.

Conclusion

The decimation and forced retreat of Communist labor organizers in the April 1927 coup did not ring down the curtain on the drama of the Shanghai workers' movement. The activism of silk weavers is ample testimony to a continuing and dynamic pattern of workers' politics. Stimulated—in rather complicated ways —by the severe depression that wracked their industry during the early 1930s, weavers were quick to fight in defense of their own interests. Initially in 1930, and then more dramatically in 1934, the battle was led by the "modern" sector of the weaving community, concentrated in the relatively prosperous Meiya Company. Later the more "traditional" weavers, located at smaller factories throughout the city, carried on the struggle—but under the aegis of officially sponsored unions.

While the early strikes had much in common with classic artisan protests, by the end of the Nanjing decade the pattern had changed. Proletarianized by hostile employers and pressured by outside organizers whose agendas had more to do with internal Guomindang politics than with worker interests, Shanghai's silk weavers shed many of the distinctive features of a "labor aristocracy."

In other parts of the world, as well, silk weavers have compiled an impressive record of protest activity. Robert Bezucha's description of the *canuts* of Lyon, France—silk weavers who launched massive strikes in 1831 and 1834—bears a strong resemblance to Shanghai strikers a century later. By Bezucha's account, these were highly educated workers (70 percent of the male weavers were literate) who enjoyed relative affluence and a distinct popular culture. Based on mutual aid societies, the weavers' strikes were "evidence not of dislocation, but of efforts at community organization. Far from being an uprooted, 'dangerous class,' they fought only when their future appeared gravely threatened."[101]

The "threat" facing Shanghai silk weavers in the early 1930s was the result of a drastic decline in the international market for their products. But global depression was certainly not the only precipitant. Changes in the Shanghai silk-weaving industry itself were another key ingredient. As the highly mechanized Meiya Company captured an ever greater share of a once competitive field, its search for profits (exacerbated, of course, by anxieties about the world depression) undermined earlier guarantees of worker welfare. Skilled workers then responded in what they took to be an act of self-defense. The situation resembled that described by Bernard Moss to explain the workers' struggles of mid-nineteenth century Paris:

---

[101] Robert Bezucha, *The Lyon Uprising of 1834* (Cambridge, Mass., 1974), p. 158.

"Industrialization had advanced far enough with respect to labor and commercial competition to threaten the security, integrity and relative value of skilled craftsmen, enough to provoke resistance and protest, but not enough in terms of complete mechanization to destroy the craft and its capacities for resistance."[102]

The early Shanghai silk weavers' strikes shared certain features in common with artisan protests that developed in other times and places, under comparable social and economic circumstances. But labor movements are not merely the product of industrial structure or market conditions. The larger political setting also acts as a critical force in shaping the pattern of worker protest. As Shorter and Tilly suggest, "We expect changes in the national political position of organized labor to cause strikes to increase. What is more, we expect the political dimension of the strike to expand over time, as the labor movement nationalizes."[103]

Shanghai silk weavers were no exception to this general proposition. Thanks to heightened interest on the part of outside organizers, silk-weaver strikes by the close of the Nanjing decade had become more frequent and more intertwined with political struggles—on both local and national levels. In the short run, the outcome was unfortunate; Guomindang-sponsored unions robbed the silk weavers' struggles of many of the defining characteristics of an artisan movement: craft pride, autonomy, moralism. But in the longer run, the twin pressures of proletarianization and politicization would breathe new life into the struggles of Shanghai silk weavers.

Within a year after the Japanese invasion, Communist Party branches had been reestablished at the two surviving Meiya factories. At Number Four, ten weavers joined the Party. At Number Nine, a three-member branch was set up.[104] Of the handful of Communist cadres responsible for rebuilding the Shanghai labor movement in 1938, two were former silk weavers.[105]

Following the Japanese surrender, silk weavers played a prominent role in the social unrest that plagued the Guomindang regime in Shanghai during the Civil War years. In March 1946, more than twelve thousand at some three hundred Shanghai silk-weaving factories initiated a strike that persisted for nearly three months. Through the personal mediation of Green Gang–cum–Guomindang labor leader Zhu Xuefan, the silk

[102] Bernard H. Moss, "Workers' Ideology and French Social History," *International Labor and Working Class History,* no. 11 (1977), p. 28.

[103] Shorter and Tilly, *Strikes in France,* p. 10.

[104] *Shanghai dijiu sizhichang,* p. 46.

[105] He Zhensheng, interview transcript in the archives of the Shanghai Number Four Silk-Weaving Factory, 1982/7.

weavers were eventually granted a wage hike. This favorable outcome was due in large measure to the reduced influence of Meiya's General Manager, Cai Shengbai. During the war Cai had quietly placed his two remaining factories in the hands of Italian and German businessmen to avoid a direct Japanese takeover. While the decision proved financially beneficial, politically it opened Cai to the charge of having indirectly collaborated with the enemy. By threatening to publicize Cai's disreputable dealings, labor leaders in the silk-weaving industry after the war were able to exert a good deal of leverage over the once powerful capitalist.[106]

Further evidence of silk weavers' activism was seen in the 1946 election of Pan Yueying as National Assembly representative. A silk weaver, Ms. Pan was also an underground Communist Party member who earlier in the year had organized a demonstration by fifty thousand women workers in Shanghai to celebrate International Women's Day.[107] The following year silk weavers were again at the forefront of protest in Shanghai. On May 8, 1947, more than ten thousand weavers marched from the Bund to City Hall to demand that the cost of living index be unfrozen, to keep pace with inflation. (In a desperate attempt to stem the runaway inflation of the day, Guomindang authorities had frozen the cost of living index so that wages would no long rise in line with price hikes.) The marching weavers distributed some 27,000 handbills en route City Hall, where they delivered a stirring petition that opened with the words "We want to live! We want to breathe! We want to continue to work for the good of the nation!"[108] This much-publicized display of silk-weaver solidarity inspired similar protests among other segments of the work force and helped convince the regime to reverse its policy.

By late 1947, more than one hundred Communist Party members could be found among the silk weavers of Shanghai. Although many of them were arrested in a Guomindang offensive of March 1948, those who escaped the government roundup remained active in the labor movement. At the time of Communist victory, the Party secretary of the underground Communist Labor Committee, Zhang Qi, was none other than a former Meiya worker (a skilled craftsman at Factory Number Six) who had been a leader in the strike of 1934.[109]

The key role that weavers eventually came to play in Shanghai's radical labor movement was very much the product of their experience during the Nanjing decade. Over the course of that difficult period, silk

---

[106] Zhang Shouyu, *Jindai Jiangnan sizhi gongye shi; Shanghai sichou gongyun shi*, p. 94.

[107] *Shanghai sichou gongyun shi*, pp.101–113.

[108] Shanghai Municipal Archives, no. 1-7-54.

[109] *Shanghai sichou gongyun shi*, pp. 130–132.

weavers lost many of their "aristocratic" privileges, but gained solidarity with other industrial workers. As Michael Hanagan has described the process elsewhere: "The growth of a proletariat did not by itself produce mass strikes.... Instead, the growth of a proletariat alongside a mass of threatened artisans, artisans who acted as catalytic agents of working-class revolt, produced mass strike protest."[110]

Developments during the Guomindang era helped to create in the silk weavers of Shanghai a "mass of threatened artisans" who would indeed come to play a "catalytic" role in the Chinese labor movement. As recent scholarship on the British labor aristocracy has made clear, factory artisans are distinguished not merely by their higher wages, but also by a distinctive popular culture that emphasizes mutual aid and inclines them quite naturally toward efforts at unionization.[111] Labor aristocrats commonly engage in collective action to maintain their privileged status. Although such activity often bespeaks a fundamental conservatism on the part of this favored segment of the working class,[112] under certain economic and political circumstances the effort to cling to customary privilege can have radical repercussions.[113] For the silk weavers of Shanghai, the Nanjing decade created just such economic and political circumstances.

---

[110] Michael P. Hanagan, *The Logic of Solidarity: Artisans and Industrial Workers in Three French Towns, 1871–1914* (Urbana, Ill., 1980), pp. 216–217.

[111] G. Crossick, *An Artisan Elite in Late Victorian Society* (London, 1980); Robert Gray, *The Aristocracy of Labour in Nineteenth-Century Britain* (London, 1981).

[112] Eric J. Hobsbawm, "The Labour Aristocracy in Nineteenth-Century Britain," *Labouring Men* (London, 1964).

[113] E. P. Thompson, *The Making of the English Working Class* (London, 1968).

Index

Aglen, Sir Francis, 31, 279
Ahern, Emily Martin, 131–32
Ai Hansong, 227n121
American Far Eastern Match Company, 51
Anfu militarists, 277, 278, 281
Anhui bankers, 18, 26
Anhui Consultative Committee, 94, 99
Anhui *tongxianghui*, 82, 99
Anti-American protests of 1905, 125n55, 129
Anti-Hunger, Anti–Civil War Movement (1947), 109
Anti-Japanese boycotts, 111; of 1915, 110n5, 129; of 1919, 94, 95, 96, 97, 98, 105, 112, 128, 130; of 1931–34, 51–52, 55, 63. *See also* May Fourth Movement; Student protest; Twenty-one Demands
Anti–U.S. Brutality Movement (1946), 111
Anti-Russian protests of 1903, 120, 129
Apprentices, 199, 205; in the silk industry, 308, 323–24, 327, 331
Arrests: drugs and gambling, 302; in labor strikes, 322, 323, 327, 328; for political protest, 222; for prostitution, 163, 172, 178–79; student, 80, 92, 94, 96, 97, 126
Assassinations, 195n29, 218
Aurora University, 111

Bang, 16, 86n18, 89; and native-place ties, 84, 86, 87–88
Bankers, modern, 15–16, 18, 19, 22–25, 31. *See also* Shanghai

Bankers' Association
Banking guilds, 15, 16, 19, 25, 33
Banking journals. See *Yinhang zhoubao*
Banking regulation, 15, 29
Banking terminology, 28–29
Bank loans, to the government, 23, 30, 32–33
Bank of China, 16–17, 21, 22, 26
Bank of Communications, 16–17, 22
Banks, 2, 15–17; foreign, 21–22, 27, 28, 30, 32; linked to Beiyang clique, 16, 18; northern, 16, 22, 23, 30; *qianzhuang*, 15, 16, 17, 18, 24, 30; relations with government, 16–17, 23, 29–30, 32–33, 193, 218
Banque Industrielle de Chine, 27, 28, 30
Baoshan, natives of, 18
Baoying native-place associations, 251
Baptist Shanghai College, 195n30
Barbers, 255, 257
Bathhouses, 245, 246n21, 254, 257, 274
Begging, 242
Bei Zuyi, 24
Beida Speech Corps, 127n61
Beijing octroi loan, 23, 33
Beijing Opera. *See* Opera
Beijing University, 22, 93n40
Beiyang clique, 16, 18
Bergère, Marie-Claire, 77
Bezucha, Robert, 338
Big Eight Mob, 270, 274, 277
Blacksmith trade, 86n19
Blue Shirts, 332, 333, 334
Bo Gu, 229

CHINA RESEARCH MONOGRAPHS (CRM)

6. David D. Barrett. *Dixie Mission: The United States Army Observer Group in Yenan, 1944*, 1970 ($4.00)
17. Frederic Wakeman, Jr., Editor. *Ming and Qing Historical Studies in the People's Republic of China*, 1981 ($10.00)
21. James H. Cole. *The People Versus the Taipings: Bao Lisheng's "Righteous Army of Dongan,"* 1981 ($7.00)
24. Pao-min Chang. *Beijing, Hanoi, and the Overseas Chinese*, 1982 ($7.00)
25. Rudolf G. Wagner. *Reenacting the Heavenly Vision: The Role of Religion in the Taiping Rebellion*, 1984 ($12.00)
27. John N. Hart. *The Making of an Army "Old China Hand": A Memoir of Colonel David D. Barrett*, 1985 ($12.00)
28. Steven A. Leibo. *Transferring Technology to China: Prosper Giquel and the Self-strengthening Movement*, 1985 ($15.00)
29. David Bachman. *Chen Yun and the Chinese Political System*, 1985 ($15.00)
30. Maria Hsia Chang. *The Chinese Blue Shirt Society: Fascism and Developmental Nationalism*, 1985 ($15.00)
31. Robert Y. Eng. *Economic Imperialism in China: Silk Production and Exports, 1861–1932*, 1986 ($15.00)
33. Yue Daiyun. *Intellectuals in Chinese Fiction*, 1988 ($10.00)
34. Constance Squires Meaney. *Stability and the Industrial Elite in China and the Soviet Union*, 1988 ($15.00)
35. Yitzhak Shichor. *East Wind over Arabia: Origins and Implications of the Sino-Saudi Missile Deal*, 1989 ($7.00)
36. Suzanne Pepper. *China's Education Reform in the 1980s: Policies, Issues, and Historical Perspectives*, 1990 ($12.00)
37. Joyce K. Kallgren, Editor. *Building a Nation-State: China after Forty Years*, 1990 ($12.00)
sp. Phyllis Wang and Donald A. Gibbs, Editors. *Readers' Guide to China's Literary Gazette, 1949–1979*, 1990 ($20.00)
38. James C. Shih. *Chinese Rural Society in Transition: A Case Study of the Lake Tai Area, 1368–1800*, 1992 ($15.00)
39. Anne Gilks. *The Breakdown of the Sino-Vietnamese Alliance, 1970–1979*, 1992 ($15.00)
sp. Theodore Han and John Li. *Tiananmen Square Spring 1989: A Chronology of the Chinese Democracy Movement*, 1992 ($10.00)
40. Frederic Wakeman, Jr., and Wen-hsin Yeh, Editors. *Shanghai Sojourners*, 1992 ($20.00)

KOREA RESEARCH MONOGRAPHS (KRM)

7. Quee-Young Kim. *The Fall of Syngman Rhee*, 1983 ($12.00)
9. Helen Hardacre. *The Religion of Japan's Korean Minority: The Preservation of Ethnic Identity*, 1985 ($12.00)
10. Fred C. Bohm and Robert R. Swartout, Jr., Editors. *Naval Surgeon in Yi Korea: The Journal of George W. Woods*, 1984 ($12.00)
11. Robert A. Scalapino and Hongkoo Lee, Editors. *North Korea in a Regional and Global Context*, 1986 ($20.00)
13. Vipan Chandra. *Imperialism, Resistance, and Reform in Late Nineteenth-Century Korea: Enlightenment and the Independence Club*, 1988 ($17.00)
14. Seok Choong Song. *Explorations in Korean Syntax and Semantics*, 1988 ($20.00)
15. Robert A. Scalapino and Dalchoong Kim, Editors. *Asian Communism: Continuity and Transition*, 1988 ($20.00)
16. Chong-Sik Lee and Se-Hee Yoo, Editors. *North Korea in Transition*, 1991 ($12.00)
17. Nicholas Eberstadt and Judith Banister. *The Population of North Korea*, 1992 ($12.00)

JAPAN RESEARCH MONOGRAPHS (JRM)

7. Teruo Gotoda. *The Local Politics of Kyoto*, 1985 ($15.00)
8. Yung H. Park. *Bureaucrats and Ministers in Contemporary Japanese Government*, 1986 ($15.00)